Democratic Thought from Machiavelli
to Spinoza

Spinoza Studies
Series editor: Filippo Del Lucchese, Alma Mater Studiorum – Università di Bologna

Seminal works devoted to Spinoza that challenge mainstream scholarship
This series aims to broaden the understanding of Spinoza in the Anglophone world by making some of the most important work by continental scholars available in English translation for the first time. Some of Spinoza's most important themes – that right is coextensive with power, that every political order is based on the power of the multitude, the critique of superstition and the rejection of the idea of providence – are explored by these philosophers in detail and in ways that will open up new possibilities for reading and interpreting Spinoza.

Editorial Advisory board
Saverio Ansaldi, Etienne Balibar, Chiara Bottici, Laurent Bove, Mariana de Gainza, Moira Gatens, Thomas Hippler, Susan James, Chantal Jaquet, Mogens Laerke, Genevieve Lloyd, Beth Lord, Pierre Macherey, Nicola Marcucci, Alexandre Matheron (1926–2020), Dave Mesing, Warren Montag, Pierre-François Moreau, Vittorio Morfino, Antonio Negri (1933–2023), Susan Ruddick, Martin Saar, Pascal Sévérac, Hasana Sharp, Diego Tatián, Dan Taylor, Francesco Toto, Dimitris Vardoulakis, Lorenzo Vinciguerra, Stefano Visentin, Manfred Walther, Caroline Williams.

Books available
Affects, Actions and Passions in Spinoza: The Unity of Body and Mind, Chantal Jaquet, translated by Tatiana Reznichenko
The Spinoza-Machiavelli Encounter: Time and Occasion, Vittorio Morfino, translated by Dave Mesing
Politics, Ontology and Knowledge in Spinoza, Alexandre Matheron, translated and edited by Filippo Del Lucchese, David Maruzzella and Gil Morejón
Spinoza, the Epicurean: Authority and Utility in Materialism, Dimitris Vardoulakis
Experience and Eternity in Spinoza, Pierre-François Moreau, edited and translated by Robert Boncardo
Spinoza and the Politics of Freedom, Dan Taylor
Spinoza's Political Philosophy: The Factory of Imperium, Riccardo Caporali, translated by Fabio Gironi
Spinoza's Paradoxical Conservatism, Franois Zourabichvili, translated by Gil Morejón
Marx with Spinoza: Production, Alienation, History, Franck Fischbach, translated by Jason Read
Time, Duration and Eternity in Spinoza, Chantal Jaquet, translated by Eric Aldieri
Affirmation and Resistance in Spinoza: The Strategy of the Conatus, Laurent Bove, translated and edited by Émilie Filion-Donato and Hasana Sharp
Reading Spinoza in the Anthropocene, Genevieve Lloyd
Spinoza and Contemporary Biology: Lectures on the Philosophy of Biology and Cognitivism, Henri Atlan, translated by Inja Stracenski and edited by Robert Boncardo
Democratic Thought from Machiavelli to Spinoza: Freedom, Equality, Multitude, Sonja Lavaert, translated by Albert Gootjes

Forthcoming
Spinoza's Critique of Hobbes: Law, Power and Freedom, Christian Lazzeri, translated by Nils F. Schott
Spinoza and the Sign: The Logic of Imagination, Lorenzo Vinciguerra, translated by Alexander Reynolds
New Perspectives on Spinoza's Theologico-Political Treatise: *Politics, Power and the Imagination*, edited by Dan Taylor and Marie Wuth
Passions and Politics in Spinoza, Diego Tatián, translated by Nicolas Allen
Althusser and Spinoza: Detours and Returns, Juan Domingo Sanchez-Estop, translated by Élise Hendrick, edited by Dan Taylor
Spinoza in Post-Marxist Philosophy: Speculative Materialism, Katja Diefenbach, translated by Gerrit Paul Jackson
Spinoza and Systems: Reception and Critique in the Age of Enlightenment, Diego Donna, translated by Brent Waterhouse
Towards a Marxist Reading of Spinoza, Jean-Toussaint Desanti, translated by Alya Ansari, edited by Stefano Pippa, Pierre-François Moreau, David Wittmann

Visit our website at www.edinburghuniversitypress.com/series/SPIN

Democratic Thought from Machiavelli to Spinoza
Freedom, Equality, Multitude

Sonja Lavaert

Translated by Albert Gootjes

EDINBURGH
University Press

Edinburgh University Press is one of the leading university presses in the UK. We publish academic books and journals in our selected subject areas across the humanities and social sciences, combining cutting-edge scholarship with high editorial and production values to produce academic works of lasting importance. For more information visit our website: edinburghuniversitypress.com

Het moderne democratie-denken van Machiavelli tot Spinoza en zijn kring, Sonja Lavaert 2020
English translation published by agreement with ASP Editions (Academic & Scientific Publishers, www.aspeditions.be)

English translation © Albert Gootjes, 2024

Edinburgh University Press Ltd
13 Infirmary Street
Edinburgh EH1 1LT

Typeset in 10/12 Goudy Old Style
by Cheshire Typesetting Ltd, Cuddington, Cheshire, and
printed and bound in Great Britain

A CIP record for this book is available from the British Library

ISBN 978 1 3995 3050 7 (hardback)
ISBN 978 1 3995 3052 1 (webready PDF)
ISBN 978 1 3995 3053 8 (epub)

The right of Sonja Lavaert to be identified as the author of this work has been asserted in accordance with the Copyright, Designs and Patents Act 1988, and the Copyright and Related Rights Regulations 2003 (SI No. 2498).

Contents

Preface	viii
Notes on Translation and Acknowledgements	xi
Abbreviations	xiii

I. Machiavelli's Example	1
1. A (re)construction	4
2. *Istorie Fiorentine*	12
3. *Parole – Il duca Valentino – I popoli della Valdichiana*	19
4. *Il Principe*	23
5. *Discorsi*	32

II. Fictions, Laws and Religions	42
1. *Theophrastus redivivus*	42
2. Artefact	48
3. Religion as political art	52
4. Institutions	56
5. Equal freedom	62

III. Lieutenants	66
1. *De jure ecclesiasticorum*	66
2. No equality without freedom, no freedom without equality	69

IV. A Political Balance (Between Passions and Reason, State Interest and the Multitude)	78
1. Johan/Pieter de la Court	78
2. *Naeuwkeurige consideratie van staet*	79

CONTENTS

3. *Consideratien van Staat* ... 84
4. *Politike Discoursen* ... 94

V. The Example of the Indians ... 107
1. Franciscus van den Enden ... 107
2. *Kort verhael van Nieuw-Nederlants Gelegentheit* ... 114
3. Plokhoy's *Kort en klaer ontwerp* ... 122
4. From the *Vrye Politijke Stellingen* to *Finis est in Holandia* ... 126
5. 'do not dare to speak with their mouth, [but] use their fists' ... 136

VI. Translation and Truth: A Dialogue ... 138
1. Adriaan Koerbagh ... 138
2. *'t Samen-spraeck* ... 141
3. Hobbes's *Leviathan* in translation ... 143
4. *Een Bloemhof van allerley lieflijkheyd sonder verdriet* ... 146
5. *Een Ligt schijnende in duystere plaatsen* ... 153

VII. Spinoza's Reversal ... 165
1. 1661–1665 ... 165
2. *Tractatus theologico-politicus*, 1670 ... 170
    2.1 First movement, first motive ... 173
    2.2 Second movement, second motive ... 176
    2.3 Third movement, third motive ... 179
3. Countermovement, 1670–1676 ... 183
    3.1 1671–1673 ... 188
    3.2 1674 ... 200
    3.3 1675–1676 ... 207
4. *Tractatus politicus*, 1677 ... 217
    4.1 The basis ... 218
    4.2 Experience ... 235
    4.3 [. . .] ... 241

VIII. Une mauvaise rhapsodie, un artifice ... 246
1. A revolutionary thesis ... 246
2. *L'Esprit de Spinosa/Traité des trois imposteurs* ... 250

CONTENTS

3. Unmasking deceit	258
4. The effectual truth for everyone	263
Counterpoint 1	265
Counterpoint 2	267
Counterpoint 3	271
IX. Quodlibet. In the Spirit of Machiavelli	277
Appendix. The Manuscript *Finis est in Holandia*	284
Editorial note	284
Transcription	286
Translation	287
Bibliography	290
Index of names	332
Anonymous texts	338

Preface

The debates and politics of today testify to a continuing search for balance between equality and freedom, the basic components of a democracy. Spinoza is generally recognised for the role he played in the development of modern democratic ideas through the treatises he wrote on politics and the freedom to philosophise. Less well known is the fact that he drew on Machiavelli for these ideas, dispelling the Machiavellian counterimage which had been created by Machiavelli's own political and Christian opponents. The geometric style of Spinoza's writings is the stuff of legend and has been addressed extensively. But there has been less attention for the evolution and changes which his thought underwent, and for the doubts that he harboured, even though they serve to indicate that he was reflecting on a complex and difficult problem – i.e. politics and powers – in the face of a living, social reality. While the robust philosophical studies that have appeared since the 1960s testify to scholarship's growing attention for the political aspect of Spinoza's thought, they often remain trapped in their admiration for his genius.

Spinoza, however, was no solitary genius. Rather, he formed part of a European movement of like-minded thinkers whom he influenced and who in turn also influenced him. Of particular interest were his direct surroundings in the Netherlands, where themes like metaphysics, religion and politics were thoroughly dissected and debated at length. The Dutch Republic saw various naturalist and materialist accounts arise, along with critiques on political theology as well as the conviction of the relevance of this critique for each and every person. Rejected were the speculations of a personified power outside the earth to unhinge the world, of a supreme being who establishes hierarchies and renders judgement. Freed from traditional notions and internal barriers, people began to shift their intellectual focus to the human condition. It is in this philosophical turn to the historical/current context

PREFACE   ix

and to the masses/multitude that the idea began to take shape that there is
no freedom without equality, and no equality without freedom. The decisive
turn in this shift occurred with Machiavelli, whose writings were distorted,
vilified and maligned as soon as they began to circulate, even before their
publication. But his revolutionary ideas were continued by freethinkers like
Vanini and in mysterious libertine manuscripts like *Theophrastus redivivus*,
which most probably dates from 1659. Between 1660 and 1662 a number of
republican writings appeared from the brothers De la' Court, and between
1662 and 1665 came the political pamphlets of Spinoza's teacher Van den
Enden – all of them written for a wide audience, in the Dutch vernacular.
The year 1665 saw the appearance of the anonymous treatise *De jure ecclesiasticorum*,
whose theoretical style and radical nature was so powerfully
reminiscent of Spinoza that he initially was often identified as its clandestine author.
Spinoza's friend Koerbagh similarly shared the conviction that
all people can emancipate themselves to autonomous critical reflection. In
1668 he published a subversive dictionary aimed at unmasking improper
language, followed by a systematic philosophical work in Dutch, which was
nevertheless seized and destroyed while still at press.

The present monograph seeks to trace the genealogy of modern democratic
thought in the movement that took shape from Machiavelli to
Spinoza and his circle, and beyond Spinoza in the *Esprit de Spinosa/Traité
des trois imposteurs*. The chapters follow these authors, their writings and the
anonymous works more or less in chronological fashion. A host of names
will come up in the process, and references will be found to many – often
anonymous – texts produced between 1513 and 1690.

The variety of languages in which the cited sources appeared, together
with the frequent existence of translations, is no accidental feature of our
narrative, but played an intrinsic role not only in the public dissemination
of the debates and unmasking ideas, but also in the radicalisation of the
ensuing critique. For this reason, I have given close attention to the interplay
between languages and sometimes offered my own translations in the
main body of the text, with references to the original source in the notes.
The source text has also been cited for unpublished works and for Latin texts
that are difficult to come by.

In an appendix, I have transcribed and translated an unpublished manuscript
of a revolutionary text which Franciscus Van den Enden wrote in the
very midst of preparations for revolt.

I dedicate this book to Rudolf Boehm, my teacher in philosophy, who
passed away late this past summer. During our final conversation, only weeks
before his death, we also spoke of this book, and I was deeply moved by his

serious and engaged interest. We spoke about the things that faced him: goodbyes to friends, family and life itself; the fear of pain; death, which he used to joke about and shrug off. Our conversation then naturally returned to life, and we ended with philosophy, which he understood as the serious art of asking questions, as critique.

My thanks go out to my students at the Vrije Universiteit Brussel whom I have had the honour of having in my philosophy classes over these past six years. I learned a lot from them. Finally, I would like to express my gratitude to all my friends with whom I was able to discuss various aspects of this study, and in particular to Jonathan Israel, Pierre-François Moreau, Antonio Negri and Winfried Schröder.

Bruges, 30 October 2019

Notes on Translation and Acknowledgements

Wherever possible, we have used existing translations for any early modern sources cited. For Machiavelli's *Il Principe*, *Discorsi* and *Istorie Fiorentine* we have opted for the work of Harvey C. Mansfield (and Laura F. Banfield/Nathan Tarcov); translations from other Machiavelli works have been taken from Allan Gilbert. For Spinoza, the translation of Edwin Curley was deemed most suitable. Full details for these translations can be found in the bibliography. Whenever existing translations have been modified, this has been indicated in the notes.

One notoriously difficult term to translate is Machiavelli's concept of *virtù*. At times we have decided to render it as 'power' or 'energy', while at other times it has been left untranslated. For Spinoza – as, in fact, for all authors who deployed a (neo-)scholastic terminology – a similar situation presents itself for the Latin *potentia* and *potestas*. Curley distinguishes the two by rendering *potentia* as 'power' and *potestas* as ''power' (i.e. with the prime symbol). While this convention has its merits, certainly for a translation of Spinoza's complete oeuvre, we have decided not to follow it in the present monograph. Instead, where the distinction is at play, we simply use the relevant Latin term, or supply the Latin in brackets, or else add a specifying adjective, such as 'natural power' for *potentia* and 'political power' for *potestas*. For more on our choice and on the terms themselves, we refer the reader to notes 1 and 227 in Chapter 7. We have, however, retained Curley's use of an italicised '*or*' for the Latin *sive* or *seu*, which generally marks equivalence, whereas an 'or' (in Roman type) is indicative of a Latin *aut* or *vel*, which is the preferred term for an alternative.

***

We would like to thank the Spinoza Studies series editor, Filippo Del Lucchese, for his optimism and enthusiastic support along the way.

NOTES ON TRANSLATION AND ACKNOWLEDGEMENTS

Our gratitude also goes out to Carol Macdonald along with her staff at Edinburgh University Press for all their work throughout the process, from coordinating the initial administrative matters to seeing the final manuscript to press.

The origins of this project must be traced back to the first meeting between author and translator at two conferences held in 2018, in Rotterdam ('De kring van Spinoza', organised by the Vereniging het Spinozahuis) and in Lyon ('Les Pays-Bas au siècle d'or', organised by CNRS-IHRIM of the ENS Lyon). Our conversations and the friendship that developed there prepared the soil and set the tone for our later collaboration on the present publication. I (Albert) am honoured that Sonja gauged my interest in translating this monograph, which truly was a joy to work on – both as an achievement in scholarship and as a captivating read. I (Sonja) am very grateful to Albert for involving me closely in the translation process, a precious learning experience and a joy to work, reflect and mull over things together.

Albert Gootjes
Sonja Lavaert

Abbreviations

Works by Spinoza
All quotations from Spinoza's works in English are taken from Curley's two-volume *Collected Works of Spinoza* [CWS]; Latin quotations are taken from Gebhardt's four-volume *Opera* [G]. Modifications in the translation, together with the use of an alternate edition or translation, are clearly indicated. For each citation, we provide an internal reference to Spinoza's text using the conventions below, as well as a reference to the *CWS* volume and page number.

CWS   *The Collected Works of Spinoza* (Spinoza 1985–2016). Roman numerals refer to volume number; Arabic numerals refer to page number.

Ep.   *Letters* (*Epistolae*). Roman numerals refer to letter number. Spinoza's correspondent is given in square brackets.

Ethics   *Ethics* (*Ethica Ordine Geometrico demonstrata et in quinque Partes distincta*). Roman numerals refer to Part number; Arabic numerals refer to Proposition number; further specifications follow the conventions below.

G   *Opera* (Spinoza 1925). Roman numerals refer to volume number; Arabic numerals refer to page number.

KV   *Short Treatise on God, Man and His Well-Being* (*Korte Verhandeling van God, de Mensch en des zelfs Welstand*). Roman numerals refer to chapter number; Arabic numerals refer to section number.

TP   *Political Treatise* (*Tractatus Politicus*). Roman numerals refer to chapter number; Arabic numerals refer to paragraph number.

TTP   *Theologico-Political Treatise* (*Tractatus Theologico-Politicus*). Roman numerals refer to chapter number; Arabic numerals refer to paragraph number.

xiv ABBREVIATIONS

App. Appendix
Cor. Corollary
Def. Definition
Praef. Preface
Schol. Scholium

Other works

All abbreviations for the works of other authors are limited to the conventional shortened titles, which follow the complete title at first mention. For example, De la Court: *Consideratien van Staat*; Koerbagh: *Een Bloemhof*; Machiavelli: *Discorsi*; Van den Enden: *Kort verhael*. The only exceptions to this rule are Van den Enden's *Vrye Politijke Stellingen*, which is abbreviated as *VPS*, and the anonymous *Theophrastus redivivus*, which we cite as *TR*.

TR *Theophrastus redivivus* ([1659], 1981). Roman numerals refer to the Treatise [Tractatus] number; Arabic numerals refer to the chapter [Caput] number.

VPS *Vrije Politijke Stellingen* (1665, 1992)

I

Machiavelli's Example

Niccolò Machiavelli offers an extensive and highly insightful description of how a sovereign can establish and maintain his dominion, if his only desire is to rule. But what the actual purpose of this description is remains unclear, as Spinoza astutely observes in his *Tractatus politicus*, although he does himself venture a guess.[1] If Machiavelli had a good end in mind when he offered this description, as one might indeed expect from 'a wise man' like him, it must have been to show how rashly people act when they try to rid themselves of a tyrant without venturing to remove the causes of tyranny, for the only effect of their actions is to intensify the oppression. Spinoza suspects that the intention of this shrewd Italian political philosopher was 'to show how much a free multitude should beware of entrusting its well-being absolutely to one person'.[2] Unless he were a fool or idle, a solitary sovereign will always fear for his power, and in order to protect himself he will assail the masses instead of seeing to their care. This theory conflicts with the negative reading and – in Spinoza's time, very common – 'Machiavellian' interpretation of Machiavelli as a cynical defender of tyranny, the author of the cruelty and deceit he describes, the messenger of the devil, and the wicked Antichrist. Compared with the tone struck by the antitexts proposing such readings, the assessment offered by Spinoza is careful and complex, but the import of his claim is indubitably subversive and breaks with the traditional interpretations. A similar, unequivocally revolutionary defence of a free democratic republic and a rejection of 'monarchical tyranny' can be found in Franciscus van den Enden's *Vrye Politijke Stellingen* (1665), where we likewise encounter a reference to Machiavelli as a 'very discerning

---

[1] Spinoza, *TP* V, 7; *CWS* II, 531. See also Chapter VII.4.1, 234.
[2] Spinoza, *TP* V, 7; *CWS* II, 531.

2   DEMOCRATIC THOUGHT FROM MACHIAVELLI TO SPINOZA

critic and observer'.[3] However, Van den Enden understands Machiavelli to be a proponent of mixed sovereignty, which he condemns in forceful terms, together with the 'filthy superstition and deceit' of which he accuses Machiavelli.[4] Was this difference in style and, to some extent, also in interpretation what Spinoza had in mind when he attempted to develop a free political theory of his own, in which he probed the human passions as they are and not as he would have wanted them to be?[5] Or was he thinking of the *Politike Discoursen* (1662) of Johan or Pieter De la Court, which share the same political theme, naturalism and republican views and can directly and positively be traced back to Machiavelli? The above texts leave us with an image of Machiavelli that is at variance with the dominant reading of the time, a 'leftist' view that can serve as an example for a political theory of freedom, equality and social justice and demands a critique of all deceptive forms of knowledge and religion.

The common view of Machiavelli facing De la Court, Van den Enden and Spinoza in the latter half of the seventeenth century followed in large measure from the fierce opposition which the philosopher's writings aroused almost immediately upon their dissemination. The dominant Machiavelli reading had in fact been invented and 'constructed' during his lifetime by his opponents, the ecclesiastical and political institutions which he had subjected to criticism and whose political choices he had warned against, namely the priests and the princes. With the exception of *Decennale primo*, *La Mandragola* and *Dell'arte della guerra*, which were intended for immediate publication, all other works Machiavelli wrote were not published until after his death. *Discorsi sopra la prima deca di Tito Livio* appeared in 1531, and *Il Principe* and *Istorie Fiorentine* in 1532, each of them coming from the presses of Blado in Rome, and, independent of the Blado edition and immediately after it, with Giunta in Florence.[6] Both Blado and Giunta introduced some

[3] Van den Enden, *Vrije Politijke Stellingen*, 223–4.

[4] Ibid. 160–1.

[5] *TP* I, 1.

[6] *Nicolai Malclavelli florentini compendium rerum decemnio in Italia gestarum ad viros florentinos incipit feliciter* (1504); *La Mandragola* (1518/19), published by an unidentified Florentine printer under the title *Commedia di Callimaco e di Lucrezia*; *Dell'arte della guerra* (1521), published by Giunta in Florence and repeatedly reprinted in the following years; *Discorsi*, first published 10 October 1531 by A. Blado in Rome and 10 November 1531 by B. Giunta in Florence; *Il Principe* first appeared with A. Blado on 4 January 1532 and with B. Giunta on 8 May 1532; Machiavelli submitted the manuscript of the *Istorie Fiorentine* to his commissioner, Pope Clement VII, in May 1525, after which it circulated in manuscript form, although it too would have to wait until 1532 before a first published edition appeared from the presses of Blado and Giunta.

changes to the original text. For example, Blado changed the Latin title *De principatibus* to the Italian *Il Principe*, and in the 'Proemio' to the first book of the *Discorsi* he replaced the term 'religione' with 'educazione', which had the effect of weakening Machiavelli's critique of religion. Even before *Il Principe* appeared in print, the text – which circulated in manuscript form as early as 1515 – began to be adapted and the myth started taking shape. Agostino Nifo, once an Averroist and later a critic of Pomponazzi, published his four-volume *De regnandi peritia* in 1523, plagiarising *Il Principe* almost in its entirety, albeit in adapted form, expanded with quotations from Aristotle and Plato and translated into Latin, before closing book IV with a condemnation of Machiavelli's treatise for its assault on the Christian virtues.[7] As such, a virtually new genre was ushered in. In Roman Catholic quarters, Machiavelli's political views were appropriated, used and disseminated in a new ideological and philosophical form and constellation, but they were at the same time also rejected for their anti-Christian nature, understood not only as moral corruption but also as a danger to the state for undermining the authority of government and crown.

But from the beginning there were also other texts that tended in the opposite direction and celebrated Machiavelli as the author of freedom and the republic. In the *Dialogi della morale philosophia* of Antonio Brucioli, the Florentine who had conspired against the Medici and moved to the freedom of Venice, scholars like Carlo Dionisotti have seen the echoes of the debates taking place in the Orti Oricellari, which Machiavelli regularly visited.[8] Furthermore, as far as Dionisotti could tell, the *Dialogi* is the only prose text written in the Florentine dialect and published in the 1520s and 1530s which can be compared to *Dell'Arte della guerra*.[9] Even if Brucioli had visited the Orti for years on end, he would never have come upon the idea of the *Dialogi* if he had not read Machiavelli's *Dell'Arte*. Dionisotti's thesis finds further confirmation in the second edition of the *Dialogi*, which dates

---

See Vivanti, '*Decennali* Introduzione', Machiavelli, *Opere* I, 813–14; Machiavelli, '*Dell'arte della guerra* Introduzione', 1132–3; Machiavelli, 'Teatro Introduzione', *Opere* III, 789–95; Gerber, *Niccolò Machiavell: Die Handschriften, Ausgaben und Übersetzungen seiner Werke im 16. und 17. Jahrhundert*.

[7] Cf. Kahn, 'Machiavelli's Afterlife and Reputation to the Eighteenth Century', 244–5; Macek, *Machiavelli e il machiavellismo*; Procacci, *Machiavelli nella cultura europea dell'età moderna*; Richardson, 'The Prince and its Early Italian Readers', 18–39.

[8] Cantimori, 'Rhetoric and Politics in Italian Humanism', 83–102; Dionisotti, *Machiavellerie. Storia e fortuna di Machiavelli*, 193–226; Procacci, *Machiavelli nella cultura europea*, 43–61; Spini, *Tra Rinascimento e Riforma: Antonio Brucioli*.

[9] Dionisotti, *Machiavellerie*, 202.

4   DEMOCRATIC THOUGHT FROM MACHIAVELLI TO SPINOZA

from 1537 and therefore follows the dissemination of the *Il Principe*, *Discorsi* and *Istorie Fiorentine* in print. In the sixth and seventh dialogues, which deal with the republic, 'Niccolo Machiauelli' explicitly appears as an example in one of the dialogue's interlocutors.[10]

1. A (re)construction

Beginning in the 1530s, the authors of the antitexts, just like the pope and the church, resolutely sided or collaborated with Italy's Spanish occupiers. The year 1539 saw the first work in which Machiavelli was explicitly identified as an anti-Christian thinker and *Il Principe* is described as the product of Satan's hand. The work in question is the *Apologia ad Carolum Quintum* of the banned English cardinal Reginald Pole. In 1542 the Portuguese bishop Jeronimo Osorio, in book III of his *De nobilitate christiana*, launched a fierce attack on Machiavelli's view that the Christian religion has led to the loss of the greatness of the soul and of military and civil virtue, establishing himself as one of the most important exponents of anti-Machiavellianism.[11] In his *De libris a Christiano detestandis et a Christianismo penitus eliminandis* (1552), Ambrogio Catarino placed Machiavelli side by side with Luther as enemies of the church, and he depicts him as an atheist and a master of political crimes. The many refutations and condemning works, of which the above are only a few examples, culminate in Machiavelli's inclusion on the first edition of the *Index librorum prohibitorum* (1559) as one of the authors whose entire corpus was forbidden.[12]

Yet Catholics were not alone in developing the anti-Machiavellian view of Machiavelli as a teacher of evil despots, since the decades following the papal ban also witnessed activity on the side of the Reformed. In 1576 the French Huguenot Innocent Gentillet published his *Discours sur les moyens de bien*

---

10 Brucioli, *Dialogi di Antonio Brucioli della morale philosophia. Libro primo*, 2nd ed., 1537. It is in this second edition, in 'Della Repubblica, dialogo sesto' (XXV) and 'Delle leggi della repubblica, dialogo settimo' (XXXXIV), that 'Niccolo Machiauelli' makes an appearance and poses critical questions, such as: 'Et a che fine tende questo?' (XXXXV). See also Procacci, *Studi sulla fortuna*, 33–42; Cambi, 'Gli Orti Oricellari: un cenacolo formativo del Rinascimento', 7–28.

11 Pole, *Apologia ad Carolum Quintum*, 1539; Osorio, *De nobilitate christiana*, 2nd ed., 1552, in *Nicolai Machiauelli Florentini Princeps ex Sylvestri Telii Fulginatis traductione diligenter emendatus &c.*, 205–24.

12 *Index librorum prohibitorum*, 1559: 'Nicolaus Macchiauellus'; see also Raynaud, *Erotemata de malis ac bonis libris*, 27–8; Bayle, *Dictionaire historique et critique*, vol. 3, 244–9; Gerber, *Niccolò Machiavelli*, 81ff.; Macek, *Machiavelli e il machiavellismo*, 180–5; Dionisotti, *Machiavellerie*, 411–44; Namer, *Machiavel*, 36–40.

gouverner & maintenir en bonne paix un Royaume ou autre Principauté, divisez en trois Livres &c. Contre Nicolas Machiavel Florentin, and in 1579 Hubert Languet, an enthusiastic defender of the Protestant cause, claimed the right of resistance in his famed Vindiciae contra tyrannos.[13] Gentillet's antitext and Languet's religiously inspired call to rebellion served to bolster the image of Machiavelli as the counsellor of tyrants, which – irony of ironies! – would subsequently be appropriated by Catholic authors to defend the papal ban. In 1589 Giovanni Botero published his Della Ragione di Stato, in which the 'Machiavellian' creeds – the end (i.e. state and church) justifies the means (i.e. violence and deceit by church and state) – are identified and translated into the notion of the reason of state. In 1592 Antonio Possevino published his Iudicium de Nicolai Machiauelli, in which he condemned Machiavelli without feeling any need to read the Florentine political theorist's works himself, preferring instead to plagiarise Gentillet's Contre-Machiavel.[14] As such, the fictive construction of the Machiavellian Machiavelli was completed. Illustrative in this regard is Tommaso Campanella's L'ateismo trionfato of 1607, in which the author attacks the reason of state and Machiavelli's anti-Christian view of religion as a fiction devised by priests and princes.[15]

Even Giulio Cesare Vanini, who was condemned to death and burned at the stake in Toulouse in 1619 for his alleged atheism, departed in his Amphitheatrum aeternae providentiae (1615) and his De admirandis naturae reginae (1616) from the view of the Machiavellian commonwealth as it had been forged by Machiavelli's Christian opponents. The same is true

[13] The Latin version dates from 1575/9; in what follows, we will cite the French translation of 1581, which has the title De la puissance legitime du prince sur le peuple, et du peuple sur le prince. Traité tres utile & digne de lecture en ce temps, escrit en Latin par Estienne Iunius Brutus, & nouvellement traduit en François. Etienne Junius Brutus was a pseudonym used by Hubert Languet; see Barker, 'The Authorship of the Vindiciae contra tyrannos'; Daussy, Les huguenots et le roi, 229–56.

[14] Possevino, Princeps, 195–205; Bayle, Dictionaire historique et critique, vol. 3, 244–9; Marchand, Dictionaire historique, vol. 1, 44; likewise interesting in this context is d'Assonville de Bouchault, Atheomastix, sive adversus religionis hostes universos (politicos maxime) dissertatio (1598), which draws a direct connection between the political interest and atheism. Toffanin points to the 'Tacitism' of the three Jesuit authors of antitexts: Possevino, Ribadeneyra and Botero; see Machiavelli e il 'tacitismo', 129–45. On Botero, see Senellart, Machiavélisme et raison d'Etat, 56–83.

[15] Campanella, L'ateismo trionfato overo riconoscimento filosofico della religione universale contra l'antichristianesimo macchiavellesco: In 2004 Germana Ernst discovered the original Italian text (which she dates to 1607–8), and published it in a two-volume critical edition with introduction and commentary; the Latin text of 1626 is not the original version, but a translation by the author.

for the other erudite freethinkers who, in Vanini's wake, read Machiavelli as an immoral atheist who refused to recognise any commandment, metonymically confusing him with the content of the truth which he unmasked, as if he himself had committed the religious deceptions detailed in his work. There is no doubt that Machiavelli is the 'prince of the atheists', so Vanini writes in his *Amphitheatrum*, but as he goes on, he turns the meaning of this commonplace entirely on its head.[16] For, so Vanini claims, in his vernacularly written *Il Principe* the Florentine thinker assumes that 'prophecies are untrue and were invented by sovereigns to train the wretched plebeians, in order that religion might bring them back to their duties when they become deaf to reason'.[17] Using literary devices like metonymy, litotes and irony, Vanini reverses the message of the antitexts. He claims to have written the *Amphitheatrum* to combat the plague of atheism spreading also among Catholic authors, who would not hesitate to call themselves politicians of Machiavellian colour. People, he continues, should not listen to Machiavelli, who questions the reality of miracles, since all books, wise men and monuments of antiquity testify to their truth. Nor should we, using some warped logic, extrapolate the Florentine philosopher's successful demonstration that some miracles were indeed the fruit of the imagination to a general denial of their reality. In this way, Vanini established an entirely different interpretation according to which Machiavelli does not recommend a political (and fictitious) use of religion to tyrannical princes, but rather shows religion to be political (and fictitious) in its very nature. By unmasking the political enterprise to its true and naked core, Machiavelli shows that the secrets, lies and deceit exploited by the temporal power constellations form the truth of each and every religion. In other words, Vanini seizes upon the reason for the rejection of Machiavelli (i.e. the claim that he was an atheist), but he accepts it – both Machiavelli's atheism and the political truth he had laid out. At the same time, Vanini participates in the debates using

---

[16] In what follows, we will reference Raimondi's bilingual edition: Vanini, *Amphitheatrum aeternae providentiae*, in *Tutte le opere*, 384: 'Nicolaus Machiavellus, Atheorum facile Princeps'; Cavaillé, 'Le prince des athées. Vanini et Machiavel', 61–3. For a portrait of Vanini and an overview of several seventeenth-century texts on his life and thought, see Donné, *Vanini, portrait au noir*. For Vanini's use of stylistic figures and shrouded writing style, see Raimondi, '*Simulatio* e *dissimulatio* nella tecnica vaniniana della composizione del testo', 77–126.

[17] Vanini, *Amphitheatrum*, 384: 'in *Commentarijs ad Titum Livium* et in perniciosissimo libello *De Principe*, vernaculo idiomate conscriptis, existimavit haec omnia falsa esse et a Principibus ad incautae plebeculae instructionem conficta ut, quam ratio non posset ad officium, religio saltem duceret'.

the same means as his Christian opponents, whom he sharply criticises using this complex but very clear method. It is, in fact, a tried-and-true modus operandi of emancipation.

As had been true a century earlier with Machiavelli, Vanini's revolutionary turn did not go unnoticed and the establishment immediately took drastic measures. In 1619 Lucilio Vanini, or, as Vanini styled himself, Giulio Cesare Vanini, was executed in horrible fashion, and his body was burned along with his books. A number of works also appeared to counteract his atheism, including Marin Mersenne's *Quaestiones celeberrimae in genesim* and François Garasse's *La doctrine curieuse des beaux esprits de ce temps*, both in 1623.[18] While Machiavelli's *Discorsi* and *Principe* continued to be reprinted and translated, albeit virtually buried beneath a thick layer of condemning antitexts which appear to have been so effective that his critics often did not dare to read the original text and bragged about that as if it were a recommendable moral quality, the two books Vanini had written were condemned to a clandestine existence. The same lot was shared by *Theophrastus redivivus* (1659), which only circulated in manuscript form and appropriates Machiavelli/Vanini's most important thesis and connects the fiction of religion to its true significance, which is primarily that of an instrument of political oppression. In a departure from the antitexts, Vanini not only writes about religion as a political art and as fiction, lies and deceit, but also addresses a polity that is not directed to the common good but to the coercion and suppression of 'the plebs, always ready to be misled, under the weight of their duties and servitude'.[19] Vanini's true concern is no doubt best captured by the words he spoke in the presence of thousands when he was being led to the stake at the Place du Salin in Toulouse:

> There is neither God nor Devil, for was there a God, I would intreat him to consume the Parliament with his Thunder, as being altogether unjust and wicked; and was there a Devil, I would also pray to him to swallow it up in some subterraneous Place. But since there is neither the one nor the other, I cannot do it.[20]

---

[18] Mersenne, *Quaestiones celeberrimae in genesim, cum accurata textus explicatione*, 1623; *L'impiete des deistes, athees, et libertins de ce temps, combatuë & renuersee*, 1624; Garasse, *La doctrine curieuse des beaux esprits de ce temps*, 1623.

[19] Vanini, *Amphitheatrum*, 330: 'ex qua originem traxisse sibi plane persuadent opiniones de Superis atque Inferis, ad concionariam plebeculam in officio servitioque continendam'.

[20] 'Il n'y a ny Dieu ny diable, car s'il y avoit un Dieu je le prierois de lancer un foudre sur le Parlement comme du tout injuste & inique; & s'il y avoit un diable, je le prierois aussi

8   DEMOCRATIC THOUGHT FROM MACHIAVELLI TO SPINOZA

There is nothing to indicate that De la Court, Van den Enden or Spinoza actually read Vanini, nor is there any factual evidence suggesting that any of them read *Theophrastus redivivus*. How, then, can we explain the powerful similarities between their arguments and reading of Machiavelli? One possibility is that Vanini exercised an indirect influence on them, through the antitexts, guiding them to another Machiavelli than that of a counsellor of tyrants. As an example, we might point to the reading offered by the theologian Gijsbert Voetius, whose *De atheismo* (1648) cites Vanini's final words and was no doubt known to every active intellectual in the Low Countries. In this disputation, Voetius does not skirt the hottest publicly debated issues: the role of the church in state affairs, the right of decision in religious matters, the heresies of the Christian sects and, in particular, the Socinians, Descartes, and the 'freedom to philosophize'. He addresses several examples of atheism, including Vanini and Machiavelli, and suggests various potential candidates – all of them Italian – for the authorship of the mythical *De tribus impostoribus*. He notes that the terms libertines, atheists, politicals and 'Machiavellistae' were used as synonyms, and, citing Mersenne, calls Vanini the 'eagle of the atheists'.[21] Voetius's *De atheismo* offers its readership in Amsterdam of the 1650s and 1660s a virtual canon of freethinkers whom he anathemises for theological-religious and/or metaphysical reasons, but also – and this actually comes down to the same thing – for the connection they draw from these theological-religious and/or metaphysical disputes to their political consequences.

But there is also another possibility. In contrast with Vanini's books (and the *Theophrastus redivivus*), which were condemned to a clandestine circulation, the works of Machiavelli on which Vanini and other freethinkers built were published in original Italian editions in 1531/32 and on top of that were reprinted numerous times, further disseminated through

---

de l'engloutir aux lieux sous terrains; mais parce qu'il ny à ny l'un ny l'autre, je n'en feray rien.' These words were recorded in the *Mercure François* (1619), 63–4, and reproduced as a long quotation in Durand, *La vie et les sentimens de Lucilio Vanini* (1717), 197–9, and in Voetius, *De atheismo* (1639), in *Selectarum disputationum theologicarum pars prima* (1648), 203; the translation is from Durand, *The Life of Lucilio (alias Julius Cæsar) Vanini*, 93.

[21] Voetius, *De atheismo*, 117: 'Dicuntur etiam synechdochica denominatione *Politici* (quam vere aut accurate hic non disquiro,) & *Machiavellista*. Ita ut synonyma sint *Libertinus, Atheus, Politicus*.'; 203: '[Est] ergo Vaninus inter eruditos atheos tanquam aquila.'

pirate editions, and also translated into English, French, Latin and Dutch.[22] The first Latin translation of *Il Principe* appeared in Basel in 1560, a year after the papal ban; this translation was the work of Silvestro Tegli and printed by Pietro Perna, two Italian Protestant refugees. Many editions of the Tegli-translation went on to appear from the presses of Perna and others, often accompanied by antitexts, including the 1580 edition in Spinoza's library, in which we also find an Italian Testina-edition of *Tutte le opere* bearing a false 1550 date, in reality dating from somewhere between 1610 and 1629.[23] Spinoza read Machiavelli directly in Italian and did not have to take recourse to what others said about his work, although he in his edition of the *Princeps* would also have found Possevino's *Iudicium*, which plagiarises Gentillet's *Anti-Machiavel*, as well as Languet's *Vindiciae contra tyrannos*. Both of these Reformed countertexts bring the anti-hierarchical perspective of freedom to bear against oppression, and as such may have stimulated a counterpoint reading of Machiavelli permeated by the notion of freedom. At the same time, Languet's call to resistance is ambiguous insofar as it is motivated by another, albeit still religious interpretation, which in the end just means that the one prince or priest is replaced by another – an observation that cannot have escaped Spinoza's notice. Another ambiguous aspect to Languet's work is that it on the one hand seeks to rebuild what Machiavelli's critique on matters of church and religion had broken down (in which Languet bases his attack on Machiavelli on Holy Scripture and ecclesiastical authority), while it on the other hand actually echoes the Florentine philosopher's views on matters of politics. A tyrant (who must be subjected to revolt and replaced), so Languet argues, is one who fills his garrisons with alien mercenaries, erects useless fortresses against his subjects and disarms his people, while a (good) king (who ought to come in the tyrant's place) is one who stands firm in the face of hostile foreign

---

[22] Cf. Gerber, *Niccolò Machiavelli*, 81–97: in the sixteenth and seventeenth centuries, the text was printed more than ninety times. From the period after the *Index* of 1559, c. 100 printed versions and manuscripts are extant, although new printed editions were all but impossible to realise in Italy during that period. The 'Wolfe's editions' appeared between 1584 and 1588, in five collected volumes printed by John Wolfe in London with a fictitious Italian publisher name and place of publication, followed by the 'Testina editions', which bore a false date (1550) and had no publisher name or place of publication. Among the Testina editions, Gerber distinguished between an original Testina A (from 1609 to 1619), a Testina B (from 1610 to 1629) and Testina C and D (between 1645 and 1650).

[23] The copy in Spinoza's library was a Testina B: *Tutte le opere di Nicolo Machiavelli cittadino et secretario fiorentino divise in V. Parti et di nuovo con somma accuratezza ristampate.*

10 DEMOCRATIC THOUGHT FROM MACHIAVELLI TO SPINOZA

rulers, seeking support in the approval of the people rather than resorting to fortresses and city walls.[24] Other passages in this tightly composed work, written in geometrical style, anticipate the naturalist genealogy of power presented in *Theophrastus redivivus* (where 'mine and yours' is said to have entered this world through war, which in turn rendered inequality, hierarchy and kings necessary) and in *De jure ecclesiasticorum* (which calls kings the 'lieutenants' of God/nature/the people).[25] As we will see later on, these two anonymous treatises likewise witness to an unequivocal shift which not only returns to the original republican ideals of Machiavelli devoid of all religious inspiration, but also goes on to radicalise them.

What might also have guided Spinoza's attention is the movement which had formed in France in the late sixteenth and early seventeenth centuries in the wake of Pomponazzi and Cardano, against the background of Machiavelli, Aristotle (read materialistically, as in Padua), and Tacitus. The work of such authors as Michel de Montaigne, Pierre Charron and Gabriel Naudé, or the French translator Jacques Gohory, reflects a radical change

---

[24] [Languet], *De la puissance*, 201–2: '[Le tiran] remplit les garnisons de soldats etrangers, bastit des citadelles contre les suiets, desarme le peuple & ne luy laisse forteresse quelconque, est accompagné de gardes composees d'estrangers ou de gens de sac & de corde, donne gages du public à des espions & rapporteurs qui vont courans ça et là par les provinces. Au contraire, le Roy se maintient plus contre ses ennemis à l'aide de la bienveillance du peuple que par la force des murailles'; cf. Daussy, *Les huguenots et le roi*, 229–56.

[25] [Languet], *De la puissance*, 130–1: 'Au reste, lors que ces mots, MIEN & TIEN entrerent au monde, que differens survindrent entre les citoyens touchant la proprieté des biens, & guerres entre les peuples voisins à cause de leurs limites, le peuple s'avisa de recouvrir vers quelqu'un qui peust & sceust empescher que les poures ne fussent foulez par les riches, & que ceux du pays ne souffrirent par la violence des estrangers. Or comme les proces & guerres croissoyent, on eslisoit celuy qui estoit le mieux estimé de tous pour la vaillance & prudence. Voila donc pourquoy les Rois furent creez iadis, c'est asavoir pour administerer iustice au pays, mener leurs suiets à la guerre, & non seulement brider les courses des ennemis, empescher le fourragement & degats de la campagne, mais aussi beaucoup plus pour chasser tous vices & meschancetez bien loin de leurs suiets.'; ibid. 22: 'Aujourdhui au sacre des Rois & Princes Chretiens, ils sont appellez seruiteurs de Dieu, destinez pour gouverner son peuple. Puis donc que les Rois sont seulement lieutenants de Dieu, establis au throne de Dieu par le Seigneur Dieu mesme, & que le peuple est peuple de Dieu & que l'honneur qu'on fait aux lieutenants ne procede que de la reverence qu'on porte a ceux qui les ont envoyez: il s'ensuit sans difficulté qu'il faut obeir aux Rois à cause de Dieu, non pas contre Dieu, & lors qu'ils seruent & obeissent à Dieu, non autrement.' For more on *Theophrastus redivivus*, see Chapter II.4 below.

in perspective on Machiavelli's writings.[26] They understood what had once been considered negative as something positive, applied an anthropological and naturalist rather than political interpretive key, and recognised the existence of a link between the theme of politics and the metaphysical question of the truth. That shift had been hanging in the air for some time and affected numerous figures, and it could hardly have escaped Spinoza, himself an attentive reader of Aristotle and Tacitus, even if he had never read any of the aforementioned French writers or Vanini. Another potential factor may have been the obscure 'French dialogues' (*Dialogues François*) we encounter in the catalogue of Spinoza's library, possibly to be identified as *Le Réveille-Matin des Français et de leurs voisins, composé par Eusebe Philadelphe Cosmopolite, en forme de Dialogues.*[27] This text, which circulated in the Netherlands (through a 1574 translation), includes a summary of Etienne de la Boétie's *Discours de la servitude volontaire*, which in its turn locates ideas (possibly taken from Machiavelli) on the relationship between the community and the sovereigns in a non-religious and neutral framework, thereby giving a new, entirely different meaning to the notions of obedience (and disobedience), power and freedom (and non-freedom).[28] As is in fact true for all of the above authors – and in particular for the French – who play a part in this complex story by which Machiavelli was thrust into history, De la Boétie is another figure who actually deserves an entire chapter of his own. He too is generally understood to be anti-Machiavellian, and yet also his *Discours* shows remarkable affinities with passages from Machiavelli's *Discorsi*.

A final figure to have contributed to the alternative, non-Machiavellian view of Machiavelli was Francis Bacon. In his *Sermones Fideles*, of which a

---

[26] Procacci, *Machiavelli nella cultura europea*, 171–212. In the wake of Garin and Procacci, Negri offered a new interpretation of the libertine *politiques*. In his *Descartes politico o della ragionevole ideologia*, he addresses how the 'Machiavellian' misinterpretation took shape in France precisely under their influence, so that progressive, critical authors (like Descartes) only knew an incomplete version of Machiavelli; see 164–5: '[qui] fait venir la tristesse'.

[27] The identification of the *Dialogues François* in Spinoza's library (no. 157 in the *Catalogus*, 32) as the *Le Réveille-Matin des Français et de leurs voisins, composé par Eusebe Philadelphe Cosmopolite, en forme de Dialogues des Français et de leurs voisin* was proposed by Olesti, 'Presencia de la Boétie en el spinozismo?', 89–105.

[28] *Der Francoysen ende haerder nagebueren Morghenwecker door Eusebium Philadelphum*, 1574; the summary of De la Boétie's *Discours* can be found in *Le Réveille-Matin*: 179–91; see also Balsamo, 'Le plus meschant d'entre eux ne voudroit pas estre Roy', 5–27; Bianchi, 'Fascino del potere e servitù volontaria', 819–33; Laudani, *Disobbedienza*, 39–67; Visentin, 'Potere del nome e potenza del linguaggio', 2–26.

12   DEMOCRATIC THOUGHT FROM MACHIAVELLI TO SPINOZA

copy could also be found in Spinoza's library, Bacon on multiple occasions refers to passages from the work of the insightful Machiavelli in order to illustrate or bolster his political theories. In fact, as Bacon poignantly observes in *The Advancement of Learning*, 'we are much beholden to Machiavel and others that write what men do, and not what they ought to do'.[29]

2. *Istorie Fiorentine*

Is Machiavelli, then, the deceiver of the people which his anti-Machiavellian opponents persistently make him out to be, or is the opposite true – namely, that his goal, as Spinoza wrote, was to discover the causes of tyranny and to sketch out the principles for a commonwealth applying to each and every person? If we consider the course of Machiavelli's life and the context of his writings, there is little room to doubt the motive and purpose of his written corpus. After the republic was established in his city of Florence in 1498, with *Gonfaloniere* Soderini at its head, the unrest, terror and corruption which had reigned, working successively back in time, in the government-less months, under Savonarola's four-year reign, and during the lengthy oligarchy of the Medici, were brought to an end for the first time in many years. It was under Savonarola's rule that Machiavelli, nearly thirty years old at the time, entered the service of the republic as political expert, observer, reporter and diplomat. He was sent out to observe and study the political situation abroad, to gather information, to make new contacts, to hold negotiations and to establish a network. During that period he wrote reports, as well as his first political writings, including *il duca Valentino* (1503) and *i popoli della Valdichiana* (1503).[30] The year 1512, which saw a change in

---

[29] Bacon, *The Advancement of Learning*, 165; *Sermones Fideles*, 64–5; 73; 218–19, cf. Morfino, *Il tempo e l'occasione*, 247–51. For positive interpretations, see again Bayle, who also refers to Bacon and devotes considerable attention to the French translators Gohory and Amelot de la Houssaye, and to Gentili and Conring: *Dictionaire historique et critique*, vol. 3, 244–9; cf. Procacci, *Machiavelli nella cultura europea*, 155ff.; 283–6; Macek, *Machiavelli e il machiavellismo*, 206–7; 246–50.

[30] *I primi scritti politici* (*Parole da dirle sopra la provisione del danaio*, *Il modo che tenne il duca Valentino*, *Del modo di trattare i popoli della Valdichiana ribellati*, etc.), *Il Principe*, *I Discorsi* and *Dell'arte della guerra* were published together in *Opere* I, the *Lettere* in *Opere* II, and *La Mandragola*, *La vita di Castruccio Castracani* and *Istorie Fiorentine* in *Opere* III. Unless otherwise noted, references are keyed to these Machiavelli editions. English translations for *Il Principe*, *I Discorsi* and *Istorie Fiorentine* have been taken from, respectively, Mansfield (trans.), *The Prince*, Mansfield and Tarcov (trans.), *Discourses*, and Banfield and Mansfield (trans.), *Florentine Histories*; all other Machiavelli translations are from Gilbert (trans.), *Chief Works*. Where necessary, translations have been

power and the return of the Medici, brought Machiavelli's political career to a premature end, and he was banned from politics, civil service and the city. He went to live 20 kilometres away, in Sant'Andrea in Percussina, near San Casciano, where he read, wrote and tried to live from the slim produce of his land and sought permission to return to the city, claiming he could not hold out long this way.[31] After writing *Il Principe*, Machiavelli did manage to secure permission to return to Florence in 1514, although he was barred from further civil service at the explicit request of Rome. He continued to write and revise the *Discorsi sopra la prima deca di Tito Livio*, which he had commenced at an earlier time but probably did not finish until 1519. The next two years, 1519–20, he was to focus on the theme of war, situating it in the context of the general political problems. *Dell'arte della guerra* (1521) is the only political work that Machiavelli himself prepared for publication, although he did also write and publish literary – or, at least, not-overtly political – works like the satirical comedy *La Mandragola* (1518), which was intended for performance during carnival.[32] With his *Dell'arte della guerra*, Machiavelli was introduced to the Medici at last (since the papal ban on civil service had not failed in its effect, effectively condemning him to years of work in poverty and silence), and this introduction earned him his first non-official commissioned work (i.e. *La vita di Castruccio Castracani*), and, in the end, also a long-coveted official assignment, in particular the writing of a history of Florence.

Machiavelli completed the *Istorie Fiorentine* early in 1525, bringing the manuscript to Rome. In spite of being commissioned, the *Istorie* first did not appear in print but only circulated in manuscript form.[33] Different hypotheses have been offered to account for this. For one, the work may not have been entirely finished – at least, his commissioner may not have been convinced it was. It is worth noting in this regard that it would have been very difficult for Machiavelli to construct a narrative to the praise and glory

---

modified. For the dating of Machiavelli's first political writings, see Vivanti in *Opere* I, 766–7; 771–2.

[31] *Lettere*, 10 December 1513, 297: 'e lungo tempo non posso star cosí che io non diventi per povertà contennendo'.

[32] *Dell'arte della guerra* first appeared from the presses of Giunta in Florence on 16 August 1521, and Machiavelli immediately sent a copy to Cardinal Salviati who read it carefully and with approbation, as emerges from his letter to Machiavelli of 6 September 1521, *Lettere*, 380; see also note 1, 1612; cf. Vivanti, 'Introduzione', *Dell'arte della Guerra*, I, 1132–3.

[33] Vivanti, 'Introduzione', *Istorie Fiorentine*, III, 866–70; Dionisotti, *Machiavellerie*, 365–409; Gilbert, *Machiavelli e il suo tempo*, 306–10.

14 DEMOCRATIC THOUGHT FROM MACHIAVELLI TO SPINOZA

of the Medici, who represented just about everything he despised, criticised and warned against. In a letter from 19 December 1525, Machiavelli wrote to Guicciardini that, now that he had received payment for the *Istorie*, he was planning to write a new work which would not fail to blame the princes openly for the terrible situation in which the Italians currently found themselves.[34] Yet nothing ever came of the plans for a new diatribe against the princely monarchy. But in the *Istorie* we do already find Machiavelli, in order to convey his actual views without openly attacking the commissioning party, ending his history of Florence with the death of Lorenzo in 1492, before the establishment of the republic and its renewed abolition with the return of the Medici. The ending is therefore hardly a celebrated and glorious ending – in fact, the situation in 1492 was very similar to that in 1525 – but Machiavelli still managed to tell the story of a seemingly glorious and illustrious past, with at its indubitable centre the great civil revolt of 1378 known as the *tumulto dei ciompi*, or 'wool workers' revolt'.

Early in the fourteenth century, Florence was already in many respects a modern republic, even though the power remained in the hands of an elite group of rich bankers, merchants and manufacturers. The wool guild defended the interests of the wool manufacturers against the wool workers (*ciompi*), who had not succeeded in organising themselves in any way and did not have anyone to defend their interests, and this circumstance represented one of the most important reasons for their revolt, which Machiavelli describes in Chapters 12–18 of book III in the *Istorie Fiorentine*.[35] Since the beginning of the fourteenth century, the wool workers had been seeking to establish a guild of their own, which would allow them to participate in the city's government. The great plague had made this an even more pressing concern, and, following an economic crisis caused by the war with Pisa, the *ciompi* went on strike in 1370. This period of social unrest coincided with a conflict between the petite bourgeoisie and the rich families who governed Florence with corruption and deceit. In 1378 the unrest escalated to a revolt, which proved so successful that the *ciompi* ended up taking power in the Palazzo, together with the petite bourgeoisie. The simple wool carder Michele De Lando, a revolution leader and hero from the war with Pisa, was appointed *Gonfaloniere di giustizia* (minister of justice) and formed one of the most democratic governments

[34] *Lettere*, 19 December 1525, 411: 'Io ebbi quello augumento insino in cento ducati per la Istoria. Comincio ora a scrivere di nuovo, e mi sfogo accusando i príncipi, che hanno fatto tutti ogni cosa per condurci qui.'
[35] *Istorie Fiorentine* III, 12–18, 442–54.

Florence would ever see.[36] He enacted laws to punish violence, to deprive the financial elite of their political power, and to curb their greed and corruption. He dissolved the producers' guild and established new guilds, among them the twenty-fourth guild for the *ciompi* which had the function of a labour union. Machiavelli describes De Lando as a person who owed his success to his *virtù* (not *fortuna*) and left the power of decision to the masses ('You see: this palace is yours and this city is in your hands. What do you think we should do now?').[37] In spite of these promising beginnings, things soon began to take a turn for the worse. De Lando had been elected *Gonfaloniere* by the poor plebeians and rich citizens together. But soon the wool workers saw that their new minister of justice did not keep his promise of equitable distribution, failed to act with power, faltered before the wealthy, and made himself their dependent, to the detriment of his credibility. Once again the *ciompi* took to the streets and spontaneously formed their own government so that the city now had two 'goverments': the official government at the Palazzo, and the revolutionary government at the piazza Santa Maria Novella. After this, De Lando abandoned the wool workers altogether, responding to the latest initiatives with repressive measures and suppressing the revolt with violence, after which the guild of the labourers was dissolved, the wool workers were disarmed and an end was made to the democratic republic.

Machiavelli describes the events of the Ciompi Revolt itself in the form of a story with fictive dialogues, using the narrative perspective of an anonymous wool worker with whom he identifies. The greater part of book III, Chapter 13 consists of a discourse pronounced by 'one of the most daring and more experienced' wool workers.[38] The use of a specific perspective for narrating history, and especially the perspective of an anonymous plebeian, represented a radical novelty at the time and evoked numerous responses. In addition, the 'immoralism' of the plebeian's words make it one of the most explosive texts from Machiavelli's entire corpus.[39] But that is not the only thing. Through the voice of a courageous wool worker, Machiavelli argues for the equality of all human beings: 'Do not let their antiquity of

---

[36] Weil, 'Un soulèvement prolétarien', 7–15; Barot, '1378 ou l'émergence de la question moderne du sujet révolutionnaire', 61–80.

[37] *Istorie Fiorentine* III, 16, 450: 'Voi vedete: questo palagio è vostro, e questa città è nelle vostre mani. Che vi pare che si faccia ora?'

[38] Ibid. 443: 'alcuno de' più arditi e di maggiore esperienza'.

[39] Villari, *Niccolò Machiavelli e i suoi tempi* III, 249; Tommasini, *La vita e gli scritti di Niccolò Machiavelli nelle loro relazioni col Machiavellismo*; Pedullà, 'Il divieto di Platone. Niccolò Machiavelli e il discorso dell'anonimo plebeo', 209–66.

16   DEMOCRATIC THOUGHT FROM MACHIAVELLI TO SPINOZA

blood, with which they will reproach us, dismay you; for all men, having had the same beginning, are equally ancient and by nature in one mode. Strip us all naked, you will see that we are alike; dress us in their clothes and them in ours, and without a doubt we shall appear noble and they ignoble, for only poverty and riches make us unequal.'[40] On the face of it, this passage seems to conflict with an insight that finds frequent repetition in the *Istorie Fiorentine* and represents one of the cornerstones of Machiavelli's theory. As he says in the first chapter of book III, there is a fundamental difference between the people and the nobles, since the nobles want to command while the people do not want to obey.[41] Throughout the *Istorie*, Machiavelli switches between the perspective of sovereign and subject and, accordingly, between optimism and pessimism. At one time he sees the conflicts as a source of violence, at another as profitable for the city's grandeur. '[T]he nobles were, first, divided among themselves; then the nobles and the people; and in the end the people and the plebs', so Machiavelli writes in the preface to the *Istorie*, and this circumstance resulted in much violence, countless deaths, many exiles and numerous torn families.[42] But just a few lines down, he also writes that these perpetual conflicts had only served to make Florence stronger, owing to the 'virtù of those citizens' and the power of their intellect.[43] While under natural circumstances equality and therefore also freedom dominate, conflicts arise as soon as power relations are established, due to the different humours related to the asymmetry between the two perspectives. Those in power seek to command and expand their power, while the subjects pursue not just rest and peace but also freedom, meaning that they prefer not to obey. There is no internal, theoretical conflict, but rather a tragic aporia.

Regardless of perspective, there is fundamentally and by the nature of the case an equality which encompasses (or coincides with) freedom. Conflicts

---

[40] *Istorie Fiorentine* III, 13, 444: 'Né vi sbigottisca quella antichità del sangue che ei ci rimproverano, perché tutti gli uomini, avendo avuto uno medesimo principio, sono ugualmente antichi, e dalla natura sono stati fatti a uno modo. Spogliateci tutti ignudi, voi ci vederete simili; rivestite noi delle vesti loro ed eglino delle nostre: noi sanza dubbio nobili ed eglino ignobili parranno; perché solo la povertà e le ricchezze ci disagguagliano.'

[41] Ibid. 423: 'Le gravi e naturali nimicizie che sono intra gli uomini popolari e i nobili, causate da il volere questi comandare e quegli non ubbidire.'

[42] Ibid. 309: 'Ma di Firenze in prima si divisono intra loro i nobili, di poi i nobili e il popolo, e in ultimo il popolo e la plebe; [. . .] Dalle quali divisioni ne nacquero tante morti, tanti esili, tante destruzioni di famiglie.'

[43] Ibid. 'Nondimeno la nostra pareva che sempre ne diventasse maggiore: tanta era la virtù di quegli cittadini e la potenza dello ingegno.'

arise as a consequence of inequality and the absence of freedom. Those conflicts are sometimes detrimental to the city, and at other times they are not. There is therefore not only a tragic aporia, but also an evil (and good) polity, and it is here that we encounter the motif of the duality of lies and deceit. Knowledge of the natural state gets in the way of the interests of the established party in power, which for that reason lies about that natural state and creates the fiction of natural inequality. The wool worker in the *Istorie* unmasks this lie and points out that power constellations can be changed and even reversed. Through his voice, Machiavelli argues that actions and decisions, for instance about the wool workers' use of violence, must not be motivated by fear of something on the other side of life: 'And we ought not to take conscience into account, for where there is, as with us, hunger and prison, there cannot and should not be any fear of hell.'[44] The oppressed and exploited need not fear God (or divine punishment). Of themselves, wool workers are not inclined to violence or lawlessness. On the contrary, says the *ciompo*/Machiavelli, 'out of conscience many of you repent the deeds that have been done and [. . .] you wish to abstain from new deeds', and need to be convinced to take up arms.[45] The question pressing itself upon the wool workers is whether, and, if so, how they are to revolt, and whether they may or must use violence. The purpose pursued by Machiavelli/the wool worker is a change, a reversal of roles, the establishment of a new order in which all oppression and exploitation are put to an end. The text is strategic and performative, making it imperative for the hearers/readers to open their eyes to the lie at the basis of their misery and oppression. The fiction of hell is unveiled in its political significance, and thus unmasked and dismantled. The question facing Machiavelli/the anonymous plebeian is whether the wool workers who currently have no power can transform themselves into a political subject.

Machiavelli presents his arguments from the narrative perspective of the wool workers, since the ideas he champions are to their interest. He very literally employs the grammatical subject of one of the *ciompi* because they are the actors of the (hi)story. He likewise ascribes the virtù, which he mentions in the Proemio and theorises in *Il Principe*, to the wool workers. In other words, the *ciompi* are a 'subject' in a grammatical as well as a

---

[44] Ibid. 444: 'E della conscienza noi non dobbiamo tenere conto, perché dove è, come è in noi, la paura della fame e delle carcere, non può né debbe quella dello inferno capere.'

[45] Ibid. 'molti di voi delle cose fatte, per conscienza si pentono, e delle nuove si vogliono astenere'.

18 DEMOCRATIC THOUGHT FROM MACHIAVELLI TO SPINOZA

political sense. They devise a tactic for taking over power and establishing a new order, with a new social strategy and on the basis of the recognition of their specific interests.[46] In the name of the new political order, the old laws are unmasked as deceit: 'all those who come to great riches and great power have obtained them either by fraud or by force; and afterwards, to hide the ugliness of acquisition, they make it decent by applying the false title of earnings to things they have usurped by deceit or by violence'.[47] The strategy therefore means both making political use of violence (which becomes *virtù*) and seizing the moment for action (*kairós*): 'Now is the time not only to free ourselves from them but to become so much their superiors that they will have more to lament and fear from you than you from them.'[48] Otherwise stated, Machiavelli summons the poor plebeians to take over power and to reverse the direction of the perspectives: 'For faithful servants are always servants and good men are always poor; nor do they ever rise out of servitude unless they are unfaithful and bold, nor out of poverty unless they are rapacious and fraudulent.'[49] To that end, they need to face the actual reality; they must pursue the 'effective truth' which unmasks deceit and violence and understands what 'is' in a perspective of change and time.

---

[46] Weil, 'Un soulèvement prolétarien', 12–13; Barot, '1378 ou l'émergence de la question moderne', 66–72. In reference to the question of 'subjectivity', Barot (67) points to the different Marxist readings of Machiavelli, including those of Abensour, *La Démocratie contre l'Etat*; Althusser, *Machiavel et nous*; Gramsci, *Note sul Machiavelli*; Lefort, *Le travail de l'oeuvre Machiavel*; Negri, *Il potere costituente*: there is as yet no comparative critical analysis, in spite of the need for one; cf. Pedullà who disagrees with Marx when he compares the plebeian's discourse to Sallust's Catilina: 'Il divieto di Platone', 229; see also Marx's general positive assessment of Machiavelli's *Istorie Fiorentine*, as found in his letter to Engels from 25 September 1857: MEW 29, 87, 193: 'Die "Geschichte von Florenz" ist Meisterwerk'. See also Del Lucchese, *Tumulti e indignatio*, Morfino, 'La question du conflit chez Machiavel', 175–92; and Raimondi, 'Les "tumultes" dans *Le Prince* et dans les *Discours*', 157–74.

[47] *Istorie Fiorentine* III, 13, 444–5: 'tutti quelli che a ricchezze grandi e a grande potenza pervengano, o con frode o con forza esservi pervenuti: e quelle cose di poi che eglino hanno o con inganno o con violenza usurpate, per celare la bruttezza dello acquisto, quello sotto falso titolo di guadagno adonestono'.

[48] Ibid. 445: 'Ora è tempo non solamente da liberarsi da loro, ma da diventare in tanto loro superiore, ch'eglino abbiano più da dolersi e temere di voi che voi di loro.'

[49] Ibid. 'perché i fedeli servi sempre sono servi, e gli uomini buoni sempre sono poveri, né mai escono di servitù se non gli infedeli e audaci, e di povertà se non i rapaci e frodolenti'.

3. *Parole – Il duca Valentino – I popoli della Valdichiana*

Historical time has a logic structured by change but also by what endures.[50] For change is no true change until it can maintain itself as a new institution of power. Regardless of the form of rule, whether it be by a single prince, an elite few or the multitude of the people, cities have always succeeded in defending themselves by a combination of military power and prudent wisdom, so Machiavelli writes in *Parole da dirle sopra la provisione del danaio, facto un poco di proemio et di scusa*. At the time of writing, in March 1503, Soderini's government was facing financial difficulties and persistently failed to enact a necessary tax reform. It was high time for a decision, and Machiavelli's 'words' may have been what Soderini hoped would finally convince the Counsel of Eighty. But it is immediately clear that the *Parole* are not just about a new tax law, but address the very essence of the way power is maintained. Prudent wisdom alone does not suffice for maintaining a position of power, and, as Machiavelli writes, also the force of weapons on its own has no effect – and if it does, the effect is not a lasting one. Perhaps this is what happened in the Ciompi Revolt, since the power of the armed revolt brought about a change that proved in the end to be no change at all, since one tyrant replaced another and the democratic government failed to endure. While the rebels did manage to seize the momentum and their actions did have an effect, that effect was not lasting in nature. What was lacking was prudent wisdom, self-reflection and the courage of investigation, knowledge and truth. What emerges from this text and others written between 1502 and 1512 is Machiavelli's constant worry that Soderini's republic will meet the same fate and fail to endure. It was, after all, his task to worry, to observe, study, analyse and report on political events, to offer advice on the basis of his findings, and to warn about possible dangers. In March 1503 he concluded that the dangers lay at a much more fundamental level than mere financial shortage. What Florence needed was military independence and an army of its own. Yet the urgency with which Machiavelli writes suggests that no one was listening. While others seek to draw wisdom from their observations of the dangers facing their neighbours, the Florentine inhabitants fail even to draw any lessons from the dangers facing them; they simply do not see or understand anything.[51] They place

---

[50] Negri, *Il potere costituente*, 56: 'Il tempo storico ha una logica interamente strutturata dalla mutazione.'

[51] *Parole da dirle*, 16: 'Gli altri sogliono diventare savi per li periculi de' vicini; voi non rinsavite per gli vostri.'

20 DEMOCRATIC THOUGHT FROM MACHIAVELLI TO SPINOZA

no faith in themselves, and have no idea how much time they are losing or have already lost. They place their trust in fortune, but 'Fortune does not change her decision when there is no change in procedure.'[52] In this text from March 1503, we already find many elements that will be developed later on in *Il Principe*, *Discorsi* and *Istorie Fiorentine*, such as the importance of knowledge and the power of arms, the need to mobilise and not just to trust in fortune or heaven, and time as the rhythm of political events.

What Machiavelli is telling us in these early texts is that time is the substance of power. According to Antonio Negri, he developed this concept of truth in motion as the 'product of an *Erlebnis*'.[53] Between 1502 and 1504 Machiavelli was sent to the court of Cesare Borgia, which would prove to be a special experience for the young observer-reporter. He put the story down on paper in the summer of 1503, only months after the events had taken place, in *Il modo che tenne il duca Valentino per ammazar Vitellozo, Oliverotto da Fermo, il signor Pagolo et il duca di Gravina Orsini in Senigaglia*.[54] Various commentators have pointed to the literary style and at times fictive character of this work, which contrasts starkly with the reporting mode Machiavelli used in his messages to the Dieci describing these same events.[55] But in *Il modo* he crafts the facts that were to leave such an impression on him into a 'story', with focalisation of perspectives and a robustly organised temporal and spatial structure.[56] After Borgia had devised the plan to conquer Bologna and to establish a dominion of his own in Romagna, several of his captains became convinced that their duke had become too powerful and for that reason decided to plot against him. In less than three years, Borgia had managed to conquer Cesena, Imola, Forlí, Rimini, Pesaro, Faenza and Urbino, and made Bologna the capital of his realm. He had also subjected Piombino, and tried to form an alliance with Siena and Pisa. In between lay Florence, accused by

---

[52] Ibid. 'perché io vi dico che la fortuna non muta sententia dove non si muta ordine'.

[53] Negri, *Il potere costituente*, 59: 'Questa verità è in Machiavelli il prodotto di una *Erlebnis*.'

[54] Cf. Vivanti, 'Introduzione', I, 766.

[55] Ibid. Chabod, *Scritti su Machiavelli*, 315–17; see, for example, the official dispatch 'Machiavelli ai Dieci' dated 1 January 1503, from Senigallia: *Legazioni e commissarie*, 778–81.

[56] The term 'focalisation', which has been borrowed from photography and film theory, was introduced to narratology by Gérard Genette to replace 'perspective' or 'point of view', so as to reflect the relationship between the presented story and the narrator's view; the theory was developed further by Mieke Bal and can be applied in reflections on Renaissance art, yielding a fascinating and fruitful interplay between the presented reality, the perspective of the author/painter and the reader/viewer: cf. Genette, 'Discours du récit', 67–282; Bal, *Narratology: Introduction to the Theory of Narrative*.

Borgia of supporting the revolt in Arezzo and the Valdichiana, trapped, anxious and under threat. The conspirators sought support for their plans among the duke's enemies, and for that reason also appealed to Florence. But the city opted for another strategy, dispatching Machiavelli to Borgia to inform him of the conspiracy. The duke then began to devise a trap for his captains, with great patience and in utter secrecy, leaving them in the delusion of his full trust and even making new alliances with and for them. Then, on New Year's Eve, with his captains unaware of any threat, their guard down and confident in the outcome of their plans, he ambushed and cruelly murdered them. After slow, patient and crafty preparations, Valentino, as Borgia was also known, struck with lightning quickness, avenging himself on his former allies in definitive, dramatic and cold-hearted fashion with a single blow. In this story, the chief role belongs to time. Valentino plays with time and shapes it according to the rhythm of his plans for vengeance. First, he slows time down in extended silences, lying in wait like a spider, then he speeds time up to a frenzied attack, cruel surprise and devastating act. Valentino thus grasped, determined and organised historical time.

That same summer, a year after the Valdichiana rebellion and only months after Valentino had settled his score with his lieutenants and turned his renewed attention to Tuscany, Machiavelli wrote *Del modo di trattare i popoli della Valdichiana ribellati*. Less celebrated than *Il modo che tenne il duca Valentino* (due no doubt to the common view of the sixteenth to eighteenth centuries, which held Cesare Borgia to be Machiavelli's hero and example), this new text is at least as important and witnesses the same concepts and approach to problems we find in his main works. As Federico Chabod has observed, on the formal and substantive levels the text is characterised by the use of dilemmas.[57] 'Politics is about acting according to alternatives, with a choice between the one *or* the other': there is no room for compromise or for steering a middle course, even though people are powerfully inclined to such compromise due to their duality: never completely good, and never completely evil.[58] The work begins with a long quotation from Livy, who in book VIII, 13 of his *History of Rome* asks what ought to be done to the cities of Latium, where revolts are constantly breaking out, to the detriment of the empire's well-being. Should increasing brutality be applied, or ought greater leniency to be

---

[57] Chabod, *Scritti su Machiavelli*, 317–18.
[58] Ibid. 318: 'In politica si ha da procedere per alternativa, scegliendo l'una *o* l'altra via' (italics mine).

preferred?[59] Empires are most stable where subjects are faithful and feel an attachment to their sovereign, and where, in situations like the present where decisions must be made, these decisions are taken quickly so that the people are not left to dangle between hope and fear. On this point, Machiavelli aligns himself with Livy and the Romans, considering all compromise harmful. 'History is the mistress of all our actions, and particularly those of princes, and the world has always been inhabited by people who always had the same passions: and there were always people who ruled and who served, who served involuntarily and who did so voluntarily, who rose up in rebellion and who resigned themselves.'[60] Therefore, anyone who wants to know the most fitting response to the rebellion of Valdichiana or wants to inquire more generally into the best way to rule would do well to follow the example of Rome. Doing so does not offer us a concrete guideline or blueprint of action (for Livy does not tell us which alternative we ought to choose), but it will indicate to us that a choice needs to be made, promptly, between either one of the two alternatives. There is no such thing as an example or blueprint that will give us a concrete answer to the question regarding the use or non-use of violence; rather, one must consider each specific case, or, as Machiavelli metaphorically writes, the specific differences in 'sins'.[61] In the final part of *Del modo*, he criticises the city of Florence for never managing to make such a choice, always opting to compromise or waiting until the matter passes, failing to distinguish the specific circumstances, and never knowing when to act. But Cesare Borgia and his father, Pope Alexander VI, 'are men who recognize the right time and know how to use it very well', and, considering whether Florence must fear an invasion by the duke, Machiavelli writes that his plan does not tend in that direction and that the moment is not right, but adding also that the duke cannot afford to

---

[59] *Del modo di trattare i popoli*, 22–3: 'Restaci ora a consultare, perché spesso ribellandosi e' ci mettono in pericolo, come noi dobbiamo per l'advenire assicurarcene, o con incrudelire verso di loro, o con il perdonare liberamente.' This is part of a lengthy quotation from Livy's *Ab urbe condita* VIII, 13, which Machiavelli also cites in Latin in *Discorsi* II, 23, I, 388; see also note 11, 1044; cf. n. 8 on Machiavelli's translation of the Livy passage, 772.

[60] *Del modo di trattare i popoli*, 24: 'Io ho sentito dire che le istorie sono la maestra delle actioni nostre, et maxime de' principi, et il mondo fu sempre ad un modo abitato da uomini che hanno avute sempre le medexime passioni; et sempre fu chi serve et chi comanda, et chi serve malvolentieri et chi serve volentieri, et chi si ribella et è ripreso.' Translation mine.

[61] Ibid. 'loro feciono giuditio differente per essere differente il peccato di quelli popoli'.

wait because his fortune is intimately connected to the lifespan of the pope, who does not have very long to live.[62]

4. *Il Principe*

In the preface to *Il Principe* Machiavelli dedicates this work to the young Lorenzo de' Medici, who had been in power in Florence since the beginning of 1513. The duality of his approach immediately shows itself: while he does honour the authority, he also announces his intention to subject the politics in the city to a critical investigation. While this work was intended as a demonstration of Machiavelli's capacities so as to facilitate his return to Florence, he does immediately go on to note that he will not write as a Medici prince might expect of a man in his position, announcing that he will write without exaggeration or embellishment, but in an unbiased manner, matter-of-factly and sensitive to reality in all of its variety. He thus counters the prince's expectations ahead of time, and introduces the metaphor of perspective. Lorenzo ought not to take it ill of him that he, a common man, would deign to speak of the art of government, for just like 'those who sketch landscapes place themselves down in the plain to consider the nature of mountains and high places and to consider the nature of low places place themselves high atop mountains, similarly, to know well the nature of peoples one needs to be prince, and to know well the nature of princes one needs to be of the people'.[63] In Florence, where the art of painting had taken off ever since the discovery and application of linear perspective, this metaphor certainly would have appealed to his audience. In their artwork, the Florentine masters achieved the most realistic depictions of (human) reality by virtue of analytic abstractions and the interplay of (mental) image, illusion and fiction. The principle of linear perspective is a fictive projection by which artists order their thoughts and sharpen their insight – that is, mental activity which in nature occurs automatically (and which artists in their work recreate in a real-life way).[64] Seeing the

---

[62] Ibid. 26: 'che siano conoscitori della occasione et che la sappiano usare benissimo'.

[63] *Il Principe*, 118: 'perché così come coloro che disegnano e' paesi si pongono bassi nel piano a considerare la natura de' monti e de' luoghi alti, e per considerare quella de' luoghi bassi, si pongono alto sopra' monti, similmente, a conoscere bene la natura de' populi, bisogna essere principe, e, a conoscere bene quella de' principi, conviene essere populare'. Translation modified.

[64] Treatises on perspective written by Machiavelli's contemporaries include Leon Battista Alberti, *De pictura*; Piero della Francesca, *De prospectiva pingendi*; and Leonardo da Vinci, *Trattato della pittura*. Several scholars hold the view that there must have

24 DEMOCRATIC THOUGHT FROM MACHIAVELLI TO SPINOZA

drawings of his contemporaries and reading the works of Alberti, it must have dawned on Machiavelli that this could be applied to knowledge, as had in fact been customary since Dante. The use of perspective was coupled with a specific (new) and complex view on nature, knowledge and art, and their mutual relationship. On the one hand, there was the notion that knowledge and art of human creation reproduces – and must indeed reproduce – nature in a real-life way. On the other hand, it was thought that knowledge and art are only established insofar as something is added to the natural, namely thought, fiction and imagination. Erwin Panofsky, and after him Carlo Ginzburg, have noted how the discovery of linear perspective in Renaissance Italy was accompanied by a new, critical stance towards the past, which we can also find in Machiavelli, as will be detailed later on.[65]

Although to date no evidence has come forth from their letters or notebooks for meetings or conversations between the two, one may safely assume that Machiavelli knew Leonardo da Vinci well and was thinking of him when he developed his metaphor. For Leonardo served as military engineer to Cesare Borgia between 1502 and 1504, and Machiavelli almost certainly spoke with him and observed him in his work during his own stay at the ducal residence from October 1502 to January 1503. At this very time, Leonardo was making preparatory studies for his maps of Imola, which he completed several months later, offering 'exceptional evidence of his ability to depict landscape from above'.[66] In May 1504 it was once again Machiavelli who, as an envoy of Soderini's government, commissioned Leonardo to produce a painting of the mythical battle of Anghiari in the Sala del Maggior Consiglio of the Palazzo Vecchio in Florence. The fresco remained unfinished, however, and was later painted over and lost for good. But what we do have are several preparatory studies from Leonardo himself, along with two copies, one of them from Rubens, and they give us an idea of the grand nature of this planned work, which depends on an analytical detachment from reality,

---

been a connection between Machiavelli and Leonardo, from which the metaphor of perspective originated: Boucheron, *Léonard et Machiavel*; Fournel and Zancarini, 'Commentaires et notes', in *De principatibus/Le Prince*, 219; Ginzburg, *Occhiacci di legno*, 171–86 (Eng. *Wooden Eyes*, 139–56); 190; Solmi, 'Leonardo e Machiavelli', 535–71; for reflections on perspective, see Panofsky, *Die Perspektive als symbolische Form*; Damisch, *L'origine de la perspective*.

[65] Ginzburg, *Occhiacci di legno*, 180–3 (Eng. *Wooden Eyes*, 148–54); *Miti emblemi spie*, 58–65.

[66] Ginzburg, *Occhiacci di legno*, 181 (Eng. *Wooden Eyes*, 150).

in line with the 'tragic awareness' that reality is as it is.[67] The extant traces of this lost artwork are reminiscent of Machiavelli's incisive, realistic ideas since, according to Roberto Esposito, Leonardo did not understand painting simply as a means of expression, but as the very form of thought itself, a kind of 'thought in images' or 'thinking imagination'.[68] According to Esposito, the overlapping between painting and ideation is characteristic of all classical Italian philosophy, and in particular of the work of Machiavelli. Moreover, since such overlapping is never perfect, it may explain Leonardo's frequent failure to complete projects.

Similarly, knowledge that is formed and stored from a collective subjective perspective would be more realistic and effective than with the abstraction of perspectives. Perspectival knowledge of political affairs implies knowledge with a concern for the specific variations and awareness of the serious nature of the matter. In this, the choice of perspective is of defining importance; Machiavelli does not choose the perspective of the sovereign but of those 'down in the plain'. *Il Principe* first came from the press in 1532, but this 'phantasy' (*ghiribizzo*) had already been written back in 1513, as Machiavelli writes to Francesco Vettori in a letter from 10 December of that year.[69] Since, as Dante says, we only have knowledge after we recall and internalise what we have understood, he decided to put his thoughts on paper and composed a 'little work, *De principatibus*, where [he went] as deeply as [he could] into considerations on this subject, debating what a princedom is, of what kinds they are, how they are gained, how they are kept, why they are lost'.[70]

---

[67] I have drawn this expression, which is highly apt for Leonardo and Machiavelli, from Ginzburg, ibid. (Eng. *Wooden Eyes*, 150): 'The tragic awareness that reality is as it is – so often interpreted as cynicism – derived from an impassioned advocacy of analytical detachment.'

[68] Esposito, *Pensiero vivente*, 87 (Eng. *Living Thought*, 87).

[69] In his letter to Vettori dated 10 December 1513 Machiavelli calls his treatise an 'opuscolo' (brochure, pamphlet) and 'ghiribizzo' (phantasy, caprice): *Lettere*, 296.

[70] Ibid. 'E perché Dante dice che non fa scienza sanza lo ritenere lo avere inteso, io ho notato quello di che per la loro conversazione ho fatto capitale, e composto uno opuscolo De principatibus, dove io mi profondo quanto io posso nelle cogitazioni di questo subbietto, disputando che cosa è principato, di quale spezie sono, come e' si acquistono, come e' si mantengono, perché e' si perdono'; cf. n. 29, 1574: Machiavelli refers to Dante, Paradiso V, vv 41–2: 'ché non fa scïenza, / sanza lo ritenere, avere inteso'; it is in the letter dated 10 December 1513 that Machiavelli first mentions this treatise. The Latin title indicates that it was written for a wide audience. Already for the first Blado edition in 1532, the title was changed into Italian. Even though *De principatibus* is therefore more correct, in what follows I have opted to use the more familiar title *Il Principe*.

While Machiavelli addresses himself to the reigning Medici prince in the preface, in the middle of the book, in Chapter 15, he turns to an unspecified person who understands what he is saying: 'since my intent is to write something useful to whoever understands it, it has appeared to me more fitting to go directly to the effectual truth of the thing rather than to the imagination of it'.[71] In the last chapter (Chapter 26), he addresses the reader a third time, now a 'redeemer' who is yet to come, someone (from among the common people) who will take over power.[72] *Il Principe* therefore turns from a treatise on princedom/monarchy to a performative text, a plea, a political programme, a pamphlet.[73] This transition is reflected in the two parts which make up this tightly composed and ingeniously constructed work. In the first fourteen chapters, Machiavelli addresses the beginning of a new political order, the takeover of power and moment of change, which requires a single agent or body. Drawing on a variety of cases, he treats the acquisition of power in different constitutions (i.e. the new institution of power can be total, shared or mixed, the result of inheritance, war, occupation, conspiracy, rebellion or election by fellow citizens, or occur by *virtù*/ personal strength or *fortuna*/chance) and with reference to all the potential dangers threatening the new power, one of the chief threats being instability: 'men willingly change their lords in the belief that they will fare better: this belief makes them take up arms against him'.[74] Most of the time, however, they discover they have made a mistake, realising that they are now worse off than before. But this 'natural difficulty that exists in all new principalities' leads Machiavelli to another observation: the moment of change is often accompanied by violence.[75] From Chapter 16 to the end, he therefore treats the maintenance and consolidation of the new established order. To maintain itself, the government must support the many of the multitude, and conversely, the government must also be willed and approved by the many – violence and the maintenance of power simply do not go hand in hand. In *Il Principe* Machiavelli does not make a choice for a specific form

---

[71] *Il Principe* XV, 159: 'Ma sendo l'intenzione mia stata scrivere cosa che sia utile a chi la intende, mi è parso più conveniente andare dreto alla verità effettuale della cosa che alla immaginazione di essa.'

[72] *Il Principe* XXVI, 192: 'uno suo redentore'.

[73] Cf. Gramsci, *Note sul Machiavelli*, 9. The term *princeps* – and, by extension, *principatus* – is difficult to translate adequately into English to reflect Machiavelli's usage; see n. 80 below.

[74] *Il Principe* III, 120: 'li uomini mutano volentieri signore, credendo migliorare, e questa credenza li fa pigliare l'arme contro a quello'.

[75] Ibid. 'una naturale difficultà, quale è in tutti e' principati nuovi'.

of government, whether a princely monarchy or a republic of the multitude (since he is only concerned to investigate the acquisition and maintenance of power in general), but rather demonstrates how each of the two forms has its own time. Monarchy is connected to the beginning or acquisition of a new power, while a republic is about the maintenance of a position of power. For maintaining its power, every form of government, including that of a monarch or prince, benefits when dominion is shared with the many.

Machiavelli proceeds from the idea that political life is always about two conflicting perspectives: the perspective of the ruling party, that is, the rulers who usually have great wealth; and the perspective of the ruled, that is, the multitude who have neither institutional power nor wealth. He also departs from the assumption that everything is contingent and subject to change, meaning, as a consequence, that the two opposing perspectives are not irrevocably joined to specific constellations, classes, families or persons.[76] In a neutral and realistic way, without embellishment or obfuscation, Machiavelli describes the different forms of conflict between sovereigns and subjects (which occasion protest, dissent, resistance, revolt, conspiracy, civil war, terror) and among sovereigns themselves (which often lead to war), seeking to understand the dynamics at play.[77] He is specifically interested in the effective truth, and for that reason his attention goes out to the living movement of the political drama. This means that he directs himself to the beginning and logic, the power and form, of a particular form of dominion, and his investigation leads him to conclude that the sovereigns are the party to resolve and process the conflict in a logic of war. Already in the preface, Machiavelli adopts the perspective of the subjects, which opposes the logic of war. He clearly depicts the shift from the violence inherent to the initial crisis to a politics based on laws, knowledge, capacities and the approbation of the people, which he understands as a powerful polity, that is, a polity that endures. For violence can be put to good or evil use: well-used violence – 'if it is permissible to speak well of evil' – is violence that only occurs a single time and thereafter transforms itself to the advantage of the subjects, while bad violence is violence that only continues to grow and renders the maintenance of power impossible.[78] Conflict is never absent;

---

[76] Cf. Galli, *Contingenza e necessità*, 16–37.

[77] Cf. Audier, *Machiavel, conflit et liberté*; Esposito, *Ordine e conflitto*; Lefort, *Le travail de l'œuvre Machiavel*; Lavaert, 'The Logic of Conflict, against the Logic of War', 105–19.

[78] *Il Principe* VIII, 142: 'se del male è lecito dire bene'. Cf. n. 3, 852: here Machiavelli introduces the radical question concerning the relationship between ethics and politics, which he develops in Chapters 15 and 18 (which are discussed below); see also *Discorsi* III, 21, 473.

28 DEMOCRATIC THOUGHT FROM MACHIAVELLI TO SPINOZA

in fact, there are conflicting humours which must come to expression albeit not through violence, and it is on this that the maintenance and success of dominion depends.[79] A new position of power can also be obtained without initial violence, as when a 'private citizen' becomes 'prince' (*principe*) by the actions and election of his fellow citizens.[80] Machiavelli calls this a 'civil principality' (*principato civile*), and in his discussion we encounter several elements that will play a role particularly in the second part of *Il Principe*, on the maintenance of power. This exposition proves to be a difficult exercise, as Machiavelli seems to stumble over the words, content and purpose of his own text. Such a 'civil principality' is not so much the result of either *virtù* or *fortuna*, but is rather established through a combination of the two, described as 'a fortunate astuteness'.[81] Civil principality is achieved either through the actions of the people or through the actions of the nobles, and in that sense there is no middle road (that is, no mixed government).[82] This is because there are always two different humours, resulting from the fact that 'the people desire neither to be commanded nor oppressed by the great, and the great desire to command and oppress the people'.[83] This conflict between two different humours (perspectives) can issue in three different circumstances: principality (*principato*), 'liberty' (a republic?), or 'license' (into which a republic easily degenerates).[84] This curious division

[79] In *Discorsi* I, 4 and I, 5 Machiavelli returns to the different 'humours' and connects them to conflicting perspectives on sovereigns and citizens/multitude. The humour of the sovereigns is expansive, aimed at the constant expansion of power, and inclined to the oppression of citizens and the attack on foreign sovereigns. The multitude, in contrast, wants rest and peace, is conservative, and directed to self-preservation, but it is also stubborn and loves its freedom, leading to a conflict between the two humours: *Discorsi* I, 4; I, 5, 209; 211.

[80] *Il principe* IX, 143: 'uno privato cittadino'. This term has an ambiguous sense to it throughout the entire treatise. The 'principe' is a monarch, a prince, but Machiavelli is clearly also referring to the Stoic meaning of a neutral sovereign. This is of significant interest given the strategic nature of this text, which moves from the one of the monarchy to the many of democratic rule.

[81] Ibid. 'una astuzia fortunata'.

[82] This conflicts with Van den Enden's claim in his *Vrye Politijke Stellingen*, 160–1.

[83] *Il principe* IX, 143: 'in ogni città si truovono questi dua umori diversi: e nasce, da questo, che il populo desidera non essere comandato né oppresso da' grandi ed e' grandi desiderano comandare e opprimere el populo'.

[84] Ibid. 'e da questi dua appetiti diversi nasce nelle città uno de' tre effetti: o principato o libertà o licenza'. In *Discorsi* I,2 Machiavelli refers to the classical trichotomy, 203: 'dico come alcuni che hanno scritto delle republiche dicono essere in quelle uno de' tre stati, chiamati da loro principato, ottimati e popolare'. Other authors speak of six forms of government, since each of the three basic forms can easily degenerate into,

reveals a tension in Machiavelli's text, which can only be understood – and Machiavelli often has no problems stating things simply as they are – as an attempt to effect a shift and to convince his readers of something new, critical and perhaps even revolutionary. 'Civil principality' is achieved either by the people or by the nobles, although, as Machiavelli goes on to note, such princedom is difficult to maintain with the nobles but certainly an option with the people.[85] A 'civil principality' shaped by the common people is based on an entirely different dynamic, where commands and obedience recede into the background, where equality has a central role, and where power depends on trust, approval and friendship.[86]

Starting in Chapter 15 and also in the second half of *Il Principe*, Machiavelli treats the duality of sovereigns, who must be able to be good and evil, to withstand violence, to use deceit and to be as sly and cunning as a fox, and to apply the game of pretence which renders knowledge and imagination so necessary.

> And many have imagined republics and principalities that have never been seen or known to exist in truth; for it is so far from how one lives to how one should live that he who lets go of what is done for what should be done learns his ruin rather than his preservation. For a man who wants to make a profession of good in all regards must come to ruin among so many who are not good.[87]

It is obvious that a ruler who keeps his word is better than a deceiver, so Machiavelli writes in Chapter 18, but experience shows that some in power

---

respectively, tyranny, oligarchy and lawlessness, ibid. 'Alcuni altri, e, secondo la opinione di molti, più savi, hanno opinione che diano di sei ragioni governi: delli quali tre ne siano pessimi; tre altri siano buoni in loro medesimi, ma sí facili a corrompersi, che vengono ancora essi a essere perniziosi [. . .] perché il principato facilmente diventa tirannico; gli ottimati con facilità diventano stato di pochi, il popolare senza difficultà in licenzioso si converte.' He frequently notes that this is the view of others, but never says anything about his own view, which nevertheless does come to expression in *Il Principe*.

[85] *Il Principe* IX, 144–5.

[86] Ibid. 144–6.

[87] *Il principe* XV, 159: 'E molti si sono immaginati republiche e principati che non si sono mai visti né conosciuti in vero essere. Perché gli è tanto discosto da come si vive a come si doverrebbe vivere, che colui che lascia quello che si fa, per quello che si doverrebbe fare, impara più presto la ruina che la preservazione sua: perché uno uomo che voglia fare in tutte le parte professione di buono, conviene che ruini in fra tanti che non sono buoni.'

30   DEMOCRATIC THOUGHT FROM MACHIAVELLI TO SPINOZA

have achieved great things even though they were masters in deception. This is because there are two ways to fight the battle: by laws, and by force. The former is characteristic of human beings, the latter of animals. But since the former, human way often does not suffice, it is good to have the other option of force. This is why a sovereign must be able to apply both the way of animals and the way of men, and even as an animal there is a duality, since he must be able to act as a fox and as a lion. A sovereign must have both the cunning of a fox, so as to protect himself against the traps set for him, and the strength of a lion, so as to defend himself against the violence of a wolf. On top of this, a sovereign must be able to colour and mask this duality of man and animal, lion and fox, good and evil, behind feigned, unambiguous characteristics that people commonly understand as good. Here we once again see a role for change and for the element of time. A sovereign must not always be faithful, honest, religious, good, compassionate and consistent, since that would impede his ability to maintain his power. Sovereigns must be ready to abandon these things and to be evil at times under the appearance of goodness. For people are so simple and ready to obey the needs of the here and now that a deceiver will always be able to find someone who is easily deceived. Everyone sees what you appear to be, and only a few sense what you actually are, but they do not dare to resist the opinion of the many, who moreover enjoy the support of the state's majesty.[88]

After its powerful announcement in the preface, the perspective of the multitude is bracketed in part I, only to return to the foreground in part II. Violence leaves the scene, and gives way to duality, fiction, lies and deceit. The choice for the perspective of the multitude is based on an anthropology of equality. In spite of this, the notion of the multitude and universal equality does not presuppose or aim at a harmonious order. To Machiavelli's mind, every person pursues self-preservation and has two faces – or, otherwise stated, every human being is both good and evil. There are no exceptions to this rule. Like other animals, people are a part of nature, in which there is no good or evil. This anthropology is accompanied by an orientation to the effective, living truth, to the truth of reality in motion. And the truth in motion is accompanied by a view of history, a

---

[88] *Il principe* XVIII, 166: 'sono tanto semplici gli uomini, e tanto ubbidiscono alle necessità presenti, che colui che inganna troverrà sempre chi si lascerà ingannare'; 'ognuno vede quello che tu pari, pochi sentono quello che tu se'; e quelli pochi non ardiscono opporsi alla opinione di molti che abbino la maestà dello stato che gli difenda'; cf. Vanini, *Amphitheatrum*, 330 and note 19, 7 above.

natural history understood as an interplay of rhythm and tension between the conceptual pair of *fortuna* and *virtù*. Natural history is based on the notion of the contingency of history, albeit rooted in natural necessity.[89] The notion of political contingency at once opposed to and comprehended within natural necessity is in the end related to a critical reflection on the role of religion. Machiavelli's elaboration of these themes can largely be found in the final chapters (Chapter 25 and 26), where he addresses the meaning of *fortuna* or (happy) fortune and *virtù* or (effective) strength. He is not unaware, so he writes, that many thought and still think that 'worldly things are so controlled by fortune [*fortuna*] and God' that there is nothing people can do to resist.[90] This view has only gained adherents in the wake of the great upheavals taking place in his time, and Machiavelli admits that he had almost come to accept it himself. Nonetheless, in his view fortune or nature – God is no longer mentioned – may govern perhaps half of our actions, but for the rest we can determine them ourselves. Human acts always depend on both *fortuna* and *virtù*, and are equally autonomous and are equally determined and not-determined by us. All of this is related to the fact that, on the one hand, everything in human history always remains the same and continually involves the same problems, giving us the impression that nothing ever changes and that history is like the seasons, an eternal cycle. On the other hand, civilisations do disappear and political powers do lose their robes of power, and each individual adult is irrevocably confronted with declining powers and the prospect of death. The relationship between *virtù* and *fortuna* is connected to this cyclical return and these irreversible changes. *Virtù* (human strength, ability, art and culture) and *fortuna* (fortune, God, nature) are at once in tension and mutually related. Machiavelli understands whatever can maintain itself and endure to be good, which in public affairs is achieved by own

---

[89] Cf. Galli, *Contingenza e necessità*, 16–37.

[90] *Il Principe* XXV, 186: 'E' non mi è incognito come molti hanno avuto e hanno opinione che le cose del mondo sieno in modo governate, da la fortuna e da Dio, che li uomini con la prudenza loro non possino correggerle, anzi non vi abbino remedio alcuno'; n. 1, 888; in the *Discorsi* Machiavelli returns to 'nostra religione'; see further below. The expression 'de la fortuna e da Dio' is remarkable, where 'fortuna' in later passages sometimes coincides with nature while God disappears from the text, in which we may see an adumbration of Vanini's (and Spinoza's?) pantheism and notion of 'deus sive natura'. Machiavelli's expression appears precisely in the context of the thesis he opposes, according to which human beings are unable to intervene in history because everything has already been determined by God and/or fortune. See also Chapter VIII.5 below.

32 DEMOCRATIC THOUGHT FROM MACHIAVELLI TO SPINOZA

energy/strength and intelligent knowledge (*virtù*). And yet there is also nature, fortune (*fortuna*), circumscribed in a chance that presents itself or in the violence of nature with its destructive power rendering things impossible. A sovereign with *virtù* is a sovereign who knows when the circumstances are favourable and seizes the chance when it is offered, while also anticipating changes in fortune so as to protect himself against them. Such a sovereign builds dykes to temper the danger of floods, knows that floods can take place and when, and arms himself against this danger.[91] Power (*virtù*) means both capitalising on and resisting fortune/nature, and doing so at the right moment. These moments do not follow a set schedule or laws. For Machiavelli, history is not cyclical but futile, and has no laws at its basis.[92] The only rule governing history is the absence of rules, that is, contingency. This philosophical reflection finally serves as the basis for his appeal in the final chapter for the division in Italy to be overcome and for power to be seized to that end, since the time is now. This reflection is also the expression of Machiavelli's materialist view on which his entire corpus rests: the course of history is dictated by fortune or chance, that is, by the confluence of different factors that effect a certain turn, although things could also have turned out differently.

5. *Discorsi*

God is only mentioned a single time in *Il principe*, at the beginning of Chapter 25, when Machiavelli opposes the common belief that people have no influence whatsoever on the course of events through knowledge. For the rest, God is replaced by fortune, nature, or what cannot be controlled and avoided. It is not until the *Discorsi* that Machiavelli explicitly calls the common faith 'our religion', also offering a critical reflection on the Christian religion.[93] In *Discorsi* II, 2 he provides a lengthy analysis of the reasons why the Romans were more attached to their freedom than his own contemporaries are and also stronger. Briefly stated, their nurture was different, based as it was on a different religion. Our religion, 'having shown the truth and the true way, makes us esteem less the honor of the world'.[94]

---

[91] The example Machiavelli gives for 'fortuna' (i.e. a flood) refers to nature and is the polar opposite of what human beings can themselves control, determine and effect: *Il Principe* XXV, 187.

[92] Galli, *Contingenza e necessità*, 19.

[93] *Discorsi* II, 2, 333: 'la nostra religione'.

[94] Ibid. 'Perché avendoci la nostra religione mostro la verità e la vera via, ci fa stimare meno l'onore del mondo.'

Our religion 'has placed the highest good in humility, abjectness, and contempt of things human'.[95] If our religion demands inner power, it 'wishes you to be capable more of suffering than of doing something strong. This mode of life thus seems to have rendered the world weak and given it in prey to criminal men'; the majority of citizens prefer to be beaten and humiliated rather than to avenge the injustice they incur.[96] Out of their concern for the afterlife (i.e. fear of the punishment of hell and the hope of heaven), people are ready to suffer slavish subjection. Machiavelli considers Christian faith in 'heaven' problematic for the way it distracts people from their interest in politics and the world around them. So too Christian faith in the 'absolute good' is problematic because when people pursue the good alone, they expose themselves to evil. This does not mean that Machiavelli skirts the question of the good altogether and makes a plea for evil. On the contrary, as he writes in a letter to Guicciardini of 17 May 1521, he, in contrast to his contemporaries, believes that 'to learn the road to Hell in order to avoid it' is the only effective way to arrive at the good. While his fellow citizens want a preacher to show them the way to heaven, he wants a preacher who bears in him all of the church's deceit, since such a preacher can show us the way 'to send the Devil back to his house'.[97] After all, also the 'lies' of the Christian institution and faith are problematic: 'Seeing, besides this, how much credit a bad man has who conceals himself under the cloak of religion . . .'[98]

Throughout the *Discorsi*, his letters and literary corpus, Machiavelli repeatedly exposes and condemns the hypocrisy of the priests and religious officials. Fra Timoteo in *La Mandragola* is an interesting and complex character, but at the same time also the second-most antipathetic figure of the carnival comedy. This sly figure, who has no qualms of moral conscience and lacks all empathy, draws up a strategy based entirely on illusions, lies and deceit, has no truth to it whatsoever and is absurd to the point of hilarity, and he does not hesitate

---

[95] Ibid. 'Ha dipoi posto il sommo bene nella umiltà, abiezione e nel dispregio delle cose umane.'

[96] Ibid. 333–4: 'E se la religione nostra richiede che tu abbi in te fortezza, vuole che tu sia atto a patire più che a fare una cosa forte. Questo modo di vivere adunque pare che abbi renduto il mondo debole e datolo in preda agli uomini scelerati.'

[97] *Lettere*, 372: 'io vorrei trovarne uno che insegnassi loro la via di andare a casa il diavolo'.

[98] Ibid. 'Vedendo, oltre di questo, quanto credito ha un tristo che sotto il mantello della religione si nasconda.'

34 DEMOCRATIC THOUGHT FROM MACHIAVELLI TO SPINOZA

to carry it out.[99] Even so, Machiavelli's critique is not limited to the deceit and corruption of his Christian contemporaries, for it forms part of a reflection on religion as such, following the path set out by the Roman authors he read, including Livy, of course, but also Tacitus.[100] Although Machiavelli never says so in so many words, his argument actually presumes that there are no gods. Religion is a means of power which is both comparable with and opposed to violence. Violence belongs to the crisis of the beginning, and it is negative in the sense that it destroys and that it elicits a movement leading to ever increasing violence. For this reason, violence must happen all at once, leaving as quickly as possible thereafter and transforming into something else. Religion, on the contrary, belongs to the maintenance of power, is positive by virtue of its ability to unite and to establish stability in spite of the contradictions (conflicts) and the short lifespan of sovereigns and their dominion (contingency). In Roman history, as Machiavelli explains in *Discorsi* I, 11, we see the importance of religion in the way an army is commanded, so as to induce the common people to obedience and to teach kings conscience and shame.[101] Moreover, 'where there is religion, arms can easily be introduced, and where there are arms and not religion, the latter can be introduced only with difficulty'.[102] Republics are made great by the religious cult, but the neglect of religion leads to their downfall. For this reason, religion

[99] The two most antipathetic characters in *La Mandragola* are Messer Nicia, the rich, selfish, provincial, foolish (and, in the end, duped) husband, and Frate Timoteo, the hypocritical, two-faced, cunning and deceptive priest. These two characters are the only ones with a title; Callimaco, Lucrezia, Siro and Sostrata do not have one.

[100] Apart from implicit references, Machiavelli on several occasions also refers explicitly to Tacitus: in *Discorsi* I, 29, 261; *Discorsi* III, 6, 426; *Discorsi* III, 19, 471; see also Toffanin, *Machiavelli e il 'Tacitismo'*. Tacitus's words in *Historiae* I, 1 which became the motto of proponents of the 'freedom to philosophise' (*libertas philosophandi*) and stood at the origins of the notion of freethought and free speech in De la Court, Van den Enden and Spinoza, do not appear in Machiavelli: 'the rare fortune of these days that a man may think what he likes and say what he thinks' ('[. . .] rara temporum felicitate ubi sentire quae velis et quae sentias dicere licet').

[101] *Discorsi* I, 11, 229: 'E vedesi, chi considera bene le istorie romane, quanto serviva la religione a comandare gli eserciti, ad animire la plebe a mantenere gli uomini buoni, a fare vergognare i rei.'

[102] Ibid. 230: 'dove è religione, facilmente si possono introdurre l'armi e dove sono l'armi e non religione, con difficultà si può introdurre quella'.

must be encouraged and fostered in a dominion; religion is a political art. At the same time, Machiavelli leaves no doubt that religion belongs to the order of the imagination: just like art, it has been devised and implemented by politicians for the consolidation of their power. As such, Machiavelli is only a small step removed from the notion of religion as deception.

Everyone knows that the uneducated are easily persuaded of a new order or opinion – that is, they are highly susceptible to deception – but so too are the civilised and highly educated who feel elevated above the plebeians by virtue of their education. The people of Florence, for example, who can hardly be called uneducated or primitive, took Savonarola at his word when he claimed to speak directly with God. Machiavelli does not want to judge the truth of Savonarola's claim, 'because one should speak with reverence of such a man'.[103] But the fact remains that an infinite number of people believed him without ever having seen anything that might have convinced them. The Florentines took Savonarola 'at his word', due to the issues he broached and the power of his words. In the aforementioned letter from 17 May 1521, Machiavelli calls Savonarola an example of 'cunning', and many years earlier, in one of his first letters, this one dated 9 March 1498, and addressed to Ricciardo Becchi, Savonarola's ability to deceive and the virtuosity of his discourses elicited the same admiration which he held for Borgia.[104] In the story of rise and fall, the two figures seem to mirror each other. Borgia, who showed great virtuosity in his strategic employment of time and his application of the evil of violence at the demand of the moment, was in the end just a prince who owed all too much to fortune as the son of a powerful father. Savonarola, who was endowed with divine virtue and had the ability to manipulate people and hold them captive, in the end failed to unite even a single person with his religious teaching and his 'light is extinguished on the pyre'.[105] Savonarola excelled in political opportunism and functional deceit, like Borgia did in effective violence. However, Savonarola's endeavour

---

[103] Ibid. 231: 'Io non voglio giudicare s'egli era vero o no, perché d'uno tanto uomo se ne debbe parlare con riverenza'; cf. Ginzburg on Hobbes's use of the term 'awe', inspired by Thucydides, the Book of Job, Tacitus and perhaps Montaigne: *Paura reverenza terrore*, 51–80; 231–45.

[104] *Lettere*, 372; 5–8: 'più versuto che fra Girolamo'.

[105] *Compendium rerum decemnio*, 97–8: 'io dico di quel gran Savonarola / el qual, afflato da virtù divina, / vi tenne involti con la sua parola. Ma perché molti temean la ruina / veder della lor patria, a poco a poco, / sotto la sua profetica dottrina, / non si trovava a riunirvi loco / se non cresceva o se non era spento / el suo lume divin con maggior foco'. Translation mine. Cf. Russo, *Machiavelli*, 183.

36   DEMOCRATIC THOUGHT FROM MACHIAVELLI TO SPINOZA

failed, and this was not due to the deceptive nature of his rhetoric (whose truth Machiavelli refuses to judge), but because 'many were afraid their country would be ruined, little by little, when they saw that his prophetic teaching failed to reunite them'.[106] Religion is a means for organising and uniting the people, a political instrument, but when the rulers see religion as their legitimate truth, the result is a corrupted religion and dubious politics, as the multitude of the people clearly understand.[107] What Machiavelli writes in *Discorsi* I, 11 does not represent a critique on the deceptive use of religion; in fact, he even defends it. What he plays with are the perspective and the roles. If Savonarola managed to convince the masses for some time, others should be capable of the same. For this reason, he advises no one to be afraid of being unable to do what others have achieved, since all people are equal, regardless of education: 'men are born, live, and die, always in one and the same order'.[108]

Machiavelli therefore does not critique religion as such, since it is a way to convince people of the laws and institutions of which one could otherwise hardly convince them. On the contrary, a sovereign must see to it that the people practise religion, since that keeps them 'good and united'.[109] In *Discorsi* I, 12 Machiavelli continues with this motif, returning to the point of departure, repeated at the end of the preceding chapter. Religion is fiction, an artefact, and is not natural, even though it does reflect natural human attributes, and this is why sovereigns make use of religion. Pagan religion thus depended on the fiction of the oracle, and it was successful for some time as the masses believed the oracle and stood before it in worship and awe. But when the oracles 'began to speak in the mode of the powerful', the common people began to see through this fiction (deceit), abandoned their faith, and rebelled and overturned the order. This is why wise sovereigns have always done everything in their power to promote whatever profits religion, even if they considered religion false. This is aptly illustrated by the example of miracles, an object of veneration 'even in false religions',

---

[106] *Compendium rerum decennio*, 97–8. Translation mine.

[107] Cf. Russo, *Machiavelli*, 184: 'Savonarola, che volle far della politica facendo il profeta, fu cattivo profeta, perché politicizzò il suo profetismo, e fu infelice politico perché non armò abbastanza la sua profezia (profeta disarmato)'. The theme of Savonarola as an 'unarmed prophet' (*profeta disarmato*) over against Moses as an armed prophet is discussed at length in Strauss, *Thoughts on Machiavelli*, and more briefly by Namer, *Machiavel*, 36–40. See also below, Chapter VIII.4 Counterpoint 1.

[108] *Discorsi* I, 11, 231: 'gli uomini (. . .) nacquero, vissero e morirono sempre con uno medesimo ordine'.

[109] *Discorsi* I, 12, 232: 'buona e unita'.

which in spite of their dubious origins were embellished by the Romans and raised to a cult.[110] Religion is a politically inspired fiction which is effective as long as the masses believe it, but it ceases to be effective when politicians confuse it with truth and/or use it to promote their own ideas (or themselves), for in this way they are unmasked and, as Machiavelli implies, unbelief arises among the masses. These ideas coincide with Machiavelli's critique on the politics of the Christian church. If the Christian leaders had managed to salvage faith in miracles, the situation in the Italian republic would perhaps not be as bad as it is now. While many consider the well-being of the Italian states to depend on the Roman Catholic Church, Machiavelli disagrees, for two incontrovertible reasons. In the first place, all religious sense has been lost due to the poor example of the papal court. The priests are to blame for the Italians losing their faith and turning evil. Secondly, Italy has in fact remained divided due to the church. The papal court proved to be insufficiently strong to conquer all the Italian states, so as to unite and protect them from outside attack. What the papal court did manage to do is to maintain itself by the support of some tyrant or other who came to its aid in order to protect his own worldly possessions. As such, the church prevented someone else from uniting Italy, thereby perpetuating its divided state. These two reasons coincide with what we saw in *Discorsi* II, 2: the problem of religion is not a universal or epistemological problem, but rather a political problem – and in particular the political problem of Christendom, which turned fiction, lies and deceit into truth, and as such impeded all true politics.

Politics is about protecting the peace and well-being of the commonwealth, and such protection is impossible without unity – division makes the Italian states prey to foreign powers which come to invade the land, to plunder it and to spread death and decay. Yet a politics founded in Christendom perpetuates division, and thus by the nature of the case also the corruption of princely tyranny, the logic of war and lies. Christendom confuses fiction with truth, and politics with a fiction of itself. Throughout the *Discorsi* Machiavelli not only criticises the politics of priests and the Christian religion, but also condemns tyranny,

---

[110] Ibid. 'l'opinione dei miracoli, che si celebrarono nelle religioni eziandio false'. Machiavelli is therefore also saying that prophecy and miracles are not an exclusive mark of the Christian religion (as it claims), but respond to the natural needs of human beings and belong to all religions. Cf. Feuerbach, *Pierre Bayle*, 51: ‚Nun findet sich aber der Mirakelglaube in allen Volksreligionen. [. . .] Das Mirakel ist ein natürliches Bedürfnis, eine Kategorie der Volksreligion.'

38   DEMOCRATIC THOUGHT FROM MACHIAVELLI TO SPINOZA

that is, the kind of unity that does violence to the freedom, multitude and diversity of the common people. He does not make a plea for mixed dominion – his preference is for the republic – but for opposition, which must be able to come to expression on the institutional level (*Discorsi* I, 2 and 4), and for the establishment of court, which will guarantee the right of accusation (*Discorsi* I, 7); both are necessary for freedom. Power always has two sides to it, a relationship in an intermediate space, fluctuating and temporary; this is why violence and (religion as) deceit both have a role. The ambiguity inherent in such a dual, by definition undecided relationship is described by Machiavelli as a condition characteristic of political life. The argument therefore goes as follows: power is about appearances, is marked by duality, and vacillates between good and evil, and for that reason violence is sometimes useful, provided that it occurs in a brief moment, and similarly religion (deceit, lies, illusions) can be useful, but must be enduring in order to have an effect. This means that religion (or, the enduring deceit of religion) may not crystallise in a story serving the individual interests of a dominion or sovereign (that is, an ideology), for when that does happen, the faith of the community will be lost and we will find ourselves in a downward spiral in which trust is abandoned. The same holds true for the concrete expression of power with the goal of threatening people, such as the fortified castles, walls or fortresses which princes or oligarchs typically build (*Discorsi* II, 24). Such material expressions of dominion are not only senseless, but also pernicious in evoking distrust and hatred, eventually leading to conspiracy and revolt. Machiavelli describes different cases demonstrating that a dominion can only maintain itself if it is based on the approval of the many as well as on trust and friendship, and not on oppression or distrust, since the latter two set in motion a downward spiral only leading to growing suspicion until all that is left is anger, envy and vengeance (*Discorsi* III, 13). The deceit of religion therefore involves an evil side for the effect of power that is inversely equal to violence: a tendency to self-affirmation which coincides with suppression of the subjects and for that reason undermines the republic (and therefore also itself). Just like violence, religion may never culminate in and lead to itself, but must perpetuate unity, faith and trust in an open and neutral movement, so that it can be put to use as a kind of means of dominion, without a concrete goal (i.e. as a game), *for* the multitude of the common people.

Throughout the three books of the *Discorsi*, Machiavelli finally discusses not only cases of dominion *for* but also *by* the multitude of the common people. The clearest passages in this regard appear in *Discorsi* I,

57 and 58. In Chapter 57 he departs from the commentary of Livy, who has no illusions in this regard, on the typical way in which the common people act: together they are strong and fierce in their rebellion, but as soon as they find themselves alone, they hasten to obey in fear and cowardice.[111] 'For the multitude is often bold in speaking against the decisions of their prince; then, when they look the penalty in the face, not trusting one another, they run to obey.'[112] For that reason, a sovereign must not allow himself to be bothered by the criticism and protests of the masses, as long as he affirms them if they agree with his polity and sees to it that they stand powerless if they do not agree. For there is no greater danger than unleashed masses without a leader, but conversely there is also nothing weaker. Masses/multitude that rise up in rebellion must therefore immediately choose a leader, organise, and close their ranks, so Machiavelli writes, for together they are strong, but if each person starts to think of the dangers facing them, they become cowards and weaklings, just as Livy had said. Once again, we can note that the perspective has shifted between Livy and Machiavelli from the perspective of the sovereign to the perspective of the masses/multitude. Machiavelli's interest lies in what the subjects must do if they do not agree with the politics of the government. For this reason, he in Chapter 58 can no longer agree with Livy when the latter claims that there is nothing more fickle and rash than the masses/multitude. The inconstancy of which the writers accuse the multitude is a shortcoming inherent to each and every human being in general and in particular to princes/monarchs, 'for everyone who is not regulated by laws would make the same errors as the unshackled multitude'.[113] This can easily be gathered from the fact that there have been very many monarchs, but few were ever good and wise. What Livy writes about the nature of the masses/multitude does not apply to the masses/multitude that are ruled by laws and have organised or united themselves. The nature of the common people is no different from that of the rulers. In fact, if someone wants to have something relevant to say about the matter, he must compare a monarch with his subjects and will no doubt discover the same cowardice, fierceness or *virtù* there. For this reason, Machiavelli

---

[111] Machiavelli quotes Livy in *Discorsi* I, 57, 314: 'Ex ferocibus universis singuli metu suo obedientes fuere.'

[112] Ibid. 'la moltitudine è audace nel parlare molte volte contro alle diliberazioni del loro principe; dipoi, come ei veggono la pena in viso, non si fidando l'uno dell'altro, corrono ad ubbidire'.

[113] *Discorsi* I, 58, 316: 'perché ciascuno che non sia regolato dalle leggi farebbe quelli medesimi errori che la moltitudine sciolta'. Translation modified.

40 DEMOCRATIC THOUGHT FROM MACHIAVELLI TO SPINOZA

concludes, 'against the common opinion that says that peoples, when they are princes, are varying, mutable, and ungrateful', that 'these sins are not otherwise in them than in particular princes'.[114] Machiavelli sees some validity in accusing the common people and their sovereigns of the same thing, since it would be a great mistake to make an exception for the latter. For 'a people that commands and is well organized will be stable, prudent, and grateful no otherwise than a prince, or better than a prince', while a prince who is bound by laws will be more thankless, capricious and reckless than the common people ever would be.[115] The difference in their actions is not dictated by a difference in nature, 'because it is in one mode in all'.[116] The difference rather results from the varying levels of respect they show for the laws under which they live. For that reason, it is clear that rule by the multitude and organised by laws is to be preferred to monarchy.

We would be betraying Machiavelli's spirit, tragic and devoid of all illusion, if we were to close this chapter on an optimistic and even triumphant tone. The serious nature of the topic at hand rather demands that we return the way we have come and consider the negative consequences of the absence of approval, trust and friendship. In *Discorsi* I, 55 Machiavelli makes it clear that a state in which the common people are honest and united can be governed quite easily, and, if there is equality, that state will be like a republic. However, if there is no equality, a republic is not possible, and if honesty is absent among the common people, we have nothing good to expect from the state governing them. Regrettably, such a situation devoid of equality and honesty is what we encounter on the peninsula of Italy. The note Machiavelli strikes in *Discorsi* I, 53 is even gloomier. Often the common people allow themselves to be deceived by 'a false image of good' which leads them to pursue their own downfall: excessive promises and an exaggerated hope can easily excite the multitude to a frenzy.[117] If there is no one to open their eyes and show them their true interests, many dangers will lie in wait for them. And if the multitude have no one to trust because of the betrayal

[114] Ibid. 317: 'Conchiudo adunque contro alla commune opinione, la quale dice come i popoli quando sono principi, sono varii, mutabili ed ingrati, affermando che in loro non sono altrimenti questi peccati che siano ne' principi particulari.'

[115] Ibid. 'perché un popolo che comandi e sia bene ordinato, sarà stabile, prudente e grato non altrimenti che un principe, o meglio che un principe'.

[116] Ibid. 317–18: 'la variazione del procedere loro nasce non dalla natura diversa, perché in tutti è a un modo'.

[117] *Discorsi* I, 53, 305: 'il popolo, ingannato da una falsa immagine di bene, disidera la rovina sua'.

they have experienced through specific events or people, their downfall is unavoidable. As Dante said in *De Monarchia*, the common people will then cry out to themselves as they all too often do: '"Life!" to its death, "Death!" to its life!'[118]

---

[118] Ibid. 'Viva la sua morte! E Muoia la sua vita!' This somewhat puzzling quotation actually comes from Dante's *Convivio* I, xi, 8, and has been adapted slightly by Machiavelli.

II

Fictions, Laws and Religions

1. *Theophrastus redivivus*

The circumstances under which *Theophrastus redivivus* was written remain entirely shrouded in mystery. We have virtually no details available to us about this idiosyncratic philosophical treatise which appears to have fallen from the sky, and know next to nothing that we cannot deduce from the content of the text, which only survives in four manuscripts.[1] Three of the extant manuscripts do bear an indication suggesting composition prior to 1659.[2] Nevertheless, for a philosophical analysis, such a dearth of information is actually a blessing. It means we can only study the content of the text itself, focusing on its themes, sources, development, theses and arguments, and consider whether there are lines to be drawn to the contents of other

---

[1] Anonymous, *Theophrastus redivivus*. 1659. Edizione prima e critica a cura di Guido Canziani e Gianni Paganini, Firenze, La Nuova Italia, 1981; henceforth cited as *TR*. This first, critical edition is based on the four extant manuscripts; two are held in Vienna at the Österreischische Nationalbibliothek (Ms 11451, siglum: W; Ms 10405–10406, siglum: H), one in Paris at the Bibliothèque Nationale de France (ms. lat. 9324, siglum: P), and a final, incomplete manuscript in Lennik in the private collection of Jeroom Vercruysse (siglum: L). On the manuscripts, see Canziani and Paganini, 'Introduzione', ibid. LXXIII–LXXVIII.

[2] In treatise II we find a reference to Joseph Scaliger's *Opus de emendatione temporum*, in which Scaliger outlines various hypotheses concerning the antiquity of the world, using the year of writing (i.e. 1594) as his point of departure. In manuscripts P, H and L, this original date has been replaced with '1659', and the Chinese view of time has been reformulated and corresponds – with a small emendation – to this new date. The date emerging from these indicators is further bolstered by several other arguments, which together offer a convincing argument for the 1659 date; see Canziani and Paganini, op. cit., LXVI–LXVII; *TR* II, 4, 317.

FICTIONS, LAWS AND RELIGIONS   43

works, whether earlier, contemporaneous or later. We have no idea of the
author's identity, know nothing about where it was written, and even have
very little to say about its readership. It was not until 1981 that *Theophrastus
redivivus* was finally published, by Gianni Paganini and Guido Canziani.
Until then, anyone wishing to read it had to spend time in the vicinity of
the French or Austrian national libraries.[3] Unlike today, this Latin work was
relatively well known in the late seventeenth and early eighteenth centuries. According to Olivier Bloch, there must have been a number of different
copies in circulation at that time.[4] The first known reference to *Theophrastus
redivivus* comes from a certain Ladvenant and dates from 1706, and the copy
which Prince Eugene commissioned for his library in Vienna appears to
come from the same period.[5] The circulation of this work is likewise attested
in the French 'translations' of the time, which are in fact no translations
at all. Rather, these pseudo-translations were a kind of imitation or forgery
inspired by what was transmitted in oral culture and appear not to have been
based on an actual reading of the Latin manuscript itself.[6]

Scholars who have studied the *Theophrastus redivivus* see in it a link
between the Italian Renaissance and Enlightenment philosophy.[7] It is the

---

[3] In his overview of the sources that shaped the thought of the young Spinoza, Stanislaus
von Dunin-Borkowski included the *Theophrastus redivivus*, which he had discovered in
manuscript form at the court library of Vienna. Nevertheless, he adds that Spinoza
need not have resorted to this 'libertine gospel of the times', since he could also have
used the original works, and since he, 'in contrast with the mockingbirds in the circle
of Van den Enden', had the ability to separate the wheat from the chaff; see *Der junge
De Spinoza*, 489–91; 602–3. Dunin-Borkowski considered the *Esprit de Spinoza* to have
been plagiarised from the *Theophrastus*; see also 'Nachlese zur ältesten Geschichte
des Spinozismus', 65–8, and Chapter VIII.3 below, 258–63. Dunin-Borkowski may
have been alerted to 'what may well be the most radical book of all times' by Abram
Deborin, who, like Georgi Plekhanov, saw Spinoza as a forerunner of materialism; see
'Die Weltanschauung Spinozas', 57–8. The Paris manuscript was discovered by John
S. Spink; see 'La diffusion des idées matérialistes et anti-religieuses au début du XVIIIe
siècle: le "Theophrastus redivivus"'. In the end, the work began to garner the attention
it deserved through Tullio Gregory's monograph *Theophrastus redivivus*, and, finally,
through the critical edition published by Canziani and Paganini.
[4] Bloch, 'Theophrastus Redivivus', 261.
[5] Ladvenant, the secretary of Louis Ferrand, refers in his foreword to the 1706 edition
of the latter's posthumously published *De la connaissance de Dieu* to the author of the
'pernicieux Manuscrit': Canziani and Paganini, 'Introduzione', LXV.
[6] Bloch, 'Theophrastus redivivus', 261.
[7] Apart from the introduction and extensive commentary in Canziani and Paganini's
edition, as well as Gregory's monograph, there are only three studies that are devoted
in their entirety to the *TR*: Gengoux, *Un athéisme philosophique à l'Âge classique: le*

44   DEMOCRATIC THOUGHT FROM MACHIAVELLI TO SPINOZA

first explicitly atheistic text in which the existence of gods is systematically denied. It links all religions to politics, thereby laying the foundation for a critique of political theology. It is a typical example of libertine erudition, an anthology of all the heterodox literature produced up to then. It is a systematic analysis which radically undermines traditional political and ethical thought. It is a theoretical text based on the notion of natural equality and freedom, a plea for the liberation, emancipation and autonomy of all who are oppressed. As John Stephenson Spink observed, this substantial compendium contains within itself all the important ideas of 'the "left wing" of the philosophical movement'.[8] Even if there is no concrete evidence suggesting that the work circulated in the Low Countries and was read by one of our authors (since everything appears to point to a French context, although some of the French of course sought refuge in the relative freedom of Holland), there are so many parallels and similarities that it must inevitably be situated on the 'left' road leading from Machiavelli to Spinoza.[9]

The classically structured, rhetorical preface reads like the state of scholarship section in research proposals today, as it demarcates the theme, explains the title and identifies its sources so as to establish the treatise's own place and purpose. The anonymous author notes that the six books which the Greek philosopher Theophrastus wrote on the gods have been lost, like so many of his other works. This is the common destiny of many books, since a raging fire or the emergence of a new ruler or religious sect often implies the destruction of old memories, statues and poetic works.[10] The fragile destiny of books and the knowledge contained in them and the meaning of the gods are themes of interest for the author, who for that reason wants to rediscover or revive the work of Theophrastus. His intention is to start on a historical investigation of the gods, or, in other words, to be a second Theophrastus, a *Theophrastus redivivus*. The programme he sketches out reads like a textbook

---

Theophrastus redivivus, 1659; Ostrowiecki-Bah, *Le Theophrastus redivivus, erudition et combat antireligieux au XVIIe siècle*; Rodríguez Donis, *Materialismo y ateismo. La filosofía de un libertino del siglo XVII*. In scholarship on clandestine philosophy, the *TR* is mentioned in the work of René Pintard, John S. Spink and Ira O. Wade. Others to deal with it include Miguel Benítez, Lorenzo Bianchi, Olivier Bloch, Jean-Pierre Cavaillé, John Chris Laursen, and Winfried Schröder. For the position of the *TR* between Renaissance and Enlightenment, see Garin, *Dal Rinascimento all'Illuminismo*, 86–7, and Gengoux and Moreau (eds), *Entre la Renaissance et les Lumières, le* Theophrastus redivivus.

[8] Spink, 'La diffusion des idées matérialistes', 250.
[9] Canziani and Paganini have convincingly demonstrated that the *TR* was written by a French author: 'Introduzione', LXV–CXI.
[10] *TR* Prœmium, 2.

FICTIONS, LAWS AND RELIGIONS 45

example of Renaissance knowledge. Apart from Aristotle, as read through the Paduan, Averroist lens of Pomponazzi and Cardano, the anonymous author's sources include the Italian naturalism of the likes of Campanella or Vanini, the ancient and modern scepticism of Sextus Empiricus, Charron and Montaigne, materialist authors like Pliny or Lucretius, and political authors like Bodin, Naudé and Machiavelli.[11] The *Prooemium* is followed by a table of contents which details the structure of the work and reads like a summary. The six lost books of Theophrastus of Eresus are echoed in the six treatises of *Theophrastus redivivus*, whose themes are identified in the keywords on the title page.[12]

The first treatise is on the gods, and begins with a reflection on people who deny the gods, followed by three chapters on the gods, who do not exist. It then moves on to providence and hell, after which the author concludes that the existence of gods cannot be proved by arguments of human reason. As we will see, the beginning of this investigation into the significance of religion for ethics and politics brings to mind the structure of Spinoza's *Ethica*.

The second treatise addresses the world. Even today, at the beginning of the twenty-first century, God is persistently connected to the question of origins: believers see God as the creator of the world, while non-believers attack this doctrine of faith by demonstrating that God is not the creator of the world. The critique of religion therefore almost always follows the

---

[11] *TR*, Fig. 1. In the genealogical tree we read the names of the following philosophers, from left to right, in the line from Theophrastus of Eresus to Theophrastus redivivus: Protagoras, Theodorus of Cyrene, Plato, Epicurus, Cicero, Pliny the Elder, Galen, Diogoras, Euhemerus, Aristotle, Lucretius, Seneca, Lucian, Sextus Empiricus, Pomponazzi, Cardano, Bodin and Vanini.

[12] *TR*, Fig. 1; Fig. 2. The title page depicts a genealogy of philosophical atheists which surrounds the following words: 'Theophrastus redivivus, or, History of the things that are said about the gods, the world, religion, the soul, hell and demons, the scorn of death, and a life according to nature. A work constructed from the opinions of philosophers, and proposed to the most learned theologians for them to destroy it.': 'Theophrastus redivivus sive historia de iis quae dicuntur de diis, de mundo, de religione, de anima, inferis et daemonibus, de contemnenda morte, de vita secundum naturam. Opus ex philosophorum opinionibus constructum et doctissimis theologis ad diruendum propositum.' See also Canziani and Paganini, 'Introduzione', LV. Alfredo Gatto has noted that the philosophers on whom Theophrastus builds his argument – i.e. Pomponazzi, Paracelsus, Machiavelli, Cardano, Charron and Vanini – are the same ones attacked by anti-libertine polemicists (Garasse, Mersenne). He adds that the *TR* furthermore proposes that atheism and materialism form the constant foundation of the entire philosophical tradition; see his 'La fictio del sacro. Il Theophrastus Redivivus e il fondamento della sovranità politica', 67–8.

46 DEMOCRATIC THOUGHT FROM MACHIAVELLI TO SPINOZA

question of origins. One might wonder, however, whether a real shift actually takes place when the question regarding the (temporal) origins of the world is *not* – or no longer – posed, for this is what we see in *Theophrastus redivivus*. It is a matter of logic, for anyone who sets out to trace the foundation and history of religion must depart from the world as a given and therefore as eternal. The second treatise then goes on to treat the various existing views on the topic of origins, noting that some people think the world was created from nothing, which it then counters with opposing arguments. Precisely the same argument for the eternity of the world and against creation *ex nihilo* can be found back in Koerbagh as well as Spinoza, although we must note a certain tension, if not contradiction, in the author of the *Ethica*, who does at times still pose the question of origins. *Theophrastus redivivus*, in contrast, is entirely consistent in this regard, and even offers a formal, logical proof in favour of his position. That the world is eternal does not mean no changes ever take place. On the contrary, there are intrusive and irreversible upheavals and revolutions that take place as a result of floods, fires and all kinds of other natural disasters, which issues in the constant cycle of renewal structuring every chronology. This view on time as a circle and a line, of contingent interventions grafted on the cycle of nature, seems to come straight from Machiavelli.

In the third treatise, the polemical theses become concrete, as pseudo-Theophrastus attacks the main theses of religion in general and of Christianity in particular. As such, it amounts to nothing less than a declaration of war on all religious faiths.[13] First, the author investigates what religion actually is and where it comes from, yielding the conclusion that it is 'in every respect a political art'.[14] Then he goes on to deal with oracles, sybils, prophets and miracles, and this recalls another of Spinoza's works, this time the *Tractatus theologico-politicus*. The anonymous author's analysis amounts to a systematic critique of religion, departing from the assumption that historical changes do not form a continuous movement but a dialectical and discontinuous process which at once leaves and wipes out its traces. As a result, history becomes archaeology, an excavation in the material and genealogy, a search for relationships.[15] Unlike Spinoza, the anonymous author

---

[13] Bloch, 'Theophrastus redivivus', 259.
[14] *TR*, VIII: 'In quo diffuse ostenditur religionem omnino esse artem politicam'.
[15] This explains the genealogical tree on the title page, which points out that the *redivivus* envisions a new kind of historical knowledge that departs from a specific view of history. Cf. Canziani and Paganini, 'Introduzione', LV; Ostrowiecki-Bah, 'Notice', in *Libertins du XVIIe siècle* II, 1490–1.

FICTIONS, LAWS AND RELIGIONS 47

does not focus on a single religion, but maps similarities and differences among the pagan, Jewish, Christian and Saracen religions as the four chief religions. He then describes their 'superstition and deceptions', and thereafter 'it is shown that every religion is good, since every religion has its origin in politics and was instituted by human beings rather than being given by God, as is commonly believed'.[16] This is the same trajectory we find running from Machiavelli through Spinoza's *TTP* to the *Traité des trois imposteurs*.

In the fourth treatise, *Theophrastus redivivus* closely investigates the soul and hell. First, 'it is demonstrated that the immortality of the soul was devised for the sake of utility', then 'the essence, substance, seat, and origin of the soul' are addressed, and on this basis the conclusion is drawn that there is no such thing as spirits or resurrection.[17] From there, the author demonstrates the mortality of the soul 'on altogether natural grounds', before going on to show that 'the places of hell and paradise' do not exist and that 'there are no demons or angels'.[18] As we will see later on, the table of contents once again anticipates the structure of Spinoza's and Koerbagh's religious critique, as well as the final chapters of the *Traité des trois imposteurs*.

The fifth treatise investigates death – what death is and what makes it so terrifying, the love of life and emancipation from the fear of death, why death does not touch us, and, finally, why death is to be wholly despised. Scorn of death and love of life are a foundational motif in all the texts whose authors we are investigating here, from Machiavelli to Spinoza, and they form an explicit building block in the work of De la Court, who is most closely and explicitly related to Machiavelli and applies the same cut-and-paste method we find in the *Theophrastus redivivus*.

Finally, the sixth treatise takes stock of the results, draws a conclusion, and moreover offers a positive account of the natural and happy life. In this treatise, the anonymous author comes closest to the naturalism of De la Court, Van den Enden, Koerbagh, Spinoza and the similarly pseudonymous *Lucius Antistius Constans*. Human beings are animals, only distinguished from them in kind, and like all other animals they are equal and inclined to community. But by their laws, the arts and the sciences, they themselves

[16] *TR*, VII: 'superstitionibus et imposturis'; 'In quo omnis religio bona esse ostenditur, cum nulla sit quae a politicâ ortum non habeat et ab hominibus sit instituta, non vero a deo data, ut vulgo persuasum est.'

[17] Ibid. 'In quo animae immortalitas ob utilitatem conficta fuisse declaratur, itemque de illâ alios aliter statuisse'; 'In quo de animae essentia, substantia, sede et origine agitur.'

[18] *TR*, VIII: 'In quo animae mortalitas rationibus naturalibus penitus declaratur'; 'In quo Inferorum et Paradisi loca nulla esse declaratur'; 'In quo nullos esse daemones sive angelos ostenditur.'

48   DEMOCRATIC THOUGHT FROM MACHIAVELLI TO SPINOZA

have destroyed this natural community and equality, thereby also abolishing freedom. Wisdom therefore means returning to nature and living according to it.

2. Artefact

Nature is governed by freedom, that is, community and equality, but this natural freedom has been lost in an artificial system of fictions, laws and religions. *Theophrastus redivivus* directs its critique against the mystifications of knowledge and religion which are by definition related to political, historical objectives, even if – or, more accurately, especially when – these objectives are denied. The analysis here is structured by a naturalistic philosophy in which there is no room for transcendence; the only thing that is, is the here and now of the world in which we live, communicate and form mental images existing as memory, imagination, representation, expectation, habit and linguistic signs. The anonymous author's critique is therefore not just directed to religion, but also to the knowledge forms, cultural fables and political laws which string their fictional abstractions together into systems and anchor them in habits and language. He categorically rejects every abstraction or fiction that dissociates itself from experience and is transformed into doctrine, even if the resulting doctrine is 'scientific' or 'rational'. This radical criticism is based on an intrinsically related anthropology and strict notion of immanence, whose constitutive elements and implications are also evidenced in the texts from Machiavelli to Spinoza. Like so many libertine authors, *Theophrastus redivivus* ascribes a central role to Renaissance thought in the rediscovery of the ancient sources. Quotations and paraphrases from ancient and modern texts are strung together to form a new knowledge that denies authority, tradition and god. As such, the *libertins érudits* of the seventeenth century, and in particular *Theophrastus redivivus*, represent a link in the chain from the Italian Renaissance to modern thought, culminating in the Enlightenment. Where the anonymous author does distinguish himself from Machiavelli, as well as De la Court, Koerbagh and later Enlightenment writers, is in his relationship to his audience. *Theophrastus redivivus* is composed in Latin, and addresses an elite of (like-minded?) intellectuals, among whom it circulated exclusively in clandestine form.[19] Accordingly, it shows

---

[19] This difference may indicate that *Theophrastus redivivus* was still stuck in premodern thought. This is similarly suggested by the contents, as when the arguments drawn from natural philosophy against the truth of miracles depend on a pre-mechanical view of nature; see Schröder, *Ursprünge des Atheismus*, 270–9. In this context, various

FICTIONS, LAWS AND RELIGIONS

itself sceptical regarding the possibility of change ('It is folly to will to move or injure even in the slightest decree what has been established by custom') and witnesses of a pessimistic view of the common people, on both points conflicting with its basic principles and its critique of religion.[20]

Though pure folly, the anonymous author does undertake a genealogical investigation of the godhead, focusing first on language. Since words 'pertain either to some object and a real thing or else signify a fiction of a thing [. . .] or are various empty words like unarticulated sounds, it must follow for us that, in investigating the name God, we will recognize what its true meaning is, and whether God is some real thing or a fiction'.[21] The author soon reaches the conclusion that 'the false and fable-like opinions on the gods have been impressed on human minds from times of old by the authority of custom and laws'.[22] God 'is about fiction, which was adapted to the need of the state and thereafter translated into myths by the authority and power of custom'.[23] All representations that correspond to something real can be established by sense perception. But whatever can be formed and imagined in the mind without the aid of the senses is nothing but a

> scholars have pointed to the elitist, politically disengaged character of the critique on religion, in which the common people are explicitly denounced; see Bianchi, 'Sapiente e popolo nel "Theophrastus redivivus"', 137–64; Ostrowiecki-Bah, 'Notice', 1490–6. Nevertheless, it cannot be denied that the critique is directed against oppressive regimes and anything supporting such oppression, or that the text has – or can have – an emancipatory effect/function. The author's use of Latin is above all indicative of his intended audience (i.e. intellectuals), as is also true for Spinoza, who in the *TTP* likewise thematises the notion of *libertas philosophandi*. Their use of Latin can be understood in two different ways: either these texts operate within a genre that to a certain extent actually undermines their effectivity, or they are addressed to intellectuals because of the authors' conviction that the critique must be formulated by intellectuals. In the latter case, the use of Latin does not get in the way of the application of their knowledge.
>
> [20] *TR* I, 1, 42: 'Quae autem consuetudine invaluêre, dementia est, vel etiam minimum movere ac laedere velle.'
>
> [21] *TR* I, 2, 50–1: 'Cum enim voces et nomina a rebus ipsis ortum ducant, et termini sint omnino positivi, id est ad rem aliquam referantur et verum aliquod ens aut figmentum admodum entis significent, priusque sit necessario quod nomine donatur, et illo qui nomen imponit, et etiam nomine ipso imposito – aut nomina sunt varia et inania, veluti inconditae et inarticulatae voces, ut supra ex Epicuro retulimus – eveniet ut, examinato dei nomine, cognoscemus quaenam sit vera eius significatio, et deum esse aut verum aliquod ens aut figmentum.'
>
> [22] *TR* I, 2, 65: 'En vides falsas et fabulosas de diis opiniones solâ consuetudinis et legum authoritate a teneris annis mentibus hominum insitas vigere.'
>
> [23] *TR* I, 2, 66: 'figmentumque esse ad reipublicae utilitatem accom[m]odatum, deinde ad fabulas traductum legum authoritate et consuetudinis potestate validum'.

50   DEMOCRATIC THOUGHT FROM MACHIAVELLI TO SPINOZA

fiction, without a real existence or independence. The thing we call God is a being of the human mind, a fabrication that only exists in our intellect. The author's argument here is rooted in the assumption that representations only correspond to reality if they can be established empirically, and in a view of language which undermines the traditional dichotomy between nature and culture. Various animal behaviours that are considered natural actually depend on training and custom, while countless human behaviours acquired by custom and discipline approximate the spontaneity of nature.[24] Human beings are a kind of animal: as with other animals, their behaviour is guided by the drive for self-preservation, which in fact also determines rationality. Nature has endowed animals no less than people with understanding and reason.

The new Theophrastus also corrects the Aristotelian definition of human beings, according to which they are distinguished from other animals by their use of language. It is a prejudice to think that the use of language is the prerogative of human beings. Animals also communicate by means of noises and with their voice. Like human beings, they too have internal and external speech. Yet a comparison between the speech of human beings and animals does teach us an important difference, which still yields a distinguishing characteristic of human speech: we see a variety of different languages spoken among people, which can each change independently and are established arbitrarily.[25] Human speech is not necessary but contingent: it can be and not be. Had human language been necessary, 'the different idioms of language which we see in use among the different nations would no doubt originate from nature. Yet they do not come from nature but

---

[24] Canziani and Paganini, 'Introduzione', XXIV.

[25] For the question of language in the *TR*, see Gensini, 'The Linguistic Naturalism of Theophrastus redivivus', 301–20. The new Theophrastus's reflections are analogous to the reversal of the traditional understanding of language effected by De Saussure and Peirce and further advanced throughout the twentieth century and down to today (e.g. Paolo Virno). Had there been no material evidence in the form of manuscripts, whose existence had already long been documented, and no scholarship on the *TR* dating back to 1910, one might well imagine the *TR* to be a late twentieth-century forgery. All these specific theories of rather recent development – i.e. the linguistic turn, historical materialism, radical Enlightenment and Romanticism, postmodern critique, etc. – are present in the text, formulated in a timeless, essential form. The exemplary attributes of a '*libertin érudit*-text', including even the ironic quip at the outset that the anonymous author is a pious Christian, make the *TR* a textbook example of forgery. As we will see, the same characteristics also mark *L'Esprit de Spinosa/Traité des trois imposteurs*.

depend on place [. . .] and they are acquired by instruction.'[26] Languages are unstable over time and subject to constant change. As a result, human linguistic signs can only be arbitrarily established. Human beings give names to things arbitrarily, and it is only by their long use and with the passing of time that the names 'obtain the power of a property attribute, although they by nature have no such power'.[27] The only privilege which human beings have over animals is this arbitrary establishment of names, which occasions various idioms. This relative superiority comes at a price, namely the instability, variability and superficiality of culture which conflicts with the constant, economical and firm foundation of nature.[28] Human beings are not elevated above animals; on the contrary, the fact that human beings have many languages is a sign of their failure and imperfection. In contrast with other animals, for human beings life is a constant process of learning and emancipation so as to become an animal that uses language and is rational and social – that is, a return to their lost natural state which is doomed never to succeed in full.[29]

This insight into the existential tragedy and the complex relationship between nature and culture means that the materialist perspective or sensualism at the foundation of the *Theophrastus redivivus* is not absolutised to a new metaphysics. It forms the basis for a critique of theology and, in fact, of *all* deceptive cultural forms, of which religion is indeed the most representative example.[30] As we may understand from the primary institution of language, the transition from natural freedom to complex culture occurs by a growing structure of fabrications and fantasies. On the basis of 'old lies', opinions take shape which 'are for the most part sanctioned by consensus

[26] *TR* VI, 2, 832–3: 'si necessaria esset, a naturâ haud dubie proficiscerentur varia linguarum idiomata quae apud varios populos in usu esse videmus. At haec non sunt a naturâ, sed ratione loci [. . .] et per disciplinam acquiruntur'.

[27] *TR* VI, 2, 834: 'igitur non sunt a naturâ, sed, ut sunt homines ad loquendum apti, eorum lingua eiusmodi a naturâ dispositionem sortita, rebus ad libitum imponunt nomina, quae longo deinde usu et tempore vim proprietatis obtinent, quamvis nullam a naturâ habeant'.

[28] Canziani and Paganini, 'Introduzione', XXIV.

[29] Cf. Virno's idea, drawing on Aristotle and Saussure, that human beings use language as a repeated self-emancipation from aphasia; see, e.g., his *Parole con parole*; *Quando il verbo si fa carne*.

[30] Canziani and Paganini, 'Introduzione', XXVIII–XXIX. This forms the basis for the critique of political theology as it is reversed (to a political theology) by conservative Restoration thinkers, from the anti-revolutionary Joseph de Maistre to the Nazi ideologist Carl Schmitt. See, for example, Assmann, *Herrschaft und Heil*; Ginzburg, *Paura reverenza terrore*; Agamben, *Stasis*.

52 DEMOCRATIC THOUGHT FROM MACHIAVELLI TO SPINOZA

and confirmed by the passage of time' and which move people much more powerfully 'than the new announcement of an unaccustomed truth'.[31] In this sense, there is no difference between the ignorant common people and educated elite: the former join the general consensus out of conformity and by their hostility to anything independent, while the latter do so because they, subscribing to a doctrine and school, follow the authority and rules (as well as prejudices) of their teachers. This is how opinions are both the cause and consequence of the world of fictions which they themselves have created.[32] This is how 'even among the philosophers, for whom it is much easier to be persuaded of the truth than it is for the uneducated, there are very few who embrace this theory [. . .] and have the courage to convert to the law of nature'.[33] The author ends his work on the same pessimistic note with which he had begun: it is pure folly to will to change and to move what has been established by custom.

3. Religion as political art

Religion is the perfect example and paradigm of that law. In the third treatise, the anonymous author draws on Machiavelli to locate the source of religion in actual human practices (i.e. religion as a human affair) and focuses on the artificial processes by which the fiction, which starts out neutral, turns into a lie and oppression (i.e. religion unmasked as an instrument of power). Throughout history, politicians have used religion to serve their power interests and to oppress their subjects; miracles and prophecies are deception. At the same time, *Theophrastus redivivus* does see religion as something inescapable and as something that must be maintained for the general good, which nevertheless takes nothing away from its fictive foundation, nor may it be confused with truth. In fact, the political usefulness of religion is related to its shadowy and illusory character, or, to put it another way, it is useful insofar as it is a fabrication and has no foundation of truth. After this general account, the author goes on to adduce concrete historical examples and testimonies exposing religion as a political art.

---

[31] *TR* VI, 4, 881: 'vetera enim mendacia plurimorum consensu comprobata et diuturnitate confirmata multo potentius movent, quam nova insolitae veritatis propositio'.

[32] Canziani and Paganini, 'Introduzione', XXVIII.

[33] *TR* VI, 4, 881: 'ita ut inter philosophos ipsos, quibus multo magis quam indoctis veritatem persuadere facile est, pauci admodum sint qui ex animo hanc amplectantur [. . .] ad naturae legem sese convertere audeant'.

FICTIONS, LAWS AND RELIGIONS

Lawgivers have performed many amazing things which 'appeared to be miracles to the people', as when they saw to it that 'their bodies were hidden after death', 'so that people would believe that they had been taken up into heaven'.[34] Moses and Christ, Aeneas and Romulus – they were all politicians whose deceit was so great

> that they also willed for people to believe that they were gods and no longer just men. For this reason, it is clear that all lawgivers and princes are deceivers and imitators, and that the religion by which they draw the people are nothing but a ruse and fabrication conceived and established to exercise dominion or gain renown; but the people, who are so easily deceived, are altogether ignorant and have no [life] experience, for otherwise religion would not stand.[35]

Politicians present themselves as exceptions, as if they are not (mortal) human beings but gods. On the basis of these two fictions – i.e. that immortal beings exist, and that they themselves are immortal beings and must therefore be different from (and better than) normal human beings – they construct the myth that their power, and they themselves in fact, cannot be questioned. The one motif is therefore religion as deceit. The author's critique is directed to the actors in this deception, the lawgivers in power, but also the people who participate in the deception by which they have been captured: 'the common people are coerced by religions as a muzzle, as it were'.[36] The other motif is that of religion as something inescapable, necessarily bound to the law and good for everyone. There has never been a lawgiver who

> did not trace [new] laws back to God as their author, since those laws would never been accepted by the people without this fabrication; for there are many useful and advantageous things that are known by and manifest to the wise alone, which nevertheless bear no evident arguments

---

[34] *TR* III, 2, 355–6: 'multa miranda visi sunt facere quae populo discernere nescienti visa sunt miracula [. . .] et post mortem curaverunt occultari corpora sua quo crederentur in coelum esse translati'.

[35] *TR* III, 2, 357: 'ut etiam deos credi voluerint qui ne quidem amplius homines esse poterant. Unde manifestum est omnes legislatores et principes esse deceptores ac simulatores religionemque qua populos trahunt nihil esse quam astutiam et commentum ad dominatus utilitatem, vel ad famam comparandam excogitatum et introductum; populum vero, cui tam facile imponitur, ignarum omino et imperitum esse, aliter enim religio non staret'.

[36] *TR* III, 2, 357: 'vulgus enim religionibus tamquam fraeno coërcetur'.

within themselves by which they can persuade others. Therefore, in order to overcome these difficulties, the prudent lawgivers pretend that their laws were given to them by god.[37]

Theophrastus redivivus follows the same line of argument we find in Machiavelli, in *Discorsi* I, 11. Religion is what ensures that the common people, who are usually ignorant, are convinced to adopt new opinions and forms of life. Religion is useful for establishing a new power and for introducing a new view to the people, because the majority of them are not open to the truth which is often complex and depends on arguments. It is worth noting that Theophrastus, like Machiavelli, points out that it is not just the uneducated plebeians who are credulous, limited as they are in their ability to reason critically, and who therefore need the story of a miracle. For the highly cultured and educated Florentines likewise allowed themselves to be persuaded by Savonarola that he communicated directly with God. Accordingly, religion has a rhetorical and propagandistic function, as it were. It constructs a fiction or myth which makes it possible for complex views to be announced in normal language. It is an exercise in metaphorical and human speech, a political art.

At times, however, speech does not suffice, and the fiction breaks through the fragile surface of the common mind, endangering the dominion of the sovereign. In the preceding chapter we saw how Machiavelli understood religion as a means of power alongside violence, where the power of dominion grows proportionally to the proper use of the combined power of weapons and religion. Theophrastus follows him in this. Since

> the mind of the common people is fickle and unstable (for it is easy to impress new opinions on them, but just as difficult to make them stay, as Machiavelli correctly observes in *Il Principe* 6), it is necessary for the prince to arrange his affairs in such a way that he constrains the people to believe by force as soon as they stop believing. Thus Moses, like all the prophets, constantly bore arms, and those who controlled the people with the combined aid of weapons and religion were always the victors.[38]

[37] *TR* III, 2, 358–9: 'qui ad deum tamquam ad authorem illas non retulerit, quia absque hoc commento numquam acceptae essent a populis; multa enim sunt utilia et commoda, solis prudentibus nota et manifesta, quae in se tamen nullas habent evidentes rationes quibus aliis persuaderi queant. Idcirco sapientes legislatores, ut has difficultates amoveant, a deo suas leges sibi tradi simulant.'

[38] *TR* III, 2, 359–60: 'Sed quia varia et instabilis est mens vulgi (ut enim facile est novas opiniones illi imprimere, sic difficile est in iisdem illum diu retinere, ut recte

FICTIONS, LAWS AND RELIGIONS 55

Yet the anonymous author also follows Machiavelli in his insistence on the priority of religion over violence. In the Roman republic, weapons always proved to be useful, but the fact that the dominion there was safe, stable and smooth must be credited to religion. Violence is often of benefit for the conquest of new territory, but it must vanish as soon as possible in order for the new power to be able to persist. If the new sovereign continues to protect his position against his opponents and subjects with the use of violence, it will have an adverse effect and the sovereign will meet his end. For violence destroys, while religion, even if it belongs to the order of the imagination, creates solidarity.

> All of these things are the true secrets of this political art; if you take them away, it may be to the great disadvantage of dominion. Therefore, as Machiavelli says (*Discorsi* I, 12), all sovereigns or republics that want to keep their dominion long intact must first devote every effort to see to it that the ceremonies of religion are not weakened in any way but kept in the highest honour. [. . .] The sovereigns must favour all matters relating to religion, even if they realize that these are false and contrived, and even increase them.[39]

In this way, wise sovereigns have fostered and propagated faith in miracles, as well as oracles, sybils and prophecies. But since these are political arte-facts, the prophecies and miracle accounts are relative, bound to context and time. They organise and construe historically contingent constellations into a meaningful narrative, and they only have this positive, binding force and function to the degree that the fiction does not become complete. In order for religion to function as a political art, it may make no claim to the truth, and cannot be anything more than the fictive example of the political rule of law, which itself similarly lacks a necessary foundation, but rather, like the many languages that people speak according to the place, time and specific

---

animadvertit Machiavellus [*in Princ. cap.* 6°] propterea necesse est principem res suas ita disponere, ut vi populum ad credendum cogat, statim atque incredulus factus est. Sic Moses, sic prophetae omnes, armati semper fuêre et victores semper fuerunt ii omnes qui armorum et religionis simul auxilio populos continuerunt.'

[39] *TR* III, 2, 362–3: 'Itaque principes omnes, inquit Machiavellus [*lib. 1° de' Discor. cap.12°*], vel respublicae, quae dominationem suam diu conservare volunt incorruptam, prospicere in primis omni cura debent, ne vel minimum religionis caeremoniae labefactentur, imo ut in summâ veneratione semper habeantur. [. . .] Cunctis etiam rebus, quae religionis gratiâ fiunt, favere debent principes, quamvis falsas confictasque illas esse perspiciant, imo illas augere debent.'

56   DEMOCRATIC THOUGHT FROM MACHIAVELLI TO SPINOZA

constellation of their community, has an arbitrary, conventional basis. The signs, figures and stories of religious faiths were devised by people; the political laws were agreed to by people. Neither involves a real foundation of truth which lends the story or law its specific form. This likewise serves to explain why oracles disappear over time and cease to exist 'as people become unbelievers. Once the deceit was discovered, as Machiavalli says (*Discorsi* II, 12), and people began to realize that they were the fabrications of princes, they became unbelievers.'[40] This too is inescapable, and as such we find ourselves back at the first motif, which is the unmasking of the deceit. The anonymous author of *Theophrastus redivivus* discusses the superstition and deceptions of the four most important religions (pagan, Jewish, Christian and Saracen), and shows that every religion is in principle good, since each has its origin in politics and has been established by human beings. The fiction of religion only becomes deception and oppressive when it dissociates itself from and elevates itself above the political laws, when it presents itself as a necessary reality, so that, covering itself with a deceptive cloak of truth, it lends those same political laws the coercive power of a necessity.

4. Institutions

The sixth treatise returns one more time to the naturalistic basis on which the critical argument of the entire work rests, and which is now connected to concrete ethical and political conclusions in counterpointed fashion. The pragmatic rationality of self-preservation yields the foundation for happiness and justice, which also implies respect for life.[41] 'There is by nature equality and community among all living creatures, and people have abolished them primarily by laws, arts and sciences. It is certain that they have also deprived themselves of natural freedom by them.'[42] This concrete explanation is surprising, new, subversive, enlightened and undeniably revolutionary. In their natural state, people are equal and free, and, because they are many, they are also inclined to community. These natural attributes coincide and form an indistinguishable blend or are synonymous. All problems begin with

---

[40] *TR* III, 3, 394: 'Haec autem, succedente tempore, evanescunt et fieri desinunt quia increduli homines facti sunt. Postquam fraus detecta fuit, ait Machiavellus [*lib. 2° de' discor. cap. 12°*], et principum esse commenta perspectum est, increduli facti sunt homines.'

[41] Canziani and Paganini, 'Introduzione', XXIX.

[42] *TR* VI, 3, 840: 'In quo aequalitatem et communitatem a naturâ inter cuncta animantia esse declaratur et homines illam legibus potissimum, artibus et scientiis sustulisse. His etiam libertatem naturalem sibi ademisse constat.'

FICTIONS, LAWS AND RELIGIONS

the institution of an authoritative power, for where there are sovereigns, there are also slaves. The dynamics are as follows: At first, the situation is governed by equality, community and freedom, which the people destroy through discord. The moment they resolve their discord with violence and war, they decide that they need to appoint leaders and sovereigns, 'and this is the first step of inequality'.[43] After wars yield division of mind, there also comes division of things. And thus 'yours and mine was born', dividing the people.[44] They 'stopped possessing all things when they wanted to have their own. The ambition and greed of individuals contributed to even greater inequality and tore the community apart. In the end, they lost their natural freedom altogether through the laws that they established, and introduced the greatest slavery among people by instituting and creating kings and princes.'[45]

In the state of nature, there is no such thing as possession – all people are equal, and so there is community, including the community of goods. In the natural state, there is equality – all people are equal, and so they have the right of existence and are all equally free. No one has a higher or lower rank than the other, no one has a greater or lesser right to anything, no one has any claim on anyone else (or on their life). Yet this does not mean that all always agree; discord arises, and such discord is sometimes addressed by means of war, for which leaders are necessary. Sovereigns have their place within a logic of war, and through the institution of such sovereigns the notion of ownership arises. Property is not something spontaneous, not a principle to be defended by war; conversely, ownership arises as a result of war.[46] And even though

---

[43] *TR* VI, 3, 854: 'qui est primus inaequalitatis gradus'.

[44] Ibid. 'Sic tuum et meum ortum est.' This line of argument can also be found, sometimes quite literally, in Languet's *Vindiciae contra tyrannos/De la puissance*, in which, as noted, Languet interprets Machiavelli as a councillor of tyrants, although he in his refutation actually echoes the Tuscan statesman's political insights; see I,1 above, 4–10. In the context of the question of the right of resistance, Languet's alter ego Brutus investigates why the people, 'who by nature love liberty', instituted kings, observing that 'ces mots, MIEN & TIEN entrerent au monde, que differens survindrent entre les citoyens touchant la proprieté des biens, & guerres entre les peuples voisins à cause de leurs limites': *De la puissance*, 128; 129–30.

[45] *TR* VI, 3, 854: 'atque omnia possidere desierunt, dum volunt sibi propria. Singulorum deinde ambitio et avaritia multo magis inaequalitatem attulerunt, et communitatem distraxerunt. Tandem libertatem naturalem legibus, quas condidêre, prorsus amiserunt et maximam inter illos servitutem constituerunt, reges et principes instituendo atque creando.'

[46] This is a reversal of Hobbes's argument, completely analogous to the line of argumentation we encounter in Rousseau.

58 DEMOCRATIC THOUGHT FROM MACHIAVELLI TO SPINOZA

by the law of nature no one is dependent on another, but all can do whatever they want without law or prohibition, after the institution of dominion they completely besieged this freedom. For the sovereigns established laws through which just and unjust were created, even though before that time these names were not known, but each person was only concerned about his preservation and satisfaction, just like the other animals, according to the precept of nature. But those who were unwilling were forced to obedience through punishment.[47]

In this way, 'man became a wolf to man; indeed, under the dominion of laws and sovereigns, men suffered even greater cruelty from their fellow men than they did from wild animals under the law of nature'.[48] By nature all things are given equally and communally, 'but with their laws the rulers made everything unequal and [a matter of] property'.[49] The sovereigns and laws have given people functions and distinguished them according to forms and levels, so that they 'appear to be different, deformed, and discoloured: and the whole, which they call a civil body, is a monster composed out of widely diverging parts, which has nevertheless always been one and uniform by the law of nature'.[50]

This image, of course, recalls the monster on the title page of *Leviathan*, and it looks like Hobbes and *Theophrastus redivivus* are each independently breaking with traditional philosophy in the same way.[51] Yet there is also the

[47] *TR* VI, 3, 854–5: 'Cum enim naturae lege nullus ab alio dependeret, sed, iniussi aut nullo vetante, omnes quidquid libuerat facerent, imperio constituto hanc libertatem penitus oppugnavêre. Leges enim condiderunt principes quibus iustum et iniustum creatum est, cum antea non essent haec nota nomina, sed unusquisque tantum ad sui conservationem atque satisfactionem, caeterorum animalium more, ex naturae praescripto, respiciebat. Invitos autem ad parendum poenis adegerunt.'

[48] *TR* VI, 3, 855: 'Sic homo homini lupus fuit; imo ab ipsis hominibus plus saevitiae perpetratum est in homines sub legum et principum imperio, quam a ferocioribus animalibus in lege naturae.' Following Gregory, Canziani and Paganini note in their footnote commentary that *Theophrastus redivivus* is here arguing against Hobbes; *TR* VI, 3, 855. Similar ideas can be found in Vanini, in *De admirandis naturae*, IV, dialogue 50, and in Machiavelli, *Istorie Fiorentine* III, 13 in the words spoken by the leader of the Ciompi; see above, Chapter I.2 and Chapter VIII.3–4.

[49] *TR* VI, 3, 855–6: 'principes vero cum legibus suis omnia inaequalia et propria fecerunt.'

[50] *TR* VI, 3, 857–8: 'ut omnino diversi, deformes et discolores esse videantur: et hoc totum quod corpus civile vocant, monstrum ex partibus dissimilibus conflatum et coagmentatum, quod naturae lege unum et uniforme semper fuerat'.

[51] For the image of the Leviathan and an analysis of the illustration on the title page of the first edition, see Agamben, *Stasis*; Bredekamp, *Thomas Hobbes: Der Leviathan*; Ginzburg, *Paura reverenza terrore*; Malcolm, *Aspects of Hobbes*, 200–33. The *TR* does

FICTIONS, LAWS AND RELIGIONS 59

imagery of the wolf, which Hobbes applied to the natural state but which is used by the anonymous author the other way around: a human being becomes a wolf to another human being *after* the institution of ownership and the transfer of power to the sovereign. We see analogy in their respective naturalistic point of departure, as well as in their adoption of Machiavelli's realism and its application as a critique of religion and traditional ethics. In the third treatise, however, we see a difference emerge, which comes to full expression in the sixth treatise. While for Hobbes the state of nature was marked by chaotic violence and therefore had to be radically eliminated, the anonymous author understands violence to become problematic precisely when the institutions totally abandon that natural state. Theophrastus too understands violence to be inherent to the natural state, but insofar as it is natural it is also considered inevitable. Organised violence, as when it structures the logic of institutions and characterises civil life, is intensified to cruelty, or, with the aid of religion and science, it is systematised to oppression. In both cases, it has turned into terror, a generalised and all-pervasive violence caused by the destruction or negation of the state of nature.

Another difference relates to the movement from unity to multitude, and vice versa. Hobbes understands there to be a natural hostility among the multitude of many different people that spontaneously degenerates into violence. In order for this natural division and terror to be put to an end, an artificial, civil unity must be established – and this is the one-headed monster whose body is made up of the natural multitude and which Hobbes finds illustrated in the image of the Leviathan in the Book of Job. Once again, Theophrastus understands things the other way around. Everyone is by nature equal and inclined to community; in that sense, the human race forms a unity. Nevertheless, it is a restless, complex and dialectic unity, not uniform or harmonious and at peace, since internal particularities, conflicts and discord are sometimes resolved through violence. The artificial civil

not include any references to Hobbes's *Leviathan*, a fact which could be explained by the anonymous author's deficiency in the English language, as the Latin translation of *Leviathan* did not appear until 1668. Nevertheless, Hobbes's ideas are known to have been circulating rather widely in France already in the 1640s, as *De cive* was extensively discussed immediately upon its appearance. This seems to bolster the account of Gregory (*Theophrastus redivivus*, 191) and Canziani and Paganini (855), who argue that the *TR* represents a confrontation with Hobbes in general. This account confirms the genealogical line of a 'leftist' radical and revolutionary trajectory as we propose and establish it here in the present monograph from *De jure ecclesiasticorum*, De la Court, Van den Enden, Koerbagh and Spinoza, against Hobbes. For Hobbes's presence in the European Republic of Letters, see Malcolm, *Aspects of Hobbes*, 457–545.

60   DEMOCRATIC THOUGHT FROM MACHIAVELLI TO SPINOZA

institution which puts an end to the natural state perpetuates and sys-tematises the violence by instituting differences between yours and mine, between people with more rights and people with less rights, between sover-eigns who are autonomous and followers who are deprived of their freedom. The unity to which the anonymous author refers is the general nature of humankind – it is human nature, which is neither good nor evil (since the latter concepts only arise after the institution of division), which is truly uni-versal and has no room for exceptions. As a result, he criticises the cultural and political institutions, which do make exceptions. *Theophrastus redivivus* and Hobbes therefore seem to describe a similar problem (of power, right, violence and religion) in different ways, with another focus and therefore also other consequences. Hobbes's critique is directed against governments which resolve their conflicts (often based on religion) in wars (against other countries) and against masses which start civil wars by rising up in rebellion (for religious motives again, or through spontaneous impulses of the mind). Religion and emotions are connected to the state of nature, and for that reason Hobbes locates the solution in a complete triumph over the state of nature. Theophrastus's critique, by way of contrast, is directed against gov-ernments and laws, which seek to remove all traces of the law of nature. The difference between Hobbes and the new Theophrastus is one of perspective: the former assumes the perspective of a sovereign confronted by the threat of war (or civil war) and rebellion, while Theophrastus assumes the perspective of the community whose freedom is suppressed. 'To this end their mandates and edicts have been instituted, their books, their sciences and disciplines, arts, educational institutions, associations, and various workshops; what people worry about day and night from the cradle is that nature is put out of operation altogether or violently strangled by erudition.'[52] Even though they proceed from the same immanent, materialist principle, Hobbes and *Theophrastus redivivus* draw opposing conclusions, which ought not to be sur-prising, in fact, because they view the matter from the opposite perspective.

Is every social order or institution of political power then doomed to a violent and destructive outcome? This does indeed appear to be what the anonymous author has in mind. 'The *corpus civile*, which the laws are

---

[52] *TR* VI, 3, 858–60: 'Ad hoc varia instituta sunt illorum mandata et edicta, libri, scien-tiae et disciplinae, artes, collegia, conventus, officinae omnis generis; atque illic noctu diuque ab incunabulis laboratur, ut natura prorsus depravetur, aut saltem eruditionibus violenter torqueatur.' The idea that laws and religions are connected in that way and supported by science and art is likewise found in Van den Enden; see Chapter V.4 below.

FICTIONS, LAWS AND RELIGIONS

said to rule and direct, what is it but a collection of imprisoned slaves who are surrounded by chains on all sides and subjected to constant fear?'[53] Theophrastus's criticism is at once also self-criticism and aims at knowledge itself, or, more specifically, at the erudite knowledge of books which, like religion, forms a hub in the abstraction of fictions to laws. As such, he draws on the typical, mutually confirming modes of Renaissance thought and modern subject thinking, which we find in each of the authors treated in this monograph. In the Italian Renaissance, resistance to doctrine and tradition was accompanied by a critique of the scholar-in-function and his wisdom of the ivory tower. In satirical poetry, Machiavelli and Ariosto denounced the pedantry of verbose academics and the cultural elite. With countless references to Dante, Petrarch and Ruzante, the young Galileo composed his anti-conformist and ironic poem 'Against Wearing the Toga' (*Contro il portar la toga*).[54] The object of their aversion was illusory knowledge, that is, a knowledge feigned with words, titles and outward display, by which scholars and teachers of the ivory tower reaped their successes in church and chancellery. Yet the conspiracy of theologians and the powerful elite could only be opposed with true, that is, critical and independent knowledge. 'There are no doubt many philosophers, but few are wise', as the anonymous author writes.[55] Many philosophers pursue fame and acclaim; they can speak eloquently and adapt themselves to their times, but the truly wise man only listens to the inner truth. Descartes's modern subject arises in the need for a knowledge that emancipates itself from success and subjective complicity, an independent, methodical investigation which finds the courage to look inwardly and thinks for itself, against the consensus. 'For this is wisdom: to turn to nature and to return from where public error has driven us.'[56]

The point is that the different institutions are intertwined and therefore mutually reinforcing; the insight which *Theophrastus redivivus* has gained here is new, uncommon and revolutionary. The most important strategists

---

[53] *TR* VI, 3, 861: 'Corpus illud civile, quod hae regere et moderari dicuntur, quid aliud est quam saevus ergastulorum coetus, quos undique vincula circumstant et quibus assiduae timendi causae subiiciuntur?'

[54] Galilei, *Capitolo Contro il portar la toga* (1589). See also the commentary from Bignami, Finucci, Rippa Bonati, Tognoni and Vergara Caffarelli in the 2009 edition produced by Tongiorgi Tomasi.

[55] *TR* VI, 4, 882: 'Sic multos esse philosophos non dubium est, paucos vero sapientes.'

[56] *TR* VI, 4, 880: 'Haec enim est sapientia: in naturam converti, et eo restitui, unde publicus error expulerit.' For Descartes in this context (and in departure from Machiavelli), see Negri, *Descartes o della ragionevole ideologia*.

62 DEMOCRATIC THOUGHT FROM MACHIAVELLI TO SPINOZA

of the fictions – i.e. the priest and lawgivers – together follow a single plan aimed at the prohibition of natural freedom and happiness. And the deceiving science of the powerful, the credulity of the plebeians and the tacit complicity of the philosophers allow the formation of a social apparatus which is based on this plan, bolsters it, and therefore brings it to realisation, and which gives all actors – lawgivers, priests, pseudo-philosophers, scientists, teachers – a power that lives on oppression, destruction and prohibition. The anonymous philosopher who finds the courage to unmask the conspiracy against the people – for what we are dealing with here is indeed a conspiracy against the human race itself – is most conscious of the mechanisms of control. Canziani and Paganini have suggested that he is trapped between the bitter pessimism of his cyclical view of eternal return and the potential of proposing that we 'must cast off the yoke of laws'.[57] At the same time, he is forced to admit that, with a view to happiness, civil disobedience is pointless. As such, Canziani and Paganini offer a powerful summary of the tension in and counterpoint nature of *Theophrastus redivivus*. Against this reading, which is itself sceptical and pessimistic in nature, we propose to ask the following questions: Do we not find here a tragic aporia intrinsic to the matter itself, a problem inherent to the human attempt to fashion just institutions and knowledge? After all, it seems fitting to see the *Theophrastus redivivus* – this compilation of critical thought, this grandiose and unconventional intellectual endeavour, this text which is so modern as to anticipate also dialectical, historical-materialistic, language-analytical and postmodern critique of modernity – as an experiment in true knowledge and as a critique of religion as a political theology, which for that reason does not skirt the aporias of reality.

5. Equal freedom

'We enjoyed an unrestrained freedom, as we already noted above, before the laws were introduced, and there was no evil except what was opposed to freedom; at that time vice and moral evil were unknown, but today natural freedom is unknown. The actions of men were in the past not yet distinguished by these words, and among them, as now among the other animals, there was nothing morally evil, nothing vicious, because nothing was forbidden; for that reason, they were not kept from any sort of actions by fear of punishment, except by the fear which they could perhaps experience

---

[57] *TR* VI, 1, 783: 'Nos vero qui legum iugum hic excutim'; Canziani and Paganini, 'Introduzione', XLIV–XLV.

FICTIONS, LAWS AND RELIGIONS

when they wanted to apply violence to someone, for they knew through natural reason, and not through any other law, that violence is opposed by violence [. . .]. Finally, all that was permitted by the natural law is now so strictly prohibited by laws that even eating, drinking and sexual intercourse (without which human beings cannot be perpetuated) have been subjected to the yoke of such laws [. . .] even though the other animals follow the natural desires in all these things.'[58] Religion was invented to abolish natural freedom. But why did this happen? Why this declaration of war on the human race? Like Theophrastus explained in the chapters on the gods (in the first treatise) and on religion (in the third treatise), 'innumerable monstrosities against nature were born: for since they have been contrived from the lust for dominion and power and with the goal of suppressing the freedom of people, they are totally opposed to nature, which made all people free and each person his own master'.[59] Nothing is by nature evil, and it goes without saying that nothing that serves to keep people alive is evil. These commands, which conflict with logic and with life itself, have only been established by laws. For this reason, the only remedy to this deplorable state of affairs is the destruction of all laws and the return to nature. This does not mean that knowledge as such must be surrendered, but it does mean that we must pursue a new knowledge that is inwardly directed, that is self-critical, and that questions fictions, laws and religions. For the only relevant knowledge is our knowledge of what is useful or harmful.[60]

The anonymous author does not, like Galileo, end his work with an ironic plea to walk naked through the streets. Instead, he closes with several concrete instructions in regard to the theme of love, which is one that many still

---

[58] *TR* VI, 3, 862: 'Insonti libertate fruebamur, ut supra diximus, antequam leges introducerentur, nec malum quidquam erat, nisi quod isti libertati adversabatur, vitia et turpia aeque tunc ignorabantur ac libertas naturalis hodie ignoratur. Actiones hominum fictitiis istis nominibus nondum distinguebantur, et inter illos, veluti nunc inter animalia caetera, nihil turpe, nihil vitiosum erat, quia nihil prohibitum: ideo nullo poenarum metu a quibuslibet actionibus arcebantur, nisi quem forte experiri poterant cum vim alteri inferre volebant, quia naturali ratione, non vero ullâ aliâ lege, sciebant vim vi repelli; [. . .] Denique, cuncta quae erant naturali lege licita, nunc adeo legibus fiunt illicita, ut vel ipsi cibo et potui et coitui, sine quibus nec individuum conservari nec species perpetuari ullo modo possunt, legum istarum iugum imponatur [. . .] cum caetera animalia naturalem appetitum in his omnibus sequantur.'

[59] *TR* VI, 3, 863: 'Verum quotquot sunt, tot monstra sunt adversus naturam exorta; nam cum imperii et dominandi cupiditate hominumque libertatis opprimendae causâ excogitatae fuerint, naturae penitus adversantur, quae omnes liberos et sui ipsius unumquemque dominum fecit.'

[60] *TR* VI, 3, 874.

64   DEMOCRATIC THOUGHT FROM MACHIAVELLI TO SPINOZA

worry about even today. Should love be organised in marriage? What does love mean for a philosopher? Theophrastus once again warns that a knowledge returning to nature will be very difficult, demands great courage, and is likely to fail. For 'who among the people would allow any of the ancient customs or opinions to be violated even the slightest bit? Who would tolerate a longstanding error to be removed?'[61] It seems like the author is applying the insights he has gained to his own life and addressing the relevant questions – i.e. How should we live? What should we do? – to himself. In nature, all people are equal and free. A wise philosopher pursues a happy life and for that reason returns to that natural state of freedom and equality. But a wise philosopher also criticises the institutions that obstruct such a life according to nature – precisely that is what defines his wisdom. But since these institutions pervade all things and even intervene in the natural life itself and, in fact, corrupt, violate and destroy that life, the possibility to change them is very small and the prospects of a happy life are very slim for the whistle-blower. In other words, the philosopher's task is virtually impossible to combine with the attainment of a happy life for himself. But the anonymous author questions himself in a more intelligent manner than we are used to from both educated academics *and* erudite libertines. Whether marriage is something for the wise is a question that, as one might expect, receives a negative answer, but it also receives another, critical dimension.

For *Theophrastus redivivus*, there are no disciplinary or ascetic motives for why the wise man ought to 'abhor marriage', as we so often see them elsewhere.[62] Marriage itself binds natural love to laws and thereby installs a power constellation, which is wrong. For centuries on end, and in three of the four leading religions, physical love, which by nature is temporal, subject to change, curious and inclined to experiment, was throttled by the fiction of a unique and exclusive union, and in the end became its own enemy by the fiction which was nailed down in the myth of a reliable accounting contract. Love became a good for which the price and rules of production and distribution were fixed. This is what the wise man opposes, and accordingly he surrenders himself to free love and polygamy. Within a libertine context, such a position is hardly unexpected or radical, and so the anonymous author goes on to subject it to critical investigation. For polygamy gives 'freedom to men alone and not to women, who by nature ought to enjoy the same right

---

[61] *TR* VI, 4, 883: 'Quis enim e populo ferret ullam ex antiquis illius consuetudinibus et opinionibus vel minimum violari? Quis toleraret inveteratum aliquem errorem expelli?'

[62] *TR* VI, 4, 895: 'Igitur a nuptiis sapiens omnino abhorrere debet.'

FICTIONS, LAWS AND RELIGIONS

of freedom as men do: and the most cruel injustice of all is the injustice that has been incurred against natural freedom and has subjected physical love to the coercion of laws'.[63] The laws that made love an accounting matter are violent and cruel, but the most incredible and cruel injustice of all consists in laws demanding 'that the libido of women, who often burn with the same lust, be restrained by the same constricting bounds'.[64] And 'for that reason, the union of a man and a woman must be free and unrestrained, so that *both* can mix with whomever they want and as often they want'.[65]

The anonymous author opts consistently for the most radical perspective of the many who have been suppressed the most, and the most often, throughout the centuries by the conspiracy of fiction, religion and laws. It is to women that *Theophrastus redivivus* gives the final word.

---

[63] *TR*, VI, 4, 893: 'Praeterea polygamia viris tantum indulget, non vero mulieribus, quae eodem libertatis iure secundum naturam frui debent, quo viri ipsi: et omnium quidem iniuriarum saevissima ea est, quae eiusmodi libertati naturali illata est quaeque venerem legibus coërcuit.'

[64] Ibid. 'quam foemina quae perpetuitatis illorum fons et origo est'. In Machiavelli the proverbial final word is likewise left to women, albeit implicitly, in the satirical carnival comedy *La Mandragola*. This explicit turn of unexpected contemporary relevance in what already constitutes a highly unusual work suggests that the anonymous author may actually have been a woman, a Theophrasta.

[65] Ibid. 'Itaque libera et soluta esse debet viri mulierisque coniunctio, ut *uterque*, cui et quantum voluerit, misceri possit' (italics mine).

III

Lieutenants

1. *De jure ecclesiasticorum*

In 1665, the city of Amsterdam saw the appearance of *De jure ecclesiastico-rum*, published under the pseudonym Lucius Antistius Constans and attrib-uted to the fictive publisher Cajus Valerius Pennatus. The central question in this work is to whom the care for religion must be entrusted, with the title already summarising the author's stance.[1] Rights can only be assigned to the church's office-bearers by the government of that republic in which the ecclesiastical offices in question are instituted. If, however, office-bearers bestow such rights upon themselves, they do so unlawfully. What moved the anonymous author to compose this treatise was the ecclesiastical officials'

---

[1] *Lucius Antistius Constans De Jure Ecclesiasticorum. Liber singularis: Quo docetur: Quodcunque Divini Humanique Iuris Ecclesiasticis tribuitur, vel ipsi sibi Tribuunt, hoc, aut falsò impièque illis Tribui, aut non aliundè, quam à suis, hoc est, eius Reipublicae sive Civitatis Prodiis, in quâ sunt constituti, accepisse:* 'Lucius Antistius Constans On the right of ecclesiastical officials. One book in which is taught that whatever divine or human right is attributed to the ecclesiastical officials, or whatever [divine or human right] they attribute to themselves, is either falsely and impiously attributed to them, or that they have received these [rights] from nowhere else but the lieutenants of the republic or state in which they have been appointed.' After the original 1665 edition, the text of the treatise was republished in 1843 in an (incomplete) anthology of works from Descartes and Spinoza edited by Carl Riedel: *Renati des Cartes et Benedicti de Spinoza Praecipua opera philosophica*. A modern French translation was produced by Butori, Lagrée and Moreau: *Du droit des Ecclésiastiques*, 1991. The translations here are my own, keyed to the pagination in the original Latin text from 1665. The original pagi-nation is also followed in the modern French translation. This chapter has appeared in a slightly revised form as: '"Lieutenants" of the Commonwealth: A Political Reading of *De jure ecclesiasticorum*', 150–64.

excessive ambition and their fraudulent abuses, which have destroyed all public religious cult. For this reason, the author also expects his work to be met with a torrent of abuse and slander from its readers and critics. Yet the anticipated negative reception does not represent the most important reason for him to publish this work under a pseudonym. Rather, 'people almost always inquire into the author of a work for the wrong reasons', in particular when such a work seeks to unmask the abuse of power.[2] In doing so, they divert the attention from the abuse to be unmasked, away from the real issue, and away from the views of authors which can only be known from what they write or by inquiring into such things as the motive and authority that drive them to compose what they write. The text of *De jure ecclesiasticorum* amounts to a political critique, and treats of such topics as the use and abuse of power, right and power, church and state, and motives and judgements. Its motive is the pernicious ambition of the ecclesiastical officials, and its authority is derived from the author's pious indignation at that ambition. *De jure ecclesiasticorum* is a fundamentally modern text insofar as its critique is mirrored in and directed towards itself.

Removed from its original political context by the 350 years which have passed since its publication, the question concerning the identity of 'Lucius Antistius Constans' now does seem to have regained a certain relevance. By far the most famous figure proposed as the potential author of the *De jure* is Spinoza, although the current scholarly consensus has relegated this to the realm of myths.[3] For many years one of the De la Court brothers also seemed to be the most plausible candidate, which explains why the *De jure* can be found in many libraries shelved alongside the *Consideratien van Staat* and *Politike Discoursen*.[4] Another convincing contender for the title of author is Spinoza's friend Lodewijk Meyer, even though this physician-philosopher and playwright never wrote anything else devoted explicitly to politics.[5]

---

[2] *De jure ecclesiasticorum*, n.p. [A2v–A3r].

[3] This was the view of Bayle, cf. Art. Spinoza, *Dictionaire historique et critique*, note L, vol. 3, 2773. Reimmann similarly supposes Spinoza to be the author; see *Versuch einer Einleitung in die Historie der Theologie*, 642. Colerus denies that the treatise was written by Spinoza; see *Korte, dog waarachtige Levens-Beschryving van Benedictus de Spinoza*, 42–5; see also Leibniz in *Essais de Théodicée*, III, §375, 339.

[4] See Baumgarten, *Nachrichten von einer Hallischen Bibliothek*, vol. 3, 25–35, who writes that the author of this 'godless work' was most likely 'Van den Hooft', that is, one of the De la Court brothers. The same was suggested by Lucas in his *La vie de monsieur Benoît de Spinosa*, in Freudenthal, *Die Lebensgeschichte Spinoza's*, 25.

[5] This has, for example, been suggested by Colerus, *Korte, dog waarachtige Levens-Beschryving*, 42–5. Thijssen-Schoute takes her point of departure in Colerus's rules, which she interprets as a sign that the authors named (Spinoza, De la Court and

68   DEMOCRATIC THOUGHT FROM MACHIAVELLI TO SPINOZA

Of course, this latter point can hardly represent a definitive argument against his authorship, since Meyer broached the most diverse fields in his other works and did so using a variety of different styles. On top of a philosophical dissertation on matter and a treatise on the passions, Meyer wrote and rewrote dictionaries, translated plays, published an anonymous Italian grammar (*Italiaansche spraakkonst*) and somewhere in there also composed his infamous *Philosophia S. Scripturae Interpres* in 1666, which the next year also appeared in a Dutch translation (*Philosophie d'Uytleghster der h. Schrifture*) that he himself presumably wrote.[6] Moreover, Meyer too was convinced that the theologians he was criticising 'will be aroused to ire'.[7]

These days *De jure* no longer enjoys the same renown it once had and has received rather scant treatment in scholarship.[8] But that was not how things always were. From the end of the seventeenth century to the beginning of the nineteenth, *De jure* may not have elicited quite the same indignation as Machiavelli's *Il Principe* or Spinoza's *Tractatus theologico-politicus*, but it did appear consistently on the lists of 'impious' books that were considered best forbidden.[9] This indignation was accompanied by speculations about the identity of the person hiding behind the initials L.A.C. Was it Spinoza, or De la Court, or perhaps Meyer? Philosophers and publicists like Leibniz, Bayle and Colerus introduced their respective audiences to the treatise and

Meyer) did *not* write this treatise; see *Nederlands Cartesianisme*, 393–4. Riedel was of the opinion that the work had been authored either by Spinoza himself or by one of his friends, among them Meyer; see *Renati des Cartes et Benedicti de Spinoza praecipua opera philosophica*, vol. II, IX–X.

[6] Meyer, *Philosophia S. Scripturae Interpres, Exercitatio paradoxa*, 1666; *De Philosophie d'Uytleghster der H. Schrifture. Een wonderspreuckigh Tractaet*, 1667. See also Bordoli, *Ragione e scrittura tra Descartes e Spinoza*.

[7] Meyer, *Philosophie d'Uytleghster*, n.p. (*2r).

[8] In recent times, the *De jure ecclesiasticorum* has been studied predominantly in the context of Spinoza or one of the candidates hiding behind the pseudonym Lucius Antistius Constans (Meyer, De la Court). See, for example: Blom, 'Le contexte historique du *De jure ecclesiasticorum*', IX–XXI; Bordoli, *Ragione e scrittura*, 29–34, 92–7; Gebhardt, 'Einleitung zu den beiden Traktaten', 238–41; Israel, *Radical Enlightenment*, 201; Lazzeri, 'L.A. Constans entre Hobbes et Spinoza', XXIIV–XLI; Lagrée, 'Du magistre spirituel à la "Medicina Mentis"', 595–621; Moreau, *Spinoza. État et religion*, 63–70; Nobbs, *Theocracy and Toleration*, 245–50; Weststeijn, *Commercial Republicanism in the Dutch Golden Age*, 313.

[9] See Baumgarten, *Nachrichten von einer Hallischen Bibliothek*, 25; Freytag, *Analecta litteraria de libris rarioribus*, 268–9; Masch, *Verzeichnis der erheblichsten freidenkerischen Schriften*, 89; Reimmann, *Versuch einer Einleitung*, 642; Riedel, *Renati des Cartes et Benedicti de Spinoza praecipua opera philosophica*, 228–30; Trinius, *Freydenker-Lexicon*, 314–15; Vogt, *Catalogus librorum rariorum*, 214.

LIEUTENANTS   69

offered their views on its authorship. Christian Thomasius devoted ample
attention to it in his lectures at the university.[10] So too the French orato-
rian priest Mathieu Mathurin Tarabaud understood Enlightenment political
philosophy, which he referred to as *philosophisme*, to be the fuse that was to
ignite the fire of the French Revolution, seeing the *De jure* as one of the most
pernicious examples of *philosophisme* leading to the rebellion. In his eyes,
the treatise defends theories that give the people, and even each individual
person, the right to cast off the yoke of the most legitimate authority and
to establish what is essentially anarchy (*anarchie en principe*).[11] Tarabaud
favoured the view that held Meyer to be the author of this insurrectionist
text. However, in his foreword L.A.C. not only indicates that such speculations regarding authorship are misplaced, but also adds that few could even
know his identity since this work is the only one he has ever written. In his
eyes, nothing has been as damaging to religion as the impiety, dishonesty
and fraudulence of the church's office-bearers, which is why he immediately announces his plan to write a second book, this one on the 'secrets
of the ecclesiastical officials' (*Arcana ecclesiasticorum*).[12] Such statements
serve to exclude the author of the *Consideratien van Staat* as a candidate
for the *De jure*, together with Meyer, although they would seem to favour
Spinoza again. In the end, we ought perhaps to heed the anonymous author's
counsel – does he not present himself explicitly as an author who does not
hide behind the mask of a person, but rather adresses readers who can use
their own reason as their guide? – and turn to study the text itself.[13]

2. No equality without freedom, no freedom without equality

As in Spinoza's *TTP*, there is a lot that happens in the text of *De jure ecclesiasticorum* through the inclusion or omission of a word and through language
itself. The treatise begins by establishing a clear distinction undergirding the
entire work, namely between inner religion and outer religion. Inner religion
is not subject to regulation by people or institutions; God's *prodii*, literally
his substitutes, *lieu-tenants*, or lieutenants, have no say at all in matters of
inner religion. While this uncommon term *prodii* at its first occurrence refers
to God's substitutes and thus the religious – that is, ecclesiastical – officials,
immediately thereafter and in fact throughout the rest of the work it is used

[10] Thomasius, *Historia contentionis inter imperium et sacerdotium*, 406–10.
[11] Tarabaud, *Histoire critique du philosophisme anglois* II, 3–5.
[12] *De jure ecclesiasticorum*, n.p. [A6v].
[13] Ibid. n.p. [A3v–A4r].

70 DEMOCRATIC THOUGHT FROM MACHIAVELLI TO SPINOZA

almost exclusively in its shifted and more neutral sense of a lieutenant or deputy authority of the republic, political government or commonwealth.[14] Moreover, once this semantic shift has taken place, the ecclesiastical officials turn out to be no lieutenants at all, since they have nothing to do with inner religion which, as we have seen, is the sole prerogative of the person whose inner religion it is. So too the ecclesiastical officials do not actually regulate outer religion, since their task is to teach such outer religion to people who are ignorant of it, and 'this is not regulation'.[15] Teaching is not commanding. In the domain of education, commands are even useless, for those who give them cannot force those who receive the instruction/command to obedience, nor can the commander/instructor ever determine whether the command/instruction has been obeyed/followed. In education one can do no more than to encourage and to give counsel, for the truth of what is being taught can only be judged by those who receive the message, that is, by the people. The ecclesiastical office-bearers are those who have been entrusted by the lieutenants or political authorities with the task of teaching religion, but that is their only privilege.

Chapter 2 immediately takes us to the core of the matter, and in particular to the 'origin and development' of the right and power of the lieutenants, that is, how the right and power of the political state is formed.[16] In the political state, all right and power resides in the hands of the lieutenants, while the citizens have no such power and right. The lieutenants are therefore more the substitutes of the citizens than they are of God. Here too we

---

[14] Ibid. 2–5.

[15] Ibid. 2–3: '[. . .] non est Procurare [. . .]'.

[16] Ibid. 7: 'Tit. II. De Origine & Progressu Juris & Potestatis Prodeorum: Ut appareat penes eos esse omne Jus & Potestatem Civitatis sive Reip. nihilque Juris aut Potestatis penes Cives esse.' According to Moreau, the 'jus circa sacra' question represented a public debate revolving around two basic views: the first, in the line of Uytenbogaert, did not hold God to have established two kinds of sovereign magistrates with spiritual and temporal power; the other posited the independence of the two powers, which in practice always meant that the ecclesiastical authorities could intervene in political matters; see État et religion, 66. On Uytenbogaert's position and the 'jus circa sacra', see also Secretan, 'Fonction du politique et jus circa sacra dans les controverses hollandaises du début du XVIIᵉ siècle', 167–85, and Bordoli, 'The Monopoly of Social Affluence', 121–49. The TTP must be situated in the context of this public debate; similarities and differences between the TTP and De jure will be treated elsewhere. Here I am proposing the thesis that the De jure actually addresses another issue, and that the 'jus circa sacra' only functions as the occasion for addressing the formation of political community and power, as well as the freedom of thought and speech, which (1) is considered necessary and (2) presupposes equality.

can observe strange shifts in the text, as the words alternate between clarity and ambiguity, until they finally yield a message so radical that it still has not been digested three-and-a-half centuries later. The origin and development of the right and power of the political state is a paradoxical and complex matter. Although the title of this second chapter would seem to suggest that it will establish absolute power, recalling *Il Principe*'s apparent self-presentation as a manual for absolute monarchs, its real and radically innovative message is that there is no freedom without equality, and no equality without freedom. This second chapter takes its point of departure in the natural right according to which 'all people are born in the same condition and are for that reason equal: God did not make one person the lord or subject of another, just as he did not make some animals lord over others'.[17] The definitions maintained by the anonymous author are of crucial importance here. To be free is no other thing than to be under one's own right and power, not subjected to the right and power of any other person. To be equal is no other thing than to 'have one's own natural right and power, and not to belong to any other person in any way'.[18] Equality therefore does not mean that people do not have specific qualities by virtue of which they differ. But what it does mean is that when two people are compared to each other and called equal, 'they each have the same right and power'.[19] By nature, all people are equal and free. But they can lose this freedom and equality in three different ways: by violence, by subjection to a greater power or by mutual agreement. The collective decision to come to an agreement is one that people can take to counteract the threat of chaos and violence as well as the dangers inherent to the state of nature. As such, they can decide to transfer their natural power, and they can transfer it to all, to a few, or to a single person. The amount of power to be transferred by such an agreement is not to be decided on by the transferring party but by the receiving party, that is, by the deputy lieutenants. On the face of it, the structure of the argument does not diverge from what we find in Hobbes, although on closer examination there do indeed appear to be differences in choice of terms and in the precise nature of the formulations, as well as in the conclusion.

---

[17] *De jure ecclesiasticorum*, 8: 'omnes homines pari conditione nascantur, ac proinde aequales sint, & hujus rei nullam aliam rationem esse, quam quod Deus hominem homini non praefecerit, nec subjecerit alii alium: uti nec caetera animalia aliis alia praeposuit'.

[18] Ibid. 9: 'Liberum esse nihil aliud est, quam sui Juris & Potestatis, nulliusque alterius subjectum Juri & Potestati esse. Et Aequalem esse, naturale illud in se Jus & Potestatem habere & nulla ex parte penes alium esse.'

[19] Ibid. 'Par enim quisque in se Jus & Potestatem habet.'

72   DEMOCRATIC THOUGHT FROM MACHIAVELLI TO SPINOZA

For the author makes various asides or tangents, and the outcome of the argument is one that we also find in Spinoza and alters its entire message.[20]

The amount of power to be transferred to the lieutenants, whether they be one, a few, or a multitude, must be sufficient for them to secure the protection and maintenance of the civil body. Nevertheless, the anonymous author adds, 'if we consider the force and efficacy of natural right and power in the natural state in which we have been constituted by Nature, that is, by God, the refusal and inability to use this right and power must be considered equivalent'.[21] There is no doubt that the phrase 'Nature, that is, God' can be reversed. Furthermore, we understand the quoted passage in such a way that, everything considered, people relinquish their natural right and natural power and transfer them to another party that uses them in their place insofar as they themselves do not have the ability to use them. Earlier on in the text we read that once people have left the state of nature and entered civil society, they are no longer considered to have their judgement and free choice to use their natural right and power. The formulation is surprising: 'they are assumed to have transferred them *as if they could also belong to another person*'.[22] But this is actually impossible; in reality people cannot transfer their power of judgement, which also explains the author's use of the counterfactual conditional. 'For such natural faculties cannot be transferred

---

[20] Our reading of *De jure* confirms the thesis that Hobbes was read in the Low Countries between 1660 and 1670 through a republican-democratic lens, and that its naturalistic starting point was adopted to emphasise general human equality, yielding a completely different view on the freedom of thought and speech in Spinoza and others compared to the Hobbesian one. This view is bolstered by the translation of *Leviathan* by Van Berkel, who moved in the circle of Spinoza. In the preface to his translation, Van Berkel noted the potential of naturalism for a republican-democratic view; naturalism opposes the widely prevalent superstition, ecclesiastical authority and revealed religion, which functioned as a binding force and propagandistic tool for the ecclesiastical officials. The preface includes clauses that can be found almost verbatim in *De jure*, such as when ecclesiastical officials are said to have no right to authority since there may only be a 'legal authority' (*Wettelijcke Magt*); see *Leviathan of van de stoffe*, n.p. [*6r]. See also Chapter VI below. See also Bordoli, *Ragione e scrittura*, 92–7; Lagrée, 'Du magistre spirituel à la "Medicina Mentis"', 608; Weststeijn, *Commercial Republicanism*, 147–57; 337–44.

[21] *De jure ecclesiasticorum*, 19–20: 'Illud enim summopere notandum est: in statu Naturali, in quo omnes a natura, id est, a Deo constituti sumus, noluntatem & impotentiam naturali Jure & Potestate utendi, pro eadem re accipi oportere, si illius Juris & Potestatis vim & effectum intueamur.'

[22] Ibid. 20: 'Iudicium quoque & Arbitrium naturali Iure & Potestate utendi dicendi quoque sunt, in status Naturalis in Civilem commutatione non retinuisse, sed quasi ea quoque alterius fieri possent, transtulisse.' Italics mine.

LIEUTENANTS

73

or acquired by others, but they can only disappear' as when we die or when we lose them *without* them being acquired by others.[23] All internal faculties, and in particular the faculties of *judgement* and *free choice*, are and remain by their very nature the possession of the person on whom nature has bestowed them. They cannot be transferred to anyone else.

The soul's internal faculties or capacities therefore remain the possession of each individual person. God, that is, Nature, has endowed every human being not only with the right and power of self-protection, of the satisfaction of their needs and of the attainment of their salvation, but it has also endowed them with reason by which they can regulate precisely this right and power. This internal faculty, which cannot, as it were, be distinguished from thought or which is that in which the substance of the soul resides, is a defining human attribute, such that reason could be said to coincide with the human soul. The internal faculties coinciding with reason 'are not, or by their very nature cannot be, subjected to the right and power of the lieutenants'.[24] The author is aware of the anomaly of these ideas. Up to now they have been articulated by few, making them completely new, with barely a political state to be found in which things happen or have happened this way. Furthermore, people are generally not aware of the origin of political right. The formulation suggests that the 'origin and development' of political right and political power (*Origo & Progressus Juris & Potestatis*) must not be understood here in a concrete historical, chronological, spatial-temporal sense, but more generally and philosophically.[25] This finds confirmation in the final six paragraphs of this second chapter, where we find a collection of statements that appear to have been derived in part from *Il Principe* and at the same time quite literally anticipate Spinoza's *Tractatus politicus*. The question at issue is of surprising contemporary relevance. Every state or city has an explicit or implicit law demanding from all who want to settle there and enjoy its public advantages (i.e. immigrants) that they surrender their natural right and power to the lieutenants. Any immigrant who does not do so will be considered an enemy and not a citizen. The clear transfer or explicit agreement is a sign of transmission of will, and it is 'only through this will and not the words, except insofar as these words signify the will,

---

[23] Ibid. 20–1: 'Re vera enim ejusmodi facultates naturales transferri non possunt & aliis acquiri, sed desinere tantum possunt maxime cum interitu ejus, cui decedunt, ut tamen aliis non acquirantur.'

[24] Ibid. 22: 'Animae facultates Prodeorum Juri & Potestati non sint suppositae, aut sui natura supponi non possint.'

[25] Ibid. 7.

74 DEMOCRATIC THOUGHT FROM MACHIAVELLI TO SPINOZA

that right and power are transferred. They are therefore no less transferred than they would be if they were transferred only in acts and not in words.'[26] Otherwise stated, people do not just retain the natural freedom of thought by the transfer of natural right and power to the lieutenants (for political authorities do not think for others), but they also retain the natural freedom of speech (for the lieutenants do not speak for others). With this, the author is convinced he has given a suitable description of how political societies are generally shaped, maintained and preserved.

The very title of the next chapter already anticipates the boldest position assumed by Spinoza in his *Tractatus politicus*. The institution of a civil society does not change anything in the natural equality of all people, and so every inequality existing between individuals in a political state must have been caused by the lieutenants. This twofold thesis was what led the political opponents of the *De jure*, including Tarabaud in 1806, to view the work as an anarchist manifesto. The transition to a civil state does not change anything in natural equality, which remains fully intact. Every inequality, including inequality in possession, standing or privilege, is contingent and historically determined by the will of the political rulers. The next step in the argument is that also the superiority of the ecclesiastical officials, like that of the other citizens who do not differ from them at all in terms of right and power, comes from and is determined by the lieutenants (or political authorities). This point is clearly hammered home when the author repeats how the terms 'right' and 'power' are connected. If people are said to be equal in the natural state and unequal in the civil state, this only applies in regard to the power to which they do have a right in the former but not in the latter. The term 'right' is only added as an indication of the legitimacy or illegitimacy of natural power. Right itself, without the support of power, has no force or effect.[27] In other words, the author seems to be suggesting that right does not as such exist on its own.

It is clear that power is exercised by bodies, and that the practices regulated by 'the right of inequality' (*Inaequalitatis Jus*), as the author calls it now, are bodily practices.[28] Who, then, could command or forbid someone to think or not to think something, or to accept or condemn certain ideas? Or who could command them to believe words and propositions that cannot

---

[26] Ibid. 35: 'non verbis, nisi voluntatem significantibus, Jus & Potestas transferantur, non minus Jus & Potestatem transferri dicendum est, quod quaeque non verbis, sed factis transferri significentur'.

[27] Ibid. 54: 'nudum Jus sive quod Potestate destitutum est, nullius vis aut momenti [est]'.

[28] Ibid. 55.

be confirmed by reason and that are unconvincing and largely dubious to them? Here we must not forget the essential difference between inner and outer religion. The power of governments and/or ecclesiastical officials only extends to outer religion, that is, the bodily practices.

> We can be commanded to assemble in a certain space, to listen to some- one teaching us, to cover our heads, to bend our knees, to open or close our hands and lift them up to heaven, to call upon and honour God or some other thing [!] with prescribed words, to regulate all other acts and gestures of our body. To produce a certain sound with our voice and tongue and to do with our body what the lieutenants who have command over outer religion – i.e. the ecclesiastical officials – command or forbid.[29]

Here the distinction between inner and outer religion is clearly reminiscent of the motif at the basis of Spinoza's *Tractatus theologico-politicus*: the incon- stance of human affections, by which people surrender themselves to rituals and outward display, such that faith degenerates to superstition. Yet we never find any of the candidates for the authorship of the *De jure*, whether Spinoza, De la Court or Meyer, giving such radical expression to contempt of faith. Covering or not covering one's head, folding or opening one's hands, making noises, moving one's lips or clacking one's tongue are only gestures by which we call upon or honour 'God or some other thing' (*Deum aliudve*).

The privileges of divine right that are normally ascribed to the ecclesi- astical officials are typically legitimised with an appeal to Holy Scripture. Yet, so the anonymous author counters, not a single rule relating to this question can actually be found in either the Old or the New Testament. It should also come as no surprise to find the treatise moving on to the topic of prejudices once it has finished with superstition. The author attempts to scour the Bible for reasons and arguments in its text, using an unprejudiced mind; once again, we see a line emerge from critique to political emanci- pation. If people question the power of the lieutenants, or rather, if they claim that these lieutenants need not always be obeyed, the next question to present itself is an obvious one: For who decides when the lieutenants should and should not be obeyed? And should this decision be left to each individual citizen? The author's surprising answer is that 'this is in any case

---

[29] Ibid. 57: 'Juberi enim possumus, ut unum in locum conveniamus, docentem aliquem audiamus, capita detegamus, genua flectamus . . . Deum aliudve praescriptis verbis invocemus & honoremus . . . certum linguae vocisque sonum efferamus.' The French translation erroneously translates 'Deum aliudve' as 'Dieu de telle ou telle façon'.

76   DEMOCRATIC THOUGHT FROM MACHIAVELLI TO SPINOZA

more reasonable than to claim that the citizens endowed with an ecclesiastical office can make this decision for all, and to maintain, as the apex
of absurdity, that the other citizens must regulate their civil life according
to the choice and judgement of the ecclesiastical officials and must obey
them when they resist the orders of the lieutenants'.[30] While the power of
the ecclesiastical officials is dismantled for and assumed by the lieutenants
(meaning here, once again, the political government), the power of the
political government, whenever and as long as it applies, is made to depend
on the decision of each and every citizen.

At the end of Chapter 6, this line of argument is brought to completion.
A citizen who refuses to obey leaves civil society through his disobedience
and returns to the natural state. This natural human being, in contrast with
what we find in Hobbes, does not surrender himself to the threat and chaos
of violence, even though, as noted at the outset of the treatise, these dangers
were what incited him to come to a mutual agreement in the first place. But
the moment a citizen refuses to obey, his refusal is legitimate and in agreement with divine or natural reason, 'since he follows his own reason, that is,
God', more than he follows public reason or the reason of the lieutenants.[31]
'The lieutenants are always considered as equals and not as leaders, that is, as
lieutenants/substitutes, whenever obedience is denied them.'[32] As such, disobedience is no longer a 'sin' that one only encounters in the natural state,
but it becomes a reality of the civil state. Of course, this also implies that
all the privileges of the ecclesiastical officials disappear, since every person,
by divine command, must obey his own reason alone and not the reason of
others, including the ecclesiastical officials. 'For every person is always justified to doubt' about what another person desires of him or her.[33] 'Whenever
we doubt, we rightly refuse to do what is demanded of us. For the doubter
it is the same thing as being asked to do something unlawful and unjust.'[34]

---

[30] Ibid. 75–6: 'Quod utique Rationi magis consentaneum est quam quod Ecclesiastici
Cives pro caeteris Civibus hoc discernerent. Et a Ratione quam maxime abhorrens,
quod caeteri Cives Ecclesiasticorum arbitrio & judicio vitam Civilem instituerent:
illisque jussa Prodeorum dissuadentibus parerent.'

[31] Ibid. 77–8: 'Et proinde recte, & divinae Rationi convenienter facit, quod Rationi suae,
hoc est, Deo magis, quam publicae, hoc est, Prodeorum obsequatur.'

[32] Ibid. 78: 'Quos utique pro hominibus sibi aequalibus, & neutiquam sibi praepositis, hoc
est, pro Prodiis habet, quoties & quatenus illis obedientiam denegat.'

[33] Ibid. 82: 'Nam justam dubitandi causam unusquisque semper habet, a quo homo alius
quidquam non suo Jure [. . .], sed alieno & quidem divino desiderat.'

[34] Ibid. 82–3: 'Quoties igitur quis dubitat, & Iure denegat, quod postulatur: quo-
niam, quantum ad dubitantem attinet, idem est, ac si indebitum & injustum ab eo
postularetur.'

In the later chapters, these bold theses are developed concretely in relation to the ecclesiastical officials' right and power, privileges and customs, albeit without any reflection on the relationship between the political government and its citizens. It is only in Chapter 12, which reads like a summary of the entire work, that we once again encounter the revolutionary thesis, this time formulated in a weaker form, that has a crucial role in the argument but was only formulated in passing. The political lieutenants now know their right and power in relation to the citizens; this right and power may appear at first sight to be absolute and irrevocable, but nothing could be further from the truth. The political lieutenants need to remember that they *receive* their right and power from the citizens, on whose acts and will they depend, and not the other way around.[35] For that reason, they should not oppose the citizens nor disappoint them in their faith in and hope for an easier and more pleasant life under the regime of these lieutenants. The political authorities/lieutenants are only subservient substitutes or deputies who do not rule to their own advantage, but for the good of the citizens and in their interest.

[35] Ibid. 159–60.

IV

A Political Balance
(Between Passions and Reason, State Interest and the Multitude)

1. Johan/Pieter de la Court

In 1660, five years before the publication of *De jure ecclesiasticorum*, the first edition of the *Consideratien en exempelen van staat: Omtrent De Fundamenten van allerley regeringe* appeared in print, commonly attributed to Pieter de la Court, although it may well be the work of his brother Johan who had recently met his death.[1] The next year saw the appearance of a second edition, with only minor textual changes, but now under the well-known title *Consideratien van Staat, Ofte Politike Weeg-Schaal*.[2] In the preface to his *Kort verhael van Nieuw-Nederlants Gelegenheit*, Franciscus van den Enden applauds the boldness of the author whose example he seeks to emulate in writing freely, although he does complain that the second edition deviates from the views of its late author by its partial abandonment of his democratic ideals.[3] Another year later, no less than four additional editions appeared, with an expanded text and a specific focus on 'practice' (*practijk*).[4]

---

[1] De la Court, *Consideratien en exempelen van staat, Omtrent De Fundamenten van allerley regeringe. Beschreven door V. H.*, 1660.

[2] De la Court, *Consideratien van Staat, Ofte Politike Weeg-Schaal beschreven door VH*, 1661.

[3] Van den Enden, *Kort verhael van Nieuw-Nederlants Gelegentheit*, 1662, iii–iv.

[4] De la Court, *Consideratien van Staat, Ofte Politike Weeg-Schaal, Waar in met veele Reedenen, Omstandigheden, Exempelen en Fabulen werd ooverwoogen; Welke forme der Regeringe, in speculatie gehoud op de practijk, onder de menschen de beste zy. Beschreven door V. H.*, 1662. ('Considerations of State, or Political Balance, in which is investigated, with many arguments, circumstances, examples, and tales, what form of government, with *particular attention* to *practice*, is best for people. Described by

A POLITICAL BALANCE 79

In this chapter, we will be using the 1661 edition, since it is listed among the books in Spinoza's library and undoubtedly influenced him in crafting his own political ideals.

Anyone who reads these *Consideratien van Staat*, or else the *Politike Discoursen* of 1662, both of which were in Spinoza's library, will immediately be struck by two things.[5] The first is the many implicit and explicit references to Hobbes, to Roman authors (and to Tacitus in particular), and to Machiavelli, who seems to serve a paradigmatic role in both works.[6] Not only are there a plethora of references to and examples from Machiavelli's *Discorsi*, but many commonalities can also be detected in structural development and textual interplay. Secondly, both the *Consideratien van Staat* and the *Politike Discoursen* anticipate in their point of departure, argumentative structure, non-normativity, general secularising tone, political perspective and radically innovative nature the naturalistic programme of the anonymous *De jure* and Spinoza's *Tractatus politicus*. The presence of Machiavelli, which is ubiquitous in De la Court and striking and carefully selected in Spinoza, raises the suspicion that Spinoza may have been citing Machiavelli through the works of De la Court, and it may well be that not a single Machiavelli quotation in Spinoza is absent in De la Court. However, Spinoza had direct access to Machiavelli's works, which were in his library. A textual relationship need not be posited because Tacitus and Machiavelli occupy a central role in the *Consideratien* and the *Tractatus politicus*, or because the arguments in these works, as in the *De jure*, reflect those of Hobbes and depart from the same basic principle, since these similarities may have developed independently. Therefore, it may well be that the anonymous author in the *De jure* and Spinoza in the *TP* shared the same sources as De la Court in developing their radically innovative ideas, but went much further than him and above all headed in a different direction.

2. Naeuwkeurige consideratie van staet

What is also not immediately clear is whether the political position of the author and/or editor who identifies himself as 'V.H.' really was all that

---

V. H.') See Weststeijn, *Commercial Republicanism in the Dutch Golden Age*, 56–7.

[5] De la Court, *Politike discoursen, handelende in ses onderscheide boeken van Steeden, Landen, Oorlogen, Kerken, Regeeringen en Zeeden. Beschreven door D.C.*, 1662. For Spinoza's library, see *Catalogus van de Bibliotheek der Vereniging Het Spinozahuis te Rijnsburg*.

[6] See also Morfino, *Il tempo e l'occasione*, 241–66; Visentin, *La libertà necessaria*, 283–327.

80   DEMOCRATIC THOUGHT FROM MACHIAVELLI TO SPINOZA

revolutionary.[7] His most famous work, the *Interest van Holland*, appeared in 1662, arguing that the republic benefits the state, in this case Holland. It has been claimed that Johan de Witt, the Grand Pensionary of Holland, read and corrected several chapters of the *Interest*. Even if this is just a matter of urban legend, it does raise the vexed question of how a work at the centre of such rumours could ever be politically revolutionary in nature. Could an author who was that close to a government, even if it be a government opposed to the prince, ever be in a position to propose radically innovative ideas? But there is also something else. The same year when the four editions of the *Consideratien* and the *Politike Discoursen* appeared also saw the appearance of another work under the same initials (V.D.H.) that Pieter de la Court used: *Naeuwkeurige consideratie van state, Wegens de Heerschappye van een vrye en geheymen staets-regeering*.[8] Anyone who happens to pick it up could easily confuse it for yet another edition of the *Consideratien*. The attribution of the *Naeuwkeurige consideratie* to De la Court has almost never been questioned, even though it, apart from the many references to Tacitus and Machiavelli, actually has little in common with either the *Consideratien* or the *Politike Discoursen*.[9] It is, as Kossman once described it, 'a somewhat scholastic booklet on the *arcana imperii*, based largely on quotations from ancient writers'.[10] Little has been written on this work in scholarship, just as one will largely have to navigate one's own way through the original texts of the De la Court brothers. Their works are not available in modern editions, thus leaving us with very little to go by in the way of philological guidance or text-critical commentary. While the leading economic and political works of the De la Court brothers have been studied at considerable length, the scarce scholarly commentary on the present work that does exist largely takes the form of a few condescending remarks.[11] Haitsma Mulier initially identified the *Naeuwkeurige consideratie* as an early text, dating perhaps as far back as the 1640s, which uses a conventional juridical

---

[7] Similar doubts have been expressed by Visentin: 'Between Machiavelli and Hobbes', 227–48.

[8] [De la Court], *Naeuwkeurige consideratie van staet, Wegens de Heerschappye van een vrye en geheymen staets-regering. Over de gantsche Aertbodem. Aengewezen door V.D.H.*, 1662.

[9] Haitsma Mulier, 'De naeuwkeurige consideratie van de gebroeders De la Court. Een nadere beschouwing', 397.

[10] Kossman, *Politieke Theorie in het zeventiende-eeuwse Nederland*, 37, cited in Haitsma Mulier, 'De naeuwkeurige consideratie', 397.

[11] See Blom, *Causality and Morality in Politics*, 168–73; Weststeijn, *Commercial Republicanism*, 57; 80.

style to convey conventional ideas about the secrets which sovereigns in all forms of state, including mixed sovereignty, must understand and/or cherish to be able to rule.[12] But when the *Naeuwkeurige consideratie* was shown to have been carefully 'plagiarized' from Gerardus van Wassenaar's *Bedekte Konsten in regeringen en heerschappien* (1657), Haitsma Mulier was forced to revisit his earlier position.[13] For why did V.D.H. publish this classical work in the reason of state tradition as if it were a companion to the *Consideratien van Staat?*

The first thing that comes to mind is that V.D.H. enjoyed playing with words and had a healthy appreciation for irony. With numerous references to Tacitus, Livy and Seneca, and after the example of Arnold Clapmar's *De arcanis rerumpublicarum*, the *Naeuwkeurige consideratie* offers an exposition of the secret actions that can be applied by a state or sovereign. It is worth noting here that the remains of Spinoza's library catalogued at his death did not include the *Naeuwkeurige consideratie*, but did house Clapmar's *De arcanis rerumpublicarum*.[14] Its perspective is traditional and assumes the vantage point of the elite or of the party in power, and it analyses various forms of state which must all be on guard against the dangers of democracy. Although the *Naeuwkeurige consideratie* was written in the vernacular, it is not clear why the author would have addressed himself to the common people, since he describes them 'as a cruel animal, equally inclined to compassion and immoderate cruelty'.[15] They cloak themselves with the 'sweet name' of freedom, and, under the guise of pursuing equal laws, they are only out to plunder and to oppress.[16] All the 'shenanigans' (*schelmerijen*) found in a monarchy or aristocracy are also manifest in a democracy, and are even much worse there.[17] The message is clear: for the sake of the general well-being, democracy must be avoided and the people must be deceived. As in Clapmar's work, the sovereign's secret action is justified in the passive nature of the people, which is at the same time violent and unmanageable. So too in matters of religion the position of the *Naeuwkeurige consideratie* is hardly innovative: The state power must

---

[12] Haitsma Mulier, 'De naeuwkeurige consideratie', 397–8.

[13] Ibid.; Wassenaer, *Bedekte Konsten in regeringen en heerschappien. Die bykans gebruyckt worden, en waer door Koningen en Princen, Edelen en Steden, die het hooghste gebiedt hebben, haer Staedt en Heerschappie vast stellen*, 1657.

[14] *Catalogus van de Bibliotheek der Vereniging Het Spinozahuis te Rijnsburg*, 21.

[15] *Naeuwkeurige consideratie*, 71: 'als een wreedt dier, soo wel als het genegen is tot barm- hertigheydt, soo onmatigh is 't tot wreetheydt'.

[16] Ibid.

[17] Ibid. 72.

82 DEMOCRATIC THOUGHT FROM MACHIAVELLI TO SPINOZA

constantly direct itself according to the established religion; God himself deceives human beings for their own good; religion and piety are the most powerful bulwarks of rule; the evil in the world does not come from religion, but has always been there.[18]

Haitsma Mulier has observed how the text in V.D.H.'s work is almost completely identical to that of Van Wassenaar's *Bedekte konsten*, with the exception that the term 'arts' (*konsten*) has consistently been replaced throughout the first part by the term 'sciences' (*wetenschappen*).[19] Even though the political message is completely different and perhaps even its polar opposite, one can begin to understand why De la Court published the *Naeuwkeurige consideratie* as an important source to accompany his own work. Two remarks can be made in this context. The first is that we need to be careful when reading a theory which speaks the truth about lies and deception, since every truth judgement is also self-referential. The author/ editor even says so himself: 'no one speaks from the heart, no one lies openly, but the truth is mixed with falsehood and adorned so as to deceive the untried more easily'.[20] The minute one opens the store of hidden arts and shines the unmasking light of truth on deceit, a pendulum movement between knowledge and unmasking is set in motion and cannot be stopped. The truth then literally becomes a matter of perspectives, an attempt to gain insight into these perspectives demanding neutrality. In other words, it becomes difficult to detect a position and to determine the truth, for if you follow the neutrality which is indispensable for the process of unmasking, you end up with a discourse that may have been devised in favour of the sovereign and the elite, as appears to be the case here, but that discourse *could* also be used in the service of an opposing standpoint. As such, knowledge is about weighing matters carefully on the balance of public life, and it is left up to the reader to use this knowledge to his or her advantage. This too is a point which the author/editor actually makes in so many words: 'the face and appearance of things often deceive, words frequently do, for which reason these hidden arts here are very useful when you appear and pretend not to understand that you understand', 'for if those who are guided [by] these ruses and coverings acquire knowledge of the matter, they with a jump often turn the state on its head, for which reason not every person is capable

---

[18] Ibid. 9–10, 34–5, 45.

[19] Haitsma Mulier, 'De naeuwkeurige consideratie', 405.

[20] *Naeuwkeurige consideratie*, 91: 'niemant spreekt na sijn herte, niemant liegt openlijck, maar de waarheyt wordt met valsheyt vermengt en opgepronkt om de onervarene lichter te bedriegen'.

A POLITICAL BALANCE 83

of such work, but in particular those who can view things from all sides and have exercised their mind and appearance'.[21]

Knowledge and insight are not accessible to everyone, but they are not beyond the reach of those who make the effort and exercise themselves in viewing things from all sides. Moreover, such exercise makes them able to turn the state on its head with a jump. For this reason, the author moves on in the next part of the *Naeuwkeurige consideratie* to an analysis of the 'arts and ways to enter the services and state', and considers how people end up doing certain acts or how they can be persuaded and convinced to do them.[22] The exposition proceeds from a view of history in which we hear Machiavelli almost verbatim: 'even though chance or Fortune virtually seems to govern the lives of all people', 'one must not believe in any way that everything is driven by foreordination or necessity': 'care and good polity join themselves to Fortune'.[23] A political arrangement is not foreordained nor is it a question of necessity, but is made by people whom you can for that reason steer and even turn in the other direction, if only you acquire knowledge about human beings. This observation is followed by an analysis of the passions based on a materialist, Hobbesian account of Descartes's theory of the affections, which one encounters throughout the text of the *Consideratien* and *Politike Discoursen*. V.D.H. must have thought it useful to introduce his audience to this work, which clearly functioned as his source (i.e. *Bedekte Konsten*, the 'Secret Arts'), in that very way – that is, as a source, as an art and secret.

We sense here an inescapable association that just might confirm the hypothesis that V(an).D(en).H(ove)./De la Court is the author hiding behind the pseudonym Lucius Antistius Constans. In the preface to *De jure ecclesiasticorum*, which was published in 1665, three years after the *Consideratien*, *Politike Discoursen* and *Naeuwkeurige consideratie*, the anonymous author announced his intention to respond to the smear campaign which his work would undoubtedly elicit with a new, separate work

---

[21] Ibid. 90; 91–2: 'het gesicht en 't wesen bedriegen dickwils, de woorden meermaal, waaromme dese bedekte konsten alhier seer nut zijn, als gy schijnt en veynst niet te verstaan datje verstaat'; 'want als de gene die dese listen en lagen geleydt worden van de sake kennisse bekomen, soo keerense den Staat met eenen spronck dickwijls het onderste boven, waaromme een yegelik tot dit werck niet bequaam is, maar die sonderling, die haar wenden en keeren konnen, en haar verstant en gelaat geoeffent hebben'.

[22] Ibid. 92–3.

[23] Ibid. 'hoewel het geval ofte de Fortuyne bykans schijnt aller menschen leven te rechten [. . .] moet men geensins gelooven dat alles door een voorschicking ofte noodtdwangh wordt gedreven [. . .] voorzichtigheydt en 't goet beleydt voeghen haar by de Fortuyne'.

84 DEMOCRATIC THOUGHT FROM MACHIAVELLI TO SPINOZA

which he or she proposed to publish under the name *Arcana ecclesiasticorum* ('the secrets of the ecclesiastical officials').[24] For the anonymous author knew and had seen through his opponents, the ecclesiastical officials, and their tricks, as well as the pernicious practices of those who resorted to doctrine rather than their own reason, so that he knew ahead of time what they would say and write. Yet, so he thought, there was no trick by which these slanderers could prevent the truth of the views proposed in *De jure ecclesiasticorum* to reach and be recognised by at least some pious and good people guided by reason. Nor can they prevent the courageous from defending the truth, so that in due time it might be appropriated for public use. Further on in *De jure*, the anonymous author announced his intention to treat at length of the arts and arguments of his opponents (i.e. the ecclesiastical officials and those who do not follow their own reason) in a *Liber singularis* with the title *Arcana ecclesiasticorum*. There are thus remarkable similarities between the themes and titles, as well as the double, self-referential game of fiction and masking. Of course, this cursory similarity in the end does not really settle anything in regard to the identity of the person hiding behind the pseudonym – although it does lend some credence to the suspicion that De la Court may have been the author hiding behind the initials L.A.C. – but an analysis of its contents and a comparative reading does yield a possible explanation for what motivated V.D.H. to publish this 'addendum to the *Politike Discoursen*' under his initials.[25]

3. *Consideratien van Staat*

In the preface to the 1661 edition, the major theses of the *Consideratien van Staat* are announced by the editor, perhaps the brother of its late author, although this may be a masquerade to facilitate his defence and plea of innocence.[26] As in *De jure*, the motive and authority for this work are laid out immediately and cannot be doubted. The author prefers freedom over monarchy, and accordingly assembles as many arguments as possible in favour of the republic and against monarchy. Yet this does not mean that monarchies are in practice all bad and republics all good, though it does mean that this is how things *can* be.[27] The author follows these observations up with a rather strange argument to thwart the attack and smear campaign he anticipates from his

---

[24] See Chapter III, 69.
[25] Geil in Haitsma Mulier, 'De naeuwkeurige consideratie', 397.
[26] *Consideratien van Staat*, n.p. [2r–5v].
[27] Ibid. n.p. [2v].

A POLITICAL BALANCE 85

opponents. Powerholders ought not to take umbrage at this critique, which does not aim at the person but more generally at the issue, nor at a political theory that takes its point of departure in human 'malice' (*boos-aardigheid*).[28] For it was precisely because he knew that also after this generation 'not angels' but 'animal-like' (*diergelijke*) people would be born that he could not be an enemy of his fellow human beings.[29] This naturally applies also to the rulers; although they are gods, they live and die just 'like other people'.[30] The nature of rulers is no different from that of their subjects, as had already been made clear by Machiavelli, one of the author's greatest sources of inspiration. On the balance of the political state we find freedom and equality. In the introduction, the work's general thesis against monarchy and in favour of the republic is illustrated with Latin and Italian quotations to the effect that one or a few only rule well when this is to the advantage of the common people and that 'in a free republic, also the tongue ought to be free'.[31]

De la Court then begins the *Consideratien*, like Machiavelli, by first turning to monarchy in his search for a specific example, that is, to self-love as the source of political activity. Self-love is the foundation and origin of all human acts, whether good or bad. Since people constantly tend to compare their situation with that of others and want to be esteemed but do not themselves want to esteem others, self-love elicits distrust and fear. Furthermore, people tend to downplay their own well-being and fortune and to exaggerate that of others, while amplifying the damage they suffer and quickly forgetting the misfortune of others.[32] De la Court locates the cause of this two-faced human inclination in the struggle between the passions and reason, which he traces back to the very womb; this struggle coincides with human nature itself. 'No one can be found who has mastered all his passions, the *best* overcome some passions, and we call *good* those who moderate all their passions and fight against them, and their number is few.'[33] For this reason,

[28] Ibid. n.p. [3r].
[29] Ibid.
[30] Ibid. n.p. [2v].
[31] Ibid. 2: 'in een vrye republik, de tong oock behoorde vry te weesen'.
[32] De la Court takes his starting point in Hobbes's well-known point of departure; see also throughout the entire argument. For De la Court's relationship with Hobbes, see Petry, 'Hobbes and the Early Dutch Spinozists', 150–70; Röd, 'Van den Hoves "Politische Waage" und die Modifikation der Hobbesschen Staatsphilosophie bei Spinoza', 29–48; Secretan, 'La réception de Hobbes aux Pays-Bas au XVIIe siècle', 27–46; Visentin, 'Between Machiavelli and Hobbes', 227–48.
[33] *Consideratien van Staat*, 18: 'Niemand vindmen die aller zijne driften meester is, de *Besten* komen eenige driften te boven, en *Goed* noemtmen de menschen, die alle haare driften maatigen, en daar tegenstrijden, welke menschen zeer weinig zijn.'

86   DEMOCRATIC THOUGHT FROM MACHIAVELLI TO SPINOZA

the political state, even in its most imperfect form, can rightly 'be called a Heaven'.[34] From there, the author concludes that the essence of a political state resides in a mutual covenant to 'protect one another against all violence from within and without'.[35] After this covenant has been established, it must be able to endure, and for it to do so, there are two conditions that must be satisfied: First, it must be determined which of the covenant partners is to hold power, and, accordingly, who must obey and be subjected to punishment in case of disobedience, and for how long. Secondly, the number of covenantal partners must be sufficiently great to warrant speaking of a real political state.

We must assume that there are no perfect governments, and this is a point of essential significance in these considerations. Precisely this is why it is so important to distinguish a good government from a bad government, which can be done quite easily: the best government is the one in which the welfare of the rulers is directly related to the welfare of the ruled, while the worst government is one that cannot favour the welfare of the subjects without itself suffering damage and can only draw benefits when it harms its subjects. There are three kinds of government (monarchy, aristocracy and democracy), whose origin the author describes in a way similar to what Machiavelli writes in his *Discorsi*: one form passes over into another in an eternal cycle of rising and falling. On the face of it, no single form is to be preferred over another, as each has its own advantages and disadvantages. Yet since

> a political state cannot exist except from an assembly of thousands upon thousands of people, and no person by virtue of an excelling wisdom or physical power has *the character of a ruler rather than a subject imprinted on his soul or body*, it automatically follows that this authority and power [to rulership] must come from the outside; and also that it can only lawfully descend on *one person or an assembly of a few* from all the members of the assembly. From this, it follows *that democratic or popular government is the most ancient and legitimate* [form of government].[36]

[34] Ibid. 20: 'een Hemel [. . .] werden genaamd'.

[35] Ibid.

[36] Ibid. 30: '[. . .] een politike Staat niet kan bestaan, dan uit een vergaderinge van veele duizenden menschen, ende niemand der zelven menschen door uitsteekende wijsheid, ofte lighaamelike kragten, *in zijn ziele ofte lichaam heeft een ingedrukt Caracter van te regeeren, en niet geregeerd te moeten werden*; soo volgd van zelfs, dat die magt ende kracht van buiten moet aankomen; alsmede, dat die niet kan wettelik afdaalen, *'t zy op een mensch, 't zy op een Vergaadering eeniger weyniger menschen*, dan van alle de Leeden

A comparison between the editions of 1660 and 1662 yields no significant textual variants, and certainly none that, as Van den Enden claimed, have the effect of abandoning the democratic spirit.[37] It is worth going through the passage one more time. The author departs from one of the two conditions he had outlined: Regardless of the concrete form it has assumed, a political community can only continue to exist if it is formed from an assembly numbering thousands of people. A multitude of covenant partners is therefore a condition. But how must that multitude be understood? According to the author, the number of covenant partners must be so great 'that a small decline or growth in power on either side does not suffice to destroy that assembly of people'.[38] Such multitude is necessary so that another large group is not tempted to oppress the smaller group. Multitude is therefore necessary against the outside threat. The author's second basic condition is the equality of this multitude of people with reference to their 'impressed character' to ruling or being ruled: not a single member of the multitude from which and in which a political community is formed has extraordinary intellectual or physical attributes that make him fit for ruling or being ruled. If there are no internal qualities by which power is conferred on the one or the other, whether a single person or an assembly of a few, then this power is assigned according to reasons that are not related to such internal qualities. Finally, power can only be conferred by *all* the people of the multitude, either on a single person or on an assembly of a few. The logical conclusion is that democracy therefore represents the most ancient and legitimate form of rule.

If this knowledge can be derived from the given facts, why are democracies not sustainable, rather passing over into other, less legitimate forms of government? For this is what always happens, in an eternal, pendulum-like movement. It is simply unthinkable for a 'popular assembly' ever to confer power on a single person and his descendants 'into eternity', since 'everyone

---

van die vergaadering, sulks wijders volgd, *dat de Demokratie ofte Populare regeering de oudste ende wettelikste is'*.

[37] In the preface of his *Kort verhael van Nieuw-Nederlants Gelegenheit* (IV), Van den Enden refers to De la Court's statement, added at the end of the second edition, as to why popular government is presented in such a positive light, 'hoewel die warelik de beste niet zij', and that aristocracy is 'gewisslik de beste Regeering': *Consideratien van Staat*, 652; 661. Yet these are isolated passages, which cannot be used to undermine the general tenor of the book, as will also become evident below.

[38] *Consideratien van Staat*, 21: 'dat eenige kleyne vermindering aan de eene, ofte aanwas van kraften aan de andere zijde, geen genoegzaame reeden zy, om die vergaaderinge van menschen gewisselik te vernietigen'.

88 DEMOCRATIC THOUGHT FROM MACHIAVELLI TO SPINOZA

knows the extent to which human beings are subject to change and death'.[39] This leads to the general and paradoxical condition that the transfer of power is by definition temporary, and that power can, or more accurately must, be recalled every so often. For one can easily imagine how 'a person who has been given the authority to protect the common people will apply all his ability and power to turn many of the inhabitants into his followers so as to make himself and his children the *master* of all'.[40] Democracy, which is the oldest and most legitimate form of government, can easily degenerate into absolute monarchy. One can also easily imagine how a 'popular assembly may confer all power for the protection of the common people *upon several of the most competent, on the condition that they from time to time replace the members of the assembly who have passed away*', so '*that aristocracies have a legitimate origin*'.[41] Nevertheless, conflicting with this legitimacy is the reality that aristocracies have come into being because 'the poorest inhabitants, who are consumed by manual labour and raised in ignorance, have already accepted too many of the opinions of the notables that serve to recommend their [i.e. the notables'] greatness'.[42] Burdened by their economic cares, the common people tend not to be sufficiently vigilant in seeing to it that the government indeed fulfils its duty. As a result, aristocratic rulers have seized the opportunity presented to them 'to draw sovereignty towards themselves, and to claim all the benefits and offices of government, to the exclusion of all the other inhabitants. This has often resulted in such oppression of the common inhabitants that they have risen up in rebellion and have sometimes been fortunate enough to restore government to a *democracy*.'[43]

---

[39] Ibid. 30: 'een yder weet hoe veranderlik, hoe stervelik de menschen zijn'.

[40] Ibid. 31: '[. . .] dat een ter gemeene bescherminge geauthoriseerd persoon, alle zijn bequaamheid ende magt zal gebruiken, om veele ingezeetenen aan zijn snoer te krijgen, ende daar door zig zelven en zijn kinderen *Heer* oover allen'.

[41] Ibid. 'populare vergaadering, ter gemeene bescherminge volle magt kan geeven, *aan eenige bequaamste persoonen gekoomen uit allen, op conditien, dat de zelven van tijd tot tijd de afstervende Leeden der Vergaaderinge zullen vervullen* [. . .] *dat de Aristokratien een wettig oorsprong hebben konnen*'.

[42] Ibid. 31–2: 'de armste Ingezeetenen, met den arbeid hunner handen bekommerd ende in onweetendheid opgevoed, al te veel de opinien der aansienelikste tot hun eige grootsheid raadende hebben ingevolgd'.

[43] Ibid. 32: 'om de Souverainiteit tot zig te trekken, ende met uitsluitinge aller andere Ingezeetenen, alle beneficien ende officien der regeeringe, van zig alleen dependent te maaken. En hier op zijn veeltijds gevolgd zoo groote verdrukkingen der gemeene intezeetenen; dat de zelve oproerig werdende, somtijds het geluk hebben gehad die regeering weederom tot een *Demokratie* te konnen brengen.'

'The Lord God takes special pleasure in monarchical government.'[44] It is not entirely clear whether this is advantageous or disadvantageous, but these words do at least seem to suggest that God is not on the side that has the greatest claim to legitimacy, nor is he connected to a political arrangement that brings welfare or happiness to the people. In the second book of part I, De la Court examines a number of concrete governments, most of them monarchical in form (Turkey, France, Spain, England, etc.), the common import being that a political community must not base itself on virtue but on the duality of human beings. The analyses are not intended as a plea against virtue, but rather as a recommendation of careful, virtuous and rational rulers *and* subjects so that human cunning, malice and passion might be recognised, and the laws governing political activity might be shaped in such a way that evil rulers and subjects are forced to behave well. In this way, the traditional line of argument has been turned on its head: politics ought not to pursue an ideal of perfection and goodness (i.e. virtue), but proceed from the fact that human beings in general, including both rulers and subjects, are not good and that laws must be enacted aiming to restrict this non-goodness. This reversal is reminiscent of Machiavelli's argument in the second part of *Il Principe*, or of the words of the Ciompi leader. It also encapsulates an implicit critique, likewise found in Machiavelli, of the church, of the Christian religion and of all those who hang on to the existence of a single truth and doctrine (and who therefore do not judge on the basis of their own reason). This critique is bolstered by various anecdotes regarding bad governments. And lest anyone imagine that 'the Mohammedan religion is the cause of this evil government and the shrinking population', the author cites so extensively from Sansovino's *Dell'Historia* 'that one can easily see that if those lands had been under a Christian religion they would have suffered even greater destruction'.[45] The cause for the lapse into tyranny was not the religion of the Turks, but the malice of the people.

As he goes on, De la Court constantly places arguments, stories and facts in the political balance, whose scales at one time favour the one and at another the other. We will not summarise the weighing of each in detail, but prefer to skip ahead to the conclusion of the *Consideratien*. It should be clear that this exercise in balancing can never be finished, that

---

[44] Ibid. 36: 'God de Heer heeft een bijzonder welbehagen in de Monarchale regeeringe.'

[45] Ibid. 184: 'de Mahometaanse Religie oorzaak deezer quade regeeringe en ontvolking zy [. . .] dat men ligtelik daar uit zal konne zien, dat die Landen, onder een Christelike Religie, nog veel meer verwoest zouden weezen'.

90   DEMOCRATIC THOUGHT FROM MACHIAVELLI TO SPINOZA

the conclusion can only be provisional and for that reason also presents itself in this provisional way. The first thing to consider is the structure of the work as a whole. Part I is about politics in general and about formation (that is, the beginning or *principle* of a political state), where various concrete monarchies are examined, similar to the way Machiavelli presented that beginning or principle in *Il Principe*. Part II is about 'freedom' (*vryheid*), and part III about 'popular government' (*populare regeeringe*).[46] The first book of part II treats freedom and republics in general, then moves on to aristocratic forms of government in general and in particular, with a number of examples, including mixed sovereignty at the end, being placed on the balance. In part III, the author first treats popular government in general, once again following the familiar pattern: what is the principle of popular government, when was it formed and what are its advantages and disadvantages? He then scours history for a specific popular government, with the title actually already indicating that no such example can be found, with the one exception of Athens, which came quite close.[47] Finally, in the third book of part III, the author considers whether monarchy, aristocracy or popular government represents the best form of government.

The disadvantages of a monarchy are clear, as the Greeks and Romans called it 'tyranny', just as they also 'called the required obedience of another person *slavery*'; in a monarchy, a subject is, like a slave, bound 'to behave in accordance with his master's desires'.[48] At the other end of the spectrum we find a political state in which people do not command one another, but are elected to take their seat in an assembly where they can cast their vote and where conclusions are drawn on the basis of a majority of votes so that certain laws are accepted and magistrates are elected to execute them. The ancients call such a political state

> *freedom*, since *no one there is bound to live according to the will of a man* (which ought nevertheless to be considered very carefully), but *in accordance with order and law*, to which all inhabitants of that state are equally subjected, just as they are to reason. As a result, both the magistrates and the common inhabitants will have to obey or to be punished, so that no one in such a *state* is either *master* or *slave*. Indeed, in such lands none of the inhabitants can really be called *subjects*, since

[46] Ibid. 255–431; 432–572.
[47] Ibid. 491.
[48] Ibid. 255.

A POLITICAL BALANCE

91

they are not subjected to anyone. Nowadays such *states* and *lands* are called *republics*.[49]

After enumerating the advantages of these republics and then their disadvantages, the author, as noted, turns to aristocracy, investigating its principle as well as its advantages and disadvantages. Once again we find echoes of Machiavelli, as one of the greatest defects of an aristocratic government is 'oligarchy, *Dominatio Paucorum*, *stato da pochi*, government of a few'.[50] Even though such a deficient government is much better than many others, as can be gathered from the majority of Dutch cities which

> *enjoyed great welfare much longer than other lands. But* there is reason to doubt *that this welfare will last long in the United Netherlands, and in particular in Holland.* For since the cities have undergone vast expansion and their numbers have grown infinitely without the councils being expanded and in some cities, in fact, even being scaled back against all good protocol, the disproportion between rulers and subjects has grown dramatically. The fear is that this *government of the few (Paucorum Dominatio)* will not last long when trade and prosperity drop, and when subjects find themselves emptyhanded and in discomfort.[51]

---

[49] Ibid. 256: '*vryheid*: alsoo *niemand aldaar verbonden is, te leeven naar den zin van een mensch,* (daar zeer wel op te letten staat,) maar *naar de zin van de ordre en Wet,* aan welke alle Ingezeetenen van dien Staat, gelijk aan de Reeden, eenpariglik onderworpen zijn. Zulks de Magistraats-persoonen, alzoo wel als de gemeene Ingezeetenen, hier moeten gehoorzaamen, ofte gestraft werden; en dienvolgende, is niemandt in zoodanige *Staat* een *Heer* ook niemand een *Slaaf*; Jaa naweliks magmen in zoodanige Landen, iemand der Ingezeetenen een *onderdaan* noemen, dewijl zy aan geen mensch onderworpen zijn. Deeze *Staaten* en *Landen* werden nu genaamd *Republiken*.'

[50] Ibid. 290: 'Oligarchie, *Dominatio Paucorum*, *stato da pochi*, een regering van weinig menschen.'

[51] Ibid. 291: '*ten respecte van andere Landen, van oover langen tijd zeer welvaarende zijn geweest. Maar of dat welvaaren, lange in de Vereenigd Neederlanden, voorneementlik in Holland,* zal duuren, is reeden te twijffelen: Want vermits de Steeden zoo zeer zijn vergroot, en in menschen oneindelik toegenomen, zonder dat de Raaden zijn vermeerderd; jaa ter contrarie teegen alle goede politie in verscheide Steeden zijn verminderd, zoo is die disproportie tusschen Regeerders en onderdaanen veel grooter geworden; en is te vrezen dat die (*Paucorum Dominatio) Heersching van weinig menschen,* by vermindering van neering, en welvaaren, by leedige en ongemakkelike onderdaanen, niet zal konnen werden lang gedragen.'

92   DEMOCRATIC THOUGHT FROM MACHIAVELLI TO SPINOZA

The most important argument against aristocracy is that rule is held by too few, such that it does not promote but hinders the general well-being and therefore cannot endure. The most important argument in favour of democracy must be located in how it is formed, namely as a remedy against the dangers and disadvantages of human malice and against the violence and suppression found in the two other forms of government, 'namely *monarchy* and *aristocracy*, which come into being through pure *violence* and deceit'.[52] Monarchies and aristocracies are established through violence and deceit and they require such oppression to maintain themselves, whereas democracies are established by opposition to such oppression. Another disadvantage of monarchies and aristocracies is that they only acquire a certain legitimacy after a very long time, not until each inhabitant living there has been born under such government and feels obligated to render obedience out of thankfulness for the protection they receive. This means that monarchies or aristocracies do not work for new arrivals, for immigrants. Whenever people migrate, whether out of poverty or in order to escape violence, they are always inclined to establish a democracy.[53] The advantages of popular government are therefore clear: it is 'not based on violence, but is natural, rational, and in and of itself equitable'.[54] It aims at the welfare of the people, while in other forms of government the welfare of the people is just a '*cloak*' to cover the ruler's agenda. Popular government alone uses 'all the *knowledge* of the inhabitants, their *passion* and *ability*', while in other forms of government the choice rather goes out to 'the most incompetent – which is only compounded by the fact that the power of rulership and servitude appears to be more closely attached to the people in [these] other governments'.[55] Finally, in a popular government, no eternal taxes are to be imposed on the people. But there are also drawbacks that must be placed on the political balance. There is much greater ignorance in a democracy than there is in other forms of rule, whose cause is not to be sought in the people themselves but is to be ascribed to the government, since 'all people enter the world

---

[52] Ibid. 436: 'naamentlik de *Monarchale* ende de *Aristokratike*, ontstaan door puur *geweld* en bedrog'. The first argument can also be found in Machiavelli, the *libertins* and Hobbes, while the second does not occur in Hobbes, appears to be there in the *libertins*, and can be found explicitly in Machiavelli, in particular in his discussion of the Ciompi Revolt (*Istorie Fiorentine* III, 13).

[53] *Consideratien van Staat*, 440.

[54] Ibid. 442: 'op geen geweld gefondeerd, maar naturelik, redelik, en in zig zelven billik'.

[55] Ibid. 443–4: 'alle *kennissen* der Inwoonders, haare *passie*, en *bequaamheid* [. . .] de onbequaamsten, en dat nog het argste is, vermits in andere regeeringen, de magt van regeeren en dienen meer schijnt aan de persoonen vast te zijn'.

in equal ignorance'.[56] The causes of 'ignorance and deceit must be located outside the *will* of the person who remains ignorant or was deceived'.[57] The ignorant and deceived are victims, and, even though they are themselves complicit in their ignorance and deception (or self-deception), they do not do so voluntarily or 'on purpose', as it were. For this reason, deceit cannot be banished from popular government, and there are more powerful passions of money and ambition – a very great disadvantage – to be faced there, and since the people under popular government are ruled by 'the majority', this effectively means '*dumb and ignorant people who have neither eyes nor ears*'.[58]

The situation therefore does not look good, *and yet* the evils of a monarchy are even worse. For a monarch to be great, the subjects have to be divided and incited against one another. In regard to aristocracy, one must consider whether the elite do not always rule to their own advantage, even if that means disadvantaging their subjects. Time and again, De la Court returns to the point that popular government, in which government is of the people themselves, is directed to the general welfare of all the common inhabitants.

Popular government is 'by nature the *first* and the *oldest*', and it only lapsed into another form of government 'through *violence* and *deceit*'.[59] 'And although these deficiencies of popular government, which arise from the deep ignorance of the most needy citizens regarding the things that serve their own welfare, are very great, from the same conclusion it still appears that the deficiencies of an oligarchy (or a state ruled by a few) are much greater.'[60]

---

[56] Ibid. 448: 'aller menschen kinderen even onweetende ter Wereld komen'.

[57] Ibid. 448–9: 'onweetenheid en bedrog moeten werden gevonden buiten den *wille* des menschen, die onweetende blijft, ofte bedrogen werd'.

[58] Ibid. 453: '*domme en onweetende menschen, nog oogen nog ooren hebbende*'. In this context, De la Court refers, atypically as it were, to Tacitus. The latter is commonly cited in support of the freedom of thought and speech by his words in *Historiae* I, 1: 'the rare fortune of a time when one may think what one likes and say what one thinks' ('rara temporum felicitate ubi sentire quae velis et quae sentias dicere licet').

[59] *Consideratien van Staat*, 556.

[60] Ibid. 561: 'En hoewel deese gebreeken der Populare Regeeringe, spruitende uit der behoeftigste Borgers, diepe onkonde omtrent saaken die tot haar eige welvaaren dienen, zeer groot zijn: so blijkt nogtans uit de zelve conclusie, dat de gebreeken eener oligarchie, ofte een Staat die door weinig menschen werd geregeerd, veel grooter zijn.'

94 DEMOCRATIC THOUGHT FROM MACHIAVELLI TO SPINOZA

4. *Politike Discoursen*

In 1662, the Leiden printer Pieter Hackius published the *Politike Discoursen* under the initials 'D.C.' on the title page, a work generally attributed to Pieter de la Court but almost certainly written by his brother Johan. In the preface we read about the 'author' that he 'passed away at the height of his life, leaving this work unfinished, and without order or title, written for the most part on loose leaves, so that it was necessary to bring some order to it'.[61] Once again, there are similarities that would seem to lend credence to the thesis that De la Court was somehow involved in the writing of the *De jure ecclesiasticorum*: an anonymous publication, an editor who still has work to do to complete the text, and an author who has spent time in distant countries abroad. Another similarity is the method of responding to anticipated criticism and slander by going on the attack. The author has a keen mind and is bold, but at the same time covers his tracks, since one ought not to despise 'a well-planted vegetable, herb and flower garden' because 'fools could poison themselves'.[62] The unmasking of (covered) violence and deceit yields knowledge of the way violence and deceit are practised. The *Discoursen*, which deal in particular with 'conspiracies, rebellion and ecclesiastical affairs', can be used by 'children and [by] greedy, foolish and wicked people to their own destruction and the destruction of their neighbour', but also by 'mature, sober, wise and kind-hearted people' who 'can put it to very good use'.[63] Moreover, the *Discoursen*, like the *Consideratien*, present us with the same naturalist point of departure, non-normative discourse, reasoning, careful weighing, and combination of existential considerations with an adapted Cartesian theory of the affections, as well as the same conclusion which continuously balances *fortuna* and *virtù*, unchangeable nature and contingency, equality and freedom. So too the *Politike Discoursen* amount to a long, nuanced, often repetitive argument in favour of the republic. But there are also differences vis-à-vis the *Consideratien*. The *Discoursen* are even closer to Machiavelli, in form as well as content; their focus is more directed to conflict, both external (war) and internal (revolt, conspiracies, suspicion); and, finally, religion, or at least the church, now forms an important theme.

---

[61] *Politike Discoursen*, n.p. [*2v]: '*koomen in sijn bloeiende Iaren te ooverlijden, latende dit alles onvolmaakt, en sonder ordre, of* Titul, *geschreeven op veele allesints van een gescheide bladen; sulks het selven eenig sints heeft moeten werden geschikt*'.

[62] Ibid. n.p. [*3v]: 'een wel-beplante Moes-kruyd-en-Bloem-Hof [. . .] dwaase menschen *sig daar mede vergiftigen konnen*'.

[63] Ibid. n.p. [*4r]

A POLITICAL BALANCE 95

The first book, which treats of city affairs, addresses in particular the benefits that accrue to a state from the multitude, from an open immigration policy, and from the welfare of the common people. Measures for fostering trade secure the presence of many wealthy subjects, which is better for a state than many poor people are, even though many poor subjects are still better than a small number of wealthy people. At all events, a city with many inhabitants is better than a city with few inhabitants, and there must likewise be many magistrates. Moreover, in the interest of the state and the maintenance of its government, these things must be 'a heavy burden which one ought to bear for the welfare of the fatherland and to the detriment of one's private affairs'.[64] Privileges, monopolies, forms of trade that only benefit the individual, and corruption are all counterproductive for the common people. The general rule is that one ought not to force matters where one does not have the necessary power. Therefore, since 'the regents cannot coerce their malicious subjects to diligence and justice, they must not attempt to do so in vain, to the detriment of the most excellent subjects. Rather, they must leave the same, complete freedom to all subjects without distinction.'[65] This freedom is particularly applicable to newcomers, to immigrants. One ought to 'give all aliens who seek to settle in the cities as much freedom as the other, old inhabitants', since their presence leads to 'large, highly populated cities', which is the best thing that can happen to a city.[66]

In the second book, which treats of national affairs, the author addresses issues of internal or domestic conflict, such as suspicion, conspiracies and revolt, in the course of which he emphasises the role of semblance and the influence of Machiavelli becomes readily apparent. In *Il Principe*, Machiavelli writes about the establishment (beginning) and essence (maintenance) of a political community in general, while he in the *Discorsi* lays out his own political view (for a republic), of course in relation to specific – that is, his own – historical circumstances. Moving back and forth between current events and a commentary on Livy's historical works, he reveals his own political view, subjects the causes of the demise of the land to critique

---

[64] Ibid. 13: 'zijn een lastig pak, dat men ten welstand des Vaderlands, en met verminderinge van sijn eige familiare saken, behoorde op sig te laden'.

[65] Ibid. 4: 'de *Regenten* hun quaad-aardige Onderdaanen tot *naarstigheid* en *oprechtigheid* niet konnen dwingen, zoo moeten zy 't zelven niet te vergeefs tragten te doen, *tot nadeel der beste Onderdaanen*; maar liever aan alle Onderdaanen zonder eenig onderscheid, de zelve volkome vryheid laaten'.

[66] Ibid. 3: '*alle vremdelingen die in de Steden willen komen woonen, zoo veel vryheids als den anderen oude ingezeetenen te geeven* [. . .] volkrijke groote Steeden'.

96   DEMOCRATIC THOUGHT FROM MACHIAVELLI TO SPINOZA

(i.e. church and the Christian religion), and produces a nuanced albeit effective political theory of democracy. In the same way, after the general considerations of the *Consideratien*, De la Court moves on in the *Discoursen* to an account that draws lines to concrete historical events and governments, citing Livy extensively, together with Machiavelli. Violence, schemes, secrets and appearances in general play an important role in the affairs of the nation. De la Court likewise moves back and forth, comparing historical events like the Revolt of the Batavi to the Ciompi Revolt as described in the *Istorie Fiorentine*.[67] Remarkable about his analysis of conspiracy and revolt is the shift in literary perspective to that of the actors, the (grammatical) subject. He posits that even though an uproar begins with the common people, the rebels' first act must be to choose a leader; that those who rise up in conspiracy or revolt must overcome fear and be valiant, must spring into action without delay; that a revolt must initially appear not to be directed against the government, but only express dissatisfaction with specific people, magistrates or officers; that a rebellion cannot stop halfway; etc.

In the third book, which treats of affairs of war (i.e. external conflicts), we likewise find frequent paraphrases of Machiavelli, whose views are defended as being of interest to Holland. It therefore decries the use of mercenary armies and the involvement of the multitude in battle, proposing instead to turn a limited number of people into soldiers. Enemies must be deprived of the power to inflict damage, among other ways by treating them well and turning them into friends. Courtesy is always preferable to cruelty. Remarkable about this book is the extensive discussion of what one should do in conquered territory, as the author points out that a war is only won if the newly acquired power can maintain itself. Once again, Machiavelli can be found on every page, for instance in the discussion of the 'castles or citadels' which are sometimes necessary or beneficial, although they in general represent dangerous means for maintaining a city.[68] After all, fortresses and strongholds give the impression that the conquered territory is still enemy territory. Yet the most important part of the *Politike Discoursen* is book IV which, as announced in the preface, treats of ecclesiastical affairs.

The first discourse of the fourth book motivates the line of reasoning by taking its point of departure in the basic human passions of joy and sadness. The fact that these passions can be observed in young children in all their intensity immediately tells us that human beings allow themselves to be

[67] Ibid. 145ff.
[68] Ibid. 276.

guided more by 'the passions' than by reason.[69] Even the wisest, who make it their goal to judge by reason on the basis of experience and investigation, never manage to control their passions completely, no matter how hard they try. In fact, the opposite can even be observed, as people derive the greatest pleasure from the satisfaction of their passions and devote all their energy, time and judgement to that pursuit. Accordingly, they remain incompetent in judgement, but since they are aware of their ignorance and do not want to be put to shame, they constantly judge by outward appearances. And since thorough investigation is difficult, they get used to prejudice and in the end are convinced that they have or had good reasons for their judgements. There are very few who recognise this deficiency in themselves and are driven, 'by the improved exercise of their mind and brains, to prescribe fixed rules for themselves so that they might know when they have been instructed, can decide by truth and reason rather than by appearances and their own passions'.[70] As we will see later on, we encounter the same argument almost word for word in Spinoza's *Tractatus theologico-politicus*. Furthermore, the author is writing here about the wisest people, and we can easily guess what to expect from those who are not as wise and who do not exercise themselves. They make all judgements by outward appearances and the passions alone. In addition, with 'lies, deception, eloquence, and whatever good or evil might be present', one can easily arouse in them a 'contrary appearance' (*contrarieschijn*) and passions so that they immediately change their judgement and appetites.[71] This fickleness results from the fact that people allow themselves to be governed by outward appearances and their passions.

The second discourse aims to demonstrate that 'public religion is necessary in a state'.[72] As long as there is 'in a civil society neither God nor a publicly authorized religion', people cannot be coerced to obedience, and since human beings – including both rulers and subjects – by nature 'love themselves, their mind, and their own passions', the rulers are primarily out to suppress their subjects to their own advantage and to the satisfaction of their private passions.[73] 'The subjects, on the contrary, fear oppression

---

[69] Ibid. 280.
[70] Ibid. 281: 'verstand en herssenen beeter oeffenende, sig selven vaste reegels voor te schrijven, om te weeten wanneer sy wel onderregt zijnde, konnen besluiten naar waarheid, en reeden, en niet naar schijn, en haare eigen passien'.
[71] Ibid. 'loogens, bedriegery, welspreekendheid, ende eenig teegenwoordig goed ofte quaad'.
[72] Ibid. 288: 'de publike Gods-dienst in een Staat noodsakelick is'.
[73] Ibid.

98   DEMOCRATIC THOUGHT FROM MACHIAVELLI TO SPINOZA

from their government and constantly hope for an opportunity to rebel.'[74] Without god or religion, one is left with oppressive rulers and rebellious subjects. Arthur Weststeijn has pointed to a difference between Spinoza and the De la Court brothers on the point of the relationship between faith and politics, which can be measured by their response to the Koerbagh-drama. While for Spinoza the gruesome fate suffered by Koerbagh became one of the most important reasons for launching a fundamental appeal for the freedom to philosophise (*libertas philosophandi*), the De la Court brothers condemned Koerbagh's 'public undermining of Christian dogma', though they did consider his punishment excessive and inappropriate in its severity.[75] While Spinoza responded to the events with the universal principle of freedom of thought and speech, which by definition extends also to biblical criticism, for the De la Court brothers the freedom of speech ends where the word of God begins: 'it is kings who should be criticised, not Scripture'.[76] For this reason, Weststeijn judges D.C.'s critique not to be as radical as that of Spinoza. The toleration and freedom advocated by D.C. is limited and does not extend to Holy Scripture (as pointed out by Weststeijn, noting that toleration and freedom of speech are understood here as the announcement of truth in the service of the republic).[77] Finally, D.C.'s critique is directed to the church rather than to religion as such. And yet this is not all there is to say. For there is such a thing as 'false' religions with gods and goddesses introduced to coerce subjects to obedience, even though they only deceive. 'And in order to keep the people in constant veneration regarding matters of religion, they had a constant stream of newly devised miracles.'[78] Some religions are pure deceit and can only maintain their status with trickery or 'secret arts', including miracles. Sometimes religions are only out for oppression, and how severe such oppression is can be gauged by the wars fought in their name. Clerics have found no better solution for ending the conflicts than violence and wars, to their own advantage, convincing the people that these wars serve to spread the true religion.

In the third discourse, De la Court argues, now with great conviction, that religion is necessary for the political life and for human happiness. This does fit in well with Weststeijn's argument. But immediately

[74] Ibid. 289: 'De onderdaanen daar-en-tegen, souden de vervolging haarer Ooverheid vreesen, en altijd hoopen op gelegentheid om te konnen rebelleeren.'
[75] Weststeijn, *Commercial Republicanism*, 341.
[76] Ibid. 342.
[77] Ibid. 337–44.
[78] *Politike Discoursen*, 291: 'En om de Gemeente noch geduurig in veneratie, omtrent den Gods-dienst, te houden, hadden sy haare gedurige nieuwe versiersels van Miraculen.'

after establishing this necessity, the author proposes that it is possible to imagine a government that emerges from a *status naturalis* or innate condition, 'without public religion'.[79] In fact, this possibility cannot just be imagined but even *demonstrated*, since 'the Indians and heathens have had very good governments, even though they had very little religion or very false religions'.[80] In his *Kort verhael*, Van den Enden likewise points to the societies of the 'Indians' where there are no gods, as exemplified in the establishment of the colony in Delaware and, by extension, all other democracies. In this observation, De la Court finds confirmation for the persistence of politics, while 'religion either grows or declines and degenerates with time'.[81] As a result, religion is not necessary for either the political life or for human happiness. Moreover, the fact that the 'Americans lived with a good polity but had no religion, or at least a very corrupt one', and that Europe is divided to the point of war between many 'sects and religious forms', should teach us that it is better not to try to convince people to embrace another faith.[82] Religious disputes and proselysation lead to bloodshed. For this reason, there ought to be no law prescribing for people what they must believe. So too the political government is to ensure that none of its citizens coerce anyone in matters of religious conviction. In other words, clerics are subject to the authority of the government and have nothing to say to their fellow citizens. They do not have a right at all, not even for giving religious instruction. To 'instruct [one's neighbour] in religious forms' is to transgress the government's injunction and therefore a 'rebellious opinion'.[83]

De la Court's position therefore seems to waver back and forth. The one moment religion is understood to be necessary (in which the author seems to be parroting Machiavelli), the next moment it is said not to be necessary at all and a political community better off without. The entire argument leads consistently to the freedom to believe and to think as one

---

[79] Ibid. 293: 'sonder publike Gods-dienst'.

[80] Ibid. 'dat'er seer goede Regeeringen onder de Indianen, en Heidenen, geweest zijn, daer seer weinig, of seer verkeerde gods-dienst was'.

[81] Ibid. 'Gods-dienst ondertusschen somtijds toe, en somtijds seer afneemd, en verbasterd'.

[82] Ibid. 'Americanen in goede Politie, maar sonder Gods-dienst, of met een seer verbasterde waren geweest'; 'secten en manieren van Gods-dienst'. This coincides with Van den Enden's critique in the *Kort verhael* (published that same year, in 1662) on the attempt of the British to Christianise North America; for more, see Chapter V.2 below.

[83] *Politike Discoursen*, 296: '[. . .] willen onderregten, in manieren van Gods-dienst [. . .] oproerige opinie'.

deems fit: 'it would be cruel to command what, as one knows, cannot be obeyed'.[84] The government has neither authority nor right over a person's inner conscience, feelings or love of neighbour. At the same time, precisely because it is impossible to obey in reason and faith, teachers are forbidden to 'advise, speak or command' in matters of religion.[85] According to Ernst H. Kossmann, these conflicting claims, this 'improvised character of the *Politike Discoursen*', is the result of the philosophical amateurism of the De la Court brothers.[86] However revolutionary and refreshing their political ideas might sound against the background of scholastic politics, they failed to develop a coherent system whose consequences they could fully accept. Kossmann attributes this failure on the theoretical level to the revolutionary character of their political views; the brothers were 'by nature pioneers and trend-setters'.[87] But against Kossmann's thesis we might note how tightly organised and composed it is for an allegedly improvised work. For in the back and forth movement of the work, we do hear the unmistakable and consistent, albeit somewhat diffuse, sound of critique against the authority of the ecclesiastical institutions and their theologians. At the end of the third discourse, this critique becomes explicit and announces the theme that will be developed in the next two discourses. The only people governed by the pope are his 'jesters; for all those who see him as a God on earth and submit to him for the sake of their freedom are fools'.[88]

'If obedience is to do and not do what is not to one's own advantage but to the advantage of another who has some superiority over us; and if one's own desire is one's delight – then all obedience was clearly caused by coercion.'[89] Having said this, the author returns in the fourth discourse to the basic motif established at the beginning of book IV, that 'all people are from birth subject to the affections of blood and the resulting passions; and [that] there are fewer people who throughout the course of their lives advance

---

[84] Ibid. 295: 'het soude een wreedheid zijn, iet te gebieden, wat men weet niet gehoorsaamd te konnen werden'.

[85] Ibid. 296: 'te raaden, te seggen, nog te gebieden'.

[86] Kossmann, *Political Thought in the Dutch Republic*, 61.

[87] Ibid. 62.

[88] *Politike Discoursen*, 300: '[. . .] Paus regeerd oover louter Narren; want alle die hem voor een Godt op aarden houden, en sig Hem onderwerpen, daar sy haare vryheid konnen houden, zijn sot'.

[89] Ibid. 'Indien gehoorsaamen, is doen, en laaten, niet 't gunt men selfs, maar 't gunt een ander, die eenighe superioriteit oover ons heeft, begeerd; en indien eens menschen zin is, eens menschen Hemelrijk: soo sietmen klaerlik, dat alle gehoorsaamheid, door dwang, veroorsaakt werd.'

A POLITICAL BALANCE

101

so far as to follow right reason by their will'.[90] Moreover, all people pursue their passions and prefer to surrender themselves to their own passions and reason rather than those of others. As a result, all people show an aversion to obedience. In the author's opinion, such disobedience manifests itself particularly among those who read carelessly and imprudently much in *Holy Scripture*, since it tells of prophets and apostles who, under the guidance of an inner divine revelation, refuse to obey the political authorities. For imprudent readers imagine themselves to be like the prophets and look to their disobedience as an example, albeit without a special revelation which they of course do not have. This disobedience is particularly common among the malevolent

> expositors of the divine Scriptures [. . .], since, although they ought to recall that all people who do not base their exposition of Holy Scripture on right reason but on their own private divine revelations deserve to be called rebels, enthusiasts, spiritualists or Quakers, and are for that reason recognised by the wise as evil hypocrites or ignorant melancholics in need of medicine, we see that they still present themselves to their hearers as the ambassadors of God, endowed with an individual and divine commission and instruction

to write, teach or preach, 'according to God's will, in the name of God and in his place'.[91] These divine ambassadors are so convinced of their position that they imagine themselves to have the right to chastise, censure and banish anyone who holds a different – and, in their opinion, erroneous – opinion. The preachers and teachers who think they know better are guided by their ambition, pride and personal advantage to the extent that they think they have the right to abuse the ignorance of the common people who hear and

---

[90] Ibid. 'alle menschen, van de geboorte af, den driften des bloeds, en daar uit ontstaan de passien, onderworpen zijnde; weer weinige menschen, geduurende de loop huns leevens, soo verre komen, dat sy de goede Reeden gewilligh souden volgen'.

[91] Ibid. 302: 'uitleggers der Goddelike Schriften [. . .], want hoewel sy behoorden te gedenken, dat alle menschen die nu de uitleggingen der H. Schriften op geen goede reeden maar op haar eige particuliere Goddelike revelatie voor-geeven te bouwen, de naam van Oproermaakers, Enthousiasten, Geest-dryvers, of Quakers, verdienen: ende dienvolgende dat sy by verstandigen, werden geschat boosaardige schijn-heilige, of wel onwetende, Melancholike, Medecijn-behoevende menschen te zijn: soo sietmen nogtans dat sy by hun Toe-hoorders sig veeltijds uitgeeven voor Gods Ambassadeurs, voorsien met particuliere Goddelike last, ende Instructie, om Godes wille, in Godes name, ende in sijn Persoon [. . .]'.

102   DEMOCRATIC THOUGHT FROM MACHIAVELLI TO SPINOZA

read and to extend their teaching to the disadvantage of the political government. This point can be illustrated with historical examples, which the author considers very evident: 'All of these things are clearly seen in the papacy and in other clerics, whose time of reckoning has come long ago.'[92]

The fifth discourse continues unabated with its critique of the ecclesiastical officials, charging that they obstruct and destroy science and elicit ignorance. Since the public teachers of religion see how their power grows and slinks according to the number of their followers, they do not restrict themselves to the instruction of their religion but despise all who do not believe in God, and they use their sermons and writings to defame both unbelievers and believers with diverging views. In this way they lead the common people to believe that jurists are bad Christians, that physicians are libertines, that philosophers are atheists, and that politicians are deceivers. The focus of their slander and religious fervour are the philosophers and savants. The religious teachers are very persistent, since, although they like all other people pursue fame and are convinced that they speak as substitutes – *lieutenants* – of God, they think that they cannot draw any useful teachings from fellow human beings and imagine themselves exempt from humility and modesty, such that they are exceptionally passionate in all they do and seek to accomplish. This passion and religious fervour serves to explain why they are not satisfied just to forbid those with diverging views – in particular the theorists, like physicians, philosophers, political thinkers and mathematicians – to speak against them in public. In order to make sure that no one says anything different even within the privacy of their own homes,

> they have the custom to banish from the land all those who are of another mind or to put them to death, and to completely eradicate whatever might bring people to fall back on such religion – everything, in fact, that could provide even the slightest bit of knowledge concerning the teaching they reject.[93]

In this way, every deviation from their teaching is immediately nipped in the bud, and all thought and speech is subject to the control of the ecclesiastical

---

[92] Ibid. 304: 'Alle het welk men, in het Pausdom, en in andere Geesteliken, wiens pot lang genoeg te vuur is geweest, oopentlick siet.'

[93] Ibid. 307: 'pleegen sy alle menschen die van een ander gevoelen zijn, uit den Landen te jaagen, ofte te dooden; ende met een uit te roejen: alles wat de menschen wederom tot soodanigen Gods-dienst soude konnen doen vervallen: ja selfs ook alles dat maar enige de minste kennisse soude geven van de Leere die sy verwerpen'.

officials. Not only are all divergent views punished with banishment or death, but every possibility for knowledge of heterodox views is cut off. While up to this point the critique seemed to be formulated especially against the institutions of the Christian religion, that is, the Christian officials under the pope as their head, in the following paragraphs the author argues that it applies to all religions and doctrinal systems. Dissident thinkers and those of other faiths are being banished and put to death, while all that might lead to another god is eliminated, and anything that could even lead to knowledge of the rejected teaching is obliterated. This is what the pagans did amongst themselves. This is what the Jews did to the pagans and Christians. This is what the Christians did to the Jews and pagans. This is what the Turks did to the Christians. And, finally, this is what the Christians are doing amongst themselves, divided as they are into their many different sects.

In the sixth discourse, De la Court suggests that the ignorance caused by the ecclesiastical officials not only destroys science, but also leads to the decay of the public religion. This decay is caused in exactly the same way as the decay of politics, especially in that excessive power is given to a single person, such as the king, for too long. What once again emerges is that religion as such is not the problem, since religion is, properly speaking, an internal affair, although on the public level it represents a binding force for the common people. Rather, the problem is the religious policy maintained by the institute of the church. For just as it is good for a land to be governed by a multitude, so too religions appear to be most steadfast when they find themselves under the republican government of a multitude.

The fifth book, which treats of justice, republic and monarchy, draws the same conclusions as the *Consideratien*, revealing the true aim of the discourses in regard to ecclesiastical affairs. Laws must be instituted in such a way that all inhabitants pursue the common welfare. That 'a republic is better than a monarchy' is illustrated by the observation, filtered and still valid in spite of many examples to the contrary, that for the subjects even the 'best monarchical government' is not as good 'as the basest of republican governments'.[94] So too 'sovereigns are in general much more malicious than other people', and 'nobles or courtiers are subject to more shortcomings than others'.[95]

---

[94] Ibid. 357: 'beste Monarchale Regeering'; and 377: 'als de geringste Republijkse Regeering'.

[95] Ibid. 388: 'de Vorsten doorgaans boosaardiger zyn, als andere Menschen'; 391: 'Edelluiden, ofte Hoovelingen, den gebreeken meer, als andere menschen, onderworpen zyn'.

104 DEMOCRATIC THOUGHT FROM MACHIAVELLI TO SPINOZA

In the sixth book, which treats of moral affairs, the argument comes full circle as we return to the starting point of the fourth book, namely the 'human passions, which one could summarily call joy and sadness'.[96] Kossmann observes that there can be no doubt about the source of De la Court's analysis of the affections, arguing that they are fully in line with the tenor of Descartes's thought.[97] The affections, which arise in the soul/inner being by a complex physiological process, are a natural phenomenon and not something voluntary or conscious. They arise of themselves, although they can still be governed, as demonstrated by the means Descartes devised to achieve this. De la Court follows Descartes on this point, emphasising the importance of reason, and offering examples of the way the affections can be harnessed by knowledge and experience. Nevertheless, as has also been observed by Kossmann, there is also an important difference over against Descartes. For the author of the *Politike Discoursen*, the conflict in the human soul is much more tragic in nature. As with Hobbes, self-preservation lies at the centre of everything, and for this reason the fear of death impresses its stamp on all human activity. This yields a sober view of human beings, who are moved by fear and whose life consists of a long struggle against death. But in the end, this illusionless view still amounts to a reason to attempt – and more than an *attempt* it cannot be, and in recognition of the mistakes that are going to be made – to follow reason – one's *own* reason, to be sure! – carefully and tentatively, with much critique and self-critique. And even then it is not so that the passions and affections must, as with Descartes, be conquered by reason, since they are a positive force and since they moreover cannot be conquered without life itself being dissolved. While reason is universal, the passions relate specifically to the life of each individual person. Reason and the passions together motivate the balance between general human equality and freedom, where the latter by definition differs for each individual. As such, Descartes's argument has been turned on its head, with the aid of Hobbes. At the same time, Descartes's positive faith in reason allows Hobbes's political perspective to be turned on its head.

The human passions, which one could summarily call joy and sadness, are so necessary that one cannot imagine the order and course of the world to exist without the passions. For if all that lives did not suffice, maintaining and nourishing life, so as to feel the passion of joy, and, on the contrary,

[96] Ibid. 404: 'passien der menschen, die men in 't kort blijdschap en droefheid zoude konnen noemen'.
[97] Kossmann, *Political Thought in the Dutch Republic*, 62–4.

warding off all that could be harmful to life, so as to avert the passion of sadness, then life would virtually be non-existent.[98]

And since 'these affections of blood, the spirits, and the external members' belong to life, they can be found in animals as well as human beings, and equally in all human beings.[99] The only difference is one that can be sensed in the rhythm of the movement. 'And for this reason, no one has a great advantage over the other.'[100] Or, for this reason, a theory of politics is a matter of judging and weighing.

The freedom for which De la Court makes his plea differs from the *libertas philosophandi* pursued by Spinoza, at least on the face of it. In the end, D.C. has no interest in matters of speculation, and religion, like everything else, is addressed only insofar as it plays a role in matters of state. Moral issues too are addressed solely from within this political perspective. On the other hand, the argument is reminiscent every step along the way of the materialist point of departure at its basis, the foundation where everything begins, namely the affections and passions which are connected to life itself and to self-preservation. It is in this repeated return to the foundation that it launches its critique on the church and on all forms of government that do not take their starting point in the multitude. But it is also in this return that the Cartesian theory of the affections and its view of reason are adapted, so that reason obtains a different significance. De la Court maintains a view of knowledge and the freedom of speech that is not so much theoretically described in the *Politike Discoursen* and *Consideratien van Staat* as it is put to practise in them. This specific knowledge, a judging and weighing, a republican 'speaking the truth' (*parrhesía*) or effective truth (*verità effettuale*), is connected to a specific rhetoric and argumentative structure. Rhetoric plays with appearances, double layers, covers and unveilings, references and self-references, and irony. The structure of the argument is one of deliberation, it is open and, above all else, non-linear. We ought not to forget that these works are written in the vernacular and that the brothers address an audience

---

[98] *Politike Discoursen*, 404: 'De passien der menschen, die men in 't kort blydschap en droefheid zoude konnen noemen, sijn soo noodsakelik, dat men niet begrypen kan, hoe des werelds ordre en loop, sonder die passien, soude konnen bestaan; want indien niet alles wat leefd genoeghen ware, het leven onderhoudende en voedende, de passie van blijdschap te gevoelen; en integhendeel afweerende alles wat schadelik aan het leven kan zijn, de passie van droefheid te ontgaan, so soude het seer haast met het leven gedaan zijn.'

[99] Ibid. 'dese driften des bloeds, der geesten, ende der uiterlike Leden'.

[100] Ibid. 'En daarom heeft de eene mensch geen groot voordeel boven den andere.'

106   DEMOCRATIC THOUGHT FROM MACHIAVELLI TO SPINOZA

of common people, the multitude of the many. According to Weststeijn, the underlying, implicit justification for their involvement in the public debate using the common tongue is that an explicit and clear determination of the brothers' standpoint shall lead to a triumph of their truth. For it is only when differences are clearly expressed that common ground can be found.[101]

This reading can be confirmed by the announcement in every preface that as many arguments as possible will be collected in favour of the republic. And that no one ought to take offence at either the critique or a political theory that takes its starting point in human malice. After all, sovereigns live and die 'like other people do'.[102] This reading is confirmed by the argument three years later in the *De jure ecclesiasticorum*, in which the thesis whose seeds have been sown here are systematically developed in crystal clear fashion, without the use of rhetoric or the vernacular. The formation of power is a matter of temporary transfer and creates substitutes – *lieutenants* – who are tasked with the duty of bringing common welfare to realisation. As temporary substitutes, the lieutenants are common people, which is why they misunderstand their task if they imagine that they may or must speak in the place of another person. They likewise misunderstand their task if they imagine themselves to be messengers of God, or, more accurately, if they forget that they, common people, can come in the place of god/nature/ the multitude of the many, and are therefore provisional and conditional. Multiple shifts take place here, and the term *prodii* is, like *lieutenants*, also a metaphorical term. This reading is likewise confirmed by the incontestable similarities with Machiavelli's works in content, form, structure, perspective, critique, rhetoric and language use. Finally, this reading is confirmed in the above quotation from the plagiarised work on the covered political arts, which can be read as a programme, commission or exercise in the new knowledge that has been experimented with here, ironic, critical *and* radical, and which lays a path from Machiavelli to Spinoza: 'for if those who are guided by these ruses and coverings acquire knowledge of the matter, they with a jump often turn the state on its head'.[103]

---

[101] Weststeijn, *Commercial Republicanism*, 343. For the concept of *parrhesía* in this context, I am indebted to Weststeijn: 'for the De la Courts the Tacitean maxim "to think as you want and to say what you think" signifies republican *parrhesía*, the ability to tell the truth and to reveal, like Actaeon, the nakedness of the unconcealed desire to rule'. See also n. 58 above.

[102] *Consideratien van Staat*, n.p. [2v]: 'gelijk andere Menschen'.

[103] *Naeuwkeurige consideratie*, 91–2: 'want als de gene die dese listen en lagen geleydt worden van de sake kennisse bekomen, soo keerense den Staat met eenen spronck dickwijls het onderste boven'.

V

The Example of the Indians

1. Franciscus van den Enden

The remarkable and successful example of the 'Politijke Consideratien', 'Discoursen' and 'Hollandtze Interesten', which all appeared in print in 1662, motivated Franciscus van den Enden to bring his *Kort verhael van Nieuw-Nederlants Gelegentheit* to press that same year.[1] One year earlier, the life of this Flemish immigrant, former Jesuit, physician, art dealer, Latin teacher, theatre writer and amateur Cartesian philosopher had taken yet another turn when he began to devote himself actively to politics. Van den Enden's life reads like a picaresque novel and has appealed to the imagination of numerous biographers and chroniclers.[2] To his contemporaries

[1] *Kort verhael van Nieuw-Nederlants Gelegentheit, Deughden, Natuerlijke Voorrechten, en byzondere bequaemheidt ter Bevolkingh: Mitsgaders eenige requesten, Vertoogen, Deductien, enz. ten dien einden door eenige Liefhebbers ten verscheide tijden omtrent 't laatst van 't Jaer 1661. gepresenteert aen A.A. heeren Burgemeesteren dezer Stede, of der zelver E.E. Heeren Gecommitteerde, enz.*, 1662. This pamphlet is included in Van der Wulp's *Catalogus van de tracaten, pamfletten*, 1867, 105, which also mentions a 1663 edition under a different title (114). Frank Mertens devoted his doctoral dissertation to this pamphlet (*Franciscus van den Enden's Brief Account*), and has published a transcription of the text on his Van den Enden website. A shorter version of the present chapter has been published in a collected volume edited by Henri Krop, *Spinoza en zijn kring: Een balans van veertig jaar onderzoek*, in the series Mededelingen vanwege het Spinozahuis: Lavaert, 'Prelude voor een democratische revolutie', 63–75.

[2] Van den Enden is mentioned in writings from authors who can more or less be considered direct witnesses, including Colerus, *Korte, dog waaragtige Levens-Beschryving*, 36–9; Goeree, *De kerklyke en weereldlyke Historien*, 617–18; 665–7; Leibniz, *Essais de Théodicée*, §376, 340. He is briefly referenced by Bayle in the 'Spinoza' article of his *Dictionaire historique et critique*, vol. 4, 255. For more recent biographical descriptions,

108 DEMOCRATIC THOUGHT FROM MACHIAVELLI TO SPINOZA

he was known as the Latin teacher of Spinoza and Koerbagh, an infamous freethinker and atheist, and an esteemed interlocutor and correspondent of other famous thinkers and intellectuals.[3] This makes it all the more remarkable that his published writings long remained in the shadows. There are two anonymous pamphlets that can positively be identified as the product of a single author: the aforementioned *Kort verhael*, which includes seven letters signed with the acronym 'H.V.Z.M.', and the *Vrye Politijke Stellingen* of 1665, whose title page is signed with the periphrasis 'Meest Van Zaken Houdt' (roughly translated into English as 'Loves Things Most'). In the preface to the latter, the author explicitly refers back to the former, which had already been published.[4] Furthermore, we know about Van den Enden that he moved to Paris around 1670, where he became involved in a conspiracy against Louis XIV before being unmasked, arrested, condemned to death and hanged in 1674 – all facts documented in the testimonies of his contemporaries and in archival material.[5] Later his life story was also recounted for a wider audience. In an article published in the *Revue des deux mondes* in 1886, for example, Alfred Maury offered a description of the republican conspiracy which Van den Enden plotted against the

see Bedjaï's edition of the *Philedonius*, 19–50; Klever's edition of the *Vrye Politijke Stellingen*, 13–86; Meininger and Van Suchtelen, *Liever met wercken, als met woorden*; Mertens, *Van den Enden en Spinoza*; and Proietti's edition of the *Philedonius*, 15–78.

[3] See the aforementioned references in Bayle, Colerus and Goeree. Leibniz himself notes that he, like Arnauld, visited Van den Enden: 'Van den Ende, qui s'appelait aussi A Finibus, alla depuis à Paris et y tint des pensionnaires au faubourg Saint-Antoine. Il passait pour excellent dans la didactique, et il me dit, quand je l'y allai voir, qu'il parierait que ses auditeurs seraient toujours attentifs à ce qu'il dirait. Il avait aussi alors avec lui une jeune fille qui parlait latin et faisait des demonstrations de géométrie. Il s'était insinué auprès de M. Arnauld; et les jésuites commençaient d'être jaloux de sa reputation. Mais il se perdit un peu après, s'étant mêlé de la consiparation du chevalier de Rohan.', *Essais de Théodicée*, 340. See also Beverland, *De peccato originali*, 116, and Stensen's Denunciation to the Holy Office from 4 September 1677, in Spruit and Totaro (eds), *The Vatican Manuscript of Spinoza's Ethica*, 68.

[4] *Vrye Politijke Stellingen, en Consideratien van Staat, Gedaen na der ware Christenens Even gelijke vryheits gronden, strekkende tot een rechtschape, en ware verbeeteringh van Staat, en Kerk. Alles kort / en beknopt / onder verbeeteringh / voorgestelt / door Een Liefhebber van alle der welbevoeghde Borgeren Even gelyke vryheit, en die, ten gemeene-beste*, Meest Van Zaken Houdt. 't Volks welvaert is de hooghste *Wet*, En des zelfs stem, *is Gods stem. Het eerste deel*, 1665. In 1992 Wim Klever published a modern edition of this treatise/pamphlet, restoring Van den Enden and his work to its rightful place. This edition is henceforth cited as follows: VPS, 126.

[5] Leibniz, *Essais de Théodicée*, 340; Bayle, 'Lettre XVIII à Mr. Minutoli, 15 décembre 1674' in *Œuvres diverses*, vol. 4, 550–1; *Procès Rohan*, Archives Nationales V/4/1474.

THE EXAMPLE OF THE INDIANS   109

French king together with the Chevalier de Rohan, the Marquis de Villars and Latréaumont.[6] Four years earlier, the second edition of Eugène Sue's novel *Latréaumont* (1st ed. 1837) had appeared in print and had made these unfortunate events of Van den Enden's life a French commonplace. The opening lines of the novel set the scene in 1669, at the Hotel des Muses in Amsterdam, offering a portrait of *maître* Affinius Van den Enden with an unpublished manuscript of Spinoza's *Traité de théologie politique* on his lap, abandoning himself to his reflections on what he has just been reading.[7] Sue emphasises that Van den Enden understood religion never to be a matter of divine origin, but always a social or political, human invention. For this reason, every religion was in his eyes subject to the human condition of birth-life-death. And since religions are historical facts which have an effect and influence on events, he could teach about every religion. Just like all other human products, religions are true and false, correct and incorrect, and participate in good and evil. Sue's portrait depicts Van den Enden as a polymath (scientist, physician and teacher of languages, philosopher and poet), but he insists that the latter's true passion was his 'political faith' (*foi politique*).[8] 'His greatest obsession was the establishment of a free society for which he had formulated statutes', and these statutes were so democratic that the United Provinces looked like an aristocracy in comparison.[9] In his essay in the *Revue des deux mondes*, Maury connects the

[6] Maury, *Revue des deux mondes*, 1886, 376–406; see also Wyzewa, *Revue des deux mondes*, 1896, 696–707. There is also a nineteenth-century edition of the *Mémoires inédits et Opuscules de Jean Rou* published by Waddington, as well as Clément, *La conspiration du chevalier de Rohan*. See also Tréhet, 'Une république normande? La dernière conspiration politique importante du règne de Louis XIV', 283–94.

[7] Sue, *Latréaumont*, 3–16.

[8] Ibid. 8.

[9] Ibid. Sue uses the phrase 'formulated the statutes' (*formulé les statuts*), which may well point to the manuscript *Finis est in Holandia*, in which the most important rules for a free constitution are drawn up in a short Latin text, although it could also mean the *Kort verhael*, which includes a constitution for the colony in Delaware, as well as the *Vrye Politijke Stellingen*. For the manuscript *Finis est in Holandia*, see also n. 15 and the Appendix below. Sue presumably based himself on Du Cauze de Nazelle's *Mémoires* and the judicial file of the *Procès Rohan* of 1674, which is held at the Archives Nationales V/4/1474. Copies of this file are held at the department of manuscripts of the BnF: Fr. 7576, Fr. 7629 and Fr. 16556. Du Cauze de Nazelle lived in Van den Enden's boarding school, the Hotel des Muses in the rue de Picpus, and played an important role in the unveiling of the conspiracy, leading to Van den Enden's arrest. He wrote an account of the events in his *Mémoires*, published by Daudet in 1899: *Mémoires du temps de Louis XIV par Du Cause de Nazelle*. The events were already long known in France: they were reported on in the *Mémoires historiques et authentiques sur*

110   DEMOCRATIC THOUGHT FROM MACHIAVELLI TO SPINOZA

story to what may also have been Sue's sources, namely the *Mémoires* of Du Cauze de Nazelle and the pieces in the judicial file against the conspirators. In his *Mémoires*, Du Cauze refers to a Latin manuscript of Van den Enden, a translation he had made for Latréaumont sketching the basic principles of a republican government. The original text, he notes, had been published 'in Flemish under the title *Vue politique libres et Considérations sur l'état [Free Political Propositions and Considerations of State]*'.[10] At his arrest, Latréaumont had not succeeded in disposing of this objectionable work in time, so that it became an exhibit in the trial against Van den Enden.

In *Spinoza en zijn kring* (1896), Meinsma devoted an entire chapter to Van den Enden, although he treated the conspiracy rather briefly and failed to mention a political-theoretical text.[11] Other writers who addressed Spinoza and his context around the turn of the twentieth century, including Dunin-Borkowski, showed themselves similarly unacquainted with Van den Enden's writings.[12] It is only rather recently that scholarship on the historical and

---

La Bastille (1789), vol. 1, 74–112, and described in *Le Mercure François*; see De la Place (ed.), *Nouveaux choix des pièces tirées des anciens Mercures*, vol. 90, 49–54. The historian Clément published on the conspiracy in 1856, and Jean Rou's *Mémoires inédits* were published the next year, in 1857. There were therefore multiple reports and witnesses from which the nineteenth-century writers could obtain their information, going back to the old sources or else copying from the work of the others. Yet the only reliable source is the aforementioned judicial file of the *Procès Rohan*.

[10] Maury, *Revue des deux mondes*, 397. It is not entirely clear whether Maury worked directly from the original judicial files or whether he cited them via Du Cauze. He correctly cites two sentences from the manuscript *Finis est in Holandia* of which Van den Enden says that they are not his, but writes about the work as if it were a translation of the entire *Vues politiques libres* (also using the same title as Du Cauze, even though the reports use the original Dutch title without translating it (except 'politique')). Interesting in this context is Maury's remark that '[l]a seconde partie dudit ouvrage avait été interdite en Hollande, en raison de la hardiesse des idées qu'elle contenait', ibid. 397. Maury also writes that the papers and books, both printed and in manuscript form, were burned at the execution of the conspirators. Finally, he includes a citation of the entire text of the pamphlet *La noblesse et le peuple de Normandie*, ibid. 398–400.

[11] Meinsma, *Spinoza en zijn kring*, 125–53; 330–3; 412–15. Meinsma first mentions the conspiracy in a footnote (125) and returns to it later on (412–15), although he dismisses it as an irrelevant, patriotic enterprise (against France), possibly with solely monetary motives, and adding that, whatever the case may be, Van den Enden's involvement was purely coincidental.

[12] Dunin-Borkowski sees in the conspiracy a sign of Van den Enden's political acumen. In the Van den Enden household, Spinoza must have breathed the 'politically charged atmosphere' (*hochpolitische Luft*), as he writes in *Aus den Tagen Spinozas*, 'das zeigte sogar der Verschwörungsplan, dem er später zum Opfer fiel', 71. As usual, Dunin-Borkowksi bases himself on solid sources, in this case Daudet's 1899 edition of Du

THE EXAMPLE OF THE INDIANS   111

intellectual context of the seventeenth century has managed to piece Van
den Enden's life together, assembling the various details scattered about in
French archives, scholarly essays, historical novels, Spinoza biographies,
colonialist literature and philosophical sources. An important step in this
regard was taken by Bedjaï and by Klever, who both claimed to have discovered around the same time, in 1990, that Van den Enden authored the
two aforementioned anonymous treatises.[13] Yet the fact of the matter is that
the German historian Malettke had already published material that would
have facilitated this identification in 1976 in his *Opposition und Konspiration
unter Ludwig XIV*, although, as so often happens, the results of this historical
research failed to make its way to scholars working in the fields of philosophy
and Spinoza studies.[14]

Cauze de Nazelle's *Mémoires*, which evidently would not have been available to
Meinsma yet. As *Buchseltenheit* he follows this up with a page from the 'Rencontre
de Bayle et Spinoza dans l'autre monde', which appeared with the (fictive) publisher
Pierre Marteau in Cologne in 1711. For this curious work, see also Saintes, *Histoire de
la vie et des ouvrages de B. de Spinoza*, 167–8, and Vernière, *Spinoza et la pensée française
avant la Révolution*, vol. II, 361.

[13] Marc Bedjaï and Wim Klever published their discovery of the *Vrye Politijke Stellingen*
at virtually the same time: Bedjaï, 'F. van den Enden, maître spirituel de Spinoza'
(1990), 289–311; Klever, 'Proto-Spinoza Franciscus van den Enden' (1990), 281–8.
Bedjaï dates his discovery to 1971, adding that Meinsma, literature on Jansenism,
and historiography on the conspiracy against Louis XIV led him to the catalogues
of the British Museum and the Bibliothèque Nationale, where he found the *Vrye
Politijke Stellingen*, and from there also the *Kort verhael* and the *Philedonius*. He
documented the road to his findings with references, adding a useful 'Bilan biblio-
graphique': ibid. 290–5; 307–11. Klever too offered a more concrete report of the
trail of his findings in: 'A New Source of Spinozism: Franciscus Van den Enden'
(1991), 613–31.

[14] Malettke, *Opposition und Konspiration unter Ludwig XIV*, 142–223; 335–43. After the
discovery of the VPS by Bedjaï and Klever, and its publication by Klever, scholarly
interest in Van den Enden grew, although it remained largely scattered and did not
cross disciplinary lines. Apart from the aforementioned introductions accompanying
the work of Bedjaï, Klever and Proietti, see also (in chronological order): Bedjaï,
'Métaphysique, éthique et politique dans l'oeuvre du docteur Franciscus van den
Enden' (1990), 291–313; Proietti, 'Le "Philedonius" de Franciscus van den Enden et
la formation rhétorico-littéraire de Spinoza' (1991), 9–82; Bedjaï, 'Pour un Etat populaire ou une utopie subversive' (1993), 194–213; Mertens, 'Franciscus van den Enden:
tijd voor een herziening van diens rol in het ontstaan van het Spinozisme?' (1994),
718–38; Klever, *Mannen rond Spinoza* (1997), 31–52; Israel, *Radical Enlightenment*
(2001), 175–84; Van Bunge, *From Stevin to Spinoza* (2001), 104–7; Van Bunge, *Spinoza
Past and Present* (2012), 56–66; Blom and Looijesteijn, 'Ordinary People in the New
World' (2013), 203–35; Mertens, 'Van den Enden and Religion' (2017), 62–89.

112   DEMOCRATIC THOUGHT FROM MACHIAVELLI TO SPINOZA

Malettke offered documentary evidence for the story as it had been told by Sue and Maury, together with a transcription of the manuscript. The original documents are held in the Archives Nationales in Paris, with copies in the Bibliothèque Nationale. Van den Enden's name comes up countless times in the 880 pages of these court records, giving us the distinct impression that both the French court system, with its royalist sympathies, and the Chevalier de Rohan sought to place as much of the blame as possible on the shoulders of Affinius.[15] According to the records of the interrogations of 26 and 27 September, and 2 October 1674, which total no less than forty-six pages, Van den Enden acknowledged that the Latin manuscript reflected conversations he had held with Latréaumont, and that the manuscript even seemed to derive from a translation of the essence of a book he had 'written in Flemish'.[16] The text of this book begins unambiguously by stating that

[15] Aside from the interrogation records (i.e. *Interrogatoire 26 & 27 Septembre, 2 Octobre 1674 François Affinius Vanden Enden, Procès Rohan*, 77r–99v), which are in their entirety related to Van den Enden, the file includes three manuscripts which have been initialled on every page by Van den Enden: a letter that appears to concern innocuous household affairs but was suspected of being a ciphered message containing secret details for the conspiracy, 69r–69v; *La noblesse et le peuple de Normandie*, 71r–72v; and, finally, *Finis est in Holandia erigere Statum*, 342r–344v. The last of these manuscripts is only found in the original files and is absent among the copies held at the BnF. Other official reports and pieces in which Van den Enden is mentioned include: 4r–11v; 28r–29v; 31r–33r; 35r–40r; 50r–52v. The entire file in the AN can be consulted on microfilm.

[16] Van den Enden denies that he wrote the manifesto *La noblesse et le peuple de Normandie*, although he does admit that he spoke to Latréaumont about a similar project 'd'une republique libre en holande qui est dans un livre escrit a la main que lui repondant a donné autres fois a le dit Latreaumont', *Procès Rohan*, 93v. The records also make mention of a manuscript, with marginal annotations, which cannot be found in the juridical file and of which Van den Enden admits 'qu'il croit que ce sont des extraits d'un livre de politique escrit a la main qu'il luy avoit presté', 94v. When asked how he could have written the words in the margin if he had never seen the text, Van den Enden responded: 'ces mots, vrye politique Stellingen en consideratien van Staat, ne sont pas des nottes sur ce qui est contenu dans cet escrit, mais que le Sr Latreaumont demandant a luy repondant ou estoit imprime la premiere partie de ce livre du politique, dont les deux autres ne sont escrites qu'a la main, le repondant escrivit sur le papier que tenoit ledit Sr Latreaumont, ces mots, vrye politique &c qui est le titre dud[it] livre', 94v. Van den Enden furthermore denies writing the manuscript *Finis est in Holandia* himself, although he does claim to recognise Latréaumont's hand, admitting moreover that the text contains an excerpt from a book which he had lent to Latréaumont, 'que ce livre est a la verite en flamant, mais que luy repondant avoir faict un extraict pour led. Latreaumont que luy respondant avoir eu translaté en latin'; to substantiate his claims, Van den Enden adduced two sentences that were not his own

THE EXAMPLE OF THE INDIANS   113

'the goal is to erect a certain democracy in the Netherlands' (*Finis est in Holandia erigere statum quemdam populi*), and ends by insisting that religion and matters of state are not to be mixed.[17] During the interrogations, Van den Enden was asked about certain words that appear in the margin of another manuscript (which is itself not included in the juridical dossier). He responded that these words, 'free political propositions and considerations of state' (*vrye politique Stellingen en consideratien van Staat*), represent the title of a book on politics which he had written, whose first part had already been published but whose second and third parts as yet only existed in manuscript form, and that he had scribbled the title in the margin at Latréaumont's request.[18] These statements in the court records leave no doubt that Van den Enden is the author of both the *Kort verhael* and the *Vrye Politijke Stellingen*.[19]

'Up to the end of the year 1661, I had never even imagined publishing anything related to politics', so Van den Enden writes in the preface to the *Vrye Politijke Stellingen*, until he was unexpectedly requested to draft a petition to the Colonial Office on behalf of some people who wanted to set sail for New Netherlands.[20] What initially fitted in a 'small clasp' gradually grew into 'books' worth of paper', which he published in 1662 under the title 'short story of New Netherlands, etc.' (*Kort verhael, van N. Nederlandt. enz.*).[21] Concretely, the petition envisaged the establishment of a colony on the shores of the South River in North America at a place called the

and that Latréaumont must therefore have added himself, 95r–95v. The Appendix below presents a transcription of the Latin manuscript, along with an English translation. In transcribing the text, we noted several orthographical errors and small grammatical errors in the manuscript, which strongly suggest that Van den Enden, a professional Latin teacher, spoke the truth when he claimed not to have written the text. The initialled manuscripts are not neat copies, like the interrogation records; they include extensive strikeout and are clearly autographs.

[17] *Procès Rohan*, 342r–344v. For more on this manuscript, see below.

[18] *Procès Rohan*, 94v.

[19] For an extensive description of the events, see Malettke. A study of the entire file of the *Procès Rohan* would undoubtedly reveal matters that are of importance for understanding the period and yield material for a carefully documented biography of Van den Enden (which is lacking up to the present). Here we have restricted ourselves to the evidence for Van den Enden's authorship of the *Vrye Politijke Stellingen*, namely his assertion in the interrogations records that he had written a work with this title, and that the work in question includes the same political views encapsulated in the Latin manuscript *Finis est in Holandia*. There is no reason to assume that the court clerk might have changed something in Van den Enden's Dutch words or that the latter would have lied about his authorship, meaning that we have a trustworthy witness.

[20] VPS, 125.

[21] VPS, 125–6.

114   DEMOCRATIC THOUGHT FROM MACHIAVELLI TO SPINOZA

Hoerenkil in present-day Delaware. The preface of the *Kort verhael* is dated 10 October 1662, while the letters and petition which Van den Enden directed to the burgomasters, Colonial Office and magistrates date between 22 November 1661 and 25 May 1662. Around the time of the final letter, Pieter Corneliszoon Plokhoy, a revolutionary utopian and Collegiant from Zeeland, published his *Kort en klaer ontwerp*, a recruitment pamphlet for a prospective colony in the same place, that is, at the Hoerenkil in New Netherlands.[22] The *Kort verhael* and *Kort en klaer ontwerp* were long both considered the work of Plokhoy. After all, he had a previous history of publishing revolutionary texts, both pamphlets were intended for prospective colonists to Delaware along the shores of the South River, and, finally, the two works show similarities in sociopolitical disposition and offer nearly identical concrete proposals. Yet in spite of the intriguing similarities, the pamphlets do have a very different focus, style and theoretical range, as well as differing views on religion. This is not, however, the place to unravel all the biographical mysteries, and so we will instead offer a comparative reading of the *Kort verhael* and the *Kort en klaer ontwerp*, followed by the *Vrye Politijke Stellingen*, and finally the manuscript *Finis est in Holandia*, so as to clarify the substantive and structural relationships between these texts, and in this way shed light on the scope and radical novelty of the political-philosophical views expressed in them.

2. *Kort verhael van Nieuw-Nederlants Gelegenheit*

When the Amsterdam government refused to accept Van den Enden's proposals for New Netherlands, he only devoted himself to the topic with greater application. In his eyes, he was not just dealing with the contingent problem of greedy regents who were refusing to surrender their right to levy taxes in the colonies, but the entire political system as such stood in need of sweeping reform. The project of a new constitution for the new colony served as the example for the formation of a new political theory as such. In the *Kort verhael*, Van den Enden assembled the seven letters which he

---

[22] Plokhoy, *Kort en klaer ontwerp, dienende tot Een onderling Accoort, om Den arbeyd, onrust en moeyelijckheyt, van Alderley-hand-werckluyden te verlichten door Een onderlinge Compagnie ofte Volck-planting (onder de protectie van de H: Mo: Heeren Staten Generael der vereenigde Neder-landen; en bysonder onder het gunstig gesag van de Achtbare Magsitraten der Stad Amstelredam) aen de Zuyt-revier in Nieuw-neder-land op te rechten; Bestaende in Land-bouwers, Zee-varende Personen, Alderhande noodige Ambachts-luyden, en Meesters van goede konste en wetenschappen &c. t' Samen gestelt Door Pieter Cornelisz. Plockhoy van Zierck-zee, voor hem selven en andere Lief-hebbers van Nieu-nederland*, 1662.

had dispatched to the Colonial Office. To these he appended a description of New Netherlands (the land), the Indians living there (their customs and political order), and the agricultural potential of the land (with a critique of slavery), and a commentary on the constitutional articles (with proposals for the maintenance of the envisioned state). In his letters, Van den Enden responded to the objections from the side of the government, but in vain. As the afterword indicates, the project was rejected. All of the letters are signed with the initials 'H.V.Z.M.', an acronym for 'Houdt Van Zaken Meest' ('Loves Things Most').[23] In the preface, he writes that the success of De la Court's appeal for a free republic prompted him to write and moreover encouraged him to 'greater freedom', nevertheless adding that he does not agree with 'the aforementioned writers' in every respect.[24] What irks him in particular is the fact that they in the second edition, 'in direct departure from the late author' (Johan de la Court?), appear in the end to undermine the 'irrefutable' thesis that democracy is the 'most natural [and] rational' form of government.[25] Although, as we noted in the previous chapter, this criticism is not altogether accurate, and while the accumulation of litotes, figures of speech and frequent use of the verb 'appear' (*schijnen*) also serve to make the argument rather ambiguous, the actual motive is announced in unmistakable terms: the best government for a land rests in an assembly consisting of all its inhabitants who have sufficient power and knowledge to secure their own well-being. In Van den Enden's eyes, 'this is the real and proper definition of a *truly popular government*'.[26] In the afterword, he likewise expresses himself in clear and combative terms. What is 'most damaging and even pestilential to a state is when inadequate freedom is left'.[27] But because there has never been greater freedom to present 'something openly to the common good' than there currently is in Holland, he dares 'no less than the separate *Discoursen* or the writers of the mutilated *Hollandtze Interest*' to take the freedom 'to give a small sample or closer taste of what we, after much earnest deliberation, have understood concerning common utility, provisionally and for the improvement of the faithful people of Holland'.[28] The playful allusion to Machiavelli's *Il Principe*, which likewise exhibits a knowledge based on extensive experience with current affairs, the constant

---

[23] *Kort verhael*, 45; 47; 50; 62; 65; 67; 67. Cfr. Klever in *VPS*, 30.
[24] *Kort verhael*, IV.
[25] Ibid. V.
[26] Ibid.
[27] Ibid. 69.
[28] Ibid.

116   DEMOCRATIC THOUGHT FROM MACHIAVELLI TO SPINOZA

study of history, and careful deliberation, is a significant hyperbole. The afterword is followed by a renewed appeal for 'freedom of writing and speech' in the back matter.[29]

Throughout the texts of the *Kort verhael*, we feel the tension between the way it establishes its contents in the facts and its literary, polemical-critical, pamphleteering style. As the title indicates, the arguments are presented as a story, which is why the text has the formal qualities of a narrative, including focus, perspective, shifts and figures situated in a lively context that has been carefully painted. Van den Enden's long and close reading, study, teaching and imitation of the literary classics had given him an exceptional knowledge of them. He read the works of the De la Court brothers, who had assembled their arguments and weaved them into a book accompanied by quotations, allusions, parables and anecdotes from the classics, drawing also extensively on Machiavelli. Van den Enden himself also read Machiavelli's work, which had its origins in a similar context and shared the same motif and goal as our 'Lucianist'.[30] And since the goal was constitutive and envisioned the establishment of a new society, and since he had 'a practical mind which could see through people with a single glance, a *homo politicus* who walked around with Machiavelli in his back pocket', he in setting out his project was undoubtedly thinking of *Il Principe*.[31] Van den Enden himself never went to New Netherlands, rather basing his description of the land, people and civil society on the travel accounts of De Vries and Van der Donck. With his highly sympathetic reading of this source material, he turned the indigenous, Indian natives (*Naturellens*) into despisers of 'not only pain and suffering but even death, which they can meet in good and cheerful spirits and with singing'.[32] In Van den Enden's view, the natives are not power-hungry aggressors, but free and noble people, for which reason they cannot bear the thought of being under the dominion of others and resist fiercely. Once again, one cannot escape thinking here of Machiavelli and of his description of the disposition of the common people who never thirst for power or coercion but pursue their well-being and freedom, for which reason they are more inclined, spontaneously and naturally, to recalcitrant doubt about the possibility of finding themselves under the rule of another. They are happy to leave dominion to another

---

[29] *Kort verhael*, VIII.
[30] Meinsma, *Spinoza en zijn kring*, 125.
[31] Ibid. 131.
[32] *Kort verhael*, 19. This attitude to death recalls classical libertine views, and in particular *Theophrastus redivivus*; see above, Chapter II.1, 47.

THE EXAMPLE OF THE INDIANS 117

person who assumes the task of rulership in their place, but after that they cannot bear the thought of actually being ruled. To the mind of the Indian *naturellens*, the distinction between people is greater and more visible in the Netherlands than anywhere else: 'They openly say with respect to our government that they cannot understand how one person can be so much more than another.'[33]

In Van den Enden's understanding, the Indians view all people as equals, so that no one person has more rights than any other. A remarkable fact about them is that they show little interest in justice and that they have no separate juridical authority. Crimes committed by 'the common man' almost always remain unpunished or are at most subjected to 'purely verbal' admonition, such that one is left wondering how it can be that 'so little evil happens'.[34] The absence of a penal system does not appear to issue in greater violence. In the nine years Van der Donck spent there, he had never even heard of any crimes committed.[35] But also more generally there is little among the Indians that is regulated by law, and the 'special rights, laws, or regulations conflicting with freedom' that one finds in the domestic civil right of the nations of Europe, which are divided into various independent nation states, are absent among them.[36] More than that, in New Netherlands one finds a natural hospitality extended to immigrants who need no protection by civil law. For the Indians are not narrow-minded or envious of 'the various nations coming to live closer to and among them'.[37] They harbour no enmity towards foreigners, and their land is open to anyone who wants to establish himself there 'as he sees fit, like the free indigents themselves'.[38]

The Indians likewise display a casual freedom in regard to matters of love, which has traditionally been regulated through civil or religious law. Marriages are as easily dissolved as they are formed without any formalities whatsoever when either one of the partners falls in love with someone else or in case of conflict. 'In that land, divorce is a very normal and common thing.'[39] Little is regulated by law or punishment, nor does religion play a role in social life. In fact, the Indians do not even have anything resembling religion or clearly distinct notions of good and evil. This leads

[33] Ibid.
[34] Ibid. 20.
[35] Ibid. 19–20.
[36] Ibid. 21.
[37] Ibid.
[38] Ibid.
[39] Ibid. 22.

118 DEMOCRATIC THOUGHT FROM MACHIAVELLI TO SPINOZA

Van den Enden to conclude that they do not understand the term 'Monitto or Ottico, explained in German or Dutch as "devil", as a reference to something substantive or independent'.[40] According to Van der Donk, the Indians use the same word for what in Dutch would be called the 'devil' for 'power, authority, or torment'.[41] As such, Van den Enden goes even further than Koerbagh was to do six years later in his entry for the term *Duyvel* in his *Een Bloemhof van allerley lieflijkheyd sonder verdriet* (1668), which reads: 'a slanderer, accuser, prosecutor [. . .] a bastardized Greek word', which is used various times untranslated in the Bible, where we also find other untranslated terms 'so that the common people do not understand and therefore do not acquire knowledge of the matter'.[42] If all words were properly translated into Dutch, the term *duyvel* would never appear in the Bible, and it would be difficult to convince people that such a thing as an evil spirit even existed. The indigenous population of Delaware has not been subjected to such teaching and is free of these delusions, so that they do not recognise any such thing as a 'devil' or 'evil' except in the sense of pain, power or authority. And they are no worse off for it.

On the contrary, the Indians even form an excellent nation that loves freedom, whom the British unfortunately tried to raise 'in a foul, confused, superstitious' manner 'by introducing dark, embellished, and for that reason all too often incomprehensible and shrewd articles of delusion', with chaos and decline as the dramatic result.[43] In the example of the Indians, Van den Enden finds concrete ideas for a democratic organisation of society which has the potential to prevent the degeneration of New Netherlands. The Indians are *Naturellens*; they do not try to overcome human nature and weaknesses. As a result, their society is not based on a normative system, nor is it defined by previously established principles of good and evil. Their society is rather natural and based on natural power and right. In line with this naturalism, the interests of the common people and of the poor in particular become an absolute priority. The Indians endeavour to improve their lot. Based on this naturalism, Van den Enden argues that slavery conflicts with the interests of the common people and is therefore to be rejected.[44] The naturalism of the Indians coincides with the principle of equality from which the necessity of equal rights derives: 'Equality (between more and less

[40] Ibid.
[41] Ibid.
[42] Koerbagh, *Een Bloemhof van allerley lieflijkheyd*, 259.
[43] *Kort verhael*, 23.
[44] Ibid. 26.

THE EXAMPLE OF THE INDIANS 119

wise, more and less prosperous, male and female, ruler and subject, etc.).'[45] The principle of equality does not imply the negation of differences, or that natural differences must be eliminated: 'by turning his nature-essence and special attribute into a world of its own, each person remains always distinguished from all other people'.[46] Any society that follows the example of the Indians will make laws that are good for commonwealth, seeing to it that 'the individual, natural, equal freedom of every person' without distinction is safeguarded.[47]

The arrangement of the texts in this work was judged by nineteenth-century historians of Dutch colonialism in America to be so strange that they could barely read it, completely losing their way after page 27.[48] But what bewildered them even more were the strange ideas which they had never encountered before, the unusual terms and the radical novelty – or, in other words, the example of the Indians.[49] Van den Enden connects the political customs of the Indians to naturalist, enlightened, and therefore new principles of political theory (equality, equal freedom, the necessity of freedom), while also using them to deduce a number of concrete suggestions for a 'robust' (*behoorlijke*) – that is, sustainable – democratic organisation for the new colony.[50] For example, the Indian authorities leave extensive time for the making of important decisions, which they always propose to the assembly first so as to convince the people, using whatever words and time are necessary to obtain their approval. What the Indians teach Van den Enden is that the colonists must form their own army (composed of citizens rather than mercenaries; cf. Machiavelli) for their defence, and that ministers and other religious teachers must be forbidden access to the colony. Education is very important, and this is why there ought to be no room for religion or the interpretation of the Bible, so that the costs for religious teachers can be spared. For the civil and moral organisation, it is necessary that 'abundant or sufficient schools be established in the society's mother tongue, for both the adults and young people, so that they can teach everything most clearly and certainly through a firm and indubitable argument derived from certain, infallible principles'.[51] They must teach language, mathematics and medicine, whose knowledge can be deduced from infallible principles, is

[45] Ibid. 31.
[46] Ibid. 30.
[47] Ibid.
[48] Klever, 'A New Source of Spinozism', 622; Asher, A *Bibliographical Essay*, 15.
[49] Asher, A *Bibliographical Essay*.
[50] *Kort verhael*, 27.
[51] Ibid. 29.

constructed with strong arguments and can be clearly laid out, and they must do so in sufficient schools, to both women and men, young and old, and in the native tongue.

Indian rule looks, in every respect, like 'a rough sketch of an Athenian or ancient Roman democracy', which Van den Enden recognises as the best form of government for the common freedom and equality of the people, and which is in the Indian context also much more easily 'conceived and put into practice' than it was in ancient Athens or Rome.[52] Van den Enden poses the question fundamentally: How can a commonwealth most fruitfully be realised not only with people who 'pursue wisdom' but also with 'predominantly unwise people who are subject to their passions (even though they do not live by superstition and do have reason)'?[53] And how can one see to it that 'every person's own passion' does not just hinder the commonwealth but actually serves to advance it?[54] Van den Enden answers that 'every person's own passion' must not be denied, never mind destroyed. In fact, the commonwealth must be founded in human self-love rather than a love for others; the entire matter must be turned on its head. For 'mutual, common faithfulness and love can hardly if at all be found among people', for which reason a government based on the faithfulness of a single person is by definition weak and doomed to failure.[55] For the formation of a political theory, one ought therefore to depart from the fact that most people do not excel in wisdom but follow their passions. One must assume that they do not pursue love for their fellow men, but always see to their own good above all else. One must recognise that they are not good, but also not evil. Here we hear echoes of both the Indians and of Machiavelli. Those who exchange what is for what ought to be are more likely to achieve their downfall than their redemption. People are dual (neither good nor evil, both good and evil), weak (in character, flesh and mind), and fickle (buffeted to and fro by their passions and fears). The risk of a government of one or a government of the elite degenerating into suppression and violence is therefore much greater than when power is held by a multitude.[56] The link Van den Enden establishes between religion and religious education is a remarkable one.

[52] Ibid. 31.
[53] Ibid. 32.
[54] Ibid.
[55] Ibid.
[56] As we have seen, this notion is developed by Machiavelli in *Il Principe* XV and the following chapters; see above, Chapter I.4 and 5. It is appropriated by De la Court in his *Consideratien van Staat* and *Politike Discoursen*, and thereafter by Spinoza in his *TP*; see also Chapter VII.4 below. See also Visentin, *La libertà necessaria*, 413–16.

THE EXAMPLE OF THE INDIANS

121

The commonwealth must not punish, correct or even tolerate human weakness and passion, but must use them as its point of departure. And the commonwealth must avoid superstition for the simple reason that it can be avoided; even if most people are ignorant and not wise, they are still open to reason.

In this context, what Van den Enden writes against the ecclesiastical officials who propagate their faith obtains a foundational significance. It would have been better if the British had not attempted to turn the Indians into Christians by their incomprehensible delusions. The Christian faith which the British tried to introduce to America is to be blamed for everything that went wrong. Many Christians are hypocritical, superstitious and confused, and they have invented their incomprehensible articles of faith; their religion has degenerated into superstition. Education is the foundation of society, but it must avoid matters of faith; faith must not be taught in the schools. It is better to save on the costs of the ministers and to forbid them from entering the colony, for they form 'an unavoidable, ruinous pest' to the peace and harmony necessary for the establishment and maintenance of a just society.[57] They represent a danger to peace and unity since they, regardless of the specific sect to which they belong, aim to turn all the different views and faith convictions into a single faith, while Van den Enden's aim is to establish 'a society of different people with conflicting views'.[58] The preachers' custom conflicts with Van den Enden's proposal, which is to educate in a knowledge that can be derived discursively and clearly from principles. A new, fragile society in particular must avoid anything that threatens equal freedom. The threat does not come from the differences and conflicting views; conversely, anyone seeking to even out the differing ideas and views so as to fashion a single opinion is a threat to peace.

In the seven letters which Van den Enden appended to his work, the project (and underlying theory) takes concrete shape. Letter A, dated 22 November 1661, includes the initial application and addresses the necessary conditions favourable for allowing the colonists to emigrate, including a minimum thirty-year tax exemption and savings on the costs for preachers. Letter B, from 20 December 1661, responds to the request for clarification. In regard to the settlement of conflicts and the punishment for crimes, Van den Enden shows some flexibility towards the Amsterdam authorities and their intervention. When he summarises the political project in three principles in his missive of 23 December, the strict nature of the principles seems to

[57] *Kort verhael*, 28.
[58] Ibid.

122   DEMOCRATIC THOUGHT FROM MACHIAVELLI TO SPINOZA

make Van den Enden himself more radical and less accommodating than he had been in his letter from three days ago. The first principle is that no one person is to have ruling power. The second principle states that no common funds are to be granted to a single person for his profit. The third principle determines that the 'least' have as many rights as the 'greatest' and must be treated like them, and, in fact, that the 'lesser' must always be viewed 'with more favour' than the 'greater' so that the 'least' have every opportunity to improve their condition. This third principle is necessary so that the 'society envisioned' may be sustainable.[59] The three principles are then translated into 117 constitutional articles which are enumerated in Letter D from 10 January 1662. The 'most important foundation of this society' is 'equality', even though it must be observed that the formulation of this foundation in Van den Enden's constitutional articles is somewhat disappointing, since it only pertains to men aged twenty-four and up.[60] All colonists must work for the commonwealth (Art. 53), and see to their own defence (Art. 100) as well as the defence of the weak (Art. 104). For 'this young and tender society' in particular, special care ought to be exercised to ensure that the weak and poor are not just protected against oppression from the stronger or richer, but there must even be positive discrimination so that no opportunity for improving their condition is passed over.[61] This principle of positive discrimination can be found reflected in many different articles. The community is to provide a liberal and generous system of aid for needy widows and orphans, for the elderly and sick, and for anyone else who cannot work, so that they not only do not live in poverty, but can even lead a good life and thereby contribute to the flourishing of the community (Art. 109).

3. Plokhoy's *Kort en klaer ontwerp*

The order of the composing parts in the *Kort verhael* and the dates of the letters give us an indication of how the work came into being. The more the government responded in negative terms, the deeper Van den Enden delved into the matter. The first application was submitted late in November 1661, and the letter with the constitutional articles dates from early in January 1662. In the next three letters, which are dated 3 March (Letter E), 5 May

---

[59] Ibid. 48–9. This way of speaking recalls Machiavelli's use of the terms 'grandi' or 'popolo grande' and 'popolo minuto'; see Chapter I above. See also Lavaert, *Het perspectief van de multitude*, 197; 213–14.

[60] *Kort verhael*, 50.

[61] Ibid. 60.

THE EXAMPLE OF THE INDIANS

(Letter F) and 25 May (Letter G), Van den Enden responded to the objections from the side of the government. He thus reflected on his own text and ideas, devised arguments, found new comparative material, examples and reasons, and gradually grew more radical in his views which he also gave a firmer foundation. With his description of the Indians, their institutions and their land, together with his commentary and arguments, Van den Enden's proposals, which originally amounted to an occasional text, developed into an actual theory. But we have an altogether different kind of text in the *Kort en klaer ontwerp*, which was written by Plokhoy, who no doubt numbered among those for whom Van den Enden submitted the proposal late in 1661. As the title indicates, it is a short and clear work, as a recruitment pamphlet indeed ought to be, as well as concrete and neither theoretical nor general. Nevertheless, the *Kort verhael* and *Kort en klaer ontwerp* were written with a view to the same concrete project to establish a colony in Delaware, and there are many similarities in their respective political visions.[62]

First of all, so Plokhoy writes, the 'multitudinous company' will be under general leadership and therefore not 'subjected' to the command of 'a private individual'.[63] According to Van den Enden's Letter C, no specific person is to have commanding power, a point that finds reflection in the first article of Letter D where the basic constitutional principle of equality is outlined. To maintain good order, Plokhoy's recruitment pamphlet prescribes how a new leader is to be chosen every other year from among those members of the male population over the age of thirty who are prepared to assume the task of government and present themselves for election. The elections take place by secret ballot, with the candidates being chosen by majority vote. Their mandate ends after one year, at which time they return to the 'communal labour'.[64] The limited term of the mandate, the use of secret ballots and the maintenance of the majority principle are described in precisely the same way in Letter D. The two texts likewise express themselves in similar ways on the communal labour: the *Kort en klaer ontwerp* prescribes that the colonists must work '6 hours for the communal benefit' every day except the sabbath, while Art. 53 in Letter D stipulates 'at least six hours [of communal labour] a day' for the first five years.[65] In his commentary on

---

[62] Plokhoy, *Kort en klaer ontwerp*, n.p. [A iv r]. For a comparative reading of Plokhoy's placard and Van den Enden's pamphlet, see Blom and Looijesteijn, 'Ordinary People in the New World', 214–27.

[63] Plokhoy, *Kort en klaer ontwerp*, n.p. [A iv r].

[64] Ibid. n.p. [A iv v].

[65] Ibid.; *Kort verhael*, 55.

124   DEMOCRATIC THOUGHT FROM MACHIAVELLI TO SPINOZA

this article, Van den Enden nuances this demand by reducing it to just two days per week of no more than 'nine hours' of collective labour, although this does not, of course, imply any change in the principle as such.[66] 'There is no room among us (where each and every person looks out for his share of the profit) for the names "servant" or "maidservant".' In case 'an alien' who does not belong 'to our society', whether an adult or a child, offers to work as a 'servant or maidservant' to one of our families for a daily wage, so Plokhoy continues, these alien labourers are likewise to 'work 6 hours a day for the community, and the rest of the time for their own master or mistress'.[67] Van den Enden speaks in this context only about the 'colonists' (*coloniers*) who are all equally expected to 'roll up their sleeves'.[68] He makes no distinction here between an alien and indigenous population, nor does he speak of servants and maidservants. In his commentary, he does briefly mention maidens and servants with reference to the task he reserves for young, unmarried women and men.[69] In regard to the 'aliens' (*Vremdelingen*), the 'outsiders of this society', Van den Enden envisages a totally different dynamic than Plokhoy.[70] In line with his positive view of the Indian community, his notion of political community is inclusive. And his demands for social justice pertain to all, and are not just reserved for the colonists. He devotes a lengthy comment on Art. 83 to the issue of aliens in relation to aspects of citizenship, such as voting rights, criminal law and the freedom of religion, as well as in relation to foreign affairs, such as the drawing of boundaries and the measures to be taken in case of invasion. At one time Van den Enden speaks strictly about the members of the society, at another he mentions the 'residents' of the colony as a reference that includes the indigenous population (i.e. the Indians). For example, in relation to religion no one there, whether an 'alien' (*Vremde*), 'simple resident' (*simple Inwoonder*) or 'citizen' (*Burger*) of the society, may be attacked for their opinion or faith by a government official.[71]

As for Plokhoy's colony, it is to 'secure all freedom of conscience' in religious matters.[72] Provisions shall be made for a general place of assembly where they will read, 'on Sundays and the Feasts, only the holy Scriptures'

---

[66] *Kort verhael*, 36–7.
[67] Plokhoy, *Kort en klaer ontwerp*, n.p. [B iv].
[68] *Kort verhael*, 49.
[69] Ibid. 37.
[70] Ibid. 37–9.
[71] Ibid.
[72] Plokhoy, *Kort en klaer ontwerp*, n.p. [B iv].

THE EXAMPLE OF THE INDIANS   125

that all Christians recognise as true.[73] Similarly, Van den Enden's second constitutional article prescribes the possibility of readings from Holy Scripture on Sundays and the Christian holidays.[74] Religion is a matter 'that does not concern the society in general'.[75] For this reason, and 'in order that equality might be respected on all sides', the public schools will teach no religion but only the 'natural sciences and languages'.[76] If there are people who want to place their children in private schools at their own costs, once again 'every person is undetermined, according to the freedom of his conscience, [and] all the more so because this has nothing to do with the society'.[77] Even conscientious objectors who do not want to carry weapons will be exempt from the duty of bearing arms, provided that they pay for this freedom and make a financial contribution to society. To this extent Plokhoy and Van den Enden agree. The differences between them pertain to religion and Christianity. Plokhoy stresses the Christian religion, but Van den Enden does not. In the latter's reflections, the Indians play a much greater role than any of the Christian sects do. Religion is abandoned entirely to the domain of the internal, and religious education is impossible simply because the teachers of religion will not be admitted to the colony. Plokhoy emphasises individual freedom, freedom of conscience, freedom of religion and tolerance. The colony on the South River is to be a religious safe harbour for the colonists; the indigenous population has no role to play there, except as a workforce that does not belong to the society itself and is therefore cut off from its rights. It is almost certain that Van den Enden initially proceeded from the same concern as Plokhoy, namely to write a convincing proposal for a colony in which people with a multitude of convictions, opinions and inner motives can live together in peace and which the Colonial Office would approve. But instead of a brief pamphlet, Van den Enden's proposal turned into a hefty volume that is supported with arguments and engages in self-reflection. In Van den Enden's work, the focus came to be on complete equality, on openness to improvement for the order, and it is to this end that he deemed freedom and therefore multitude of thought and critical education to be necessary.

[73] Ibid.
[74] *Kort verhael*, 51.
[75] Plokhoy, *Kort en klaer ontwerp*, n.p. [B iv].
[76] Ibid.
[77] Ibid.

4. From the *Vrye Politijke Stellingen* to *Finis est in Holandia*

A shift can be detected from an instrumental text written at the commissioning of a small group of prospective colonists to a theoretical reflection on a freedom-based society benefiting each and every person without distinction. The same movement from contingency to necessity, from a concrete case to a theory and the development towards a universal perspective can be seen in moving from the *Kort verhael* to the *Vrye Politijke Stellingen of Consideratien van Staat*. Prior to the end of 1661, Van den Enden had never involved himself in political affairs, but upon accepting the commission that led to the *Kort verhael*, he had experienced such a wide variety of astonishing things and the political substance in his observations had become so complex, that he began to fear in 1665 that he would never be able to finish his work. This did not dampen his spirits, however, nor did it shake him in his conviction that the Dutch nation could become invincible 'through a good and free government' and export its wealth to other continents so as to contribute to the gradual, 'endless improvement' of the entire world.[78] This was a grand ambition, rooted in a reversal of perspectives; after all, the alternative to the ambitious conviction that the world can be improved by reflection and reason is catastrophe. For it is the 'nature of all human affairs that nothing can remain in a single state, but everything is necessarily subject to change. And so, wherever human affairs are not established, by wisdom, to constant improvement, there they must, by deterioration, in the end plunge themselves into inevitable corruption'.[79] What Van den Enden writes is not motivated by a utopian pursuit of a perfect order, but is necessary because this perfect order is both impossible and undesirable. It is necessary to pursue improvement, for otherwise catastrophe lies in wait. Reason and wisdom serve the constant concern for improvement, and thus also the assumption that all government is, by definition and without any exceptions, liable to improvement. This motif is entirely analogous to that of Machiavelli: since all things are always changing, one must take matters into one's own hands, with reason or intelligence, for otherwise matters will turn out for the worse.[80] This too is related to the determinist perspective harboured by both Machiavelli and Van den Enden that everything,

---

[78] VPS, 127.

[79] Ibid.

[80] See especially *Il principe* XXV and *Discorsi* I, 2, 186–9; 202–7. For more on this topic, see Lavaert, *Het perspectief van de multitude*, 225–9; 243–7, and Morfino, *Il tempo e l'occasione. L'incontro Spinoza Machiavelli.*

THE EXAMPLE OF THE INDIANS 127

including factual events as well as ideas, is causal, and that matter operates on mind and mind on matter. Apart from God there is nothing that is not caused, and as we can establish every day again, 'just like the one act or operation is the cause of another, so too the one thought is caused by another thought, and also, in combination, the one operation is the cause of a thought, or, conversely, that thought the cause of an operation, etc.'[81] To prevent a weak government from plunging the Dutch nation into ruin, a political theory must be developed – and this was indeed what Van den Enden did in the 'Free Political Propositions' (*Vrye Politijke Stellingen*), which he addresses to the 'common people of Holland', who for their survival and welfare depend on a free popular government, 'which alone is the source of the kind of welfare one might wish upon all people'.[82] He directs himself to the equal, freedom-loving citizens, and announces a theory of freedom which is necessary for the promotion of the good of each and every person.

To achieve such freedom, one must first understand, globally, what common interest consists in, and this can be done by an examination of human nature. By nature, all people, both men and women, 'are born free, and not under any obligation whatsoever except their own interest'.[83] This is why people, just like other timid animals, actually prefer to stay by themselves and avoid contact with others. But since they are, on their own, weak and unable to secure even their basic needs, they are constrained to seek the aid of others. And so we see that people are, by their own nature, 'necessarily driven to mutual sociability [*gezelligheit*] and cohabitation with their fellow human beings, first out of necessity and for their own welfare, and thereafter also out of enjoyment of greater passion and pleasure'.[84] It is moreover clear that people have the ability to do what they are driven to do by their own nature. Only the 'shrewd bootlickers of the courts' and 'schoolish pedants' claim that most people are cruel and repulsive by nature, unable of themselves to form a political community.[85] For such claims aim to please the tyrants, condemning everyone 'to complete slavish coercion'.[86]

In Van den Enden's understanding, people are naturally inclined to sociability, albeit in a twofold manner, since their social inclination is not just

[81] *VPS*, 125.
[82] *VPS*, 128.
[83] *VPS*, 138.
[84] *VPS*, 139.
[85] Ibid.
[86] Ibid.

128   DEMOCRATIC THOUGHT FROM MACHIAVELLI TO SPINOZA

positive, harmonious and amiable. Nor are people 'like a wolf', however, unambiguously cruel, repulsive, resentful and hostile, for if they were, they would always show themselves this way, while experience shows that this is not the case.[87] Van den Enden's basic principle is the same as that of Hobbes: human beings are inclined to self-preservation, and think primarily of themselves. The position Van den Enden deduces from this, however, is a reversal of Hobbes. All evil passions derive from the fact that people live under a violent government, are deceived, and prey to a superstition which they have inherited by a malevolent upbringing that keeps them in their ignorance. Evil and hostile passions have their origin exclusively in an 'evil government of the republic', but the opposite is also true, especially that any good people meet in their lives 'depends absolutely on the government of the republic'.[88] Although all people pursue their own preservation and are motivated by their own well-being in everything they do, they are not by nature enemies, nor are they always friends. They are by nature timid, prefer to stay on their own, and swing back and forth between enmity and friendship. By their fear of the other as an enemy, they make that person their friend. They initially unite out of necessity (avoidance of pain), and once they have discovered the pleasure and joy of association, they do so out of passion and enjoyment (desire for pleasure). This means that they have no norms or values imprinted on them in the state of nature, but that there is a natural neutrality or indifference, by which Van den Enden breaks with the Christian tradition and traditional notions of natural law. The traditional views on good and evil are called into question, resulting in ambiguity and a pendulum movement: human beings vacillate between timidity and sociability, between good and evil. They are neither good nor evil, they are both good and evil, at one time the one, at another the other. What also changes is the meaning of good and evil.

---

[87] VPS, 140. The argument here is similar to that of *Theophrastus redivivus*; see above, Chapter II.4, 56–62.

[88] VPS, 140–1. This is a paraphrase of Machiavelli, *Discorsi* III, 29: 'Che gli peccati de' popoli nascono dai principi.' Cruelties and crimes committed by the people are the result of the 'tristitia di quelli principi, non dalla natura triste degli uomini'. Violence, crimes, and chaos among the multitude are a consequence of the audacity of the rulers (who give the example), not of an allegedly evil human nature. In this context, Machiavelli cites Livy and draws a connection to the question of the maintenance/ decline of religion: 'Timasitheus multitudinem religione implevit quae semper regenti est similis' (V, 28), 'Timasitheus filled the multitude, which is always like its ruler, with religious scruples', 489–90. Spinoza held exactly the same view in *TP* V, 2; see below, Chapter VII.4.1.

THE EXAMPLE OF THE INDIANS

This original pendulum motion which swings back and forth between good and evil as a result of natural neutrality is then translated into politics. 'Deceivers and deceived, coercers and coerced' are both positions to be avoided by those who love freedom.[89] For deceit and coercion are bad not only for the oppressed, but also for the oppressor. This follows from the nature of political dominion, which necessarily depends on the nature of human beings. There is no other reason for us human beings to form a civil society than 'to acquire and obtain our good and well-being in the safest and most certain way'.[90] This also means that there is no other reason to assume any obligation or to conform to a law.

> For one's own, individual welfare is the highest reason that can be found in nature for us human beings to do or to refrain from doing something. And where our welfare ends due to the inner evil disposition of a republic or society, there also every cause for our obligation to that assembly ends.[91]

Since there is no other reason for accommodating oneself to a law than the pursuit of one's own welfare, the duty to follow the law no longer applies when the government inflicts harm or when it no longer fosters that welfare. Politics is a complex dynamic which takes place in two mutually dependent directions, but is nonetheless not symmetrical in nature (for which reason it cannot be captured by or derived from a mathematical formula). Moreover, that dynamic is also determined in that a human being, given that he or she 'consists of a body and a soul', has 'twofold interests of welfare' which 'are so closely intertwined that when either one [i.e. the body or the soul] lacks welfare, that entire person suffers in differing degrees, with the weakest in soul being most subject to suffering and deception'.[92] Human nature is not only twofold in view of people's inclination to either isolate themselves from others or to be open to them so as to avoid pain and pursue pleasure, but also in view of their existence as body and with an inner life of thoughts and feelings (which is here called the soul), as it is reflected in two kinds of welfare: a material or physical welfare, and an immaterial or moral welfare. What Van den Enden deduces from this is that people suffer most when their inner life is at its worst state, when they are not free in mind and are victims of deceit.

---

[89] VPS, 141.
[90] VPS, 143.
[91] VPS, 144.
[92] Ibid.

130 DEMOCRATIC THOUGHT FROM MACHIAVELLI TO SPINOZA

All the theologising, moralising and philosophising of today is unable to free people from harmful feelings, so Van den Enden writes, since where one person is a devil, deceiver or tyrant to others, there no one experiences pleasure or rest 'but rather an incessant bumping and jolting', a war of all against all which is disastrous for everyone.[93] Outside a commonwealth, all human passions, even positive ones like love and happiness, remain 'bottled up, as it were', and without effect.[94] A commonwealth is necessary, that is, a political order based on the principle of 'equal freedom' (*even-gelijke-vryheidt*) in which 'such equality in order, law and assistance [is devised] through reason and experience between wiser and less wise people, between the more prosperous and less prosperous, between men and women, between adults and children, between masters and servants, or between rulers and subjects' that everyone is not just not weakened or disadvantaged, but even strengthened.[95] Van den Enden formulates the need for every person's natural 'equal freedom' in a variety of ways.[96] For the commonwealth, which is the only alternative to prevent conflict from degenerating into the disaster of an all-out war, it is necessary that all be given the opportunity to pursue their own welfare by their own rational pleasure and desire. In other words, everyone must be given the opportunity to participate in public life. 'If people cannot be given a task in the republic matching their own desire, rational pleasure, and inclination', differences of opinion will degenerate into direct conflicts plunging them into constant misery and issuing in their downfall.[97] A commonwealth is the sum total 'of each person's best', and no one can be excluded from it without 'harming the common [good]'.[98]

The greatest danger that could threaten a republic based on the principle of equal freedom is located in deceit, the spreading of falsehood and prejudice. These practices are above all the work of the 'pretended religions', which reduce human beings to slaves devoid of will, 'to the advantage of the deceivers and perpetrators of violence', by instilling fear

---

[93] VPS, 146. As with *Theophrastus redivivus*, a war of all against all is seen as the consequence of oppressive politics and deceit. However, in departure from this clandestine Latin treatise, the commonwealth is seen here as a necessity, for the sake of natural, equal freedom.

[94] VPS, 145–6.

[95] VPS, 146. The formulation is partly identical to that in the *Kort verhael*.

[96] VPS, 147.

[97] Ibid.

[98] VPS, 149.

THE EXAMPLE OF THE INDIANS   131

in them or raising the illusory hope of a hereafter.[99] What also leads to deceit and prejudice is the use of titles 'for grades of pretended learning', like the 'names of "doctor" and "professor"' which for that reason ought to be avoided 'in a republic or commonwealth that pursues truly equal freedom'.[100] For it cannot be denied that anyone active in art or science who, like today's 'theologians, jurists and physicians', simply appeals 'to what someone else has said or written', is not really practising science or art at all.[101] Finally, language itself can be a means for spreading untruth. Those who, after the custom of the Jews and papists of today, use 'the old and worn-out book languages', do so only to hide their real intentions from the common people so as to be able to deceive them. In this context, Van den Enden defends the use of a 'common language' like French – i.e. the most widely spread vernacular language in Europe at the time – which ought to be taught without charge to each and every person, 'both women and men, daughters and young men, so that they can speak, read and write'.[102] Pretended religion is an impediment to autonomous thought because it paralyses people with fear or blinds them with myths. Pretended erudition, which tricks the people using titles and authority, demands of them that they blindly repeat what they hear and replaces knowledge with imitation and submissiveness. Knowledge that is only disseminated in the languages of the books is not understood by the general public and is at best ineffective – most often, in fact, the use of book languages is aimed at misleading the readers (as Koerbagh in particular was to make clear). These processes of artifice, arrogance and deception have a mutually reinforcing effect and become power dispositives.[103] Self-formed knowledge, self-tested art, vernacular translations, and instruction in knowledge, art and languages represent the best way to avoid the deceit, superstition and deception threatening a free republic.

[99] VPS, 150. See Machiavelli's critique on (self-)deception through religion in *Discorsi* II, 2, which he also assimilates into the speech of the wool worker on the eve of the rebellion, in *Istorie Fiorentine* III, 13; see above, Chapter I.5 and I.2, 32–41; 12–18. See also Lavaert, 'The Logic of Conflict, against the Logic of War', 105–19.

[100] VPS, 152. As we have already seen, critique on the scholar-in-function and his illusory erudition was a Renaissance trope; see above, Chapter II.4, 60–62.

[101] VPS, 153. Cf. Spinoza's distinction in the *Tractatus de intellectus emendatione* (Gebhardt *Opera* II, 10; *Korte Geschriften*, 449–50) between four kinds of knowledge, the first of which depends on 'report' or on another sign.

[102] VPS, 156.

[103] Cf. *Theophrastus redivivus*; see Chapter II.4 above; this mutually reinforcing effort of the discourse to power dispositives is a theme likewise found in Foucault, *L'ordre du discours*.

132   DEMOCRATIC THOUGHT FROM MACHIAVELLI TO SPINOZA

Even though Van den Enden's political propositions show themselves indebted to Machiavelli's work and spirit, he appears to have misunderstood this Italian political philosopher's actual message. In his critique of 'monarchical tyranny' and aristocracy, Van den Enden identifies the author of the *Discorsi* as a 'real and open proponent of all filthy superstition and deceit', a disciple of Polybius who defended the notion of mixed government.[104] He charges that Machiavelli failed to understand that all the good which is alleged to follow from a mixture of the three forms of government must actually be 'ascribed to the co-rulership and authority of the people' alone.[105] As such, Van den Enden mistakes Machiavelli's thesis that opposition is necessary in every form of government (which notion Van den Enden himself still accepts, paralleling his notion of freedom of thought, speech and improvement) for an actual appeal for a mixed government, which notion may not be entirely foreign to the *Discorsi*, albeit only as a remnant of Machiavelli's preference for the widely read Roman political authors in a discourse that for the rest constitutes an unequivocal plea for a free democracy. The result of this misguided reading of Machiavelli is that it leaves Van den Enden's revolutionary and new argument all but snowed under, especially his point that only a government of the people, a 'free government, the only one that by its very nature admits of constant improvement', can be stable and good for all parties.[106]

Van den Enden continues by anticipating various objections, some of which remain familiar today, including, first of all, the argument of the ignorant multitude. He admits that such ignorance is problematic, but counters that it ought not to deprive the people of their right to knowledge so as to be left 'blindly following another, even better but individual knowledge', for in that case their minimal knowledge is far more preferable and to their own best interest.[107] If the common people blindly follow what they are told, they will undoubtedly be deceived and end up in the worst misery and slavery. Van den Enden builds on the same foundation at the bottom of the critique on the privileges of the ecclesiastical officials (and, by extension, on religion itself) uttered in the anonymous *De jure ecclesiasticorum*. The situation in politics is the same as it is in education; authority is determined by the judgement of those to whom education is given, the receivers. The authority of a political government is determined by the judgement of the subjects,

---

[104] *VPS*, 160–2.
[105] *VPS*, 163.
[106] *VPS*, 162.
[107] *VPS*, 167–8.

THE EXAMPLE OF THE INDIANS 133

the common people. Formulated even more generally, one could say that the authority in a specific affair belongs to the one to whom the judgement on that affair belongs. And it is to the 'people that the judgement of the commonwealth belongs, and so also the highest authority and the administration of that authority'.[108] Another possible objection raised by Van den Enden is that the multitude, together with the variety in what the multitude wants and thinks, will lead to delays in decision-making, to poor decisions, and even to paralysis. Van den Enden counters that not 'the multiplicity and variety of wills', but the interests of a council, even if it has 'few heads', are the cause of quarrelsome deliberations as well as decisions that are adverse in nature and sluggishly enacted.[109] In general, one can argue that the ills of political decision-making and public affairs always have their origin in the conceit and 'monarchicalness' of isolated individuals and not the masses. 'For all people together neither want nor can will anything but pure commonwealth, nor can it, stimulated to such commonwealth, fail to pursue it to the best of their knowledge and ability.'[110] If someone were to object that all people 'are by nature intractable, unmanageable, repulsive [and] inflexible, or rather that they only or largely represent furious, predatory and therefore unsociable animals, who for that reason need to be led and guided by all manner of deceit and violence, then that person must prove it'.[111] Van den Enden therefore reverses the burden of proof. Anyone who charges that people must be deceived or coerced because they are by nature unmanageable must first provide proof of this. The burden of proof does not lie with those who, like Van den Enden himself, insist that people in general are born free, as the wisest of all animals, gifted with the ability to speak so as to be able to communicate their ideas to others, flexible, amenable and susceptible to reason and therefore fit to fashion a civil society.

Even though the *Vrye Politijke Stellingen* are permeated with terms that honour the Christian religion, they announce an unmistakable critique on the church, the privileges of the ecclesiastical officials, religious education, as well as religion itself. For example, Van den Enden writes that the papal hierarchy, which is much more cunning than all pagan superstition, idolatry and deceit together, can be a symbol for every other superstition because of the many threats it issues and the excessive promises it makes for a life in the hereafter, thereby depriving people of their freedom and courage

[108] *VPS*, 168.
[109] *VPS*, 171.
[110] *VPS*, 172–3.
[111] *VPS*, 174.

134 DEMOCRATIC THOUGHT FROM MACHIAVELLI TO SPINOZA

and alienating them.[112] As another example, he writes that he can understand and agree that the true religion represents the most unbreakable bond between people and commonwealth, but he does not understand why it should also be 'the first foundation of a republic'.[113] In a footnote he explains himself further, asserting that he understands religion as 'a necessary and pretended sacred deception'.[114] And while he had criticised Machiavelli at an earlier point in this work, he now identifies him as one of the few who had a proper understanding of things. For Machiavelli simply understood religion as 'superstition and a necessary deceit'.[115] A third example is Van den Enden's claim that no nation has come closer to liberation from this 'papist deceit' than his Dutch contemporaries. For they have exposed 'the manifold deceit of pilgrimages, confession, indulgences, masses for the dead, false miracles, constraint of conscience, and the ensuing burnings and charrings, drownings, hangings and stranglings of many, together with the unbridled annihilation of all the welfare of one's fellows', and most Dutchmen are impassioned, determined and highly engaged in their opposition to this religion.[116] Van den Enden finds an alternative to this 'papist deceit' in a Christian faith that is rational and does not consist in external gestures and irrational assent or obedience, but in a clear and distinct exposition of reasons for a specific conviction that is to the advantage of 'all the nations of the earth', regardless of the particular ceremonies, rules and laws to which they adhere.[117]

It is impossible to determine whether Van den Enden lost his faith in the Dutch inclination to reason, what his precise ambitions in France were, or whether his intentions were anything other than revolutionary and anti-monarchical. What is clear, however, is that his religious critique returns in all of his writings, also in the outline which he appears to have dictated to Latréaumont in 1674 and which is appended to the court records together with his statement. During the trial which eventually led to his hanging, Van den Enden did not deny that the content of the six pages of the Latin *Finis est in Holandia* originated at least in part in his 'Vrye politique stellingen en consideratien van staat' (Free political propositions and considerations of state), which he had lent to Latréaumont and whose essence

---

[112] VPS, 188. Cf. Machiavelli's critique in *Discorsi* II, 2; see above, Chapter I.5, 32–41.
[113] VPS, 195.
[114] VPS, 194.
[115] VPS, 195.
[116] VPS, 197.
[117] VPS, 201.

THE EXAMPLE OF THE INDIANS

135

he had also translated for him from the Flemish original.[118] He did deny that he had written the Latin manuscript himself, picking out a number of phrases that were not his own, as when it says that citizens 'shall recognize no other government than noble and free people' or that 'no distinction shall be made between Catholics and Reformed'.[119] If these two sentences are not his, one might rightly infer that the rest are. Those include the following statement: 'The end is to establish in the Netherlands a certain democracy which cannot be seized by weapons, which is always flourishing and growing, through unity and like-mindedness in a single commonwealth and the equal and universal freedom of all.'[120] This constitutes nothing less than a revolutionary charter written on campaign, sketching out in clear lines the institutional rules for a democratic republic based on the principle of the equal freedom of all, where citizens even make the rules and have a written guarantee that they can change and renew those rules when they deem such change necessary. Compared to the proposals drawn up in the constitutional articles of the *Kort verhael*, these rules are radical and they coincide more or less with the social rules of the Indian *naturellens*; in comparison with the *Vrye Politijke Stellingen*, they are simple and concrete. Immediately after power has been taken over through revolution, the citizens will assemble unarmed, and the principle of freedom and its guarantee will be proposed. This means that 'no office, sentence or judgement' will be overturned 'until the people themselves, together with the nobles, have chosen governors for themselves who have decided to renew these [laws] in accordance with the laws established by them and at a time agreed upon'.[121] A military council and a civil council will be established, both by ballot. The civil council will act in accordance with the instructions of the community and deal with matters of economy, finance, culture, heritage, urban development, social welfare, justice, education, foreign affairs, and war and peace. The military council will hold responsibility for the use of weapons. There will be a constant exchange between the two councils, and mutual representation. All the seats in the civil council will change hands every year. No one can

---

[118] *Procès Rohan*, 94v–95v. It is in reality five pages and one line. For a transcription and translation, see the Appendix below.

[119] According to Van den Enden, Latréaumont added the following lines to the text: 'non alium noscant superiorem nisi nobilitatem et populum' and 'nullam facere distinctionem inter catholicos et reformatos', *Procès Rohan*, 342r; 344r.

[120] Ibid. 342r. In this introductory sentence, we immediately recognise the basic components of Van den Enden's political vision as it is expressed in his *Kort verhael* and *Vrye Politijke Stellingen*.

[121] Ibid. 342r.

136 DEMOCRATIC THOUGHT FROM MACHIAVELLI TO SPINOZA

be elected for two consecutive terms, since members can only be re-elected after an absence of at least two years. To be eligible for election, one must be above the age of twenty-one and have completed at least three years of military service. Nothing is said about the eligibility of women, seemingly suggesting that women are not excluded. Religion is not mentioned until the final sentence of the work, where it in fact says that religion shall have no role in politics. No distinction is to be made between the various religious sects, provided that their adherents act as good citizens and do not mix religion and politics.

It is clear that Van den Enden's project for the reform of politics was still alive in 1674, that the example of the Indians still appealed to him, and that his concern went out for principles that must be realised everywhere, whether in Holland, Delaware or France – that is, a democracy governed by equal freedom, where children are raised in the free arts and 'in particular in knowledge of common freedom', where 'common freedom' is respected and therefore 'religion and political affairs are not mixed'.[122]

5. 'do not dare to speak with their mouth, [but] use their fists'

In the afterword of the *Kort verhael*, Van den Enden came to the conclusion, after 'constant deliberation and reflection', that the establishment and maintenance of a 'free colony' in New Netherlands would not succeed unless the necessary reforms were first taken in Holland itself. The entire political system stood in need of urgent reform. For 'a state cannot pass on the good that it does not itself have, and so we deem it absolutely impossible for freedom-loving people in a state to expect or hope for something good from a rather corrupted state unless it is first reformed or improved'.[123] For what is most harmful to a state is when the 'appropriate freedom is not left'.[124]

The extensively argued plea for the reform of a state without equal freedom is closed with a final exposition showing how absurd it is to ban the people from speaking about reform. As such, the rhetoric comes full circle, and ironic self-reflection turns into clear critique. If no one were to be allowed to speak of reform any longer, so Van den Enden writes, it could only mean that there is no need to enact reform.[125] Nevertheless, experience

[122] Ibid. 343v; 344r–344v.
[123] *Kort verhael*, 68–9.
[124] Ibid. 69.
[125] Ibid. 80.

teaches us that this is not the case (since reform is indeed necessary), nor will it ever be the case (since reform will always be necessary). People are fickle of disposition, the economy will have its ups and downs, poverty and war are constantly lurking, princes become unruly, rulers end up corrupt and leaders govern poorly. Improvement is always necessary, and not only from the perspective of the common people, for Van den Enden also explicitly addresses the leaders. For the fact of the matter is that when a state is poorly governed, the chaos will become so widespread that fear is transformed into the desperate courage of those who 'do not dare to speak with their mouth, [but] use their fists'.[126] It is when they do not dare to speak 'with their mouth' that they take up their weapons to bring an end to the chaos issuing from the poor rule. This is how civil wars break out, which have frequently ended in the downfall of the most powerful of empires. Violent rebellions and civil wars do not arise because of the freedom of speech. Rather, the freedom of speech prevents a state from degenerating into chaos and violence.[127]

[126] Ibid.
[127] Ibid. 83.

VI

Translation and Truth: A Dialogue

1. Adriaan Koerbagh

How happy indeed is the land / whose governments have achieved such wisdom / that they have not founded their rule on the pillar of some religion / whose preservation constantly requires them / to banish / to curse / to hang / to burn / and to kill, but only on good laws and just rule / permitting / that which serves the prosperity and welfare of the land / [namely] that every bird may sing its own song.[1]

This sounds like something Van den Enden would say, fitting in seamlessly with the rhetorical and thematic dialectics of his *Kort verhael*. In reality, these lines form part of the entry for the noun 'Excommunicate' (*Excommuniceerde*) in Adriaan Koerbagh's *Een Bloemhof van allerley lieflijkheyd sonder verdriet* (A Flower Garden of All Kinds of Loveliness Without Sorrow; 1668). An 'Excommunicate' is someone who has been banished and

---

[1] Koerbagh, *Een Bloemhof van allerley lieflijkheyd sonder verdriet, geplant door Vreederyk Waarmond, ondersoeker der waarheyd, Tot nut en dienst van al die geen die der nut en dienst uyt trekken wil. Of Een vertaaling en uytlegging van al de Hebreusche, Griecksche, Latijnse, Franse, en andere vreemde bastaart-woorden en wijsen van spreeken, die ('t welk te beklaagen is) soo inde Godsgeleertheyd, regtsgeleertheyd, geneeskonst, als in andere konsten en weetenschappen, en ook in het dagelijks gebruyk van spreeken inde Nederduytse taal gebruykt worden*, 285–8: 'Maar o! hoe gelukkig is het land / welkers Overheden tot die wijsheyd gekomen zijn / datse hun land-bestier niet gegrond hebben op den suyl van eenderley Gods-dienst / om welke staande te houden men geduurig van nooden heeft / te bannen / te vloeken / te hangen / te branden / en dood te slaan: maar alleen op goede land-wetten en billik land-bestier / waar by sy toelaaten / 't welk strekt tot bloey en welvaaren des lands / dat ieder vogelken mag singen na dat het gebekt is.'

TRANSLATION AND TRUTH: A DIALOGUE 139

cast out, so the author of this dictionary of loanwords writes, rejected from the community of believers for an 'offensive' doctrine, and many excommunicates are found in places where the Roman religion is considered a pillar of the state. There this anathema, which has often proved to be 'nothing less than a death sentence', is readily applied to anyone who holds a view differing from that of the clerics, even if it is based on the sacred Scriptures which those same clerics have decreed to be a legislative text.[2] These clerics fail to realise that the diversity in upbringing and education makes it impossible to come to a single, united view in matters of faith.[3] They relentlessly impose unintelligible doctrines on one another, contesting reason and the existing diversity, and end up putting others 'to death', or anathemising and banishing them.[4] One can draw a straight line from the final plea in the *Kort verhael* of 1662 (the worst thing a state can do is to leave insufficient room for the requisite freedom), to Latréaumont's notes in the *Procès Rohan* (the goal is the establishment of a state in which common freedom is respected, such that religion and public affairs are not mixed), and to the unfortunate lot Van den Enden met in 1674 (execution for a republican conspiracy). Van den Enden was put to death for the political ideas he espoused, literally and tragically demonstrating their very truth. Something similar happened to Koerbagh. The topic he addressed in his writings was likewise indicative of his destiny: his efforts in unmasking and in vernacular translation (that is, the unambiguous statement of the truth) brought him to the Rasphuis of Amsterdam, where the truth of his words was tragically confirmed. Soon after *Een Bloemhof* appeared, Koerbagh himself became an 'excommunicate'.

Reconstructing the chronology of the Koerbagh brothers' life and relationships once again involves a certain amount of conjecture, although in this case a number of clear details are available.[5] Both brothers first studied

---

[2] Ibid. 286.
[3] Ibid.
[4] Ibid.
[5] For the details of Koerbagh's biography, see Bordoli, 'Account of a Curious Traveller on the Libertijnen Milieu of Amsterdam', 175–82; Israel, *Radical Enlightenment*, 192–6; Jongeneelen, 'Adriaan Koerbagh, een voorloper van de Verlichting?', 27–34; Klever, *Mannen rond Spinoza*, 87–106; Leeuwenburgh, *Het noodlot van een ketter*; Mauthner, *Der Atheismus und seine Geschichte im Abendlande*, II, 340–6; Meinsma, *Spinoza en zijn kring*, 293–327; Mignini, '*Een ligt schijnende in duystere plaatsen*: Adriaan Koerbagh tra averroismo e libertinismo', 167–200; Thijssen-Schoute, *Nederlands Cartesianisme*, 362–7; Vandenbossche, *Adriaan Koerbagh en Spinoza*; Van Bunge, 'Introduction' in Koerbagh, *A Light Shining in Dark Places*, 1–38; Wielema, 'The Two Faces of Adriaan Koerbagh', 57–75. For Johannes Koerbagh, see Van Heertum, 'Reading the Career of Johannes Koerbagh', 1–57. For an attempt to situate Adriaan Koerbagh relative

140 DEMOCRATIC THOUGHT FROM MACHIAVELLI TO SPINOZA

philosophy in Utrecht, then went on to the University of Leiden in 1656, where Johannes studied theology and Adriaan law and medicine. It may have been there, in Leiden, that they first met their friends Bouwmeester, Meyer and Van Berkel, with whom they were to form the hub of the radical scene in Amsterdam during the 1660s. Another figure often mentioned as a participant in those radical discussions was Van den Enden, along with the Socinian Jan Knol and, of course, Spinoza himself. Adriaan Koerbagh soon established himself as the leading spokesman of the new naturalist intellectual movement, which opposed the widespread superstition, the church's claims to authority, and the use of revealed religion as a uniting force and propagandistic tool to support the power of the ecclesiastical officials. From the very outset, Koerbagh's published writings testify to an exceptional sensitivity to issues of language, which was to become a defining characteristic of enlightened modern thinking. Enlightenment does not consist in the critique of traditional metaphysics and religion alone, but also in the public debate on such philosophical matters. From the beginning, Koerbagh sought to present his ideas to a wide, or more accurately, a general (universal) audience – that is, to everyone. A crucial role in this endeavour was reserved for the multiplicity of language and vernacular translation. Accordingly, in 1664 he published 't Nieuw Woorden-Boek der Regten (New Dictionary of Law), his first attempt at the dictionary form, supplying Dutch translations for numerous terms encountered in Grotius.[6] This dictionary's focus on legal terms is likewise indicative of Koerbagh's political interests. That same year saw the appearance of an anonymous pamphlet entitled 't Samen-spraeck tusschen een Gereformeerden Hollander en Zeeuw. Waer in de Souverainiteyt van Holland ende West-Vriesland Klaer ende Naecktelijck werd vertoont, whose title page bears the name Vrederyck Waermont (Peaceland True-Mouth), a periphrasis we also encounter on the title pages of Een Bloemhof and Een Ligt schijnende in duystere plaatsen, alongside the label 'investigator of the truth' and the name Adr. Koerbagh.[7] This circumstance was an important initial

---

to Spinoza and clandestine philosophical literature, see Lavaert, 'Entre clandestinité et sphère publique. Le cas Koerbagh', 33–48. See also Lavaert, 'Koerbagh, Adriaan', Dictionnaire des Pays-Bas au siècle d'or, 409–11.

[6] Koerbagh, 't Nieuw Woorden-Boek der Rechten: ten dele uyt de Schriften van H. en W. de Groot versamelt ende ten dele nu eerst uyt het Latyn in Nederduyts overgeset, 1664.

[7] Anonymous, 't Samen-spraeck tusschen een Gereformeerden Hollander en Zeeuw. Waer in de Souverainiteyt van Holland ende West-Vriesland Klaer ende Naecktelijck werd vertoont. Tot Refutatie van den verresen Barnevelt; bedunckelijcken Brief; 't Samen-spraeck tusschen een Rotterdammer en Gelderman, Kaats-Bal en andere onlangs uytgegevene Laster-schriften, belangende een Formulier van 't Bidden, &c. Eerste Deel. Door Vrederyck Waermont,

indicator for Gerrit Jongeneelen to attribute this 1664 political pamphlet to Koerbagh.[8]

2. 't Samen-spraeck

Jongeneelen's comparative reading led him to conclude that the similarities in the syntactical anomalies of *'t Samen-spraeck* and *Een Ligt* confirm Koerbagh's authorship of the pamphlet, notwithstanding the remarkable stylistic differences he also detected, although he ascribed the latter to such external factors as the changed historical context. Between 1664 and 1668, the Orangist party had grown in power, and France began to harbour ambitions towards Holland, making the reality of a French-English coalition an imminent danger for De Witt.[9] These changes indeed yielded other priorities, urgencies and foci, a sharpening and radicalisation of positions, and thus variations in textual production. There are, in other words, no arguments excluding Koerbagh from authorship of *'t Samen-spraeck*, but does that really mean he actually was its author? In spite of the remaining uncertainties, we follow Jongeneelen, along with Wielema, Van Bunge, Mignini and Bordoli, in the attribution of this pamphlet to Koerbagh, while being open to the distinct possibility that it may just as well have been authored by his friend Van Berkel or by the anonymous author sheltering behind the pseudonym Lucius Antistius Constans. The similarities found could just as well reverse the order of the assumptions, such that the anonymous author of the *De jure*

1664; *Een Ligt Schijnende in Duystere Plaatsen / Om te verligten de voornaamste saaken der Gods geleertheyd en Gods dienst / Ontsteeken door Vreederijk Waarmond / ondersoeker der Waarheyd. Anders Mr. Adr. Koerbagh / Regts-gel. en Genees-Mr.*, 1668. Only two extant copies have been discovered to date, both held at the Museum Meermanno-Westreenianum in The Hague. After the printing process was halted and the book was forbidden, a number of copies must have eluded the authorities and circulated. Clear indications for its circulation can be found in Pieter de la Ruë's *Aantekeningen* (1720); see Post, 'De aantekeningen van Pieter de la Ruë', 405–20. There is also evidence for this in Vogt, *Catalogus historico-criticus librorum rariorum*, 383; Uffenbach, *Merkwürdige Reisen durch Niedersachsen Holland und Engeland*, II, 66; and Lilienthal, *Theologische Bibliothec*, 1129. The only (modern) edition appeared in 1974, edited by Hubert Vandenbossche for the Centrum voor de Studie van de Verlichting en van het vrije denken in Brussels. Unless otherwise noted, Dutch text and English translation have been taken from the bilingual edition edited by Michiel Wielema: *A Light Shining in Dark Places, to Illuminate the Main Questions of Theology and Religion*, 2011. In 2014, Wielema also published a modern Dutch edition: *Een licht dat schijnt in duistere plaatsen.*

[8] Jongeneelen, 'An Unknown Pamphlet of Adriaan Koerbagh', 405–15.

[9] Ibid. 409.

142   DEMOCRATIC THOUGHT FROM MACHIAVELLI TO SPINOZA

may have written 't Samen-spraeck, or even that Koerbagh might have been the *De jure*'s anonymous author. Alternatively, various authors emerging from the same network, like Spinoza's circle or the radical scene, may have drawn on the same pool of pseudonyms, periphrases and metaphors.

Whatever the case may be, the anonymous pamphlet comes in the form of a dialogue between a Reformed *Hollander* (inhabitant of the province of Holland) and a *Zeeuw* (inhabitant of the province of Zeeland), who debate the authority of the state in religious matters and the authority of the ecclesiastical officials in matters of state and religion. It evinces the same Hobbesian views of Cartesian bent which De la Court defended in 1662 and which appeared in the *De jure* a year after the publication of 't *Samen-spraeck*.[10] It is also worth noting that Van den Enden seems to proceed from the same basic assumption regarding the place of theologians in the dialectics of sovereignty. The Zeelander asks critical questions regarding the evolution of power constellations ever since the Reformation in Holland, which the Reformed Hollander seeks to counter with rather extensive answers in the form of reasons and arguments. Overall, the work reads like an anticlerical pamphlet and a critique on the ecclesiastical officials and the violence they perpetrate on truth and politics. The one leads to the other: deceit, error and ignorance all lead to violence. The betrayal of virtue and truth is the worst and most malicious seed which Satan has planted in the hearts of human beings 'to help suppress the truth and to quash the defenders of right and justice', and it is most evident in 'those sanctimonious theologians' (*dien schijn-heylighe Theologanten*).[11] For this reason, the author considers it necessary to 'warn the ignorant about those works of filthy slander', in the hope that 'the blinds may be removed from their eyes' and they 'may gaze upon the truth in all its splendour'.[12] It is necessary to unmask the slander, lies and deception as an antidote to the 'unjust deportation, condemnation, tyrannical expulsion and banishment' of the defenders of the truth, to the bloodshed resulting from the 'ambition of the ecclesiastics' who merely proclaim their views in an effort to maintain 'the hierarchy they claim over the churches'.[13] The author will show that predestination was just a 'pretext'.[14] In the pamphlet's twofold programme, which comprises the unmasking of

---

[10] Cf. Van Bunge, *From Stevin to Spinoza*, 100–1.

[11] Anonymous, 't *Samen-spraeck*, n.p. [*2r.]: 'Sathan tot onderdruckinge der Waerheyd, ende om de Voorstanders van recht en gerechtigheyd van kant te helpen.'

[12] Ibid. n.p. [*3v]; [*4r].

[13] Ibid. n.p. [*2v].

[14] Ibid.

TRANSLATION AND TRUTH: A DIALOGUE 143

deceptive knowledge with its hidden agenda of power and the dissemination of knowledge to the ignorant by the use of the vernacular, along with the metaphor of light in the kingdom of darkness, we already recognise all the major ingredients of Koerbagh's two chief works.

3. Hobbes's *Leviathan* in translation

What we also recognise is the programme of Enlightenment envisioned by Abraham van Berkel when he in 1667 published his Dutch translation of Hobbes's *Leviathan*.[15] Initially, it comes as a surprise to find Hobbes cited as a source of inspiration by these radicals in discourses defending the freedom of expression and claiming the right of disobedience. After all, the English philosopher appears to stand on the opposite end of the spectrum, on the side of the absolute monarch who alone has the right to decide what people may say and publish. And is his sovereign not that one-headed monster on the title page, who waves his sceptre over city and countryside while holding a threatening sword in the other hand, who thinks and speaks for all?[16] The chronology and choice of target language show that Van Berkel did not complete the translation for De la Court or Koerbagh, Van den Enden or Antistius Constans. Rather, it was together with them, at their side, and for the sake of their common republican cause that Van Berkel translated the English text for the general public and therefore into the common tongue. In the preface to the *Leviathan, of van de stoffe, gedaente, ende magt van de kerkelycke ende wereltlycke regeeringe*, we read the same message we find in '*t Samen-spraeck* almost verbatim. Van Berkel's interest, just like that of Koerbagh, went out to the sovereignty of the Dutch Republic, which makes his use of Hobbes and *Leviathan*, rather than *De cive*, as Theo Verbeek has noted, entirely understandable.[17] After all, the sovereignty of Holland was under siege from the church, a band of deceivers who sought to secure their power with false and obscure theories that extinguished the light of nature as well as Scripture.[18] In these words of Hobbes, one could find a like-minded thinker and read him as a supporter of the republican

[15] Hobbes, *Leviathan, of van de stoffe, gedaente, ende magt van de kerkelycke ende wereltlycke regeeringe*, 1667.

[16] For a discussion of the image and illustration on the title page of the first edition, see Malcolm, *Aspects of Hobbes*, 200–29; see also Agamben, *Stasis*.

[17] Verbeek, 'Hobbes, Spinoza, et la souveraineté de la Hollande', 165–7. See also Wielema, 'Abraham van Berkel's Translations as Contributions to the Dutch Radical Enlightenment', 204–26.

[18] Hobbes, *Leviathan, of van de stoffe*, IV, 44, 623–4.

144 DEMOCRATIC THOUGHT FROM MACHIAVELLI TO SPINOZA

cause. The key here is not Hobbes's theory of sovereignty (although, going by what Van Berkel writes in the preface, it too in a certain way), but his critique of the ecclesiastical officials, their misguided interpretation of Holy Scripture, and their propagation of false theories and phantasms. This critique was rooted in his view on the use and abuse of language, as laid out in Chapter 4 of *Leviathan*.

In a commonwealth, the most necessary knowledge is for the political government to understand 'the foundation of its sovereign right', so Van Berkel writes, and for the subjects to be 'instructed well as to whom they must see as their sovereign rulers'.[19] It is on this political knowledge of government and subjects that the existence and welfare of a state depend. It should be noted, however, that the subjects cannot simply be reproached for the shortcomings in their political knowledge, since their ignorance results from the poor education they were given by the government. This is the problem Van Berkel hopes to address with his translation, so that 'the thick membranes and blinds of ignorance' (*de dicke Vliesen en Schellen van ontwetenheyt*) may be removed from the eyes of those who, 'by a shrewd persistence and harmful, erroneous passions, or else by simplicity, folly and incompetence, have remained in an abyss of deep darkness'.[20] In his *Leviathan*, so Van Berkel writes, Hobbes offers a concise and cogent proposal for sovereignty and lawful rule in general, regardless of its particular form, and for the freedom and duties of the subjects.[21] Since that process induced him to address matters of faith, with which he, in spite of his starting point in Holy Scripture, dealt in a radically different way than the Christian theologians did, people everywhere – 'not only in England, but also in France, Italy and Holland' – started to vilify him as 'one of the greatest and shrewdest heretics' (*een van de grootste ende snoodste Ketters*).[22] This should hardly come as a surprise, considering that he struck the ecclesiastical powers where they were most vulnerable: their teaching of the common people, that is, their phantasmagoric dominion of the air. Hobbes unmasks the church's unfounded slander and attacks, its 'impenetrable and unfathomable pretension and deceptive sanctimony', its teaching which is not intended to bring truth but to keep the common people in dark ignorance.[23] Hobbes moreover shows that the

[19] Van Berkel, 'Voor-reden', in Hobbes, *Leviathan, of van de stoffe*, n.p. [*3r].
[20] Ibid. n.p. [*5r–*5v]: 'door een snoode hartneckigheyt, en schadelijcke verkeerde Passien, of andersins oock door eenvoutigheyt, onnoosele, ende onkunde, in een afgrondt van diepe Duysternisse gebleven zijn'.
[21] Ibid. n.p. [*5v].
[22] Ibid.
[23] Ibid. n.p. [*6r].

church's officials have no right to power, since there ought to be only a 'lawful power' (*Wettelijcke Magt*).[24]

This unmasking function explains why Van Berkel translated *Leviathan* for a wide audience, and so he places extra emphasis on this function in the preface. The critique of knowledge is necessary for the success of a commonwealth and is accompanied by a new, naturalistic and materialist anthropology (treated in part 1), a new, immanent and dialectical theory of sovereignty (presented in part 2), and a new, critical interpretation of religious practices and Holy Scripture (developed in part 3). In part 4, Hobbes finally arrives at the theme that is his ultimate concern: the knowledge or philosophy needed in a commonwealth. He demonstrates that the kingdom of darkness is caused by a misguided interpretation of Scripture, and that the 'devils', conceived by an 'idle philosophy and fable-like traditions', are nothing but 'phantasms and apparitions which come to reveal themselves in the air'.[25] Devils are products of the mind without being rooted in matter; they are groundless, unfounded, illusionary and deceptive, and as such they disappear as soon they are unmasked. They are also 'spirits of deception': some benefit from idle philosophy and fable-like traditions and will do everything within their power to maintain them, so that what initially was an illusion or empty air becomes deception which, if not unmasked, yields oppression and violence.[26] The knowledge necessary for a commonwealth must therefore determine who benefits from such idle philosophy and fable-like traditions. Who are the princes of the powers of the air? For Hobbes, the answer is very clear: it is the pope, bishops, priests, monks, theologians and teachers of the Christian religion, briefly stated, the ecclesiastical officials, the so-called 'public servants of God' who think they have the power to rule the church 'and therefore (since church and state consist of the same people) also to be rulers of the state'.[27]

Since the common people have so little experience in the knowledge that distinguishes truth from lies and they for that reason hope for or fear the wrong things, only exacerbating the ignorance of their inexperienced minds, Van Berkel by way of epilogue adds a translation of the first chapter of Thomas Browne's *Pseudodoxia Epidemica*, a work whose contents 'largely coincide' with *Leviathan*.[28] He closes the work with a bookmark

---

[24] Ibid.
[25] Ibid. 685; 623.
[26] Ibid. 624
[27] Ibid. 710.
[28] Ibid. 737.

146 DEMOCRATIC THOUGHT FROM MACHIAVELLI TO SPINOZA

(*Bladt-Wyser*) which can be read as a rudimentary dictionary, with some entries and texts returning in Koerbagh's dictionary in a more developed form. For example, the bookmark describes 'idolatry' as that which the papists do 'in the administration of the Eucharist'.[29] In *Een Bloemhof*, idolatry is described as placing one's trust in something other than the being without beginning or time, the one true God. Is that not the very thing papists do when they 'turn a man into a God apart from the one true God'?[30] In the 'Eucharist' or 'Mass', it is claimed that a 'small, round piece of bread or wafer' is a man, or rather, a 'God-man'. Is this not a clear example of how an idea (image, figure, example, concept) degenerates into an idol (graven image)?[31] Is it not clear as day that all these things are deception? Even though 'the round wafer is and remains the same without even the slightest change / the clerics (who do know better) still claim that it has changed into a God-man'.[32] The Hobbesian inspiration in Koerbagh's *Een Bloemhof* is nowhere more evident than in the entry for 'Leviathan', which people claim to be the name for a great sea monster. But if one is attentive to the improper use of speech more common in Scripture, it is much better understood as an association or community of people, a commonwealth.[33]

4. *Een Bloemhof van allerley lieflijkheyd sonder verdriet*

In Hobbes/Van Berkel, 'devil' (*duyvel*) is not a proper but a generic name, and we have already seen how he reads this generic name, sometimes called 'satan' in Holy Scripture, as a delusion, spirit of deception or ruler of the air.[34] Koerbagh similarly does not understood 'Devil' (*Duyvel*) as a proper name but as the generic noun for a person who slanders, charges or accuses. It is a loanword, derived from the Greek *diabolos*, which has been left untranslated in the Dutch translation of the 'Bible', itself a problematic term, 'but in Scripture there are more non-Dutch words that have been left untranslated / so that the common people might not understand them / and

---

[29] Ibid. n.p.: "Afgoderije wat die is? 666, 671. [. . .] Sy wort van de Pausgesinde bedreven in het bedienen van d'Eucharistie. 674'.

[30] Koerbagh, *Een Bloemhof*, 345–6.

[31] Ibid. 345.

[32] Ibid. 448–9: 'het rond stukje meel-gebak het selve is en blijft sonder datter an geschied is eenige de minste verandering / so willen sy geestelijken evenwel dat het verandert is (trouwens sy geestelijken weeten wel beeter) in een Godmensch'; 345–6.

[33] Ibid. 403–4.

[34] Hobbes, *Leviathan, of van de stoffe*, n.p.; 468; 657–8.

come to knowledge'.[35] Yet 'we', the 'common people', are being convinced that 'the *devil* is an evil spirit [. . .] although we do not read a single word about it in all of scripture', for it is actually an invention of the theologians.[36] The linguistic critique applied by Koerbagh here has a structure we see returning throughout the entire work. People invent a word for some thing or for the attributes of a collection of entities situated in a specific historical context. Later that word is cut off from that context and ascribed an objectivity it does not actually have. As such, a generic name is transferred to another historical context but left untranslated, so that the term is confused for a proper name and given a new, ideal albeit groundless significance. The devil, for instance, is an invention that has been awarded a material, real-objective status. Koerbagh's criticism therefore consists in going back on the road travelled, uncovering the original meaning, and, if possible, showing who was responsible for inventing and secretly introducing the new meanings and when. The way back is like a labyrinth, often taking one along a 'bastardized form' which has undergone a similar process and forms the basis for the ideological edifice which must itself be subjected to such an analysis. It must have occurred to Koerbagh while reading Hobbes's *Leviathan* in Van Berkel's translation that the dictionary form is very well suited to the labyrinthine structure of this verbal arsenal and ideology constructed on it. After all, the key is translation, and as for the theme, content, approach and archaeological route – all these elements of the Hobbes/Van Berkel-project return in Koerbagh. The centre of the stage is dominated by the critique of the ecclesiastical officials who interpret Holy Scripture falsely and spread false theories and delusions to sustain their imperium. All idols and delusions, and above all that great sea monster of the title of Hobbes's work, lead to Holy Scripture. The way back in the secret cabinet of the (Christian) religion leads to politics, and, of course, vice versa, religion and politics secretly reflect each other. An 'error' arises from an erroneous interpretation of Scripture and from a misunderstanding regarding eternal life, so Hobbes/Van Berkel writes.[37] Scripture says nothing about 'angels', a term better understood as 'envoy and messenger'.[38] In the same way, *Een Bloemhof* describes an angel as a loanword deriving from the Greek *aggelos*

---

[35] Koerbagh, *Een Bloemhof*, 259: 'dog daar staan wel meer onduytse woorden inde schrift dewelke men on-overgeset laat staan / om dat de gemeene luyden deselve niet souden verstaan / en daar door tot kennis van saaken komen'. See also Den Boer, 'Le dictionnaire libertin d'Adriaen Koerbagh', 105–29.

[36] Koerbagh, *Een Bloemhof*, 259.

[37] Hobbes, *Leviathan, of van de stoffe*, n.p.; 625.

[38] Ibid. n.p.; 412; 416.

148   DEMOCRATIC THOUGHT FROM MACHIAVELLI TO SPINOZA

which has been left untranslated in the Dutch Bible, a generic noun for any kind of human messenger or envoy. The theologians abused this generic name when they employed it 'as a proper name for the spirits' and appealed to Holy Scripture in support, 'even though one will fail to find even a single word about it in Scripture'.[39]

According to Hobbes/Van Berkel, we do not know who the writers of Scripture were, and there is at any rate no evidence supporting Moses' authorship of the books that bear his name.[40] 'Who the writers of the Jewish scriptures are / cannot be known', so Koerbagh writes. 'Some of the most excellent theologians hold the opinion / that a certain *Esdras* copied them out from various Jewish writings.'[41] In Hobbes we likewise encounter the view of Ezra as the author of the Pentateuch. He did not deny that Moses himself wrote certain parts, as Noel Malcolm observes in *Aspects of Hobbes*, but his main point was that Moses was a lawgiver and civil ruler.[42] The entire history of the authority of Scripture was 'a chronicle of discontinuities, punctuated by political acts'.[43] The same story is repeated with the Ezra-hypothesis, as politics once again proves to be the key. One of the most important theses Koerbagh was to propose in *Een Ligt schijnende in duystere plaatsen* is that not Moses but Eszra was the author of the Bible.[44] Yet the same idea also appears in other entries of *Een bloemhof*, including 'Deuteronomy' and 'Exodus', every time with the same recurring structure.

The word *exodus*, or *exodos*, is a good Greek word / and means / as I have said / departure / but in the Dutch translation it is left untranslated: in fact so much is left untranslated / that it is not just about this one case. I trust / that the clerics would consider it a great injustice or sin / to make the effort / to translate everything into Dutch: for the common man, so

---

[39] Koerbagh, *Een Bloemhof*, 268–9.

[40] Hobbes, *Leviathan of van de stoffe*, n.p.; 394.

[41] Koerbagh, *Een Bloemhof*, 96: 'Wie de schrijvers zijn van de Joodsche schriften / kan men niet weeten [. . .] eenige der uytsteekenste Gods-geleerden meynen / datse eenen *Esdras* uyt meer Joodsche schriften uytgeschreven heeft.'

[42] Malcolm, *Aspects of Hobbes*, 383–431: 'Hobbes, Esra, and the Bible: the History of a Subversive Idea'.

[43] Ibid. 425.

[44] Koerbagh, *Een Ligt*, 286–91; 398–401. We find a remark on Koerbagh's Esdras-hypothesis from Müller in his *Atheismus devictus* of 1672, 186: 'XXV. Friedrich Wahrmund in seinem Atheistischen Büchlein Blumenhoff genandt / giebet für / dass der Nahme Moses stehe für dem Exodo oder andern Buch Mosis nicht aber der Meynung / als ob Moses Autor wäre / sondern nur darumb / dieweil von Mose und seinem Thun darinne gehandelt wäre. Es sol Esra dasselbige Buch geschrieben haben.'

TRANSLATION AND TRUTH: A DIALOGUE 149

they fear, would become too wise. [. . .] The book departure [i.e. Exodus] /
or the book of the departure is also called the second book of Moses, as if
Moses had written it / although the wisest and most erudite men posit /
that a certain *Esdra* wrote it

even if the true identity of the author actually cannot be determined.[45]
In this way, Koerbagh introduces subversive views to a wide audience,
extremely dangerous theses, in fact, which undoubtedly led to his excom-
munication and destruction. He himself was poignantly aware of this danger:
'were Scripture not maintained through the violence / of fire and sword / it
would fall'.[46] In spite of this, he had the courage to completely unravel the
authority of the Bible. That word, 'Bible', is in fact a normal word, 'a bastardized Greek term' meaning 'a book / any kind of book / even Reynard the
Fox or [Till] Eulenspiegel'.[47] The theologians abused this word when they
applied it to the Holy Scriptures, which are themselves nothing but 'some
books or writings' that treat of the Jewish religion and history.[48]

In *Een Bloemhof*, things are called by their true name. Koerbagh clears up
misunderstandings in religious matters, corrects erroneous interpretations of
scripture, and exposes the ecclesiastical officials' abuse of power, and he does
so by putting his finger on erroneous translations or improper language use.
Every case involves the same misleading processes, such that the naming
of things by their proper name exposes the oppression and violence hidden
behind the improper use of language. Apart from the deliberate confusion
of generic names and proper names (of which 'Adam' is another example),
there are also the non-translated terms, such as 'Christendom', 'Cleric',
'Genesis', 'Easter' (*Pinxter*), 'Jesus' and 'Satan'. But Koerbagh did not limit
himself to critique in his dictionary, but also set out a positive materialist
ontology, once again following in the footsteps of Hobbes. According to

[45] Koerbagh, *Een Bloemhof*, 292–3: 'Het woord *exodus*, of *exodos*, is een goed grieks
woord / en betekent / gelijk ik gesegt heb / uyttogt / dog dat laat men inde nederduytse
oversetting al onovergeset staan: trouwens men laat'er so veel onovergeset staan /
dat het op geen een ankomt. Ik vertrouw / dat de geestelijken het voor een groote
ongeregtigheyd of sonde soude rekenen / dat se die moeyten op sik soude neemen / om
het alles in 't nederduyts over te setten: want de gemeene man vreesen sy sou te wijs
worden. [. . .] Het boek uyttogt / of het boek des uyttogts word ook genoemt het tweede
boek Mosis, als of het Mose soude geschreven hebben / alhoewel de wijste en geleerste
luyden het daar voor houden / dat het eenen *Esdra* geschreven heeft.'
[46] Ibid. 95–7: 'ten waar de Schrift door gewelt / van vuur en swaard / staande gehouden
wierd / sy soude in 't kort vervallen'.
[47] Ibid. 95.
[48] Ibid. 96.

150   DEMOCRATIC THOUGHT FROM MACHIAVELLI TO SPINOZA

the author of the *Unschuldige Nachrichten* (1714), Koerbagh, under the pretence of translating everything into his mother tongue, lumped together not only the entire Christian religion but also all religions in general to make a mockery of them. 'He appears to have been, if not a wicked atheist, at least a crass naturalist.'[49]

Some see in Koerbagh a disciple of Van den Enden by virtue of his naturalism (or atheism), and indeed, many of the dictionary entries are reminiscent of the ideas of Van den Enden who, as we saw in the preceding chapter, like De la Court takes his starting point in a Hobbesian naturalism, although he, now unlike Hobbes and perhaps also De la Court, undeniably follows a revolutionary democratic programme. Van den Enden's optimistic view of the multitude – ignorant, albeit not by definition so, not through their own fault, and still susceptible to the truth – yields an emphasis on education and the notion of freedom of speech as a necessary element for the improvement of every political order which is by definition susceptible to improvement. With his dictionary project, Koerbagh proceeds from the same assumption. Had the 'common people' not been susceptible to truth, a vernacular translation or the kind of dictionary he was writing would have been useless. And there is more. In the entry on the Bible, Koerbagh points to the endless quarrels among the theologians, which had been a reason for Van den Enden not to admit them to the colony in Delaware. The quibbles over biblical interpretation arise from the prejudiced teaching of the Christian prelates, which is in fact nothing but a mask for the way they abuse political power, and reduces politics to the waging of war. Accordingly, Koerbagh describes a 'Bishop' as an

> overseer of the church / overseer of religion. [. . .] But later they gradually assumed increasing power / majesty and profit / indeed! dominion / not only in the spiritual / but also in the worldly. And in the end they even managed / to become lords of countries and cities / who, instead of teaching the church, / went to wage war out of pride.[50]

---

[49] Anonymous, *Unschuldige Nachrichten von alten und neuen theologischen Sachen*, 1714, 231–2. The *Unschuldige Nachrichten* included a number of entries in German translation, which earned Koerbagh and his *Een Bloemhof* a certain renown in Germany. *Een Bloemhof* is referenced by Edelmann (*Abgenöthigtes Jedoch Andern nicht wieder aufgenöthigtes Glaubens-Bekentniß*, 288) and Leibniz (*Nouveaux essais sur l'entendement humain*, III, §5).

[50] Koerbagh, *Een Bloemhof*, 99–100: 'opsiender der Gemeente / opsiender der Godsdienst. [. . .] Maar naderhand hebben sy allenskens hun meerder en meerder magt / grootsheyd en voordeel / ja! heerschappij angemaatigt / niet alleen in't geestelijke /

TRANSLATION AND TRUTH: A DIALOGUE 151

To persevere, a political order established 'on the pillar of some religion' constantly needs to 'banish / curse / hang / burn / and kill'.[51] Nevertheless, 'no one is powerful enough to / judge a *heresy* / since every person is, by his own prejudice, inclined to his own persuasion / [thinking] it to be the best', and this is why each persuasion accuses the others of heresy, 'ultimately making them all heretics'.[52] The Dutch word for 'heretic' (*ketter*) means 'follower', and of course we are all followers of our own persuasion. People would have the word 'heresy' mean 'unbelief' or 'bad faith', but this is not the meaning the word has. Who, in any case, can judge the faith of another? Like Van den Enden, Koerbagh emphasises the multiplicity and diversity of the religions. Each nation has a different religion, and each nation claims and believes that its religion is the best, and, in fact, will attempt to sustain it, not with reason and truth,

> but with the violence of fist and sword / gallows and wheel. And each damns and curses the other as the most unbelieving and godless / because there is no agreement on religion or religious views. This is great proof indeed / that the true, reasonable religion does not exist in the world: for it would not need to be maintained through violence.[53]

It indeed seems, as the author of the *Unschuldige Nachrichten* claimed, that Koerbagh's criticism or indifference extends to all religions and that he proceeds from a materialist ontology or naturalism. Apart from the religious concepts, which are deconstructed to their political significance, often meaning their deceptive or oppressive instrumental character, there are also the concepts appealing to religion which are deconstructed to an absurd meaninglessness. For example, *Christendom* means 'territory of the anointed', *Christians* 'anointed ones' and *Christ* 'Anointed one'. An anointed one is a person 'who has been anointed with some fragrant tree sap / or oil / or had it

---

maar ook in 't waereldlijke. En zijn eydelijk soo veer gekomen / datse zijn geworden heeren van landen en steden / die dikwijls in de plaats van de Gemeente te onderwijsen / uyt grootsheyd gingen oorlog voeren.'

[51] Ibid. 285–8.

[52] Ibid. 337–9.

[53] Ibid. 556–7: 'maar met geweld van vuyst en swaerd / galg en rad. En elk vloekt en scheld den ander om 't seerst voor ongeloovig en godloos / om datter soo effen op een stipken geen overeenkoming is in de Godsdienst of in eenig gevoelen de Godsdienst raakende. Een groot bewijs voorwaar / dat de regte redelijke Godsdienst niet inde waereld is: want die had niet van noode door gewelt staande gehouden te worden.'

poured over them'.[54] Or how would you conceive of a God who is *schepper*? Playing on the homonymy of the Dutch verb *scheppen*, which can mean both 'to create' and 'to scoop', Koerbagh writes that a *schepper* is someone who 'scoops something / whether water from the trough / or freely from the pot / or else a tool for scooping'.[55] The entire creation story thus appears 'farcical and odd' to him, and he charges that its writer must have thought he was only writing for 'very dumb, slavish Jews' who could be convinced of anything, and that if they only persist long enough in that belief, many others will follow them, which history indeed proves to have been the case.[56] Yet another example is transubstantiation, a concept used by Roman Catholic clergy to maintain the possibility of 'incarnation' (*Godmenschmaaking*) from a small piece of bread that nevertheless remains normal bread. And since substance means 'that which stands under', transubstantiation would, logically speaking, mean 'that which stands over-under'.[57] Metaphysical concepts are stripped to their absurd, even comical core using the same process. Substance means 'that which stands under', meaning it is dependent on something else, and therefore does not mean independence, as people would have it mean. A similar 'independence' that exists of itself, is not caused, and does not depend on anything else, only applies to the being that never began, is not susceptible to time, and is called God by Koerbagh, that is, 'ipstance' (*Ipstantie*).[58]

As a philologist/philosopher, Koerbagh is particularly attentive to the use of prepositions in compounds. For example, he carefully dissects the term *metaphysica* as a compound from *meta*, meaning after or behind, and *physica*, the study of nature. Yet it is often translated with the wrong preposition as 'the study of that which is above nature', as if such a thing as knowledge above and beyond nature could exist, even though nature is 'all that is'.[59] Moreover, if people really did mean 'above', they 'ought to say *hyperphysica*, not *metaphysica*'. But since there is only one nature, and nothing beyond it (which is comprehended in the language), there can also only be natural

---

[54] Ibid. 138–40. Matthias Knutzen used the same blasphemic words ('geschmiert [. . .] Christ und geschmierter') to disparage Christianity. See Schröder's commentary on this with respect to the *Epistola* (*Amicus Amicis Amica!*), in his edition of the *Schriften und Materialien*, 60.

[55] Koerbagh, *Een Bloemhof*, 207: 'die iets schept / 't zy water yt de bak / of vry uyt de pot / het betekent ook een tuyg waar men mede schept'.

[56] Ibid. 577–81.

[57] Ibid. 630.

[58] Ibid. 381.

[59] Ibid. 444.

science, which in turn means that both words – i.e. '*hyperphysica*, the science of that which is above nature / and *metaphysica*, the science of that which is behind nature' – are useless.[60] Koerbagh knows, of course, that the term comes from Aristotle who wrote books that went on to bear that title. In Aristotle, the title does not refer to something that supposedly stands beyond natural knowledge (for there is nothing there), but to the order in which the books are to be read: the books on *metaphysica* after the books on '*Physica*'.[61] Most of the ideas and arguments developed in *Een Bloemhof* – i.e. the genealogy of concepts, the critique of false theories and of those who benefit from them, naturalism – return in a slightly revised form, or more often the same form, in *Een Ligt schijnende in duystere plaatsen*, likewise dating from 1668, which can for that reason be considered a systematic exposition, or again a 'translation' as it were, of the same critical reflections. 'Metaphysics' is the wrong word for what people mean by it, and it should be called 'hyperphysics', but such a thing is an absurdity. 'For although people say that that science treats of God and the spirits, both good and evil, and the souls of human beings, etc., we say that all nature is God, nature is not above nature', and so physics must treat of the soul as well as of God. All other things of which so-called metaphysics treats are idle words 'that have no meaning'.[62]

5. *Een Ligt schijnende in duystere plaatsen*

There are two kinds of reasoning, as Koerbagh writes in the beginning of *Een Ligt*, internal reasoning and external reasoning.[63] Internal reasoning is reason or thought, an act of the mind which seeks to grasp its objects and

---

[60] Ibid.

[61] Ibid. 444–5.

[62] Koerbagh, *Een Ligt*, 474 noted: 'Want alschoon men segt, in die wetenschap word gehandelt van God en de geesten, so goede als kwaade, en van de ziel des menschen enz. wij seggen de gantsche natuur is God, de natuur is niet boven de natuur'. As we have noted, in Hobbes we find the same critique that language abuse leads to error, illusion, deceit and oppression. Hobbes too sees in the use of Latin (or the absence of translations for Latin words) in the vernacular a structural example of language abuse, and, of course, wrote and published his own *chef-d'oeuvre* in the English vernacular. See *Leviathan*, Chap. IV, Of Speech. The same critique of the use (abuse) of language as a power dispositive can be found in De la Court, Van den Enden and Koerbagh, but in Hobbes this critique does not serve a political preference for the republic but for the king and the monarchy (which also entails a divergent view on the freedom of press and expression).

[63] Koerbagh, *Een Ligt*, 56.

154   DEMOCRATIC THOUGHT FROM MACHIAVELLI TO SPINOZA

their names. External reasoning is the expression or interpretation of what we have understood internally, which we must use to communicate our internal reasoning to others. In order to do so, we of course need to use well-known and intelligible words, or else speech or writing would be pointless. Since Koerbagh has taken it upon himself to write on matters of theology and religion, a topic of interest to everyone (which is why he addresses 'all people'), he has opted to use the 'language that is known to everyone', namely Dutch.[64] In departure from De la Court, for whom the link between language and politics relates to the rhetoric of the Italian Renaissance, for Koerbagh the question of language has multiple layers. Here he writes in the vernacular and as such addresses himself to a general (universal) audience, and he does so, like De la Court and even more so Van den Enden, from the perspective of a republican/democratic programme. Furthermore, Koerbagh composes dictionaries, of two kinds: *'t Nieuw Woorden-Boek der Regten* and *Een Bloemhof*. In the former, linguistic purism also has a political, republican-democratic dimension. In the latter, the political-critical standpoint of the linguistic purism is – still – supported by and interwoven with a revolutionary philosophical view, a naturalistic perspective like that of Hobbes and Machiavelli, which we encounter in contemporary works like *Theophrastus redivivus* and *De jure ecclesiasticorum*. As such, the question of language is posed on the theoretical level and at the same time plays a role in the formation of (radically new) theory. Otherwise stated, there is a turn that takes place, which not only plays out on the surface but is intrinsically connected to the new perspective and is determinative for its content. The linguistic critique is executed on the basis of the materialist perspective, which is at the same time itself shaped by a philological analysis and/or focus on the externality of the language. An essential aspect of this process is the thematisation of the distinction between internal and external reasoning and internal and external religion. And although *De jure ecclesiasticorum* was composed in Latin (and as such not addressed to everyone, which therefore prevents it from earning a label as politically radical), the connection between naturalism and the internal-external distinction may have inspired Koerbagh to place language praxis/translation at the centre of his politics *and* ontology. His critique of religion and metaphysics evinces the political and epistemological critique to which Renaissance naturalism had brought the anonymous author of *Theophrastus redivivus*. This clandestine treatise, written in Latin, is explicitly not intended for a general (universal) audience; on the contrary, its contents are, somewhat

[64] Ibid.

contradictorily, addressed exclusively to an educated elite. The fact that *Theophrastus* only circulated in a highly clandestine fashion (as no one appears to have read the text, nor even written about or referenced it) and was written in isolation from and independently of the radical Dutch scene, turns the similarity in content into a powerful argument for the solid grounding of its contents, which break with each and every tradition. On the other hand, it is undoubtedly because the clandestine manuscript was ensconced in the most secret of cabinets and did not divulge its epistemologically and politically radical message to a general audience (which therefore did not receive or discuss that message) that it did not take the next step, which Koerbagh does take.

For what is it that remains once the critique has been completed, after both religion and metaphysics have been deconstructed to their hidden political power agendas or tragicomic futility? For Koerbagh, the next step is a reflection on general principles, categories and distinctions, an analysis of concepts and linguistic expressions and communicating the results to others. If there is no God distinct from nature, it means that there are only natural laws, and this materialist ontology (the result of internal reasonings) paradoxically brings us back to the symbolic order of language (the external reasonings). The first theme addressed by Koerbagh once he has distinguished between internal and external reasonings, noting also that this theme is of interest to the multitude and explains his choice for the vernacular, is 'Being, *Jehova* in Hebrew, which is simple, unique, eternal, infinite, without beginning, omnipresent, independent, immutable, omniscient, all-powerful and absolutely perfect.'[65] The Hebrews called that being Jehova 'because it is truly essential, essence or being. It does not simply exist in itself, but it is also the essence and being of all things.'[66] The first theme on which he focuses is 'being', all that is, in its capacity of being, or, that which is at the foundation of everything that is. It seems as if Aristotle's articulation and philosophical analysis of this most universal being does not suffice for Koerbagh, at least not along the path he has chosen to follow. 'This Being (which is called God, a word deriving, with slight alteration, from an old Dutch composite word 'i od' meaning he on high) is infinite, having eternally been all in all or the essence of all modes of being, and consisting of infinite attributes.'[67] Our problems have their origin in a misguided understanding of the Bible, both the books

---

[65] Ibid.
[66] Ibid. 56–8.
[67] Op. cit., 58.

156 DEMOCRATIC THOUGHT FROM MACHIAVELLI TO SPINOZA

themselves and the words we find in them, beginning with that which we call 'God'.

'The Apostle John conceives of God as a spirit (. . .) but he does not say or explain what a spirit is or in what the essence of a spirit consists.'[68] In the footnote, Koerbagh observes that the original text actually speaks of 'breathing, blowing or wind', which leads him to conclude that the Greeks or biblical authors did not know what a spirit is, for if they had, they would have written – and correctly so – that 'a spirit is a thinking thing'.[69] While the theologians would object that God's spirituality is to be interpreted differently, as improper speech, Koerbagh counters that there are only two possible reasons for someone to write improperly or ambiguously: the first is out of ignorance, and the second is in order to deceive (which, so Koerbagh ironically adds, could not apply here). 'The main attributes of this Being are extension and thought.'[70] Since extension and thought have always been what they are and did not suddenly come into existence (as is clear from the nature of the case, nor do we find anything about the matter in Scripture), it remains a mystery why some claim that 'there has been an act of creation out of nothing'.[71] According to Koerbagh, the deception of some is clearly exposed in this way: they think that, because they are theologians, they can just do and say whatever they want, convincing the simple-minded of anything and keeping them in ignorance. Extension and thought are universal categories, abstract principles. Whether being was before the world is a totally absurd question. When you say 'being', you are talking about all possible modes of existence/being in general, in its capacity of extension or thought. When you say 'earlier', you are talking about something that started existing before something else, neither of them eternal or existence/being in general. When you say 'world', you are talking about the 'entire reality of the world' (*gantse wesentlijkheyd des waerelds*), which is something infinite; the world in general cannot be conceived as finite. For where would the world's outermost boundaries be, and what would be immediately adjacent to it? What, then, are we talking about when we say 'being' or 'world'? Koerbagh once again applies a philological analysis, and does not explain the opening words of Scripture as the theologians normally do, but according to their sense and the truth of the matter. Accordingly, he reads '*beraeschit*' in Genesis 1:1 as two words,

[68] Ibid. Translation modified.
[69] Ibid. 58–60.
[70] Ibid. 62.
[71] Ibid.

TRANSLATION AND TRUTH: A DIALOGUE 157

'b meaning in and *raeschit* meaning main; the original, or root word *rosch* also means head, chief, supreme. Head, as everyone knows, is also generally used for some chief or supreme thing. As such, it does not speak here of a beginning or time, but of chief.'[72]

The essence of Koerbagh's critique is the exposure of the method used by the theologians in their interpretation of Scripture, not because they do not know any better but because they want to keep the simple in dark ignorance. They explain a concept expressing a reflection on general attributes as something existing in space and time. The most general attribute of all existing things is the fact *that* all these things exist, and the word by which this most universal (chief, primary, supreme) attribute is expressed is 'being'. Of course, the concept – this 'being' – does not refer to a thing that came into existence at some point in time. At the beginning of his exposition, Koerbagh had made it clear that his argument was intended for the multitude of common people. It is of utmost importance for all people to gain insight into the true meaning of Scripture and into what it means to reflect on general attributes. That he does not intend to erect a new metaphysics or religious structure is clear from the turn the text takes. While the theologians go on about the multiple fiction of a being subject to passions that created the world out of nothing, Koerbagh analyses the opening words and phrases of Genesis so as to arrive at a totally different meaning, both logically and politically. He reads *bara* as 'gave shape', which cannot be understood as making something out of nothing, and certainly not as *scheppen*, the Dutch term typically used for 'creating', which is more properly reserved for – Koerbagh plays here on the homonymous significance of *scheppen* as 'creating' and 'scooping' – the ladles of a kitchen maid. *Elohim* means 'powerful', a term that does indeed apply to the being, albeit as an 'adjective', while the theologians commonly understand it as a noun.[73] 'The word *elohim* is also used for rulers who are powerful through their lawful use of power derived from the consent of the people', or it is applied to tyrants and despots who through the 'abuse of power', which they claim for themselves and obtain through violence, are indeed often terrifyingly powerful, 'and the more ignorant and simple a people are, the greater and more unlimited is the unlawful power that such a government can wield, but the more knowledgeable and intelligent a people are, the smaller and more limited is the government's potential to abuse its power'.[74] Koerbagh adds two footnotes to the terms 'lawful power' and 'abuse

---

[72] Ibid. 66. The final two sentences of this quotation are absent in Wielema's translation.
[73] Ibid. 68.
[74] Ibid. 68–70.

158 DEMOCRATIC THOUGHT FROM MACHIAVELLI TO SPINOZA

of power'. A lawful use of power is 'when the government uses the power vested in it by the people in all matters relating to the condition of the country, to protect the freedom, prosperity and interest of the people. And these men are truly powerful, though not above the power of the people.'[75] Lawful, legitimate government power does not transcend the power of the people but is aimed at their welfare and freedom. Abuse of power is

> when a government starts to abuse, to the detriment and disadvantage of the people (that is, to the impairment of the people's freedom), the power that is bestowed on the government by the people in all matters pertaining to the country to protect the people and the people's freedom. And power is also abused when a government, unsatisfied with the power bestowed on it (. . .) seeks to seize even more power beyond that power, whether by devious means or by the force of foreign allies, to impair the people's freedom and prosperity.[76]

Consequently, in Genesis, which is about the powerful, the term obviously refers to 'powerful people', and the adjective *elohim* is most clearly not just to be identified with *Jehova*. Anyone who 'judges without prejudice' will understand what Koerbagh wants to say.[77]

Unfortunately, this was also understood by Koerbagh's opponents – the governments that were not satisfied with their power, did not protect the prosperity and freedom of the people, and for that reason preferred to keep them in ignorance. In *Een Ligt*, Koerbagh systematically deconstructs all religious principles of Christendom, and since the systematic nature of his unmasking means that nothing is posited in their place, the work represents a serious threat to those in power who are out for abuse. As Michiel Wielema has demonstrated, Koerbagh shows that Scripture does not support theology, but then goes on to deconstruct the authority of the theologians and the Bible alike.[78] In fact, he does even more. All essential doctrines of the Christian faith are dismantled so that the entire Christian teaching is completely swept aside. Yet he also breaks with the foundational teachings of the three monotheistic religions, making him an atheist. Koerbagh's critique of religion is (onto-)logical, does not aim to replace one faith by another, and is as such political and radical. His philological reflections

---

[75] Ibid.
[76] Ibid. Translation modified.
[77] Ibid. 72.
[78] Wielema, *The March of the Libertines*, 86–7.

read like a mathematical equation with atheism at the centre, which fully occupied his opponents and drew their attention away from the outcome of the equation, which is the abuse of power by those in power. The story recounted by Zacharias Konrad von Uffenbach in his *Merkwürdige Reisen durch Niedersachsen Holland und Engeland* is illustrative in that regard:

> It is said that this Koerbagh was an excellent mathematician but a bad bird who, during his incarceration for these writings in the Amsterdam prison where he was to succumb to illness, upon being addressed by the preachers for this atheism, only answered them that two times two is four, and two times four is eight, in order to show them that he would not listen to or accept anything but mathematical demonstrations.[79]

In Chapter 2 of *Een Ligt*, Koerbagh demonstrates the absurdity of the Trinity through a simple mathematical demonstration (three times one cannot be one), adding that one will not find anything about a Trinity in Scripture. It is the church's 'masters and teachers' who think they can paralyse simple people with this absurdity – but the wise have always fiercely resisted it. The simple are full of prejudices and can be convinced of anything, and the majority of people are, of course, simple. Koerbagh is not talking about the poor here, but about 'people of ordinary knowledge, judgement and education' who, had they been more experienced in knowledge, judgement and erudition, would not have so many prejudices, be less trusting, and immediately see 'that they are being misled'.[80] The same process of critique is then applied to the Christ, the son of God: 'No human being can become God (. . .); consequently the reverse must be also true, that God cannot become a human being or assume humanity.'[81] Christ or Jesus, the anointed, is not a saviour, he has accomplished nothing by his death, his mother cannot have conceived him as a virgin, he cannot have risen from the dead, and he is not the saviour awaited by the Jews.

By the end of Koerbagh's analysis, nothing is left of the basic principle of the three Abrahamic religions, by which God is understood as a person who rewards and punishes and as such forms the foundation of good and evil. Once again, he takes his deconstruction a step further. To date, no 'legislator, lawyer, theologian or anyone else' has succeeded in explaining

---

[79] Uffenbach, *Merkwürdige Reisen*, 66.
[80] Koerbagh, *Een Ligt*, 78.
[81] Ibid. 110.

160 DEMOCRATIC THOUGHT FROM MACHIAVELLI TO SPINOZA

why something is good or evil.[82] To date no thesis has been proposed for deducing a fixed normative criterion to determine what is good and what is evil. Koerbagh also explains why no such fixed criterion can in fact be found: 'For one and the same activity can be good or evil, and why will it now be good, and now evil, other than in relation to something or other.'[83] On the basis of this neutral relativity, he posits the general and practicable rule that 'all of someone's activities are good when they are advantageous to himself and to his neighbour as well, or when they are advantageous to himself and not harmful to his neighbour, or not harmful to himself and advantageous to his neighbour'.[84] In that light, the regulations of the ecclesiastical officials are 'purely and simply trivia and deceit in conflict with Scripture and human freedom'.[85] Moreover, the ecclesiastical officials 'have no lawful power to burden us or our consciences with unnecessary nonsense and concoctions'.[86] The fact that the ecclesiastical officials have indeed managed to (be able to) do so is a result of the ignorance of the people, their gullibility, and their negligence in the search for the truth. The clerics forbid pleasure, but what harm could anyone suffer himself or inflict upon anyone else by going to the theatre from time to time or by enjoying dance, music and song? Koerbagh poses questions that remain relevant in contemporary debates concerning culture, religion and one's public appearance. What harm could there be 'when someone wears their hair somewhat longer, reaching down to the ears, or, as some would have it, to the middle of the ear? Or when someone wears some kind of stitching or collar or some bows, ribbons or lace on their clothes'?[87]

Everything that can be advantageous to a person 'consists of words and deeds', and the same is true for all that by which someone can inflict harm upon his neighbour.[88] With thoughts no one can do either good or evil to another. Even if one were to think good or evil thoughts about a person for a hundred years, they would not be advantageous or harmful to that person. But when these thoughts are expressed in words or put into action, the resulting words or acts can indeed be harmful or advantageous. On the other hand, it is possible to harm *oneself* with mere thoughts. If one harms oneself through hate, envy, malice, jealousy, or avaricious or lustful desires,

[82] Ibid. 206.
[83] Ibid.
[84] Ibid. 208.
[85] Ibid. 210.
[86] Ibid. 212.
[87] Ibid.
[88] Ibid. 214.

or burdens one's own conscience through angry and vindictive passions or other improper thoughts, one 'does wrong and sins most against oneself'.[89]

All these things lead Koerbagh to conclude that true religion must come from reason, but since people are lazy in the pursuit of knowledge and rather apply themselves to thoughts that are harmful to them, they have fallen 'from a rational religion to a religion full of superstitions, fictions and fabrications'.[90] Turks, Jews and the various currents of the 'anointed' (Christians) which Koerbagh each gives separate treatment – all of them appear to suffer from the same superstition of war and all are convinced that violence and death can serve their God. They also believe in miracles. And although the Socinians reject the Trinity, they still believe miracle stories and worship a human being, making them guilty of idolatry.[91] That the Roman Catholic religion is completely unreasonable is beyond dispute, but all forms of the Christian religion, including the Reformed, participate in slander and insults. The problem is that the clerics (of all religions) make not only the laws pertaining to religion but thereby often also the laws pertaining to the state, 'which ought not to happen' since that right and power accrues to the government, as Hobbes has also shown in *Leviathan*.[92] Religions that preach violence or fantasies cause distrust among the people, and where there is no trust there can be no love, and where there is no love 'there cannot be unity, and where there is no unity there cannot be a stable state, and where there is no stable state people live in constant fear of each other, and where people live in constant fear of each other they are constantly in a state of unhappiness'.[93] To Koerbagh's mind,

> the clergy, with their factions, conflicts and horrific violence, as well as the governments that help them in this, openly demonstrate either that they hate the truth because of advantage and pleasure and do not wish

---

[89] Ibid. 216.

[90] Ibid. 218.

[91] For Koerbagh and Socinianism, see Salatowsky, 'Socinian Headaches: Adriaan Koerbagh and the Antitrinitarians', 165–203.

[92] Koerbagh, *Een Ligt*, 252.

[93] Ibid. 274. This phrase fits in flawlessly with the argument of Hobbes in the *Leviathan* that had inspired Koerbagh, as he had himself already explicitly indicated. Nevertheless, Koerbagh's formulation is such that it passes flawlessly into a matching democratic political theory, which therefore differs from Hobbes, also on the philosophical level, in particular with respect to the state of nature. For Hobbes, the state of nature is the source of violence and something that must be overcome, while for Koerbagh, the state of nature is neutral and violence is the result of religious fictions and a specific political intervention/fiction/dominion.

162 DEMOCRATIC THOUGHT FROM MACHIAVELLI TO SPINOZA

to bring it into the open, or that religions are just a lot of fabrications and chatter to keep bad people in check (as Machiavelli and some others would have it), and that people therefore have to uphold the religion that is in a country with fire and sword, no matter which religion that is, and that there is for them no true, reasonable and only God.[94]

It is the theologians who maintain their religion through violence and governments that aid them in their deception – both parties in pursuit of their own advantage rather than the welfare of the multitude.

The manuscript of *Een Ligt* was brought to the publisher in 1668, the same year that saw the appearance of *Een Bloemhof*, both signed on the title page with the same periphrasis: 'Peaceland True-mouth / investigator of the Truth' (*Vreederijk Waarmond / ondersoeker der Waarheyd*). In both works, Koerbagh presents explosive, critical ideas on religion and politics within a materialist framework. Just like Spinoza would do in his *Ethics*, he deduces this immanent perspective logically, proceeding from principles that are universally valid for everyone. The criticism takes the shape of a philological analysis connecting theoretical and religious statements with their (political or other) intention. As we have shown, his purpose in *Een Bloemhof* and *Een Ligt* is to expose the truth to the common people so that they might be stimulated to intellectual study of their own and no longer allow themselves to be deceived and oppressed by power-abusing governments. Deception and violence are related to an erroneous interpretation of Scripture by which power is ascribed to theologians, and so the Scriptures must be interpreted anew. Koerbagh takes a stance in all the important debates of the 1660s, and he does so using logical arguments demonstrating the necessity of his radical views: in favour of total freedom of speech or the *libertas philosophandi*, against the power of the ecclesiastical officials, in favour of a naturalist anthropology and ontology, against the teachings of Christendom (and, by extension, Islam and Judaism), and in favour of reason and a free republic. His works are replete with references to Hobbes's *Leviathan*, which had appeared a year earlier in Van Berkel's translation. Of course, there were also the works of De la Court that appeared between 1660 and 1662 and went back to Hobbes, albeit less unambigous in their democratic radicality and less explicit in their theoretical foundation. There were the pamphlets of Van den Enden from 1662 and 1665 with their unambiguous plea for general (universal) freedom and equality. And there was the Latin treatise of the anonymous Antistius Constans from 1665, whose critique of ecclesiastical

[94] Koerbagh, *Een Ligt*, 274.

TRANSLATION AND TRUTH: A DIALOGUE 163

power is connected on the theoretical level with the naturalism of Hobbes. Finally, Koerbagh's work cannot be considered apart from the fierce debates over the interpretation of Scripture evoked by Lodewijk Meyer's *Philosophia S. Scripturae Interpres*, which appeared in Latin in 1666 and the next year in Dutch translation.

Meyer was the first to proclaim the notion that truths are expressed improperly in the Bible, making philosophy necessary to interpret them properly. Koerbagh continues on this trajectory when he discusses the theme of God as the origin from which everything proceeds. Should someone ask him why he does not use the term *schepper* (i.e. creator), his answer is 'that God is improperly called a *schepper*', since a *schepper* is someone who 'scoops' (*schept*) something from a container or jar of water.

> Furthermore, the world is not created (or rather made or given form and shape) from nothing / but the world in general has been from eternity / and anyone who does not believe this / must be able to refute / the rule / [that] from nothing comes nothing / with sharp arguments / either from Scripture or from the wisdom of the world.[95]

Creation out of nothing cannot be demonstrated on the basis of Scripture, since it does not contain a single phrase relevant to the matter. Nor can it be demonstrated on the basis of worldly wisdom, since it conflicts with reason. It is the theologians who would have people believe that the world was created or made out of nothing, even though they actually know better and even though this proposition conflicts with Scripture. 'For from nothing comes nothing': that has always been true and will always be true. It holds true in religion as well as worldly wisdom, for the simple reason that there is only a single kind of wisdom, such that 'the term wisdom of the world comprehends all the wisdom / science and knowledge there is'.[96] In other words, there are not two truths; there is only 'worldly knowledge', and nothing comes from nothing, God/Being is not the creator of the world. The theologians claim so many things that they would have us believe about God/Being, although they can only be said of human beings.

---

[95] Koerbagh, *Een Bloemhof*, 207.
[96] Ibid. 135–6. Mignini draws a line from Koerbagh's work, his view on the world which is not created (but eternal), on the impossibility of thinking about 'nothing', and on the double truth theory (which he refutes) to Averroism. In this way, Mignini emphasises the importance of the work of Koerbagh, Hobbes and Spinoza for the radical Enlightenment; see '*Een ligt schijnende in duystere plaatsen*: Adriaan Koerbagh tra averroismo e libertinismo', 167–200.

164 DEMOCRATIC THOUGHT FROM MACHIAVELLI TO SPINOZA

Koerbagh not only translates theological, traditional and religious concepts to their true, worldly and social-ethical significance, but he also does so systematically, step by step, arguing towards an immanent view of the world. Along this route, he arrives at radically subversive conclusions – that sins are mistakes and evil spirits evil thoughts, that things without bodies have no appearance, that imagination can deceive, and that ignorant people are easily misled. Religions are shown to be irrational, only able to maintain themselves in politics with deceit or violence. For this reason, they have to be limited within the commonwealth, interpreted with worldly wisdom, unmasked and exposed, so that their power evaporates. Immediately after Koerbagh brought the explosive manuscript of *Een Ligt* to the printer, he was arrested and sentenced to the Rasphuis penitentiary in Amsterdam, where he died in 1669, less than a year later, broken, sick and ruined by the devastating circumstances.

VII

Spinoza's Reversal

1. 1661–1665

Spinoza's earliest extant letter dates from September 1661 and was addressed to Henry Oldenburg. At the time Spinoza was living in the town of Rijnsburg, where the London-based German philosopher had visited him, after which he requested him to continue their philosophical discussion by way of correspondence. In this first letter, Spinoza can already be found referring to the geometric manner of demonstration and offering a definition of God, on which basis he adduces three theses that we also encounter in part I of the *Ethica*: 'First, that two substances cannot exist in nature unless they differ in their whole essence. Second, that a substance cannot be produced, but that it is of its essence to exist. Third, that every substance must be infinite, *or* supremely perfect in its kind.'[1] The modern philosophers Bacon

---

[1] *Ep.* II [to Henry Oldenburg]; *CWS* I, 166. Translation modified. Where applicable, we reference Gebhardt's edition of Spinoza's *Opera* as follows: *Ep.* II, G IV, 7–9. For issues of language and translation, see Akkerman, *Studies in the Posthumous Works of Spinoza*; 'La pénurie de mots', 9–38; Steenbakkers, *Spinoza's Ethica from Manuscript to Print*; Lagrée and Moreau, 'Spinoza ou la puissance de la traduction', 377–92. In Curley's translation, an italicised *or* indicates a Latin *sive* or *seu*, which generally marks equivalence (rather than alternative, for which *aut* or *vel* is the preferred term); see Preface, *CWS* I, xv. Furthermore, the use of the terms *potentia* and *potestas* by Spinoza – and, more generally, in scholastic and neo-scholastic writings – is subject to extensive debate. In volume 2 of his translation, Curley renders *potentia* as power and *potestas* as 'power (i.e. with the prime symbol). See the entry for 'Power' in the 'Glossary-Index' in *CWS* II, 649–50; the view Curley expresses there in volume 2 is slightly adapted from his earlier view in *CWS* I, 651. We have chosen not to follow this convention, but we either simply use the relevant Latin term, or supply the Latin in brackets, or else add a specifying adjective, such as 'natural power' for *potentia* and 'political power' for *potestas*.

166   DEMOCRATIC THOUGHT FROM MACHIAVELLI TO SPINOZA

and Descartes, he adds, erred in their understanding of the first principles, and failed to grasp the true nature of the human mind and the true cause of human error.[2] Their lack of insight, misunderstanding and failures can all be traced back to this one error of Descartes, that 'the human will is free and wider than the intellect'.[3] Descartes was obviously on Spinoza's mind those days, since it was during that same time that he held philosophical discussions with his friends and 'students', dictating Cartesian teaching to them on the basis of his notes which he at their request turned into a book published in 1663. Yet this first letter to Oldenburg, along with subsequent letters from late 1661, reveal that Spinoza actually held views of his own on first philosophy, God and method, which distinguished him from Bacon and Descartes. He was likewise working on turning these views into a book which he himself would nonetheless never publish out of his fear for the response it would evoke from the theologians and ministers. Oldenburg too did not immediately agree with what he read and therefore plied him with questions and objections, to which Spinoza responded by insisting that people 'are not created, but only generated, and that their bodies already existed before, though formed differently'.[4] Each subsequent letter contains different formulations intended to make Spinoza's own, radically new views more explicit. The bottom line is that Spinoza did not distinguish God from nature as everyone known to him had done.[5] In July 1662, Oldenburg tried to convince him to publish his ideas 'both in Philosophy and in Theology', 'whatever rumblings there may be among the foolish Theologians', noting that the Dutch Republic is very free and 'gives great freedom for philosophizing'.[6]

Spinoza's earliest extant correspondence coincides closely in time with Van den Enden's efforts to launch his project for a new colony in Delaware which, in spite of its failure, still issued in his *Kort verhael van Nieuw-Nederlants Gelegentheit*.[7] Van den Enden's first letter to the Colonial Office dates from 22 November 1661, and the last one from 25 May 1662. By the latter date, it was clear that the projected colony would fail, but Van den Enden had still become so enthralled with politics that he continued to develop his political reflections, first in the *Kort verhael* and then more systematically in the *Vrye Politijke Stellingen* which appeared three years

---

[2] *Ep*. II [to Henry Oldenburg]; CWS I, 167.
[3] Ibid.
[4] *Ep*. IV [to Henry Oldenburg]; CWS I, 172.
[5] *Ep*. VI [to Henry Oldenburg]; CWS I, 188.
[6] *Ep*. VII [from Henry Oldenburg]; CWS I, 189.
[7] See above, Chapter V.2.

later. As we have seen, in the afterword of the *Kort verhael* Van den Enden concluded that the establishment and maintenance of a free state in New Netherlands will not succeed unless the necessary reforms have first been enacted in Holland itself. For if a state does not grant equal freedom and prohibits all talk of reform, it has nothing to offer a freedom-loving people that wants to settle in another place. In fact, the prohibition of speech is strange, also in the colonising country itself and in every political respect. If no one in a state is allowed to mention political reform, it can only mean that this state does not stand in need of improvement – but this is absurd. For improvement is by definition always necessary due to the dynamics of political relationships and given also the very constitution of human nature. Human beings are always susceptible to mood changes, resulting in conflicts that have the potential to escalate to war or to threaten rulers so that they resort to violence or corrupt and malicious rule. For the sake of its own stability, a government must always be open to improvement. A badly governed state plunges itself into a chaos which generally only snowballs and yields greater dangers, such that people end up being subject to ever growing fears that morph into the desperate courage of those who 'do not dare to speak with their mouth, [but] use their fists'.[8] Rebellion and civil war are not the result of the freedom of speech. On the contrary, freedom of speech works to *prevent* degeneration into violence.

In his anonymous *Vrye Politijke Stellingen* (1665), Van den Enden arrives at a similar conclusion, albeit via another route. The greatest danger facing a free republic based on the principle of equal freedom is deceit, when falsehood and prejudices are spread about. Such practices are commonly applied by the so-called religions which use their 'lieutenants' (i.e. the theologians and preachers) to instil fear of or irrational hope for the hereafter in the people, reducing them to a slavish condition. Falsehood and prejudices are sustained by the so-called erudite who use their titles, tradition and accumulated authority to establish hierarchies, thus replacing knowledge with subjection and submission. After all, deception, prejudices and superstition depend on and are spread by the use of veiled or mystifying language. Regardless of the specific form assumed by deceit, the deceived party is always complicit in its own deception, illusion and slavery. The victims' only available defence against such deceptive practices is the acquisition of knowledge and the fulfilment of their duty to exercise the freedom to philosophise.

---

[8] Van den Enden, *Kort verhael*, 83; cf. Koerbagh, who speaks of 'abuse of power' in *A Light*, 68–70; see above, Chapter VI.5.

168   DEMOCRATIC THOUGHT FROM MACHIAVELLI TO SPINOZA

In early 1665, Spinoza received another letter inviting him to an epistolary exchange, this one from Willem van Blyenbergh, a grain merchant living in Dordrecht and, more importantly, a diligent reader of his book on Descartes's *Principia*.[9] He responded immediately, in Dutch. Van Blyenbergh wrote that he was stumbling over Spinoza's views on the relationship between God (as creator) and human acts and emotions as Lodewijk Meyer had set them forth in a pithy summary included in his preface. Even though Spinoza is teaching the philosophy of Descartes in this work, so Meyer had noted there, he actually disagrees with him on many points. The example Meyer offers is the human will which Spinoza, in departure from Descartes, does not consider any different from the intellect and certainly not free.[10] Van Blyenbergh is uncomfortable with this position, noting that it would seem to imply either that there is no evil in the human soul, or, if there is, that God himself is its cause. Does Spinoza really claim there to be no evil hiding in the human will and soul? And how can this be rhymed with the message revealed to the prophets concerning Adam, the first man? Spinoza responds that Scripture must be read as a text written for a general readership, implying that it 'continually speaks in a human fashion'.[11] All the things God is claimed to have 'revealed' to the prophets as necessary unto salvation actually have a political significance. The prophets wrote a whole parable, depicted God as a king and lawgiver, called causes 'laws' and represented 'Salvation and destruction', which are only fictions following from the means, as reward and punishment.[12] They then presented this parable as truth and 'ordered all their words more according to this parable than according to the truth. Throughout they represented god as a man, now angry, now merciful, now longing for the future, now seized by jealousy and suspicion.'[13] Philosophers who follow virtue, not because they have to as some instituted law, but rather because their reflections cause them to recognise it as the best way, do not have to heed such words.

In his next letter, from late January 1665, Spinoza attempted to bring greater clarity to his views. The disagreement between them 'is located in this alone: whether God as God – i.e. absolutely, ascribing no human attributes to him – communicates to the pious the perfections they receive', which

[9] For Blyenbergh, see Van Dalen, 'Willem Laurensz. van Blyenbergh', 307–29; see also Deleuze, *Spinoza. Philosophie pratique*, 44–62.
[10] Meyer, 'Praefatio', in *Spinoza Opera*, G I, 131–2; *Korte Geschriften*, 23–31; *Ep.* 18; *CWS* I, 354–7.
[11] *Ep.* XIX [to Willem van Blyenbergh]; *CWS* I, 360.
[12] *Ep.* XIX [to Willem van Blyenbergh]; *CWS* I, 360.
[13] Ibid.

is the view he holds, or whether God does so as a judge, as Van Blyenbergh maintains.[14] Significantly, Spinoza does not deny that prayers are useful, but that does not mean his view would be harmful. On the contrary, 'it is the only means of attaining the highest degree of blessedness for those who are not in the grip of prejudice or childish superstition'.[15] Spinoza repeats that Scripture speaks about God in human fashion and expresses its meaning in parables. In the third letter, which Spinoza sends in March, he keeps hammering home the point that philosophy and theology each has its own manner of speaking. Theology has good reasons to depict God as a perfect human being, but in philosophy 'words of this kind have no place, and we cannot use them without confusing our concepts very much'.[16] Even though all the acts of human beings, regardless of whether or not they believe, follow from God, that is, from eternal laws, and in that sense depend on God or eternity, human beings do not differ from God gradually but essentially, just like a mouse differs from an angel and joy from sadness. Startled by this reply, Van Blyenbergh once again cites the troubling passage from Meyer's preface in an effort to come to understanding, but the only conclusion he can draw is that Spinoza, like the atheists, understands the human mind to be finite and to disintegrate together with the body at death, which would seem to suggest there is no difference between killing and giving charity. Accordingly, he asks Spinoza to explain his ethics to him. Spinoza responds three months later by ending their correspondence and asking Blyenbergh to relieve him of that request. His ethics are indeed founded on metaphysics and physics, depending entirely on that first question, which is the necessity of things. If anyone fails to understand that, there is no sense continuing the discussion.[17]

In September 1665, Oldenburg wrote to Spinoza: 'I see that You are not so much philosophizing as (if it is permissible to speak thus) Theologizing; for you are recording your thoughts about Angels, prophecy and miracles.'[18] Spinoza had started to work on his *Tractatus theologico-politicus* at the time, temporarily laying the *Ethica* aside. Was he moved to do so by Van Blyenbergh's persistent incomprehension? Or was he rather stimulated by Van den Enden's appeal to assume the pressing task of freedom? Or did Oldenburg's optimistic words perhaps convince him to show his hand in the

---

[14] *Ep.* XXI [to Willem van Blyenbergh]; *CWS* I, 376.
[15] *Ep.* XXI [to Willem van Blyenbergh]; *CWS* I, 379.
[16] *Ep.* XXIII [to Willem van Blyenbergh]; *CWS* I, 388.
[17] *Ep.* XXVII [to Willem van Blyenbergh]; *CWS* I, 395.
[18] *Ep.* XXIX [from Henry Oldenburg]; *CWS* II, 11.

170   DEMOCRATIC THOUGHT FROM MACHIAVELLI TO SPINOZA

most pressing philosophical and theological debate of the time, which concerned the *libertas philosophandi?* In his response, Spinoza points particularly to the events, the wars and political turmoil, noting that they moved him 'neither to laughter nor even to tears, but to philosophizing and to observing human nature better'.[19] He does not have the *right* to mock nature or to complain about it, since human beings, just like all other existing things, are just a part of nature, and since he does not know how each part of nature coheres with all the other parts. Spinoza confirms that he has started composing a treatise on his view of Scripture, having been moved to do so by three things: (1) the 'prejudices of the theologians' which hinder people from applying themselves to philosophy; (2) the 'opinion of the common people' which they have of him, never stopping to accuse him 'of atheism'; (3) the 'freedom of philosophizing and saying what we think, which I want to defend in every way; here the preachers suppress it as much as they can with their excessive authority and aggressiveness'.[20] Spinoza was therefore incited to the composition of the *Tractatus theologico-politicus* by recent political events, although they also coincided with his three other motives.

2. *Tractatus theologico-politicus*, 1670

The appearance of the *Tractatus theologico-politicus* would have to wait until 1670, when Spinoza brought it to press anonymously. When he started writing in 1665, the *De jure ecclesiasticorum* had just appeared, perhaps strengthening him in his resolve. But the publication of the latter was followed by several major disruptions in his immediate surroundings leading to fireworks that were so brazenly extinguished that he may have been moved to greater caution. In 1666, Lodewijk Meyer anonymously published his *Philosophia S. Scripturae Interpres*, which investigates the meaning of Scripture, the tools for interpreting it at our disposal, and the respective tasks of philosophy and theology. Meyer's work aroused an enormous controversy eliciting a long line of refutations, as appeals for the banning of his work were submitted to the provincial states by the synods of North and South Holland. In spite of this, a Dutch translation appeared the very next year under the title *Philosophie d'uytleghster der h. Schrifture* which, given Meyer's own interest in translation, may have been his very own work. In 1668, Adriaan Koerbagh's *Een Bloemhof van allerley lieflijkheyd sonder verdriet* saw the light of day, only for its author to be incarcerated in

---

[19] *Ep.* XXX [to Henry Oldenburg]; CWS II, 14.
[20] *Ep.* XXX [to Henry Oldenburg]; CWS II, 14–15.

the Rasphuis and coerced to silence several months later, even before the printing of his *Een Ligt schijnende in duystere plaatsen* had been completed. While Koerbagh aligned himself more closely with Hobbes's naturalism and political focus, the latter dimension was absent from Meyer's work which rather continued to build explicitly on Descartes.[21] In spite of this, their respective work does contain a number of common themes and points of focus shared with Spinoza. For instance, they ascribe the obscurity of Scripture to the improper, metaphorical style of writing with which the Bible, itself just another book, had addressed the common people. Both Meyer and Koerbagh seem to waver, being somewhat unclear as to whether the existence of differing linguistic practices adapted to specific audiences also implies that there are two truths. Conversely, they are both unequivocal in their plea for rules of interpretation based on reason, focus unmistakably on the unveiling power of language and translation, and address a common audience in their books, dictionaries and translations. In that light, they seem indeed to consider the common people capable of truth and of critical knowledge free from prejudice.

Spinoza, on the contrary, has doubts in this regard. As he explains in the preface to his *Tractatus theologico-politicus* (*TTP*), he wants to dismantle superstition. But he too is aware that 'it's as impossible to save the common people from superstition as it is from fear'.[22] They are not controlled by

---

[21] For Meyer and the PSSI, see Bordoli, *Ragione e Scrittura tra Descartes e Spinoza*; Israel, *Radical Enlightenment*, 197–205; Klever, *Mannen rond Spinoza*, 61–85; Krop, 'The *Philosophia S. Scripturae Interpres*', 90–120; Lagrée, 'L. Meyer et la *Philosophia S. Scripturae Interpres*', 31–43; Meinsma, *Spinoza en zijn kring*; Moreau, *Spinoza. État et religion*, 93–106: 'L. Meyer et l'*Interpres*'; Thijssen-Schoute, *Nederlands Cartesianisme*, 394–404; Thijssen-Schoute, *Lodewijk Meyer en diens verhouding tot Descartes en Spinoza*.

[22] *TTP* Preface; CWS II, 75. Where our translation departs from Curley's translation, we will refer directly to the Gebhardt critical edition of Spinoza's works, using the following style: *TTP* Praef., G III, 12. In 1693 and 1694, two independent Dutch translations of the *TTP* appeared: The first was published as *De rechtzinnige theologant* (1693), and represents the translation completed by Glazemaker before Spinoza forestalled its publication in 1671; in the mid-nineteenth century, a seventeenth-century manuscript of this translation was discovered, bound with the manuscript of the *Korte Verhandeling van God, de Mensch en deszelvs Welstand* (*Short Treatise*). This manuscript is currently held at the Koninklijke Bibliotheek in The Hague, under the shelf mark 75G15. The second was printed as *Een rechtsinnige theologant* (1694); the translator, context and history behind this translation are all shrouded in mystery. Glazemaker's 1693 translation was referred to by Duijkerius in *Vervolg van 't Leven van Philopater* (1697), which also notes the existence of 'one or two amateur translations' (*een stuk of twee vertaalingen* [. . .] *uit liefhebbery geschied*)' as well as corrupt copies; see ibid. 194–6. On the early translations of the *TTP*, see also Van de Ven, "Van bittere galle by een

172 DEMOCRATIC THOUGHT FROM MACHIAVELLI TO SPINOZA

reason, but allow themselves to be swept along to accept or reject something on a whim. They are impressionable, capricious and unstable, and when they do show themselves steadfast, it is pure stubbornness.[23] This is why Spinoza explicitly does *not* address the common people but the philosopher, to whose judgement he submits his views and arguments. In the preface to the *Tractatus theologico-politicus*, he offers a synopsis of his argument. He begins with so-called faith occasioned by the fact that people have no control over their fate and are tossed between hope and fear. Empty religiosity comes from a fearful heart, and all human beings are susceptible to it. The ease with which faith (or superstition) is formed is only matched by the persistence with which people abide by it, and this explains the institution of worship services, ceremonies, rituals, rules on attire and external adornment which in turn have the effect of reducing the religions to them. Moreover, what passes as religion aims to keep people in their error and fear, and that fear is used – by a monarchical government – to rule and suppress 'and to cloak [that fear] in the specious name of Religion'.[24] That may work under monarchical rule where people fight for their slavery as if it concerned their survival and consider it honourable to give their life to the glory of one man, but in a free republic nothing is more disastrous. This is what Spinoza wants to show: it is 'completely contrary to the general freedom to fill the free judgement of each man with prejudices, or to restrain it in any way'.[25] He not only wants to demonstrate that free judgement can be permitted without endangering piety and political peace, but to show that it *must* in fact be permitted since free judgement is a necessary condition for peace. After all, rebellions only occur 'because laws are made about speculative matters, opinions are considered crimes and condemned as wicked'.[26] Having completed his reversal of this pressing question, Spinoza goes on to dismantle the prejudices that are being disseminated by the theologians and ecclesiastical officials, and then to investigate Holy Scripture in freedom and without prejudice. This investigation will serve to show that Scripture 'has nothing in common with Philosophy', that 'revealed knowledge has no object but obedience', that it 'is entirely distinct from natural knowledge, both in its content and in its foundation and means', and that therefore 'each

gebonden': over de laat zeventiende-eeuwse Nederlandse vertalingen van Spinoza's *Tractatus Theologico-politicus*', 107–18.

[23] *TTP* Preface, CWS II, 75.

[24] *TTP* Preface; CWS II, 68.

[25] *TTP* Preface; CWS II, 69.

[26] Ibid.

SPINOZA'S REVERSAL   173

person must be allowed freedom of judgement and the power to interpret the foundations of faith according to his own mentality [*ingenium*]'.[27] On the basis of each person's natural right, which extends as far as that person's desire and power do, no one is 'bound to live according to another person's mentality [*ingenium*], but each one is the defender of his own freedom'.[28] Spinoza announces that he will show that governments are to defend and explain both civil right and sacral right, 'that *they* alone have the right to decide what is just, what is unjust, what is pious and what impious'.[29] Finally, his view is that the sovereign powers 'retain this right best, and can preserve their rule safely, only if everyone is allowed to think what he will, and to say what he thinks'.[30]

2.1 First movement, first motive

In the first six chapters of the *TTP*, the prejudices of the theologians hindering them in their application to philosophy are systematically demolished. Spinoza proceeds exactly as he had announced in his letter to Oldenburg; this is the first of three movements. In his examination of prophecy, he shows that we ought to believe the prophets only in regard to 'the end and substance of revelation', and not their literal words.[31] The prophets excelled primarily in their vivid imagination. They did not prophecy knowledge but love, and offered moral guidelines for upright behaviour and a happy life. When Spinoza asks whether the gift of prophecy was peculiar to the Jews, he is occasioned to reflect on human strivings in general which, so he argues, relate to three aims: understanding things by their first causes; acquiring virtue and controlling the passions; and living securely and healthily.[32] From there, the focus slowly shifts to the sphere of politics. The best means to living securely and avoiding injuries (from others) is 'to form a social order with definite laws, to occupy a definite area of the world, and to reduce the powers of all, as it were, into one body, the body of the social order'.[33] The election of the Jewish nation was only due to the excellence of their social order. From there, Spinoza pauses to reflect on the twofold use of the term 'law': there is the law that depends on (or follows from) the necessity of

[27] *TTP* Preface; CWS II, 73.
[28] *TTP* Preface; CWS II, 74.
[29] Ibid.
[30] Ibid.
[31] *TTP* II, 53; CWS II, 109.
[32] *TTP* III, 12; CWS II, 113.
[33] *TTP* III, 14; CWS II, 114.

174 DEMOCRATIC THOUGHT FROM MACHIAVELLI TO SPINOZA

nature, and there is the law that depends on the decision of people (which they prescribe for themselves and others).

> For example, it is a universal law of all bodies, which follows from a necessity of nature, that a body which strikes against another lesser body loses as much of its motion as it communicates to the other body. [. . .] But [the law] that men should yield, or be compelled to yield, the right they have from nature, and bind themselves to a fixed way of living, depends on a human decision.[34]

It was in this context that people began to call God a 'ruler, a lawgiver, a king' and started imagining him as merciful and just, even though these are actually human attributes.[35] One can only speak of God's decrees and volitions if one speaks according to 'the common people's power of understanding'; in reality, God's laws are 'eternal truths'.[36] Spinoza insists that it would not be difficult to explain the story of Adam, 'that whole story, *or* parable, of the first man from this foundation', but will not do so himself because he cannot be absolutely certain that his explanation agrees with the writer's intention and 'because most people will not grant that this story is a parable'.[37]

In Chapter 5, Spinoza turns to consider the function of external religious ceremonies and concludes that they serve the stability and well-being of the social order. They do not relate to blessedness, and their only aim is for subjects to constantly recognise their subjection to show reverence. The structure of the argument is the same as the one we encountered in *De jure ecclesiasticorum*: internal and external religion are distinguished from each other; questions about right and authority can relate to external religion alone, after which the question shifts to the nature of right and authority, that is, to the state. At this point, Spinoza offers an explanation of the function of a social order and deduces its attributes from that function. He introduces the perspectives of the ruler and of the ruled, which two perspectives or aspects structure his entire analysis of the function, attributes and possible forms. In this Spinoza went a step further than any of the other authors from his milieu had done – further than Hobbes, and also further than the anonymous author of the *De jure*. A social order is necessary, so Spinoza

---

[34] *TTP* IV, 2; *CWS* II, 125–6.
[35] *TTP* IV, 30; *CWS* II, 133.
[36] *TTP* IV, 37; *CWS* II, 134.
[37] *TTP* IV, 39; *CWS* II, 135.

writes, 'not only for living securely from enemies, but also for doing many things more easily. For if men were not willing to give mutual assistance to one another, they would lack both skill and time to sustain and preserve themselves as far as possible.'[38] An individual would not have the required power and time if he had to do everything himself, 'not to mention now the arts and the sciences which are also supremely necessary for the perfection of human nature and for its blessedness'.[39] If people always followed sound reason and desired only what reason prescribes, society would have no need for any laws. But all rather pursue their own interests, not according to the prescription of reason, but while being dragged along by their passions. This is why no society can continue to exist 'without authority and force, and hence, laws which moderate and restrain men's immoderate desires and unchecked impulses'. On the other hand, 'human nature does not allow itself to be compelled absolutely'.[40] Three things follow from this conflict: First, it means that either the entire community collectively possesses the power, such that no one is subject to anyone but only to himself, or else that power is held by a few or by a single person, who 'ought to have something above ordinary human nature, or strive with all his might to persuade the common people of this'.[41] For Spinoza, therefore, an aristocracy or monarchy must appeal to something surpassing normal human nature, such as a transcendent God, or they must at least pretend that there is such a thing and convince the common people of it. This is not so in a democracy, however. Secondly, 'in each state the laws must be so instituted that men are checked not so much by fear as by the hope of some good they desire very much'.[42] And thirdly,

> since obedience consists in someone's carrying out a command solely on the authority of the person who commands it, it follows that obedience has no place in a social order where sovereignty is in the hands of everyone and laws are enacted by common consent, and that whether the laws in such a social order are increased or diminished, the people nevertheless remains equally free, because it does not act from the authority of someone else, but by its own consent.[43]

[38] *TTP* V, 18; *CWS* II, 143.
[39] *TTP* V, 19; *CWS* II, 143.
[40] *TTP* V, 22; *CWS* II, 144.
[41] *TTP* V, 23; *CWS* II, 144.
[42] *TTP* V, 24; *CWS* II, 144.
[43] *TTP* V, 25; *CWS* II, 144–5.

176 DEMOCRATIC THOUGHT FROM MACHIAVELLI TO SPINOZA

A democracy has no place for obedience, nor does it need to face the problem of two truths and two ways of speaking.

The sixth chapter treats of miracles and occupies a key position within the structure of the entire work. Spinoza's main argument is that nothing that happens is in conflict with nature. People often call something they cannot explain a divine act, imagining that God intervenes wherever nature no longer operates according to its normal order. They thus imagine the power of God and the energy of natural things to be different, even mutually exclusive. But this is a prejudice, for in reality the power of God and the power of nature coincide; they are one and the same thing. On this basis, Spinoza goes on to explain how the miracles reported in the Bible must be interpreted.

2.2 Second movement, second motive

In the second part of the *TTP*, which covers Chapters 7 through 15, Spinoza pauses to consider the meaning of Scripture, accomplishing three things at once: First, he reads and interprets the *Old Testament* as he had announced he would in the first part. In that process, he further demolishes prejudices and paves the way for an entirely new construction. Secondly, this demolishing process does have a positive movement as well insofar as Spinoza uses philological criticism to show how the biblical text can and must be read. As such, his philological investigation becomes an attempt to formulate the teachings of faith that can still be rescued after the deconstruction has taken place – a minimal creed. In this way, he addresses the second motive in writing this work as he had described it to Oldenburg, writing that he intended to refute the view of the common people who consider him an atheist, and that he would do so robustly. Nevertheless, the shoe continues to pinch in that the faith teachings only obtain their significance within a political context, and, as we will see, there is nothing specifically Christian to them. Spinoza never stops talking about the two ways of speaking, connects the common people's power of understanding to deceit, oppression and slavery, and contrasts that with the freedom of philosophy. And so, thirdly, in his own deconstructive reading Spinoza demonstrates the radical separation between philosophy and theology.

For the interpretation of Scripture, Spinoza proceeds from another principle than Meyer had done in his *Philosophia S. Scripturae Interpres*, though their language-critical reflections remain similar and the consequences of their views tend in the same direction, even if Spinoza goes further than Meyer and shows himself more radical. Determining the meaning of

Scripture means unravelling the intention of the writer of the text, and this can only be done by turning to the scriptural text itself. This text must be systematically analyzed and described. That analysis therefore consists in the first place in an investigation of the nature and attributes of the language in which the books of the Bible were written, as spoken by their authors. This applies to the *Old Testament*, of course, but also to the *New Testament*, since the language of the latter is likewise coloured by Hebrew. After this general linguistic investigation, one must 'collect the sentences of each book and organize them under main headings'.[44] This method yields numerous problems for the interpretation of Scripture, which Spinoza then discusses. One problem is inherent to language. Languages are preserved and transmitted by the common people together with the learned, but 'books and the meanings of utterances' are only preserved and transmitted by the learned.[45] How, then, can someone living in the 1660s ever achieve a complete knowledge of ancient Hebrew? Moreover, Hebrew as a language is full of ambiguities, beginning with the letters themselves, since some gutturals are used interchangeably. So too conjunctions and adverbs have multiple meanings, vowels are not marked, and punctuation marks are absent. Another problem is that we do not know the authors of Scripture, a factor which in turn is compounded by the fact that the books of the Bible have only been handed down to us in translation. In spite of these difficulties, Spinoza is convinced that his method of interpretation is the best one: it is based on natural reason, which all people have, and not on some supernatural criterion or on an external authority. Moreover, it is not so difficult as to be the special prerogative of philosophers, but aims rather at the common human disposition so that it can be used by all. Spinoza's method and the concrete interpretation of Scripture which he proposes in Chapters 8 through 12 betray clear differences vis-à-vis Meyer's method and reading, although we do recognise certain similarities with Koerbagh's project in *Een Ligt schijnende in duystere plaatsen*. The deconstruction of prophecies and miracles is confirmed, suggestions concerning the supernatural are systematically refuted, and stories are systematically classified as moral teaching that can easily be grasped with natural reason. Not only is the sanctity of the biblical books dismantled, but the very concept of 'sanctity' is itself called into question. Words 'have a definite meaning only from their use', so Spinoza writes, and if they are used such that they incite people to piety, they are holy, and so are the

---

[44] *TTP* VII, 16; *CWS* II, 173.
[45] *TTP* VII, 42; *CWS* II, 179.

178 DEMOCRATIC THOUGHT FROM MACHIAVELLI TO SPINOZA

books in which they are used that way.[46] But if this use is lost or if the books are no longer given attention, 'then neither the words nor the books will be of any use'.[47] Alternatively, if the books are used in a different way and obtain an opposite significance, then words and books that once were sacred become 'unclean and profane'.[48] In Chapter 13, Spinoza then summarises his argument thus far, in particular that Scripture's only intention is to teach obedience.[49]

In the two chapters that follow, he zooms in on the main argument that actually pervades the entire work, namely the separation of faith and philosophy. He defines faith as 'thinking such things about God that if you had no knowledge of them, obedience to God would be destroyed, whereas if you are obedient to God, you necessarily have these thoughts'.[50] Faith on its own is not salvific, but only from the perspective of obedience, and, conversely, a person who is obedient necessarily has a true faith. A person's faith can only be judged by its works. Since each person's faith can only be judged pious or impious by reason of obedience (or disobedience) and not by its truth (or falsity), and since people differ and therefore hold a multitude of views with a multitude of effects on their hearts, the catholic or universal faith cannot include teachings on which people hold diverging opinions. Accordingly, Spinoza presents a list of seven teachings necessarily assumed by obedience to God, the only teachings that one can accept without debate – a minimal creed or common denominator to which all religions can subscribe – and that agree with the fundamental principles aimed at by the whole of Scripture. These seven doctrines are that (1) God exists, (2) is unique, (3) omnipresent and omniscient, (4) is independent, has supreme right and is free; (5) worship of (that is, obedience to) God consists only in love towards one's neighbour (that is, love for *human beings*); (6) everyone who obeys God is saved, while those who abandon themselves to pleasure are lost; and (7) God pardons sins, for 'no one is without sin'.[51] A remarkable feature of this list

[46] *TTP* XII, 11; CWS II, 250.
[47] Ibid.
[48] Ibid.
[49] *TTP* XIII, 6; CWS II, 258.
[50] *TTP* XIV, 14; CWS II, 266.
[51] *TTP* XIV, 25–8; CWS II, 268–9. On the face of it, the seventh rule appears to conflict with Spinoza's view of a non-personal, non-active God. At the same time, in his vision God represents nature (the laws of nature), and sins can only be committed within a social order; in the natural order, there is no such thing as good or evil. Accordingly, the claim that God/nature forgives – i.e. does not punish – sins is a truism. From a language perspective, an impersonal subject (like a natural phenomenon, thing, idea)

SPINOZA'S REVERSAL 179

is that there is nothing specifically Christian to it: there is no mention of a hereafter with rewards and punishment, no Christ, no Trinity, no resurrection. For that matter, *what* God is, whether fire, spirit, light or thought, is unrelated to faith: 'It's all the same, whatever each person maintains about these things.'[52] Finally, Spinoza shows that there is no relationship between faith and philosophy. The goal of philosophy is truth, while the goal of faith is obedience. The foundations of philosophy are the universally accepted concepts which are derived from nature, while the foundations of faith are the histories and the language which are derived from Scripture. For this reason, faith 'grants everyone the greatest freedom to philosophize, so that without wickedness he can think whatever he wishes about anything'.[53] Theology and philosophy are entirely different and cannot be reduced to each other, nor can the one serve the other. Dogmatists and sceptics debate whether faith must be adapted to reason or the other way around, but Spinoza considers both foolish, the one with and the other without reason. For reason governs the sphere of truth or wisdom, theology the sphere of obedience. How the dogmas of faith are to be understood in terms of their truth is therefore a matter for philosophy, and conversely Spinoza, as a philosopher, accepts the foundation of theology with sound judgement, 'even though [it] cannot be shown by a mathematical demonstration'.[54]

2.3 Third movement, third motive

With the separation of philosophy and theology in place, it is time to turn to the freedom to philosophise, the third motive which Spinoza had announced in his letter to Oldenburg. By now the authority of the preachers and ecclesiastical governments has been undermined, and there no longer is any reason to tolerate their harsh suppression of free speech. But what about the freedom to philosophise in its relation to the state? How much freedom does politics grant people to say what they think? In investigating this question, Spinoza begins with an analysis of the principles of politics, preceded by a study of

in an active clause acts as a 'cause' and not as an 'agent'. The most important aspect of this seventh rule therefore appears to be the addition according to which there is no one who does not sin, which serves to emphasise Spinoza's principle of improvability. For the question whether an atheist could accept this seventh rule and, more specifically, whether it is a 'beneficial lie'; see Laursen, 'Spinoza et les "mensonges officieux" dans les manuscrits clandestins', 81–98.

[52] *TTP* XIV, 30; *CWS* II, 269.
[53] *TTP* XIV, 39; *CWS* II, 271.
[54] *TTP* XV, 36; *CWS* II, 280.

180   DEMOCRATIC THOUGHT FROM MACHIAVELLI TO SPINOZA

natural right. He understands the right or established practice of nature 'as the natural rules of each individual, according to which we conceive each thing to be naturally determined to existing and having effects in a certain way'.[55] It goes without saying, of course, that the supreme right to do everything belongs to nature, since the power of nature is the power of God, which has the supreme right over all things. Since the total power of nature is the same as the power of all individuals collectively, it follows 'that each individual has a supreme right to do everything it can'.[56] The right of each natural thing likewise extends as far as its naturally determined nature does.

> Now the supreme right of nature is that each thing strives to persevere in its state, as far as it can by its own power, and does this, not on account of anything else, but only of itself. From this it follows that each individual has the supreme right to do this, i.e., [. . .] to exist and have effects as it is naturally determined to do.[57]

Spinoza sees no difference between human beings and other natural things in this respect, nor between rational and irrational people, nor even between those who are mentally impaired or ill and those with sound reason. For whatever each person does according to the laws of his own nature, he does with supreme right, because he acts as he has been determined by his nature and can therefore do no other. The right or established practice of nature under which all are born and under which they most often live forbids nothing, except what no one desires or can do. The right or established practice of nature therefore does not prohibit conflict, hatred, anger or deception; it does not prohibit anything urged by appetite. Nature is not constrained by the laws of human reason, and does not, like human reason, aim at the advantage and preservation of human beings. Following the same argument we have seen in Hobbes, De la Court and the author of the *De jure ecclesiasticorum*, Spinoza likewise holds the opinion that people due to the *mala* in the human condition must agree as one (*in unum conspirare debuisse*) so that they 'have collectively the natural right each one had to do all things. It would no longer be determined according to the force and appetite of each one, but according to the power and will of everyone together.'[58]

---

[55] *TTP* XVI, 2; CWS II, 282.
[56] *TTP* XVI, 3; CWS II, 282.
[57] *TTP* XVI, 4; CWS II, 282–3.
[58] *TTP* XVI, 13; CWS II, 284–5. Spinoza's argument only *looks* like that of Hobbes, but in reality it is about something totally different, as we notice in the next step, since

SPINOZA'S REVERSAL 181

Yet Spinoza observes that this argument remains in many respects 'merely theoretical [*merè theoretica*]'.[59] No one will ever transfer his power and, consequently, his right to another person in such a way as to cease to be a human being. Nor will there ever be a government that manages to perform all things precisely as anyone wishes. People have never surrendered their right and transferred their power to another without being feared by those who have received their right and power. A state fears its subjects more than the subjects fear that state. For this reason, the power of the state does not consist in its ability to compel by fears and threats, but rather in the obedience which people render because *they are glad to offer it*. Drawing on the history of the Jews, Spinoza goes on to argue, like De la Court, Van den Enden and the author of the *De jure ecclesiasticorum*, how 'ruinous it is, both for religion and for the Republic, to grant the ministers of sacred affairs the right to make [religious] decrees or to handle the business of the state'.[60] Moreover,

> how dangerous it is to make purely speculative things a matter of divine right and to make laws concerning opinions, which people usually debate about, or can debate about. For that government which makes it a crime to hold opinions – which each person has a right to hold, a right no one can surrender – is the most violent of all.[61]

He points to the example of the Pharisees and other hypocrites who are incited by madness 'which they call zeal for divine right', publicly anathematise the views of the virtuous and stir up the masses against them, an 'impudent license' which they mask with 'the deceptive appearance of religion'.[62] How can anyone reading these words not think of the lot of Koerbagh? Or of Vanini, whose name Spinoza no doubt encountered in Voetius's disputation on atheism?[63] And how can anyone fail to ponder the ghastly fate that

---

he is not talking about 'right' in the common sense of the term but as a psychological necessity. See Menzel, who demonstrates in *Beiträge zur Geschichte der Staatslehre* that the state's coming into existence is in Spinoza not explained on the basis of a contract – which is insufficient – but by a *Faktum*, namely the actual transfer of power (350–66). We reached the same conclusion in our own close reading of the text, which is why we in the context of this passage recall Spinoza's earlier remark concerning the twofold use of the term 'law'; see *TTP* IV, 1–3; CWS II, 125–6.

[59] *TTP* XVII, 1; CWS II, 296; G III, 201.

[60] *TTP* XVIII, 22; CWS II, 327.

[61] *TTP* XVIII, 23; CWS II, 327.

[62] *TTP* XVIII, 24; CWS II, 328.

[63] See Verbeek, 'La demonizzazione di Vanini: Voetius, Schoock e Descartes', 183–201.

182 DEMOCRATIC THOUGHT FROM MACHIAVELLI TO SPINOZA

the De Wit brothers were soon to face, which Spinoza seems to announce prophetically here? Spinoza also identifies other related problems. In a passage recalling *Il Principe*, he exposes the dangers that follow when people overthrow a tyrant, which is why they 'can often change the tyrant, but can never destroy him, or change a monarchic state into another, of a different form'.[64] Spinoza was to return to this theme later on, in his *Tractatus politicus*.

The right over religious affairs belongs entirely to the state. While internal religion is a matter of each person's individual right, external religious worship must serve the advantage of the state and can therefore only be determined by it. Spinoza eventually applies the same argument, in a way once again recalling the anonymous writer of the *De jure*, to the question of the relationship between the freedom of speech and the political system. If it were just as easy to govern the thoughts as the tongue, the governing body would not be threatened and have nothing to fear, and 'no rule would be violent'.[65] 'Everyone would live according to the mentality of the rulers; only in accordance with their decree would people judge what is true or false, good or evil, right or wrong.'[66] But that is impossible, since the assumption is a misguided one. It cannot happen that 'a mind should be absolutely subject to the control of someone else. Indeed, no one can transfer to another person his natural right, *or* faculty, of reasoning freely, and of judging concerning anything whatever. Nor can anyone be compelled to do this.'[67] This is why a political power that wants to rule thoughts is violent, and it abuses its power when it prescribes for everyone what they must accept as true and reject as false, or by what 'opinions everyone's mind ought to be moved in its devotion to God. These things are subject to each individual's control. No one can surrender that even if he wants to.'[68] Regardless of its specific form, a state will 'never be able to stop men from making their own judgment, about everything according to their own character, and from having, to that

[64] *TTP* XVIII, 32; *CWS* II, 329.
[65] *TTP* XX, 1; *CWS* II, 344.
[66] *TTP* XX, 2; *CWS* II, 344.
[67] Ibid.; see also *De jure ecclesiasticorum*, 20–2.
[68] *TTP* XX, 3; *CWS* II, 344. Here we only address the relationship between Spinoza and Hobbes sporadically and as a side note; it will be treated at somewhat greater length in our discussion of the *Tractatus politicus*. Hobbes came to a different conclusion on the freedom of expression than Spinoza, and their political views in fact opposites. In spite of this, their arguments have more similarities than has commonly been assumed, even in the way they treat the traditional theme of the right of resistance (see *Leviathan*, XXI). There is extensive scholarship on the relationship between the two, including the collected volume Bostrenghi (ed.), *Hobbes e Spinoza. Scienza e politica* and the thematic issue *Studia Spinozana* 3.

extent, this or that affect.'[69] Nature does not supply any prohibition or norm, and so every state has the full right to rule with violence. But since a state endangers itself when it abuses its power, suppresses the freedom of speech, and acts violently, Spinoza is ultimately convinced that it does not 'have the absolute power to do such things'.[70] If 'no one can surrender his freedom of judging and thinking what he wishes, [. . .] it follows that if the supreme powers in a republic try to make men say nothing but what they prescribe, no matter how different and contrary their opinions, they will get only the most unfortunate result'.[71] This completes Spinoza's argument. He closes by stating that the goal of politics is freedom, that the individual must follow the political rules in his acts, but not in his reasoning and judgement. In a democracy, which comes closest to the natural condition, all contract 'to act according to the common decision, but not to judge and reason according to the common decision. Because not all men can equally think the same things, they agreed that the measure which had the most votes would have the force of a decree, but that meanwhile they'd retain the authority to repeal these decrees when they saw better ones.'[72]

3. Countermovement, 1670–1676

On 8 May 1670, soon after the publication of the *Tractatus theologico-politicus*, the German academic Jacob Thomasius already produced a first response which set in motion a major countermovement.[73] Nothing about his *Programma adversus anonymum, de libertate philosophandi* suggests he envisioned any other goal other to warn his students and colleagues at the University of Leipzig against what he saw as a dangerous defence of the freedom to philosophise. At the time of writing, he did not yet know that

---

[69] *TTP* XX, 6; *CWS* II, 345. Translation modified.

[70] *TTP* XX, 7; *CWS* II, 345.

[71] *TTP* XX, 8; *CWS* II, 345.

[72] *TTP* XX, 38; *CWS* II, 351.

[73] Thomasius, *Programma adversus anonymum, de libertate philosophandi*, 571–81; see also Zenker, *Denkfreiheit*, 101–9; Israel, 'The Early Dutch and German Reaction to the *Tractatus Theologico-politicus*', 72–100. Below, we will address the antitexts that were of possible influence on Spinoza for the formation of and shift in ideas towards the *TP*. As a result, we will only be investigating the polemical works with which Spinoza could have been directly acquainted and that were disseminated between 1670 and 1676 in his geographic region and in the languages accessible to him. We therefore omit exchanges on the *TTP* between various third-party actors. A bibliography of primary responses from the period in question can be found in Luisa Simonutti, 'Bibliographie primaire, 1670–1677', 253–4.

184 DEMOCRATIC THOUGHT FROM MACHIAVELLI TO SPINOZA

'the author is Benedictus Spinoza, a former Jew, a blasphemous and formal
atheist', as he would write in a note added to the text when it was published
two years later together with another academic antitext, the latter written
by Dürr.[74] It was his own pupil Leibniz who informed him of Spinoza's
authorship.[75] One may therefore assume that this first polemical text only
came to be known outside Leipzig in 1672, before finding a wider readership
in 1693 when Christian Thomasius, the author's famous son, included this
brief Spinoza-refutation in a collection of his father's shorter writings he
published. In spite of this, Thomasius's attack was not an isolated piece,
but formed part of a wave of reactions that would come or were already in
the making, all of them aiming to counter Spinoza's new and revolutionary theses.[76] Thomasius compared the *TTP* to the plea for the freedom to
philosophise which Edmund Dickinson had made at Oxford in 1653 and
which had been reprinted multiple times since and also translated into
German. But he added that there is also an important difference between
the two: while Dickinson sought to introduce his Pandora's box to the
philosophical schools alone, the author of the *TTP* had aimed his arrows at

[74] Thomasius, *Programma adversus anonymum*, 572: 'Cognovi tamen posteà, impii hujus
scripti autorem esse *Benedictum Spinosam*, Exjudaeum blasphemum, & formalem
Atheum'; for Dürr, see below.

[75] In October 1670, Leibniz wrote the following to his teacher Jacob Thomasius: 'I
recently saw the Leipzig academic programme, no doubt yours, in which you treated
that intolerably liberal booklet on the *libertas philosophandi* as it deserved' (*Vidi nuper
programma Lipsiense, haud dubie tuum, quo libellum intolerabiliter licentiosum de libertate
philosophandi, pro eo ac merebatur, tractasti*). Thomasius then sent him a copy for his
perusal; see Leibniz, *Sämtliche Schriften und Briefe*, II, 1, 106. In April 1671, Leibniz was
informed of the anonymous author's identity by Graevius, professor at the University
of Utrecht: 'Johann Georg Graevius an Leibniz, 12./22. April 1671', in Leibniz, ibid.
I, 142. Leibniz in turn shared this information with his former teacher in a letter from
early 1672: 'Leibniz an Thomasius, 21./31. Januar 1672', in Leibniz, ibid. II, 1, 320.
What Leibniz omitted to mention in that letter is that he had by that time attempted
to enter into correspondence with Spinoza, and that in his response the latter had
even offered to send him a copy of the *TTP*. See Otto, *Studien zu Spinozarezeption in
Deutschland im 18. Jahrhundert*, 16–17; Israel, 'The Early Dutch and German Reaction',
80–1. It is worth noting that Leibniz had his own copy of the *TTP*, which still
survives and contains numerous annotations from his hand; see Goldenbaum, 'Die
Commentatiuncula de judice', 61–127.

[76] Thomasius, *Programma adversus anonymum*, 575; note also Israel, who in regard to
Batelier and Limborch speaks of a 'concerted effort, almost an official Remonstrant
group response, to the "Theologico-Politicus"'; see Israel, 'The Early Dutch and
German Reaction', 84. Likewise interesting is the fact that Jakob Thomasius's son
Christian, who published his father's *Programma*, had the *De jure ecclesiasticorum* in his
library; see *Bibliotheca Thomasiana*, 309–10. See also above, Chapter III.1, 68–69.

the 'sanctuary of theology', used the term *libertas philosophandi* as a cover for the 'boundless, unrestrained freedom of all religions', and reduced religious faith to 'nothing more than obedience and upright moral behaviour'.[77] This, so Thomasius charged, opened the door to atheism. Since his colleague Rappolt was likewise working on a refutation for which he was honing in on the question of naturalism, Thomasius announced his intention to focus on politics. According to Spinoza, the freedom to formulate and announce new views fits 'not so much a monarchy or aristocracy but a democratic rule (which in his view amounts to a free republic)'.[78] Thomasius does not want to challenge the claim that there is an inherent relationship 'between the popular form of state and this Babel of naturalism', but the arguments adduced by Spinoza are so general as to apply to every form of state.[79] Thomasius agrees that democratic rule indeed has no power over internal thoughts, but also considers that Spinoza moved on all too hastily to the external act of speaking, that is, to the mediation of thoughts by other signs. Spinoza had argued that a person is allowed to disagree with the government's view and to give expression to that disagreement, provided that this is done with reason rather than hate or anger. Thomasius, on the contrary, holds the view that every statement against the government is a crime, even if it is made in clandestine fashion or if the dissenters make it clear that they still intend to subject themselves to the government. The moment venomous words are spoken, it matters little whether those who uttered them do or do not subject themselves to the judgement of the physicians, for the damage has been done and 'there will already be many corpses before the physician arrives'.[80] As we have seen, Spinoza's argument is critical: he shows that those who oppose the freedom of speech depart from a false assumption. Thomasius ignores this argument completely. Spinoza had nuanced his position by adding that one may not express opinions that issue in rebellion, but Thomasius interprets this to mean that all opinions destructive to religion are allowed: there is no law forbidding 'each and every raging

---

[77] Thomasius, *Programma adversus anonymum*, 572: '[. . .] alter ille potius in Sacraria Theologorum introducere laboravit. [. . .] omnium *Religionum* infinitam licentiam hoc eum nomine occuluisse [. . .]. Nimirum *fidei* vocabulum ad solam obedientiam, [h.e. si eventum rimeris, ad externam in humano foro honeste vivendi disciplinam] arctavit.'

[78] Ibid. 575–6: 'Observamus initio, tametsi libertatem istiusmodi non tam Regis aut Optimatum statui, quam Democratico regimini (hoc enim ipsi est *Resp.* libera) convenire innuit'.

[79] Ibid. 576: 'populari formae cum illa Naturalismi Babele maximam intercedere sympathiam'.

[80] Ibid. 579: 'Antequam adveniat Medicus, jam turba cadaverum erit'.

186 DEMOCRATIC THOUGHT FROM MACHIAVELLI TO SPINOZA

fool to spew forth his anti-religious poison openly'.[81] While Spinoza understands freedom to be necessary for the development of the arts and sciences, Thomasius, ever the good Lutheran, defends a 'moderate slavery' which does not force anyone to deny the views of his own mind, but does forbid people to oppose the publicly accepted teachings.[82]

This first attack was immediately followed by that from another academic in Leipzig, Friedrich Rappolt, who devoted his inaugural *Oratio contra Naturalistas* of June 1670 to an attack on naturalism and deism. In departure from his colleague, and also as a result of his choice to restrict himself to metaphysics, Rappolt shows no interest for the novelty of the *TTP*, which is its unique perspective on politics and state formation. He does not address the impact of words, but only the status of God and religion. It is furthermore worth noting that the *Oratio* does not explicitly mention the *TTP* but only alludes to it indirectly, while Thomasius's *Programma* of 29 May 1670, which already announced Rappolt's oration, does identify the *TTP* as an example of the naturalist view which claims that it is possible to obtain knowledge of God through reason alone (*naturae lumine*):[83] 'Precisely this is the view of the anonymous writer, whose *Tractatus theologico-politicus* on the freedom to philosophize, a very wicked book, recently appeared: that religion does not judge according to the norm of heavenly truth but according to the norm of nature, and peace and the advantage of the republic.'[84] This is evident from the author's covert views, so Rappolt writes, such as when he charges that the natural religion contains nothing that does not agree with reason, that the object of revealed knowledge is simply obedience, and that Scripture only condemns the disobedient but not the ignorant. Furthermore, that God desires no other knowledge of himself than the knowledge of his divine justice and love; that people may be entirely misguided concerning the attributes of God; that a person's faith can only be judged to be pious or impious according to their obedience or disobedience; and that the universal faith does not include any doctrines concerning which respectable

---

[81] Ibid. 'Sic ergo per te nulla lex vetabit, quo minus furiosissimus quisque virus in religione suum evomat publice'.

[82] Ibid. 581: 'temperata Servitus nostra neminem cogit, animi sensa dissimulare, tantum vetat publice receptis per contumaciam obniti.'

[83] Rappolt, *Oratio contra Naturalistas &c. Junii a. 1670*; Rappolt, *Programma ad audiendam orationem inauguralem* [29 May 1670], in *Opera Theologica*, 1383–1407; 2160–8.

[84] Rappolt, *Programma*, 2162–3: 'Nec alia mens Anonymi, cujus Tractatus Theologico-Politicus de libertate philosophandi, pessimae notae liber, religionem non ad coelestis veritatis normam, sed naturam & qualemcunque pacem atque utilitatem in Republica exigens, his ipsis nundinis in lucem prodiit.'

people disagree. And, finally, that there are seven dogmas, which Rappolt then lists.[85] In short, Rappolt offers a reliable summary of Chapter 14 of the *TTP*, and stumbles over Spinoza's liberal view of faith and God. According to the author of the *TTP*, everyone is free to judge: 'Everyone must be left the freedom to judge and the capacity to interpret Scripture according to his view, and even to worship God according to that view.'[86]

Based on his study of the intellectual background of the *TTP* and Meyer's *Philosophia*, Samuel Maresius (or Des Marets), professor of theology in Groningen, concluded that Spinoza was the author hiding in anonymity and that the latter's aim extended beyond religious toleration alone. Later that year, Maresius published the results of his investigation in his *Vindiciae dissertationis suae nuperae de abusu philosophiae Cartesianae*. Using the very same words which Thomasius was to add in a note to his *Programma*, Maresius insists that Spinoza, 'an ex-Jew, a blasphemous and formal atheist', is the author of this '*Tractatus Theologico-politicus pro libertate philosophandi*, which clearly leans on the hypotheses of Cartesian philosophy as well as the theories of Hobbes, the English Machiavelli'.[87]

One can only guess whether Spinoza was still regularly in touch with Van den Enden in 1670, and whether the radicalisation of the latter's political views and his move to Paris sometime that same year related to the publication of the *TTP*. Given its content and focus, it is hard not to make that connection. As we already observed above, Spinoza's *TTP* can also be seen as a response to Van den Enden's call for people to exercise the freedom to philosophise. The German and Dutch countertexts that now face Spinoza's treatise seem to confirm that he was on dangerous footing and that this was not just a purely academic debate. In July and August 1670, the synods of The Hague, South Holland and North Holland submitted appeals against the *TTP* to their respective governments.[88] As we will see later on, Spinoza responded by persisting in his controversial views. The philosophical and/ or political freedom, the logical and naturalistic arguments, the new view of God, the interpretation of the Bible, the connection between faith and

---

[85] Ibid. 2163.

[86] Ibid. 'Unicuique enim sui judicii libertatem & potestatem Scripturam ex suo ingenio interpretandi, imo ex suo ingenio Deum colendi, reliquendam.'

[87] Maresius (Des Marets), *Vindiciae dissertationis suae nuperae de abusu philosophiae Cartesianae*, 4: 'Spinosa, Exjudaeo blasphemo & formali Atheo, authore tractatus Theologico-politici pro libertate philosophandi, quem totum niti & Cartesianae Philosophiæ hypothesibus, & Hobbesij, Machiavelli Anglici, theorematis, luce meridiana clarius est'; see also Israel, 'The Early Dutch and German Reaction', 77.

[88] Freudenthal, *Die Lebensgeschichte Spinoza's*, 122–4.

188   DEMOCRATIC THOUGHT FROM MACHIAVELLI TO SPINOZA

obedience, and the illusionless idea of a universal human nature in the colourful and contradictory diversity of faith convictions, urges and passions, are countered by his opponents en bloc, prompting Spinoza to attempt to repeat the original motives in ever clearer fashion. Spinoza persists in his view that it does not matter what exactly one believes, provided that the image of God one fashions does not form a hindrance to equal freedom. The story that runs from the publication of the *TTP* to the first reactions and down to the ban in the summer of 1674 coincides with Van den Enden's move to Paris, the revolt he conspired against the French king, his betrayal and arrest, and the sham civil trial issuing in his execution at the Place de la Bastille in October 1674. But also the politically controversial content of the treatise, the campaign launched against it, and Spinoza's persistent (but futile?) response run parallel to the tragic story of Van den Enden's project. Spinoza published the *TTP* in the spirit of his teacher's new political-philosophical ideas and revolutionary project, and it hit like a bomb, eliciting an orchestrated counteroffensive as a consequence. Did this counteroffensive change Spinoza's political ideas to the extent that he decided to publish them again, in a new form and in a new treatise, the *Tractatus politicus*? The first responses came from German and Dutch faculties of theology, but soon these were accompanied by reflections from philosophers and humanist scholars to whom Spinoza had explicitly addressed himself and who were actually struggling with many of the same questions. They too debated religion and politics, right and power, war and peace, Descartes and Hobbes, the role of the Bible, and, of course, the freedom to philosophise. What exactly emerges from their processing of Spinoza's *TTP*, and how did Spinoza respond?

3.1 1671–1673

On 24 January 1671, Lambert van Velthuysen wrote a letter to Jacob Ostens in which he offered his commentary on the widely debated *TTP*.[89] Ostens then sent that letter (or a copy of it) to Spinoza, who read it carefully, drew up notes in the margin and then wrote up a response. Van Velthuysen could identify with – and in fact approve of – the author's main purpose, namely to examine 'the opinions which make men divide into factions and form

---

[89] *Ep.* XLII [Lambert van Velthuysen to Jacob Ostens]; CWS II, 374–85. See Van Bunge, 'Van Velthuysen, Batelier and Bredenburg on Spinoza's Interpretation of the Scriptures', 49–66.

parties' and issue in violence.[90] To that end, the anonymous author must rid himself of all prejudices, but, so Van Velthuysen charges, he has gone too far in demolishing; to avoid the charge of superstition, the author of the *TTP* has in fact put off all religion. That is, while he does acknowledge the existence of God, he understands God, like nature and the world order, as necessity. As a result, there is no room for precepts or commands, and it is 'human ignorance that has brought in terms of this kind, just as the common people's lack of sophistication has given rise to ways of speaking which attribute affects to God'.[91] Van Velthuysen writes that the author of the *TTP* does not understand God as an agent with a will who intervenes, nor does his God perform miracles violating the laws of nature. Every paragraph and every sentence in the anonymous treatise is an ironclad propositional reflection. Every critique or argument that is brought to expression forms one link in the chain of logic leading to the argument in the final chapters, that 'it's the right of the Magistrate to establish what divine worship is to be publicly maintained in the state' and that it is its duty to allow its citizens to think and speak of religion as their minds and hearts tell them to.[92] This view, so Van Velthuysen continues, is based on the understanding that God is indifferent to the thoughts people cherish concerning him and the religious practices they publicly exercise. As a result, there is no longer any room for 'any divine governance or providence; the whole distribution of punishments and rewards is destroyed'.[93] Accordingly, one must not apply oneself to virtue from fear of punishment or hope of reward in the hereafter, but rather from inherent reasons, the understanding and joy one obtains from virtuous activity. On the basis of this argument, says Van Velthuysen, the authority of Holy Scripture is completely overturned and it even follows 'that the Koran must be regarded as equal to the Word of God'.[94]

In February 1671, Spinoza wrote a response to Van Velthuysen's critique. How could the latter accuse him of casting off all religion? How, then, does *he* understand religion? Is one irreligious if one locates the reward of virtue in virtue itself, and the punishment for licentiousness and folly in folly itself? Spinoza thinks he knows where the shoe pinches for Van Velthuysen: 'He finds nothing in virtue itself, or in understanding, which delights him, and he would prefer to live according to the impulse of his affects, if one thing

[90] *Ep.* XLII [Lambert van Velthuysen to Jacob Ostens]; *CWS* II, 374.
[91] *Ep.* XLII [Lambert van Velthuysen to Jacob Ostens]; *CWS* II, 375.
[92] *Ep.* XLII [Lambert van Velthuysen to Jacob Ostens]; *CWS* II, 379.
[93] *Ep.* XLII [Lambert van Velthuysen to Jacob Ostens]; *CWS* II, 385.
[94] Ibid.

190 DEMOCRATIC THOUGHT FROM MACHIAVELLI TO SPINOZA

did not stand in his way: he fears punishment.'[95] As usual, Spinoza debates matter-of-factly, focuses on the issue at hand, and recognises that he and Van Velthuysen do not agree there. His opponent appears to see reason and virtue as a torment which none would pursue of their own accord, and evil actions as something desirable, so that people only deprive themselves of them 'reluctantly and with a vacillating heart', like a slave, unwillingly. Spinoza has an opposite understanding of things. His argument on God and necessity means that 'freedom does not consist in indifference, but that we are most free when we assent to the things we perceive clearly and distinctly'.[96]

That same month, Spinoza also wrote a letter to his friend Jarig Jelles, noting that he had heard that his 'theological-political treatise' (*Godgeleerdstaatkundig vertoog*) had been translated into Dutch and that someone wanted to bring it to publication. Spinoza urgently begged Jelles to stop the printing, fearing that his treatise would be prohibited if it were to become available in the vernacular. In this same letter, Spinoza mentions a booklet entitled *Homo Politicus*, which he had recently read and considered 'the most harmful book men can devise'.[97] In his magisterial work on Spinoza, Koenraad O. Meinsma addressed the philosopher's comment at considerable length and cited the letter to Jelles virtually in its entirety, along with three and a half pages from the offensive booklet itself.[98] According to a list of rare books which Georg Hermann Schuller, who in 1671 had yet to become one of Spinoza's friends, found among the papers the philosopher left at his death, the author of this work was Franciscus Datisius. For many years Spinoza's biographers had no interest in Schuller and were unaware of the role he played in his life, correspondence and material legacy, and in bringing his posthumous works to press. The list with rare works which he found among Spinoza's papers therefore remained unknown until the end of the nineteenth century, and it was not until the publication of Leibniz's correspondence was underway that Ludwig Stein decided to study the letters between Schuller and Leibniz with a view to Spinoza, allowing the treatise to be identified as the 'Latin book in-quarto, with the title' *Homo politicus*,

---

[95] *Ep.* XLIII [to Jacob Ostens]; CWS II, 387.

[96] *Ep.* XLIII [to Jacob Ostens]. Translation mine. In his original draft, Spinoza struck out the latter passage quoted here, which is why it was not included in the *Opera Posthuma* and is thus absent from Curley's translation. The manuscript draft is currently held in Amsterdam, Stadsarchief, 169 (Archief van het Weeshuis der Doopsgezinde Collegianten de Oranjeappel), inv. No. 454, and can be consulted online at http://spinozaweb.org/letters/75.

[97] *Ep.* XLIV [to Jarig Jelles]; CWS II, 390–1.

[98] Meinsma, *Spinoza en zijn kring*, 337–41.

hoc est: consiliarius novus, officiarius et aulicus, secundum hodiernam praxin, auctore Pacifico a Lapide (1668).[99] But why was Spinoza so outraged by it? The 'Author's supreme goods are money and honor', he writes to Jelles, and to that end one must internally reject all religion but externally confess the religion that best serves one's own interests.[100] This encourages one to perform, to lie, to break promises and to deceive in order to achieve this goal. When Spinoza had read these things, he 'thought about writing a little book indirectly against it' and to show 'that Republics which have an insatiable desire for honor and money must necessarily perish'.[101] As a counterexample he adduces, rather surprisingly, Thales of Miletus, and he explains it, even more surprisingly, not in Hobbesian fashion using neutral geometry but with an anecdote showing 'that it is not by necessity, but voluntarily, that the wise possess no wealth'. The real debate is about the ends to be pursued.[102] Meinsma observes that Spinoza, 'instead of refuting the *Homo politicus*, started at this time with the composition of the *Tractatus politicus*'.[103] Against the background of the campaign that had been launched against the *TTP* and the ensuing debates that Spinoza must have played out in his head, scholars have been inclined to draw a line from the reasons for his critique to the composition of the *Tractatus politicus*. But what he writes to Jelles may not explain his fierce aversion to the latter work entirely. In this context it is worth noting that the subtitle of the booklet describes the *homo politicus* as 'the new councillor, official, and courtier by today's practice', and that the opening paragraphs immediately identify the Jesuits as the author's teacher and example.[104] They are the ones who teach that 'religion is a superstitious piety, even pure deceit, which the *homo politicus*, if indeed he wants to achieve his goal, ought not to value highly' and that the true political religion consists in 'believing differently with the mouth than with the heart'.[105] They teach that the *homo politicus* must be able to 'simulate and

---

[99] Ibid. 338; Stein, 'Neue Aufschlüsse über den literarischen Nachlass und die Herausgabe der Opera Posthuma Spinozas', 554–65. For Schuller's role in the publication of the *Opera Posthuma*, see also Steenbakkers, *Spinoza's Ethica from Manucript to Print*, 50–63.

[100] *Ep.* XLIV [to Jarig Jelles]; CWS II, 391.

[101] Ibid.

[102] Ibid.

[103] Meinsma, *Spinoza en zijn kring*, 340.

[104] Anon., *Homo politicus, consiliarius novus, officiarius et aulicus, secundum hodiernam praxin*, 4.

[105] Anon., *Homo politicus*, 5: 'neque tc Religio avocet, persuasio quaedam est, & superstitiosa Pietas, imo pura puta deceptio, quae homini Politico, si finem suum assequi vult, non magni aestimanda'; 'aliter nempe ore, aliter corde credendum'.

192   DEMOCRATIC THOUGHT FROM MACHIAVELLI TO SPINOZA

dissimulate' – terms borrowed from Machiavelli, whom the author indeed mentions alongside the Jesuits as the great example of a 'modern political practice'.[106] Spinoza must have been very upset by the way Machiavelli – the Italian forerunner of Hobbes, the defender of a free democratic republic, and after his death the thorn in the Spanish oppressor's side – was put on one line with Loyola. Datisius made a caricature of Machiavelli by presenting his work as a cynical lesson in individual egoism and by twisting its motive and goal. To Spinoza's mind, the way the author pressed Machiavelli in the service of the Society of Jesus was an abuse of Machiavelli, resting on the fiction of the Machiavellian representation which those same Jesuits had so successfully devised. In the meantime, Datisius's treatise also makes a carica-ture of the political life itself, which he claims to aim not at the public good but at the private interest of individual figures, officials and courtiers – the *homo politicus* – and thus to be merely self-serving.

On 30 June 1671, Johann Konrad Dürr gave an oration in Altdorf at the occasion of the graduation of twelve students of philosophy, which is in its entirety devoted to a refutation of the *TTP*. The *Oratio De praeposterâ et impiâ libertate Philosophandi* was not printed until a year later, in 1672, together with Thomasius's *Programma*.[107] Dürr was greatly influenced by Thomasius, and for that reason we see a number of points return that should by now be rather familiar to us.[108] He accuses the author of defending licen-tiousness and abandon to an unbridled libido under the guise of the *libertas philosophandi* and 'covered with the name of freedom'.[109] This reckless aban-don renders impossible the reverence owed to both God and sovereigns as well as other important figures. Dürr charges that there are parallels between the *TTP* and Hobbes's *De cive*, but is primarily concerned about the view of 'our democratic anonymous [writer]' that democracy is best adapted to human nature and that subjects must be freed from the bonds of laws so as to manage their own affairs.[110] Even though Johannes Georgius Graevius, professor in Utrecht, had already unveiled the identity of the *TTP*'s author to Leibniz in a letter from April 1671, Dürr (like Thomasius and Rappolt) still seems not to be aware of Spinoza's name.[111] Yet the shield of anonymity

---

[106] Ibid. 6: 'simulare dissimulareque'; 'moderna Politices praxi'.
[107] Dürr, *Oratio De praeposterâ et impiâ libertate Philosophandi* (30/6/1671), in *Actus Panegyricus impositae merentibus*, 1672.
[108] Zenker, *Denkfreiheit*, 107–8.
[109] Dürr, *Oratio*, n.p. [B1r]: 'ne ista libertas in licentiam vertat'.
[110] Ibid. n.p. [C1v]: 'ad Democraticum nostrum Anonymum'.
[111] 'Johann Georg Graevius an Leibniz van 12./22. April 1671' in Leibniz, *Sämtliche Schriften und Briefe*, I, 142.

SPINOZA'S REVERSAL

193

disappeared when Johann Melchior published his *Epistola Ad Amicum, Continens Censuram. Libri, cui titulus: Tractatus Theologico-Politicus*, also in 1671, becoming the first to name the author publicly, albeit in mutilated form as 'Xinospa' and 'Zinospa'.[112] Melchior, a theologian who had been trained in Groningen under Maresius, criticised the new philosophy, which undermined revelation, as well as Spinoza's biblical exegesis, which, like that of the Socinians, leads to atheism. He demonstrated this using the author's view of faith, which is not a religious faith but 'nothing other than obedience' and which consequently stands in the service of a practical philosophy.[113] There is, therefore, nothing new here, although Melchior does emphasise that he discovered errors in the *TTP* that had not been observed before, for instance in relation to the fall into sin. His analysis of the *TTP* is concrete and progresses systematically through the entire work. He comments on Spinoza's view concerning the lively imagination of the prophets, his critique of miracles, biblical hermeneutics, the Ezra-hypothesis, and the seven doctrines, which he deems insufficient for a religion.[114] In a postscript, he pauses to address the theme of politics: Spinoza's views on religion serve to destroy the very foundation of the state. Melchior cites the *TTP* and paraphrases it, evidently considering that the passages he considers most shocking suffice to show that the work must be rejected. Most appalling of all is the anonymous author's insistence that every person has a right to whatever he can and wills to do, that natural right forbids nothing, that human beings have no duties before God, that the power of God is the same as the power of nature, and that the government controls religion.

To our knowledge, Spinoza never responded to Melchior's *Epistola*, even though the refutations and accusations kept coming closer to him and could not have escaped his notice. On 9 November 1671, he did, however, write a response to Leibniz, who a month earlier had sent Spinoza a most courteous letter, asking him a question about optics in which Spinoza, as he had been told, was highly skilled. In a postscript to his response, Spinoza added the following comment, without any prompting by Leibniz: 'If the *Theological-political treatise* has not yet reached you, I'll send a copy, if you don't mind.'[115] Up to that point in time, the only effect which the antitexts appeared to have

---

[112] Melchior, *Epistola Ad Amicum, Continens Censuram*, 6; 44. See also Otto, *Studien zur Spinozarezeption in Deutschland*, 18; Meinsma, *Spinoza en zijn kring*, 329; Israel, 'The Early Dutch and German Reaction', 77–8; Gootjes, 'The First Orchestrated Attack on Spinoza: Johannes Melchioris and the Cartesian Network in Utrecht', 23–43.

[113] Melchior, *Epistola Ad Amicum*, 10: 'nihil praeter obedientiam'.

[114] Ibid. 26; 33–4; 34–5; 16; 17; 19.

[115] *Ep*. XLVI [to Gottfried Wilhelm Leibniz]; CWS II, 395.

194 DEMOCRATIC THOUGHT FROM MACHIAVELLI TO SPINOZA

had was to contribute to Spinoza's fame, to the point where a year and a half later Charles Louis, Elector Palatine, was moved to offer him a position as *professor extraordinarius* of philosophy at Heidelberg, with an annual salary to match. In an ironic twist, the zealous Calvinist Johann Ludwig Fabritius was the one commissioned to write to Spinoza and to communicate the elector's offer to him. Fabritius had already read the *TTP* two years earlier, concluding that its entire goal was to destroy church and state. Due to the work's most dangerous nature, he wove a less-than-subtle warning into the letter of invitation.[116] Spinoza, he writes, will have all the freedom necessary to perform his task, provided that he does not abuse this freedom 'to disturb the publicly established religion'.[117] As such, the Heidelberg offer became an act within the polemical debate, pushing Spinoza to refuse it in a letter to Fabritius dated 30 March 1673. If he wanted to instruct the youth, he wrote, he would have to stop advancing in philosophy. He would not know 'what the limits of that freedom of Philosophizing might have to be' for him not to be seeming to intend to disrupt the publicly established religion.[118] For conflicts and schisms arise 'from men's varying affects, or their eagerness to contradict one another', as he has already experienced while living 'a private and solitary life'.[119]

The year 1673 also saw the posthumous publication of the *Vindiciae miraculorum*, written by Johannes Batelier, a pastor and theologian from the Hague. Focusing on Spinoza's critique of miracles, this refutation does not touch on the theme of politics at all, and rhetorically wonders whether this 'new philosophy' has replaced God with nature.[120] In the spring of 1674, the

---

[116] In June 1670, the *TTP* was already circulating in Heidelberg. After reading it in 1671, Fabritius wrote the following to his friend Heidegger (who later quoted this passage in his Fabritius biography of 1698): 'Mir graust, wenn ich sehe, dass eine so zügellose Willkür eingeräumt wird, öffentlich darzulegen, was immer (einem) in den Sinn kommt, und die Christliche Religion selbst und die heiligen Schriften so offen zu lästern. [. . .] Das alles läuft auf den Tod sowohl der Kirche als besonders des Staates hinaus, der bei fest verankerter Religion nicht in gefährlichster Weise erschüttert werden kann. Die belgischen Aristokraten scheinen anderer Ansicht zu sein. Vielleicht hat ihr Staat auch eine andere Grundlage. Dass aber derartige Schriften nach Deutschland hineingetragen und unter den Studenten verbreitet werden, halte ich für äußerst gefährlich', Gebhardt (ed.), *Spinoza – Lebensbeschreibungen und Dokumente*, 248–52; Freudenthal, *Die Lebensgeschichte Spinoza's*, 219.

[117] *Ep.* XLVII [from Johann Ludwig Fabritius]; CWS II, 396.

[118] *Ep.* XLVIII [to Johann Ludwig Fabritius]; CWS II, 397.

[119] Ibid.

[120] Batelier, *Vindiciae miraculorum*; see Van Bunge, 'The Absurdity of Spinozism: Spinoza and his First Dutch Critics', 21; Van Bunge, 'Van Velthuysen, Batelier and Bredenburg', 59–61; Israel, 'The Early Dutch and German Reaction', 84–6.

Adversus anonymum Theologo-politicum of the Utrecht professor Regnerus van Mansvelt was published, it too posthumously. Like his predecessors, Van Mansvelt was troubled by Spinoza's view of God which equates him with the universe, eliminates all freedom and admits only a fatalist necessity.[121] If God is not distinguished from nature, the present world, which is merely composed of individual things, is the only one that exists, and God's power is nothing but the power of those individual things. Van Mansvelt considers this a monstrous view and nothing short of a lie. What the author of the *TTP* – Van Mansvelt does not mention Spinoza by name – really aims at is the completely absurd confusion of God and his creatures. Nor is he fighting for the freedom to philosophise, but for the profane and unbridled freedom to commit all possible kinds of errors, and to defend and disseminate them, as a direct threat to the peace of the state. Spinoza, so this critic continues, uses diabolical trickery to establish the atheism which Descartes had first managed to conquer with a heroic effort.[122] With his *Adversus anonymum Theologo-politicum*, Van Mansvelt therefore offers a response to the *TTP* from the allied Cartesian camp in which the theologians invariably placed Spinoza.[123]

Spinoza counters also this critique coming from the moderately progressive camp, which nevertheless approached the criticism of the theological conservatives Melchior and Batelier as well as the Lutheran response from Thomasius, Rappolt and Dürr, by persistently and explicitly connecting his view of God (or nature) with politics. The result is revolutionary and surpasses even Hobbes in its radicality. The 'difference you ask about, between Hobbes and me', so he writes in a letter to Jelles on 2 June 1674, 'is this: I always preserve natural Right unimpaired, and I maintain that in each State the Supreme Magistrate has no more right over its subjects than it has greater power over them. This is always the case in the state of Nature.'[124]

---

[121] Van Mansvelt, *Adversus anonymum Theologo-politicum liber singularis*, 272–3.

[122] Van Mansvelt, *Adversus anonymum Theologo-politicum*, 4.

[123] According to Israel ('The Early Dutch and German Reaction', 84–6), Van Mansvelt's refutation was intended to thwart the attempts of Voetius and Maresius (who was of significance for Batelier and Van Limborgh) to link Spinoza's philosophy and the philosophy of Descartes, and thus to free and purify the new philosophy from this uneasy alliance. Yet his primarily political and moderately progressive refutation only ended up bolstering the conservative theological camp and led to cooperation between the conservative and moderately progressive countermovements. See also Blyenbergh, whose refutation brings these two lines together.

[124] *Ep.* L [to Jarig Jelles]; CWS II, 406. Spinoza originally wrote this letter in Dutch; the text in the *Nagelate Schriften* represents a slightly edited version of it, while the *Opera Posthuma* include a Latin translation, as indicated by the term *versio* there;

196 DEMOCRATIC THOUGHT FROM MACHIAVELLI TO SPINOZA

The Cartesian Van Mansvelt considers the way Spinoza equates right and power unacceptable. Spinoza also writes to Jelles that he had seen the work of the late Van Mansvelt in a shop window, but, based on the little he had been able to read from it there, deemed it 'not worth reading, much less answering'. He therefore left the book lying there, 'along with its author'.[125] Nevertheless, the *Adversus anonymum Theologo-politicum* did number among the books Spinoza left at his death in 1677. He must therefore have abandoned his earlier indifference to the work, or else received it as a gift, giving careful attention to its extensive analysis of the *TTP*.[126]

Mansvelt agrees with the *TTP*'s efforts to separate philosophy and theology, although he is of the view that its anonymous author, like Meyer, in the end abandoned this project himself by failing to respect that separation. The simple notion of faith as obedience does not suffice. The biggest problem with the anonymous author's view is the significance he attributes to a number of theories (like determinism) and texts (like those of Paul), which Van Mansvelt himself nevertheless uses as his own starting point, only to draw different conclusions from them; the inferences made in the *TTP*, he charges, are tenuous, deceitful or dangerous to the state. Van Mansvelt puts his finger on the major question in Spinoza's project, but his critique of what is admittedly a difficult and tricky albeit novel contribution to the matter undermines that very novelty and ends up falling back into the old pattern. 'It is rightly said that people can do something other than they do, although they cannot do anything against divine determination' – as such, Van Mansvelt finds

---

see G IV, 239. The autograph has been lost, so that the slightly edited version in the *NS* brings us closest to Spinoza's source text and Dutch usage. The matter became more complex when Gebhardt (1925), following Van Vloten, decided to take the Latin of the *versio*-version as Spinoza's own and, consequently, as the original formulation. There is no evidence or support for this choice, which was rather based on a misguided assumption in regard to the Latin conceptual apparatus in the margins, as was rightly pointed out by Akkerman in *Studies in the Posthumous Works of Spinoza*, 47–50. For more ample treatment of this topic, see Proietti and Licata, *Il carteggio Van Gent-Tschirnhaus*, 67–71. For a similar question involving similar methods and the reconstruction of the *Korte Verhandeling*, see Boehm, '"Dieses war die Ethic und zwar Niederländisch, wie sie Spinoza anfangs verferttiget"', 175–206; Lavaert, 'Metafysica van het subject, een misleidende spraakverwarring', 141–72.

125 *Ep.* L [to Jarig Jelles]; CWS II, 407.

126 For the inventory of the books Spinoza left at his death, drawn up on 2 March 1677, see Freudenthal, *Die Lebensgeschichte Spinoza's*, 158–65, here 161. See also *Catalogus van de bibliotheek der Vereniging Het Spinozahuis te Rijnsburg*, 26.

himself back at square one.[127] Since 'ignorance and mental weakness are liable to guilt and all the appetites must be governed by reason, it conflicts with natural law when a rational creature does not follow the guidance of reason but [the guidance] of the appetites', so Van Mansvelt insists over against Spinoza, who had placed the mentally impaired and the ignorant on the same level as prudent people who follow reason.[128] The way Spinoza defines natural right by appetite and power is nonsense, for it 'is a contradiction [to say] that something is just and not of sound reason'.[129] Against Spinoza's view that natural right does not forbid anything except what no one wishes or is able to do, Van Mansvelt argues that man, as a rational being, 'is obligated to order all his acts according to the laws and rules of sound reason'.[130] The crucial point of his critique is located especially in the contradiction he sees between Chapters 16 and 20 of the *TTP*, in the extent to which freedom must be granted and in the freedom which Spinoza allows for errors to be made. Using a contradictory formula that rivals the very contradiction he claims to detect in the *TTP*, Van Mansvelt writes that 'freedom perishes through excessive freedom or irrational licentiousness'.[131] Or, even though false ideas cannot be eradicated, the government must still restrain and curb them, lest they infect others as well. For if one allows the argument advanced in the *TTP*, it follows that even atheists must be protected in their freedom to think and say what they want, which is absurd. A limited freedom does not harm the state; rather, 'very many disadvantages arise from the licentiousness to propagate errors of all kinds', as the anonymous author of the *TTP* would have it, who 'has even denied God'.[132] Moreover, 'it does not suffice to say that these things are to be feared less in a democracy'.[133]

On 6 May 1674, less than a month before Spinoza sent his disparaging remarks about Van Mansvelt to Jelles, the University of Jena hosted a

---

[127] Van Mansvelt, *Adversus anonymum Theologo-politicum*, 274: 'merito dicitur quod aliud possint agere quam agunt; quamvis dici nequeat quod possint agere contra determinationem divinam'.

[128] Ibid. 'Nam cum ipsa ignorantia & animi impotentia culpabilis sit, & omnes appetitus ratione regendi sint, juri naturae manifeste repugnat creaturam rationalem non rationis sed appetituum ductum sequi.'

[129] Ibid. 275: 'Nam contradictorium est, aliquid esse justum & non sanae rationis.'

[130] Ibid. 276: 'creatura rationalis [. . .] naturaliter obligata est, omnes suas operationes secundum leges & regulas sanae rationis instituere'.

[131] Ibid. 358: 'Nam libertas nimia libertate seu licentia irrationali, perit.'

[132] Ibid. 363: 'qualia plurima debent creari ex profana, quam petit Anonymus, omnis generis errores propagandi licentia'; 'imo post abnegatum toties ipsum Deum'.

[133] Ibid. 282: 'Nec eadem de causa sufficit, quod minus timenda sint in Democratico imperio, nam cum repugnent, nunquam jure possibilia debent statui.'

198   DEMOCRATIC THOUGHT FROM MACHIAVELLI TO SPINOZA

disputation on the *TTP* and the question of the *libertas philosophandi*, with Johannes Musaeus as the presiding professor and Christian Friedrich Knorr as the student respondent: *Tractatus Theologico-Politicus, Quo Auctor Quidam Anonymus, conatu improbo, demonstratum ivit, Libertatem Philosophandi* [. . .] *tolli non posse; Ad veritatis lancem examinatus*. When the text, which had already been printed in April, in the weeks leading up to the oral disputation, was republished in 1708, the first part of the title was changed to read: *Spinosismus, Hoc est, Tractatus theologico-politicus, quo Benedictus Spinoza, connatu improbo, demonstratum ivit, Libertatem Philosophandi* [. . .] *tolli non posse; Ad veritatis lancem examinatus*. In addition, the preface was left out of this second edition, and it was no longer clear that it had actually been authored by the respondent Knorr.[134] Since Johannes Colerus in his Spinoza biography of 1705 likewise identified Musaeus, who was a Lutheran professor of theology of some renown, as the author, this mistake has continued to be repeated in all critical and bibliographical literature on the subject down to this very day.[135] Colerus was lyrical of the sharp pen of Knorr/alias Musaeus, and expressed his amazement that this refutation 'is hardly known in Holland and hard to find'.[136] He therefore summarised the disputation, highlighted its most important points, and cited 'Jure merito quis dubitet &c.' which he then translates: 'That is, "One would be right to doubt whether the myriads hired by the devil to thwart divine and human rights ever included someone who has worked more eagerly to their destruction as this imposter, who was born to the great misfortune of the church and to the detriment of the state"'.[137] But Colerus makes small mistakes, is not always careful in his work (also when he cites the title: *Tractatus Theologico Politicus ad veritatis lumen examinatus*), and speculates and fantasises at will, as when he claims that Spinoza must have seen Musaeus's work, 'since it was found among the books he left at his death'.[138] Whatever the case may be,

---

[134] See Zenker, *Denkfreiheit*, 113–14.

[135] Colerus, *Korte, dog waarachtige Levens-Beschryving van Benedictus de Spinosa*, 86–8. The scholars who mention Musaeus alone as the author include: Israel, *Radical Enlightenment*, 631; Grunwald, *Spinoza in Deutschland*, 25; Han-Ding, *Spinoza und die deutsche Philosophie*, 42; Van der Linde, *Benedictus Spinoza. Bibliografie*, 91. See Zenker, *Denkfreiheit*, 112–19.

[136] Colerus, *Korte, dog waarachtige Levens-Beschryving*, 88.

[137] Ibid. 86–7: 'Jure merito quis dubitet, num ex illis, quos ipse daemon, ad divina humanaque jura pervertenda, magno numero conduxit, repertus fuerit, qui in iis depravandis operosior fuerit, quam hic impostor, magno Ecclesiae malo & Reipublicae detrimento natus.'; Knorr/Musaeus, *Spinosismus*, §III, 6.

[138] Colerus, *Korte, dog waarachtige Levens-Beschryving*, 86–7.

the arguments used by these Lutheran theologians have a familiar ring to them, and we may assume that they were not unfamiliar to Spinoza. Knorr agrees that no one can surrender his natural right of judgement, but it is quite another matter when a person espouses views on religion that conflict with sound reason and revelation.[139] His refutation is primarily based on the by now classic argument that the distinction Spinoza drew between internal and external acts is untenable. After all, so Knorr insists, the state can govern minds indirectly: with 'the threat of punishment [. . .] it brings the minds of people to produce internal acts and to avoid contradictory internal acts'; it can use institutions and education to incite or discourage its subjects, and apply other appropriate measures to bring them to recognition of the true religion; when false teachers 'have the audacity to spread false teachings and to whisper them into the minds of the simple, the government has the duty to coerce them with punishments or else to banish them'.[140] Spinoza too does recognise this, but at the same time he holds the view that the multitude and differences can never be completely wiped out and homogenised. And, as Dürr's reaction makes clear, this is in the German student's mind the problem of that theory:

> How much the *libertas philosophandi* threatens the right of the government [. . .] and the very peace of the state can be seen from the fact that nothing divides the minds, both between the magistrates and subjects and among the subjects themselves, as much as what arises from this [*libertas philosophandi*], namely the multitude of religions.[141]

This argument from Dürr is not a theological but a political one, and it is also somewhat new in the polemics: the problem of (philosophical/political) freedom is multitude and/or diversity.

---

[139] Knorr/Musaeus, *Spinosismus*, §CIII, 84.

[140] Ibid. 85: 'comminatione poenarum [. . .] moventque hominum animos ad [actus] internos, regulae convenienter eliciendos, & oppositos cavendos'; ibid. 88: 'Quod si doctores falsi irrepant, qui doctrinas erroneas spargere, easque simpliciorum animis instillare ausint, summarum Potestatum est eos prohibere, &, si in proposito pergant, poenis coercere, vel etiam ex ditionibus suis ejicere'.

[141] Ibid. 90–1: 'Et sane quantopere obsit libertas illa philosophandi Potestatum summarum juri [. . .] atque adeo ipsi Reipublicae paci, vel inde intelligitur, quod nihil magis animos, cum Magistratuum & subditorum, tum subditorum inter se, distrahat, quam quae ex illa nascitur, religionis diversitas'.

3.2 1674

The countercampaign proved effective, such that on 19 July 1674, the Court of Holland banned the *Tractatus theologico-politicus* along with *Leviathan*, the *Philosophia S. Scripturae Interpres*, and the 'Socinian books' of the *Bibliotheca Fratrum Polonorum*.[142] On 7 August, that ban was also adopted by the synod of North Holland, on 8/12 September by the synod of Utrecht, and on 11/13 September by the synod of South Holland.

Around that same time, in September 1674, Spinoza's former correspondent Willem van Blyenbergh published the first refutation of the *TTP* to be composed in Dutch, under the title *De waerheyt van de christelijcke godts-dienst*. This work too would be found among the books Spinoza left on his death. In the preface, Van Blyenbergh compares the treatise to other blasphemous books, like Koerbagh's *Een Bloemhof*, the mythical *De tribus impostoribus* and the works of Machiavelli which, as he claims, have succeeded in convincing many in the cities of Holland. He aims to thwart Spinoza's plans to destroy the foundations of the Christian religion and what is built on them. For Spinoza does not just restrict himself to a critique of the Christian religion, but wants 'to completely overturn and eradicate humanity, or reason, which is that in which humanity consists', and he does so by spreading his view according to which the natural right of each person extends as far as his power.[143] This ultimately equates human beings and animals and means that belief in divine punishment is undermined, resulting in lawlessness and corruption of life. Van Blyenbergh sums up the aim of the *TTP* in four main points. The author (1) denies prophetic revelation; (2) topples the authority of Holy Scripture; (3) extols the natural light of reason, such that anyone who desires a supernatural light is subjected to mockery; and (4) argues 'that in a free commonwealth one is allowed to think whatever one wants and to say whatever one thinks'.[144] According to Van Blyenbergh, the dismantling of religion will lead to political unrest and the overthrow of the government. He also fails to understand how it can be that a text with such designs is tolerated. Of course, this final remark is in a way too late, since the *TTP* had indeed been banned by the time *De waerheyt* emerged from the press.

Van Blyenbergh's refutation is thorough, closely follows the structure, chapters, logic and arguments of the *TTP*, offering lengthy quotations in

---

[142] Freudenthal, *Die Lebensgeschichte Spinoza's*, 139.

[143] Blyenbergh, *De waerheyt van de christelijcke godts-dienst en de authoriteyt der H. Schriften*, n.p. [b2].

[144] Ibid. n.p. [b2–c2r].

SPINOZA'S REVERSAL 201

the process so that its readers actually received nothing less than a compendium of the *TTP* in Dutch translation, even though it had itself not yet been published in the vernacular by then and was actually banned. In this way, Van Blyenbergh unwittingly contributed to the dissemination of reprehensible ideas among a wider audience, that is, the common people. He lists the most important chapters of the *TTP* whose refutation people absolutely need to read, as well as the parts they can skip if they happen to be short on time. To Van Blyenbergh's mind, the most important chapters are: Chapter 4, on divine law; Chapter 6, on miracles; Chapter 8, on the writers of the sacred books; Chapter 11, on whether the apostles wrote as teachers; Chapter 13, which argues that Holy Scripture teaches only the simplest matters; and Chapter 16, on the foundations of the republic. He sees in the critique of revelation, miracles and language, the reading of Scripture, and the view of faith a disguised attempt to introduce atheism. Van Blyenbergh also defends Descartes, who had understood that to will is to understand and had taught that there are eternal truths which do not flow from God's nature but do have God as their cause, such that they do not follow from the necessity of his nature but from the perfection of his intellect and will.[145] Spinoza's clear aim, on the contrary, is to overthrow the Christian religion and the Bible. What Van Blyenbergh furthermore considers unacceptable is the *TTP*'s insistence on the political significance of ceremonies and its claim that the moral law is not revealed but inscribed in human nature.[146] Spinoza's atheism conflicts with the 'Christian way of government' which 'rests on the foundations of religion'.[147] Van Blyenbergh does not agree that the divinity of Scripture only consists in its moral teachings, since this would imply that the Bible has no more significance than the writings of Socrates, Plato and Cicero. Nor does he admit Spinoza's claim that the Bible or faith only relate to obedience (rather than truth) and that a person's faith can only be judged by its works. Obedience does not, as Spinoza had argued, determine faith, but faith rather comes first and determines obedience.[148] In this context, Van Blyenbergh compares the *TTP* and Meyer on the interpretation of Scripture, showing the extent to which they diverge. He also charges that this issue broke the long-time friendship between the two authors.[149]

[145] Ibid. 112–13.
[146] Ibid. 143.
[147] Ibid. 166.
[148] Ibid. 376.
[149] Ibid. 387–8.

202 DEMOCRATIC THOUGHT FROM MACHIAVELLI TO SPINOZA

Even though Van Blyenbergh claims he has little to say about Spinoza's political vision – since his critique of religion and biblical hermeneutics are his most important target – and will address it only insofar as it discredits the Christian religion, the refutation of the final five chapters of the *TTP* actually make up the clearest part of *De waerheyt*. Van Blyenbergh holds the view that, in order to identify the natural law of the rational creature (i.e. human beings), we must return to his origin, that is, to his essence at the moment of his creation by God and of his sin against innate reason. This, he claims, is what Spinoza himself actually meant in Chapter 4 when he wrote that sin consists in allowing the animal-like in us to rule over reason. Van Blyenbergh similarly sees no disagreement between Spinoza and himself in regard to the equality of all human beings or the rule of not doing to others what you yourself do not want others to do to you. Where he and Spinoza do clash rather relates to the latter's claim 'that the natural right of each person must not be determined by sound reason but by desire and power'.[150] In Spinoza's view, whatever a person considers useful to himself, whether by reason or by affect and passion, can be desired with supreme right and pursued by all possible means. Van Blyenbergh is outraged by this: 'Does this not turn people into animals, and reason into a slave of desire and violence?'[151] In his counterargument, he draws on arguments that had figured in their earlier correspondence. It is not because a being does not do what is in its nature from the moment of birth that this thing is not of its nature, like a cat which catches mice (but not immediately at birth), and the same applies to a human being who lives and acts according to reason. Adam was from the start created in all perfection, 'his body stood in the service of his will, and the will in the service of the advising intellect', and it is 'a most astonishing folly to couple the natural right of man to his desire or power rather than to reason'.[152] The way Spinoza equates right and power is linked to the idea that literally all people are equal and consequently enjoy equal rights – children as well as adults, fools and the mentally impaired as well as the prudent and rational. Precisely this naturalistic indifference to reason (and to the presence or absence of certain ideas) is what Van Blyenbergh fiercely contests, outraged and not infrequently stooping to an insult-laced tirade: 'hellish vomit, the sea into which all streams of godlessness flow: here we see man turned into a wild animal and his reason into wanton lust; here not only Christendom, and not only all civil government, but all humanity

---

[150] *TTP* XVI, 7; CWS II, 283; Blyenbergh, *De waerheyt*, 427.
[151] Ibid. 428.
[152] Ibid. 436–7.

SPINOZA'S REVERSAL 203

is eradicated; here atheism, indeed complete impertinence, is placed on the throne'.[153] Van Blyenbergh ends his analysis of Chapter 16 by pointing to Grotius, who had expressed himself better than Spinoza on all these points, and to Hobbes, who had used the same premise of natural right to come to an opposing conclusion, charging for instance that people must always stay true to their word.[154] Van Blyenbergh then treats Chapters 17 through 20 as one unit, presenting them as a conclusion: here 'religion is not derived from God but invented by the civil government'; 'here all the bonds of virtue and justice are untied, and virtue and religion become a bridle for simpletons and a mask and toy for the wise'.[155] Spinoza wants to spread that notion 'that religion and justice are just a toy and invention of the wise, to deceive simpletons or, at best, to keep them under the demands of obedience'.[156] In the final chapter, so Van Blyenbergh charges, Spinoza argues that in a free republic everyone must be allowed to think what he wants and to say what he thinks. Van Blyenbergh does agree with the first part, for all people indeed have this right, provided they refrain from doing the second part. The freedom to philosophise ought not to be pushed so far that people can *actually express* thoughts that 'overturn the pillars and foundations of the state', as when the Christian religion is eradicated and replaced by a natural or political religion.[157]

The correspondence between Van Blyenbergh and Spinoza from nearly a decade earlier already left little doubt that the two had different views on the most fundamental issues: good and evil, the freedom of the will, biblical hermeneutics, God, Descartes's new philosophy, and the meaning of the words and concepts used. The reading of the *TTP* now revealed to Van Blyenbergh that their polemics ultimately also had a political significance and concerned the social order. With the transmutation of what initially appeared to be a purely theoretical debate to the public and common (universal) domain, along with the panicky rejection of the *TTP*, the ensuing accusations, and, ultimately, the ban, the polemics from the fall of 1674 obtained a tragic significance. And once again, as we already observed in the case of Vanini and Koerbagh, the countermovement did not just limit itself to theoretical debate but actually intervened. It slandered, condemned and forbade, and brought to realisation the very reason for Spinoza's critique, which was

---

[153] Ibid. 438.
[154] Ibid. 448–9.
[155] Ibid. 461–2.
[156] Ibid. 463.
[157] Ibid. 466.

204 DEMOCRATIC THOUGHT FROM MACHIAVELLI TO SPINOZA

bitterly materialised. Antitexts continued to be published in the following years, but, as we shall see, they did not offer any new arguments but only served to consolidate the countermovement. A number of Spinoza's friends, some of whom he used to show fragments of his work which he debated with them, went on to convert to the Roman faith, thereby joining the ranks of his enemies. In the meantime, Spinoza heroically, or perhaps desperately and against his better judgement, tried to thwart the accusations in letters, seeking to shift the focus back to the issue itself and constantly searching for ways to clarify his arguments and reasons.

The questions on the free will which Ehrenfried Walther von Tschirnhaus sent to him in a letter dated 8 October 1674, are highly reminiscent of Van Blyenbergh's concerns, and yet they were formulated in a clear and fresh manner. With this letter, Tschirnhaus initiated an exchange of ideas that not only was to play an important role in his own intellectual development but also accompanied Spinoza throughout the writing of his *Tractatus politicus* and to his premature death early in 1677. And perhaps – I submit this as a careful suggestion – this exchange partly inspired Spinoza to lay out his vision once again, this time without the extra baggage of questions relating to biblical hermeneutics and religion. Tschirnhaus, a young German aristocrat, had studied law in Leiden from 1669 to 1672, but Spinoza first got in touch with him through this letter, which was delivered to him by Georg Hermann Schuller. Schuller, a young German physician, had studied in Leiden at the same time as Tschirnhaus, but by October 1674 already figured as a loyal and full member of Spinoza's Amsterdam circle. Schuller's friends included Jan Rieuwertsz and Pieter Van Gent, and he was to be a constant presence in the final two and a half years of Spinoza's life. Moreover, the physician at Spinoza's deathbed probably was not Meyer, as some biographers have claimed, but Schuller, who likewise represented the first executor of Spinoza's will and was to play an important role in the publication of the *Opera posthuma* and the *Nagelate Schriften*.[158] He corresponded frequently with Leibniz, regularly informing him of the latest news from the Dutch intellectual scene and especially of what was happening at Spinoza's desk and in his circle. The same applies to Tschirnhaus, whom Schuller had already befriended during his student days; both were eager devotees of Descartes's new philosophy and found Spinoza's revolutionary and more radical variant of that new philosophy highly stimulating. What struck Tschirnhaus was

---

[158] See Proietti and Licata, *Il carteggio Van Gent-Tschirnhaus*, 51–74; Stein, 'Neue Aufschlüsse', 554–65. The biography which Proietti and Licata primarily reference in this context is that of Colerus.

SPINOZA'S REVERSAL
205

Descartes's and Spinoza's opposing views on the freedom of the will, noting that 'both those who argue for it and those who argue against it seem to me to speak the truth, that is, as each conceives Freedom'.[159] He confronts Spinoza with the relativity of intellectual content that follows from naturalism, from an argumentation not based on norms, and from the multitude of perspectives. The same question occurred to others as well, and at first sight Tschirnhaus's remarks seem to connect to the moralistic observations of Van Mansvelt and Van Blyenbergh. Tschirnhaus expresses his agreement with Spinoza's idea that 'in all things we are determined to something by a definite cause, and thus that we have no free will [as you understand "free will"]'.[160] But he also agrees with Descartes that we are not compelled in certain things 'and so we have free will [as he understands "free will"]'.[161] Ultimately, the question has three parts to it. The first is whether we in an absolute sense have power over the things outside of us, and the answer is a clear 'no'. The second is whether we in an absolute sense have power over the movements of our body that follow from the determination by our will. The answer is 'yes' this time, provided that we have a healthy body. The third is whether we in an absolute – that is, free – sense can apply our mind when we have the ability to use it. The answer is a resounding 'yes', for who could prevent me from thinking in my thoughts that I will to do or not to do something. In this instance, we are not compelled by external things, and if we are, as Spinoza – in contrast to Descartes – assumes, then virtue could no longer be acquired as a personal attribute. If we, like Spinoza, affirmed this, 'all wickedness would be excusable'.[162]

Spinoza did not send his response to this three-part question directly to Tschirnhaus but via Schuller, and it resembles what he had written to Van Velthuysen in February 1671. He does not understand freedom as his critics do, but his view is the exact opposite. His critics apparently do not consider the good to be good because they desire it and are attracted to it of themselves, but must be compelled to it. And the things to which they are attracted of themselves and for internal reasons, these things they consider not good. Spinoza charges that his critics have a strange view on freedom, and then goes on to explain how *he* understands freedom: 'I say that a thing is free if it exists and acts solely from the necessity of its own nature, and

---

[159] *Ep.* LVII [from Ehrenfried Walther von Tschirnhaus]; *CWS* II, 425.
[160] *Ep.* LVII [from Ehrenfried Walther von Tschirnhaus]; *CWS* II, 425.Words in square brackets from Curley.
[161] Ibid. Words in square brackets from Curley.
[162] *Ep.* LVII [from Ehrenfried Walther von Tschirnhaus]; *CWS* II, 425–6.

206 DEMOCRATIC THOUGHT FROM MACHIAVELLI TO SPINOZA

compelled if it is determined by something else to exist and produce effects in a fixed and determinate way. E.g., even though God exists necessarily, still he exists freely, because he exists from the necessity of his own nature alone.'[163] He therefore does not locate freedom 'in a free decree, but in a free necessity'.[164] His critics, he adds, are victims of a deep-seated prejudice, according to which they can freely choose and control their appetites. The fact that all people are born with this prejudice means it is difficult to abandon it. Just as a drunk thinks he freely decides to say what he says when he is drunk (but which, once sober, he wishes he never had said), so too people think they master their desires and can arouse or control them. On the basis of this argument, Spinoza goes on to respond to Tschirnhaus's objections. If he, following Descartes, calls free the person who is not compelled by an external cause, and considers compulsion to mean acting against one's wish, then Spinoza admits that we have a free will in that sense. But if he understands a compelled act as an act not against one's wishes but still necessary, then Spinoza denies that we human beings are in any way free. The point of the debate lies in the third part of Tschirnhaus's argument: Spinoza denies that we are absolutely free in the use of our intellect, as Tschirnhaus maintains. What kind of a consciousness is Tschirnhaus talking about when he makes this claim? 'For my part', Spinoza ironically responds, 'unless I contradict my consciousness, i.e., contradict reason and experience, and unless I encourage prejudices and ignorance, I deny that I can think, by any absolute power of thinking, that I will to write and do not will to write.'[165] But he appeals to Tschirnhaus's own consciousness, for the latter undoubtedly knows from his own experience that he in a dream does not have the power to think that he wills to write and does not will to write. And so, Spinoza continues,

> I also don't believe that he's learned from experience that the mind is always equally capable of thinking of the same object. [Rather, I think he's learned from experience] that, as the boy is more capable of having an image of this or that object stirred up in it, so the mind is more capable of contemplating this or that object.[166]

---

[163] *Ep.* LVIII [to Georg Hermann Schuller]; *CWS* II, 427.

[164] Ibid. For this notion of freedom and its consequences for Spinoza's political thought, see Visentin, *La libertà necessaria*.

[165] *Ep.* LVIII [to Georg Hermann Schuller]; *CWS* II, 429.

[166] Ibid.

SPINOZA'S REVERSAL

To those who claim that his argument excuses every form of evil he responds: 'For evil men are no less to be feared, nor are they any less harmful, when they are necessarily evil!'[167]

3.3 1675–1676

In the correspondence from the final two years of Spinoza's life and in the antitexts that were published in 1675 and 1676, we see a shift in focus from questions on Bible and faith to the more abstract level of physical (metaphysical) principles. This shift is accompanied – certainly in the correspondence – by the circulation of the text of the *Ethica*. In his letter from 5 January 1675, Tschirnhaus asks Spinoza when he will publish his treatise on epistemology and 'General matters in Physics'.[168] He already knew that Spinoza had made progress on the epistemological front, but his reading of the *Ethica*, more specifically the corollaries joined to part 2, had shown him that Spinoza also had a lot to offer for physics. In his response, Spinoza refers to *Ethica*, I, definition 6.[169] In June and July 1675, hopeful news reached him from London, when Oldenburg wrote to tell him that he had changed his mind about his earlier criticism of the *TTP*. Having given the entire matter renewed thought, Oldenburg was no longer convinced that Spinoza was attacking true religion or solid philosophy. For that reason, he asked Spinoza to renew their correspondence and intellectual exchange. On 5 July 1675, Spinoza sent a response (which no longer survives), in which he expressed his resolve 'to publish that Five-part Treatise' (i.e. the *Ethica*), to which Oldenburg responded rather worriedly on 22 July (in a letter which does survive), admonishing him not to include anything in this work that could convince his readers that he wants to overthrow religion.[170] He adds that he has no objection to Spinoza sending him several copies of the *TTP* for clandestine distribution in England. In the meantime, Schuller wrote to him from Amsterdam with several critical questions concerning the *Ethica* that had occurred to him and Tschirnhaus, who was staying in London at the time and had put in a good word for Spinoza and the *TTP* with Boyle and Oldenburg. Spinoza responded concretely to each of these questions.

---

[167] *Ep.* LVIII [to Georg Hermann Schuller]; CWS II, 430.

[168] *Ep.* LIX [from Ehrenfried Walther von Tschirnhaus]; CWS II, 430.

[169] *Ethica* I, Def. 6; CWS I, 409: 'By God I understand a being absolutely infinite, i.e., a substance consisting of an infinity of attributes, of which each one expresses an eternal and infinite essence.'

[170] *Ep.* LXII [from Henry Oldenburg]; CWS II, 435.

208 DEMOCRATIC THOUGHT FROM MACHIAVELLI TO SPINOZA

In August, Tschirnhaus wrote to Spinoza from London himself and addressed his remark regarding *Ethica*, II, proposition 7 again, to which Spinoza immediately responded.[171] In a letter from November 1675, Schuller returned yet again to his friend's critique regarding that same proposition – at the time, Tschirnhaus himself was travelling through France, where he spoke about the *TTP* with Huygens and Leibniz. Through Schuller as his intermediary, Tschirnhaus also asked Spinoza whether he would be allowed to discuss the *Ethica* with Leibniz, most expert 'in Physics, and especially in Metaphysical studies concerning God and the Soul'.[172] But Spinoza responded that he wanted to know what exactly this Leibniz figure was doing in France, and that he preferred for Tschirnhaus to get to know him a little better first.

Spinoza, of course, had his reasons for being careful. Even though his newest work had not come to press yet, the situation was still heating up. And the campaign against the *TTP* continued unabated. After the encouraging news from London, Spinoza also received sad news from Italy. In September 1675, Albert Burgh, a friend and fellow philosopher from the University of Leiden who had likewise studied Latin with Van den Enden, wrote a letter to Spinoza from Florence announcing his return to the Catholic Church. It is a long letter, numbering at least ten sides, and amounts to an attempt to convince Spinoza to follow Burgh's own example.[173] Another letter, it too written from Florence in the year 1675, was sent to Spinoza by Nicolaas Stensen, a former student of anatomy at Leiden who had converted to Catholicism in 1667. This lengthy, urgent letter likewise sought to persuade Spinoza to lend a 'receptive ear to our Church'.[174] Stensen did publish this letter but may never actually have sent it to Spinoza, which quite likely explains why it was not included in the *Opera posthuma*.[175] 'In the Book they say you have authored – which I myself also suspect, for various reason, that you have authored – I notice that you bring everything back to the public security, *or* rather, to your security, which, according to you, is the goal of public security.'[176] Did Stensen send

---

[171] *Ethica* II, 7; CWS I, 451: 'The order and connection of ideas is the same as the order and connection of things.'

[172] *Ep.* LXX [from Georg Hermann Schuller]; CWS II, 463.

[173] *Ep.* LXVII [from Albert Burgh]; CWS II, 441–51; see also Ed Curley, 'Editorial Preface' with 'Letters: January 1671–Late 1676' in *The Collected Works of Spinoza*, II, 366–7.

[174] *Ep.* LXVIIA [from Nicolaas Stensen]; CWS II, 452.

[175] Curley, 'Editorial Preface Letters', 366–7; Totaro, 'Niels Stensen (1638–1686) e la prima diffusione della filosofia di Spinoza nella Firenze di Cosimo III', 147–68; Spruit and Totaro, 'Introduction', in Spruit and Totaro (eds), *The Vatican Manuscript of Spinoza's Ethica*, 6–26.

[176] *Ep.* LXVIIA [from Nicolaas Stensen]; CWS II, 451.

him a veiled threat when he suggested that the means Spinoza had used in his *TTP* conflict with the security desired, for which he saw clear evidence in the fact that Spinoza has thrown everything into disarray and 'exposed himself to the greatest danger'?[177] In the summer of 1677, this same Stensen was to turn the manuscript of the *Ethica*, which he had (presumably) obtained from Tschirnhaus, over to the Holy Office so that Spinoza's works came to be placed on the Index of Forbidden Books. Oldenburg's warning had therefore not been groundless, as Spinoza himself was to find out. Just as he received Oldenburg's letter from 22 July 1675, he set out for Amsterdam, intending to commit the *Ethica* to press. But while he was occupied with this, as he writes in his response to Oldenburg from September/October 1675, a rumour was being spread that 'a certain book of mine about God was in the press [. . .] to show that there is no God'.[178] When Spinoza learned of this, he decided to delay the publication and to wait to see how the events would play out. 'But every day the matter seems to get worse', he wrote, adding he no longer knew what to do.[179]

When Johannes Bredenburg observed in his *Enervatio Tractatus theologico-politici* (1675) that Spinoza's views in the *TTP* aim to eradicate all religion completely, everyone by that time could agree.[180] In order to refute the treatise, so this Collegiant writes, it is not necessary to discuss every single detail, but it suffices to refute the foundations of the argument, namely the identification of God and nature. After analysing several passages and quotations to show that Spinoza indeed understands nature as God, Bredenburg himself demonstrates that nature is not the same thing as God, using the geometric style and entirely after the example of the *Ethica*.

While the refutations became increasingly focused, radical, theoretical and abstract, as well as longer, the polemics were at times also politicised, and more often so in these later years. This time also saw a political debate that actually had little to do with Spinoza's *TTP*, even though it did represent an incidental occasion for it. The debate was sparked by the 1675 publication of *La veritable religion des Hollandois*, written in French by Jean Brun (Johannes Braun), a Walloon minister who hailed from Germany, had been educated in Leiden, and served in Groningen as professor of Hebrew and the oriental

---

[177] Ibid.

[178] *Ep.* LXVIII [to Henry Oldenburg]; *CWS* II, 459.

[179] Ibid.

[180] Bredenburg, *Enervatio Tractatus theologico-politici*, 4; Van Bunge, 'The Absurdity of Spinozism', 21; Van Bunge, 'On the Early Dutch Reception of the *Tractatus theologico-politicus*', 225–51.

languages. This work represented a response to *La religion des Hollandois*, which had been composed two years earlier by Jean-Baptiste Stouppe, a Swiss Walloon minister who had first pursued a political career in England, thereafter entered the service of the French king and then ended up in the Netherlands as a lieutenant in the French army. While in the Netherlands, he composed this brief work – or, perhaps more accurately, this apology for the French occupation of the Netherlands – in which he expressed his amazement at the many sects that could be found there.[181] Before becoming professor in Groningen, Brun/Braun had been an instructor at the École illustre in Nijmegen, but his tenure there came to an abrupt end as a result of the cruel French invasion in which Stouppe played an important role. Brun/Braun responded to Stouppe's work with what is essentially an apology for the religion confessed in the United Provinces, in turn a vindication of the Netherlands as such. The polemics are inherently political. Both works use Spinoza's *TTP* as an example. Both authors had travelled extensively throughout Europe, lived, worked and studied in different countries, and participated in public life using various vernacular languages. Stouppe's *La religion des Hollandois* consists of eight letters, was published in Utrecht in 1673 and also appeared that very same year in Cologne and in Dutch translation in Amsterdam. Spinoza cannot be absent in a list of religious sects, he writes – 'a Jew by birth [. . .] who did not renounce the Jewish religion' and 'has a great number of followers'.[182] We find in this work the well-known objections to the *Tractatus theologico-politicus*, including its description of God as the 'power of nature', its framing of religions as 'inventions for state use', etc.[183] But Stouppe's point is that Spinoza lives in *this* country and that not a single Dutch theologian has shown the courage to try to refute him, such that one can only conclude that the Hollanders themselves deny God, approve of Spinoza's ideas, or else lack the strength and courage to thwart them. Brun/Braun in his turn criticises Stouppe's portrayal of the situation more than he attacks Spinoza or the *TTP*. Stouppe, he insists, is seriously mistaken when he claims that Spinoza has not renounced the Jewish religion. Not only does Spinoza hold aberrant views, but he has also withdrawn himself from the ceremonies, eats and drinks whatever is offered to him, including bacon and wine, and is in reality totally indifferent to each and every religion. Brun/Braun furthermore observes that the *TTP* was being sold in England, Germany, France and Switzerland, adding he is not

---

[181] Stouppe, *La religion des Hollandois*, 1673; *De gods-dienst der Hollanders*, 1673.

[182] Stouppe, *De gods-dienst der Hollanders*, 25.

[183] Ibid. 26.

SPINOZA'S REVERSAL 211

sure whether it has been banned in any of those countries. For this reason, Stouppe has no reason to single out the Netherlands, since its government did take immediate steps against it, eventually resulting in a ban. Brun/Braun furthermore asks why the theologians in the Netherlands are held more accountable for refuting the *TTP* than others are, even if the work was published in their country. 'Heresy is a gangrene infecting the entire body of the church', Catholics as well as Lutherans, and it does not respect any borders, so that *all* theologians, whether German, French, Swiss, English or Dutch, have the obligation to respond critically.[184] Moreover, so Brun/Braun asks, can Stouppe himself escape his own criticism? Why did he not compose a thorough refutation instead of engaging in plundering and murdering? 'I am convinced that Spinoza's work is no more pernicious than [Stouppe's]; for if the former teaches atheism openly, the latter does so secretly.'[185] Stouppe is a hidden enemy of religion, which makes him even more dangerous than Spinoza, who at least declared war openly. Stouppe, who was responsible for the carnage at Bodegraven, was using a more effective means to kill religion than Spinoza had done, and his *Religion des Hollandois* is therefore deserving of much greater criticism. On top of this, the *TTP* has been refuted excellently by Van Mansvelt. Brun/Braun then singles out several passages from the *TTP* and expresses his indignation over them, for instance in relation to the events in Japan, the ceremonies that were reported to have been instituted there with a view to the entire community, and the Dutchmen living there who were required to abstain from ceremonies at the order of the Dutch East India Company. Brun/Braun completely ignores the fact that Spinoza cites this example in an argument which is about teaching 'a whole nation – not to mention the whole human race –', and that this must necessarily be for the most part accommodated 'to the power of understanding of ordinary people'.[186] Spinoza is addressing a global issue and all people, while Brun/Braun is talking about what is advantageous to the Dutch. This is why Brun/Braun is troubled by Spinoza accusing the Dutch not just of irreligiosity, but also – with reference to the Amboyna massacre – of cruelty.[187]

---

[184] Brun/Braun, *La veritable religion des Hollandois*, 161.
[185] Ibid. 162.
[186] *TTP* V, 37; CWS II, 148.
[187] The term Amboyna Massacre refers to the 1623 execution of nine Japanese, one Portuguese and ten Englishmen who were in the service of, respectively, the United East India Company and the British East India Company following an extrajudicial trial that involved torture and was performed by an ad hoc court appointed by the United East India Company's governor on Ambon Island. The English saw these executions as murder, resulting in very tense relations with their Dutch competitors

In fact, he wonders why Spinoza deigns to say anything about the matter at all, noting that Holland acted in accordance with a judicial verdict. That the English complained about this verdict is only to be expected, he adds, just as all criminals always try to accuse their judges of injustice.

In 1675, the second edition of Museaus's *Ableinung der ausgesprengten abscheulichen Verleumbdung* appeared, which included a critique of Meyer's *Philosophia* and the *TTP*.[188] The publication of this book was occasioned by Matthias Knutzen, who on 5 and 6 September 1674 had spread three handwritten pamphlets in Jena announcing the rise of a new sect called the *Conscientarier* or *Gewissener* (The Conscientious) in leading European cities, including Jena itself. This was in reality just Knutzen's way to announce his own highly subversive ideas. In these pamphlets he questioned the Bible's reliability on the basis of the many contradictions found in it as well as the multitude of interpretive possibilities that present themselves to the reader due to polysemy, etc. This is followed by an attempt to deduce his own blasphemous ideas from Scripture. He thus denies the existence of a rewarding and punishing God, explicitly approves atheism, and denies Christendom (for which he, like Koerbagh, uses the term 'anointed').[189] He argues that people must follow the guidance of natural reason, science and the conscience, that all people are equal and therefore deserving of the same, such that wealth must be distributed equally. The pamphlets caused a major uproar and brought upright citizens into turmoil. Alarmed by the course of events, Musaeus immediately wrote his *Ableinung*, which went on to appear in the fall. One year later, a second, more critical and more cogently argued edition appeared, expanded with new analyses of recent books propounding similar (subversive) ideas, namely the *Philosophia* and the *TTP*. These events have led some to call Knutzen the 'first German Spinozist', though others see no direct link between the texts or else consider their contents a commonplace of anti-Christian literature.[190] Regardless, there are a number of

which would ultimately number among the factors leading to the outbreak of the First Anglo-Dutch War. See *TTP* 5, 180–1; *TTP* 16, 365.

[188] Musaeus, *Ableinung Der ausgesprengten abscheulichen Verleumbdung*, in Knutzen, *Schriften*, 91–284; for discussion, see Schröder, 'Einleitung', in Knutzen, *Schriften*, 10–32.

[189] See Schröder, 'Kommentar', in Knutzen, *Schriften*, 60; Koerbagh, *Een Bloemhof*, 139–40; see also above, Chapter VI.5, 152.

[190] In his 'Einleitung' (19), Schröder charges that the claim which makes Knutzen the first German Spinozist who literally took things over from the *TTP* is pure fantasy and myth. To support his view, he appeals to Baeck who insists in *Spinozas erste Einwirkungen auf Deutschland*, 36–41, that these are commonplaces of

SPINOZA'S REVERSAL

things that strike us. The temporal vicinity of their appearance and the dramatic commotion elicited by the *Philosophia*, *TTP* and Knutzen's pamphlets lend themselves rather easily to a story, not to mention the aura of scandal surrounding both the *TTP* and the pamphlets and their common political dimension. At times Knutzen uses the same terminology as Koerbagh. And in the second edition of his *Ableinung*, Musaeus lists virtually all the critically formulated arguments from the *TTP* which Knutzen had given a farcical rendering. What is left when all the secrets of the Christian religion are rejected and all miracles are discarded?[191] The author of the *TTP* questions not only the common interpretation of Scripture but Scripture itself, and he even openly writes that the word of God 'does not consist in paper and ink'.[192] According to him, religion is not to be found in certain books, but is universally inscribed on the hearts of all people. For that reason, people need not attach any value to the announcements of the prophets, since they too just follow their own phantasy, erroneous conceptions and imagination. Miracles either can be given a natural explanation or else are simply deceit and lies. The books said to be written by Moses date from long after his lifetime, and the apostles wrote their epistles by recourse to reason and science. Each author, of either testament, devised a way that he himself deemed best for teaching. This is why the Christian religion is built on many different foundations together with the many resulting conflicts.[193]

anti-Christian literature; see also Otto, *Studien zur Spinozarezeption in Deutschland im 18. Jahrhundert*, 77.

[191] Musaeus, *Ableinung*, 186 (92).

[192] Ibid. 187 (93)–188 (94): 'Der andere aber zeucht nicht allein die gewöhnliche Art und Weise die heilige Schrifft zu verstehen und zu erklären in Zweifel / sondern auch die Bücher Altes und Neuen Testamentes / oder die heilige Schrifft selbst / und komt endlich so weit / dass er unverhohlen schreibt / Gottes Wort bestehe nicht in Papier und Tinte / nicht in einer gewissen Anzahl Bücher / sondern es sey in die Herzen der Menschen geschrieben / und bestehe in der von Natur aller Menschen Herzen eingepflanzten allgemeinen Religion.' In two places in *TTP* XXII, Spinoza in a critical section on Scripture uses precisely this same expression 'paper and ink': 'I, on the other hand, fear that in their excessive zeal to be holy they may turn Religion into superstition, and indeed, may begin to worship likenesses and images, i.e., paper and ink [*hoc est chartam & atramentum*], in place of the Word of God', *TTP* XXII, 5; *CWS* II, 249; G III, 159; 'In the same way, also, Scripture is sacred and its statements divine just as long as it moves men to devotion toward God. But if they completely neglect it, as the Jews once did, it's nothing but paper and ink [*nihil est praeter chartam, et atramentum*]. They completely profane it, and leave it subject to corruption', *TTP* XXII, 13; *CWS* II, 251; G III, 161. See also section 2.2 above for the way Spinoza questions the concept of 'holiness'; 177–8.

[193] Musaeus, *Ableinung*, 188 (94)–189 (95).

214 DEMOCRATIC THOUGHT FROM MACHIAVELLI TO SPINOZA

Even though Spinoza must have heard such charges often enough, in September/October 1675 he wrote to Oldenburg asking him to point out those passages in the *TTP* 'which have caused learned men to have misgivings'.[194] In response, Oldenburg wrote: 'I would think that these include especially those passages in the work which seem to speak ambiguously about God and Nature.'[195] He added that Spinoza was thought to rob miracles of their authority, to question revelation and to cast doubt on the resurrection of Christ. Spinoza remained convinced that people just did not really understand what he had written, and in his next letter insisted that he holds another view of God and nature than modern Christians do. In his view, 'God is, as they say, the immanent, but not the transitive, cause of all things.'[196] As a result, divine revelation cannot be based on miracles, and Christians who do hold that position 'are distinguished from non-Christians [. . .] only by delusion'.[197] Similarly, those who profess that God assumed a human nature in the person of Christ 'speak no less absurdly than if someone were to say to me that a circle has assumed the nature of a square'.[198] Oldenburg wrote back: 'You seem to build on a fatal necessity of all things and actions. But once that has been asserted and granted, they say the sinews of all laws, of all virtue and religion, are cut, and all rewards and punishments are useless.'[199] Spinoza, in turn, responded: 'But I do not in any way subject God to fate, but I conceive that everything follows with inevitable necessity from the nature of God.'[200] This 'inevitable necessity of things does not destroy either divine or human laws, [. . .] nor will the bad things which follow from evil actions and affects be any less to be feared because they follow from them necessarily'.[201] And, finally, 'whether we do what we do necessarily or contingently, we are still led by hope and fear'.[202] These assertions seem to suggest that Spinoza was unaware that he was actually confirming his opponents' worst suspicions. During that same period early in 1676, Spinoza also wrote a response to Albert Burgh:

---

[194] *Ep.* LXVIII [to Henry Oldenburg]; *CWS* II, 459.

[195] *Ep.* LXXI [from Henry Oldenburg]; *CWS* II, 464.

[196] *Ep.* LXXIII [to Henry Oldenburg]; *CWS* II, 467.

[197] *Ep.* LXXIII [to Henry Oldenburg]; *CWS* II, 467–8.

[198] *Ep.* LXXIII [to Henry Oldenburg]; *CWS* II, 468; Spinoza uses the same example as Hobbes in *Leviathan*, Chap. IV: 'the word *round quadrangle* signifies nothing; but is a meere sound'.

[199] *Ep.* LXXIV [from Henry Oldenburg]; *CWS* II, 469.

[200] *Ep.* LXXV [to Henry Oldenburg]; *CWS* II, 470.

[201] *Ep.* LXXV [to Henry Oldenburg]; *CWS* II, 471.

[202] Ibid.

I grant that the organization of the Roman Church, which you praise so highly, is well-designed politically, and profitable for many. I do not believe there is any order more suitable for deceiving ordinary people and controlling men's minds, unless it would be the order of the Mohammedan Church, which surpasses it by far. For from the time this superstition began, no schism has arisen in their Church.[203]

The identification of the power of God with the power of nature can only be understood such that Spinoza equates God and nature, and in those days that could only mean one thing: atheism. What did not help Spinoza's cause was the way he judged Christianity and Islam by the same norm, even questioned Christ himself, read the Bible through a political-historical lens, and claimed that everything flows with an inevitable necessity from God, nature, or the nature of God. As Wiep van Bunge has pointed out, once it had been established that Spinoza really was an atheist, one could only conclude that the views he had set forth in the *TTP* were simply a lie, a deception with a hidden (political) agenda. The Socinian Frans Kuyper, himself the publisher of the *Bibliotheca fratrum polonorum* which had been banned together with the *TTP*, already said as much in the title to the refutation he published in 1676: *Arcana atheismi revelata*, that is, 'the secrets of atheism exposed'. Spinoza, so he insisted, is an atheist who 'understands true religion as nothing but a life lived by the demands of the state and the political laws'.[204]

The countertexts and correspondence of the final two years of Spinoza's life were increasingly explicit about what he kept hidden in his *TTP*, namely the underlying physics (metaphysics) which he did explicitly address in the *Ethica*. No wonder Leibniz was so curious and tried to get his hands on the manuscript, whose virtues he extolled to Tschirnhaus, while keeping his misgivings to himself. In his letters, Leibniz had for some time already been writing that the *TTP* required a powerful refutation, one not laced with emotion and hostilities, but a thorough, lengthy, robust and erudite refutation, for the very reason that the *TTP* witnesses of an author with a sharp intellect and great erudition. When, in the early spring of 1672, no such antitext had yet appeared (since Van Mansvelt's work was still waiting to be published), he wrote to the Lutheran theologian Gottlieb Spitzel, whose

---

[203] *Ep.* LXXVI [to Albert Burgh]; *CWS* II, 477.

[204] Kuyper, *Arcana atheismi revelata*, n.p. [§3v]: "ipsum [i.e. Spinozam] per veram Religionem nihil praeter vitam, ex usu Reipublicae, secundum leges Politicas [. . .] intelligere'; Van Bunge, 'The Absurdity of Spinozism', 21; Israel, 'The Early Dutch and German Reaction', 96–9.

216 DEMOCRATIC THOUGHT FROM MACHIAVELLI TO SPINOZA

knowledge of Hebrew and other oriental languages made him, in his mind, the right person for the job, asking him to dismantle the work thoroughly.[205] Spitzel, however, responded less than enthusiastically to Leibniz's request, noted that Thomasius and Rappolt had already refuted the work, and waited another four years before devoting some critical observations to the *TTP* in his *Felix literatus ex infelicium periculis et casibus* (1676). What is more, Spitzel actually did the very opposite of what Leibniz had suggested, as he too launched into a tirade, attacked the 'light-eschewing author of this unfortunate miscarriage (they say it is Benedictus Spinoza, a Jew by birth, apparently with a misshapen face, an enthusiast, estranged from all religion)', and in the end simply repeated the well-known, emotion-laced refrain.[206] In short, Spinoza ascribes prophecy to the deceptive imagination of the prophets, denies the existence of miracles, and thereby attacks Holy Scripture and overturns revelation. In his discussion of miracles, Spitzel included a footnote with a reference to Batelier's *Vindiciae miraculorum* as well as Knorr/ alias Musaeus's refutation. He then went on to add his own accent, which, in the context of the early countertexts, may well be expected but is still unique and new. We have to be careful, he writes, lest these errors (i.e. scepticism of prophecy, the denial of miracles) spread further in Germany and establish themselves in Italy, France and the Low Countries.

> In order to prevent this, it is necessary to read most carefully from the books of the MACHIAVELLIANS, THAT IS, THE PSEUDO-POLITICIANS, who connect all religions with political art and devote every effort to placing the kingdom of God in repugnant subjection to worldly dominion, the church to the world, and piety to civil politics. They consider religion as nothing more than a chain for controlling the masses, as reins for restraining the rebels' attack, as a deterrent for those who do not sufficiently recognize the government's authority [. . .], such that princes and magistrates are said to choose the religion of which they think that it best matches the state and is most suited to their judgment. And it is especially these diabolical tunes to which Machiavelli danced in his *Discorsi* and *Principe*.[207]

---

[205] Leibniz, 'Brief an Spitzel', 27. Februar /8. März 1672, in *Sämtliche Schriften und Briefe*, I, 193; see also Israel, *Radical Enlightenment*, 504–6.

[206] Spitzel, *Felix literatus ex infelicium periculis et casibus*, 143–4: 'ferunt autem Benedictum Spinosam esse, natione Judaeum, hominem ut res ipsa loquitur perfrictae frontis, fanaticum, & ab omni religione alienum'; see also Israel, *Radical Enlightenment*, 504.

[207] Spitzel, *Felix literatus*, 145–7: 'Cujus evitandi causa magna imo maxima cum cautione ipsis legendi evolvendique; sunt LIBRI MACHIAVELLISTARUM SEU

SPINOZA'S REVERSAL   217

4. *Tractatus politicus*, 1677

In the last year of his life, starting somewhere in the spring of 1676, Spinoza tried to assemble the insights he had up to that time put on paper in his correspondence, in the *TTP* and in the unpublished *Ethica*, which was already circulating in manuscript form. He must have thought it necessary to give better formulation to his views and to clarify them in the face of the persistent incomprehension and unwarranted attacks of his critics, or, even better, to demonstrate their internal coherence and irresistible logic. In the latter half of 1676, he wrote to a friend that he had been working on his *Political Treatise* for some time, and had already completed six chapters.[208] The first chapter provides something of an introduction to the work, the second treats natural right, and the third the right of the supreme power. The fourth addresses what matters of state depend on the supreme power, the fifth the ultimate thing a state can pursue, and the sixth 'how a Monarchic Government must be set up, so as not to fall into Tyranny'.[209] At the time of writing, he was working on the seventh chapter, in which the main points of the preceding chapter were to be demonstrated. He added that he would also be treating aristocratic and democratic forms of government – but Spinoza never ended up finishing the treatise. He died in February 1677, continuing his work on the *Tractatus politicus* until the end. By the time of his death, he had managed to complete the section on aristocratic rule and reached the introductory section of Chapter 11, where the analysis of democracy was to

---

PSEUDO-POLITICORUM, qui omnem Religionem ad artes referre politicas, omnique id agere studio conantur, ut terrenum regnum Regno DEI [*sic*! The final four words here clearly represent a printer's error: Spitzel reproaches the 'pseudo-politici' for subjecting the 'Regnum DEI' to the 'terreno regno', and not the other way around], Ecclesia seculo, pietas civili politiae foeda servitute subjiciatur. Religionem illi duntaxat pro vinculo habent, quo vulgus hominum coerceatur, pro froeno, quo perdomentur rebellium insultus, pro terrore, quo percellantur qui Magistratus authoritatem non adeo magni aestiment [. . .], ut sic Principes ac Magistratus eam amplecti debeant religionem, quam & statui congruam & suo juidicio consentaneam intelligant. Et [. . .] tibias hujusmodi diabolicas potissimum Nicolaus Machiavellus inflav[it] libris *Discursuum* ac de *Principe*.'

[208] *Ep.* LXXXIV [to N.N.]; *CWS* II, 488; according to Curley, letter 84 was probably addressed to Jelles and therefore originally written in Dutch, and Spinoza began composing the *TP* very early on in 1676 or even late in 1675; see *Collected Works*, II, 488; 'Editorial preface TP', 491–502. For a philological reflection towards a critical edition, see Proietti, 'La tradizione testuale del *Tractatus politicus*. 'Examinatio' per un'edizione critica', 125–53.

[209] *Ep.* LXXXIV [to N.N.]; *CWS* II, 488.

218 DEMOCRATIC THOUGHT FROM MACHIAVELLI TO SPINOZA

begin. What had been the aim of his entire oeuvre, the outcome of his reversal, the complex coherence he had tried to lay out critically and neutrally, moving forward and then stepping back, revising and polishing, building up and breaking down – all of this ended with a lacuna, an ellipsis.

The fierce and enormous countermovement which had followed upon the publication of the *TTP* rattled Spinoza, and yet he remained convinced that the only thing he needed to do was to repeat his views and to formulate them more clearly. His opponents' reactions confirmed what he had wanted to make clear in the first place – they were persisting in the error, confusion or illusion which he had sought to unmask – and this formed a reason for him to try, once again, to change their minds. His claims were not made out of personal motives, but he adduced intrinsic and universal reasons for his positions which, in his understanding, were for the good of everyone. Or, to put it another way, the errors of his opponents were also working to their own disadvantage, while Spinoza's views served a stable political order favourable to both rulers and subjects. All the texts he had written represented pieces in that puzzle, as he now wanted to make clear. Like the *Ethica*, his political theory pursues freedom and equality, the natural condition of all human beings, there where all people are and feel safe. This theory is likewise based on the conceptual framework of the *Ethica*, its ontology and anthropology. For this reason, the essential theoretical parts of the *Ethica* are appropriated and incorporated in the *Tractatus politicus*. In just the same way, the essential insights of the *TTP* are taken up into the *TP*, whose new theoretical focus also offers them an additional, radical significance.[210]

4.1 The basis

1. In spite of this, in the opening chapter Spinoza shows himself anything but optimistic about the political knowledge theorists and philosophers have produced thus far, and this scepticism moves him to focus on the field of politics. The first reason why philosophers and theorists have shown themselves unsuited to writing something worthwhile about politics is their conception of 'the affects by which we're torn as vice, which men fall into

---

[210] The following is the result of a close reading of the *TP*. The section devoted to the first five chapters (i.e. 4.1) has been published in a slightly revised form in Dutch as 'Multitude. De omkering van Spinoza, in de geest van Machiavelli', in Van den Eede and Verstrynghe, *De maakbare moraal*, 71–108.

by their own fault'.[211] They think they serve God and attain to the height of wisdom when they extol a human nature that does not exist and bewail human beings as they are. Here we hear echoes of Machiavelli: philosophers 'do not conceive people as they are, but as they want them to be'.[212] A second reason for their failure to comprehend anything about politics is that they close their ears to the lessons that can be drawn from political practice. Philosophers think political practitioners are out to trap people. Similarly, philosophers – and theologians in particular – imagine political powers, like private individuals, to be subject to the rules of piety, and so they look upon them as enemies of religion. Nevertheless, political practitioners have written much more accurately about political affairs than any philosopher, political theorist or theologian ever has. Moreover, Spinoza is convinced that everything has already been devised and tried out in political practice. People have always lived in some form of common law since that is their natural constitution: they cannot live without a political order.

For this reason, Spinoza writes that he does not intend to advance any new form of state (which is at any rate impossible) but to analyse what experience teaches us and to connect this to human nature. Furthermore, he wants to investigate politics and the affections 'with the same freedom of spirit we're accustomed to use in investigating Mathematical subjects'.[213] This is why he has contemplated the 'human affects [*affectus*] [. . .] not as vices [*vitia*] of human nature, but as properties which pertain to it in the same way heat, cold, storms, thunder, etc., pertain to the nature of the air'.[214] The mind derives as much joy from knowledge of these inconvenient affections as it does from knowledge of things that are pleasing to the senses. As such, Spinoza offers a key for reading the geometric method – as free, not burdened by assumptions or the conscience, but neutrally, flexibly, hypothetically, for the sake of comprehension, analytically – and for reading the *Ethica*. He lists the most general conclusions: In his *Ethica*, he has demonstrated that people are necessarily subject to the affects. This is true for all without exception. Moreover, people are 'so constituted that they pity those whose affairs are going badly, and envy those who are prospering; they're more inclined to vengeance than to mercy'.[215] Furthermore, everyone wishes

---

[211] *TP* I, 1; CWS II, 503 In the following, some of Curley's translations have been slightly adapted to achieve greater consistency with the original Latin.

[212] *TP* I, 1; CWS II, 503; Machiavelli, *Il Principe* 15; *Discorsi* I, 3. See above, Chapter I.4, 39. See also *Ethica* III, Praef., and the commentary from Gebhardt in G V, 133.

[213] *TP* I, 4; CWS II, 505.

[214] Ibid.

[215] *TP* I, 5; CWS II, 505.

220 DEMOCRATIC THOUGHT FROM MACHIAVELLI TO SPINOZA

that others would live as he himself has chosen to live, to approve what he approves, to reject what he rejects. And since 'everyone wants to be first, they fall into quarrels and try as hard as they can to crush each other'.[216] In spite of this, religion still holds the opposite view, even though it has little power against the affects, except where illness is conquering health or at the point of death. Another thing Spinoza has demonstrated in the *Ethica* is that the affects can be restrained by reason, but that this is difficult to do. It is an illusion to think that the multitude (*multitudo*) can be convinced to live according to the prescripts of reason. And since all people throughout the world form some sort of a civil order, one must not seek its causes and foundations from reason but from the common human condition.

*

2. 'In our *Theological-Political Treatise* we treated both Natural Right and Civil Right, and in our *Ethics* we explained what sin, merit, justice, injustice and finally, human freedom are', so Spinoza writes in the opening lines of Chapter 2, which is why he has resolved 'to explain them again here, and to demonstrate them rigorously'.[217] He then repeats step by step how he had arrived at the above conclusions in the *Ethica*. In what follows, we will closely follow the line of his argument.

Every natural thing can be conceived adequately, whether it exists or not. As a result, it is not possible to derive its definition (and thus its essence) from its coming into existence or perseverance. From this it follows that 'the power [*potentia*] by which natural things exist, and so by which they have effects, can't be anything but the eternal power of God itself [*Dei aeterna potentia*]'. In Spinoza's view, God's power stands for natural power, that is, a power that is not 'created', as he makes clear in the next sentence: a created power would not be able to preserve itself or the natural things, since it would require the same power that was necessary to be created to persevere in its existence. Spinoza writes like a geometer and his statements must be situated against the positions from which he distances himself. When the argument is read that way, it fits in seamlessly with the definitions and propositions in part I of the *Ethica*.

Spinoza is speaking about God when he refers to nature or to that which is not made, is not subject to time, and coincides with necessity. He is speaking about God's power when he refers to a power that is not created, that is, a natural power that is eternal and not subject to time, and coincides with

---

[216] *TP* I, 5; CWS II, 505–6.
[217] *TP* II, 2; CWS II, 507.

necessity. It is important not to confuse the categories, as people often do out of ignorance. Necessity is not the same thing as purposiveness, and even though people are part of nature, human nature is not divine. So too people often 'do not distinguish between the modifications of substances and the substances themselves, nor do they know how things are produced. So it happens that they fictitiously ascribe to substances the beginning which they see that natural things have.' They 'easily ascribe human affects to God, particularly so long as they are also ignorant of how those affects are produced in the mind'.[218] All their confusions and prejudices 'depend on this one: that men commonly suppose that all natural things act, as men do, on account of an end; indeed, they maintain as certain that God himself directs all things to some certain end for they say that God has made all things for man, and man that he might worship God'.[219] Nevertheless, 'not many words will be required now to show that Nature has no end set before it, and that all final causes are nothing but human fictions'.[220]

From the interchangeability of God and nature (defined, posited and demonstrated in the *Ethica*) the right of nature (*jus naturale*) is derived:

> For since God has the right over all things, and God's right is nothing but his power itself, insofar as [his power] is considered to be absolutely free, it follows that each natural thing has as much right by nature as it has power to exist and have effects [*tantum juris ex natura habet, quantum potentiae habet ad existendum et operandum*].[221]

Spinoza defines 'free' as being determined by an inner necessity: 'That thing is called free which exists from the necessity of its nature alone, and is determined to act by itself alone.'[222]

Natural right is the same thing as the laws of nature, that is, the rules according to which all things happen,

> i.e., the very power of nature [*naturae potentiam*]. So the natural Right of the whole of nature, and as a result, of each individual [*uniuscujusque individui*], extends as far as its power does. Hence, whatever each man does according to the laws of his nature, he does with the supreme right

---

[218] *Ethica* I, 8, Schol. 2; CWS I, 413.
[219] *Ethica* I, App.; CWS I, 439–40.
[220] *Ethica* I, App.; CWS I, 442.
[221] *TP* II, 3; CWS II, 507.
[222] *Ethica* I, Def. 7; CWS I, 409.

222 DEMOCRATIC THOUGHT FROM MACHIAVELLI TO SPINOZA

of nature [*summo naturae jure*]. He has as much right over nature as he has power [*tantumque in naturam habet juris, quantum potentia valet*].[223]

But since people allow themselves to be led more by their blind desire (*cupiditas*) than by reason, the natural power of people, and thus their right, must not be defined from reason, but from all possible inclinations by which they are incited to act and strive to preserve themselves.[224] The desires that do not arise from reason, however, 'are not so much human actions [*actiones*] as passions'. This is of little consequence for the political theory, since, 'whether a man is wise or ignorant, he's a part of nature', and he does nothing except according to the laws of nature.[225] Up to this point, Spinoza has been speaking about natural power (*potentia*), which must be distinguished from actual activity.

The next section marks a break, opens with a 'but' and outlines the view of many which Spinoza nevertheless rejects:

> But most people [*At plerique*] believe that the ignorant disturb the order of nature rather than follow it, and they conceive men in nature as a dominion within a dominion [*imperium in imperio*]. For they maintain that the human Mind was not produced [*produci*] by any natural causes, but was created [*creari*] immediately by God, so independent of other things that it has an absolute power to determine itself [*absoluta . . . potestas sese determinandi*] and to use reason properly.[226]

In presenting the view he intends to refute, Spinoza introduces a political element, namely dominion (*imperium*), and speaks for the first time about *potestas* (institutional power) rather than *potentia* (natural power), which is the term he uses when he speaks of the natural condition.[227] His own view is

---

[223] *TP* II, 4; CWS II, 507–8.

[224] *TP* II, 5; CWS II, 508.

[225] *TP* II, 5; CWS II, 509.

[226] *TP* II, 6; CWS II, 509. Translation slightly modified.

[227] For the difference between the concepts of *potentia* and *potestas*, see Negri, *L'anomalia selvaggia*, 225–37; Rehmann, 'Power ≠ Power: Against the Mix-Up of Nietzsche and Spinoza', 1–14; Reitz, 'Der politische Traktat in der Diskussion der Gegenwart', 171–202; Terpstra, *De wending naar de politiek*; Terpstra, 'An Analysis of Power Relations and Class Relations in Spinoza's *Tractatus politicus*', 79–105; Walther, 'From *potestas multitudinis* in Suárez to *potentia multitudinis* in Spinoza', 129–52. For the translation of these terms, see n. 1 above. Studies that focus on the notion of *multitude* consistently pay attention to this distinction; see especially the work of Del Lucchese, Morfino and Visentin. See also Balibar who discusses what he refers to as

that human beings do *not* have the absolute power to determine themselves and to always use reason, and he establishes it in three ways: by experience, from absurdity, and through the incoherence of the opposing position. First, experience 'teaches all too well that it's no more in our power to have a sound Mind than it is to have a sound Body'.[228] Secondly, one would not be able to explain why, if people could determine themselves absolutely and freely, they do not always allow themselves to be led by reason. Thirdly, the theologians cannot substantiate their claims with their theory of original sin and the first man. If indeed the first man could determine himself absolutely, why then did he fall into sin? And if he was deceived by the devil, who then deceived the devil? The first man himself, if we assume he existed, must not have had the power to make proper use of reason, and, just like us, he must have been subject to the passions. All strive to persevere in their existence, and they *have no free will* – that is the point. Whatever is indicative of inability or weakness in people cannot be ascribed to freedom. And, conversely, people are free when they act according to the laws of nature and reason, of themselves and by inner determination.

In this way, Spinoza concludes that not everyone is always able to use reason and to achieve freedom. But everyone does strive to persevere in their existence and everyone's right extends as far as their power. From this it follows that

the Right and established practice of nature [*jus & institutum naturae*], under which all men are born and for the most part live, prohibits nothing except what no one desires and no one can do; it does not prohibit disputes, or hatreds, or anger, or deceptions, and it is absolutely not averse to anything appetite [*appetitus*] urges.[229]

In the following sections, Spinoza focuses on the core of the political question and investigates what it means when people have power (*potestas*) over one another. An individual is under another person's right (*alterius esse juris*) to the degree that he is under another person's power (*alterius*

---

the 'dogmatic approaches' to this problem of Matheron, Rice and Negri, as well as the 'critical approach' of Moreau: '*Potentia multitudinis, quae una veluti mente ducitur*', *Spinoza politique*, 245–83. See also Cristofolini, 'Le parole-chiave del *Trattato politico* e le traduzioni moderne', 23–38; Curley, 'Troublesome Terms for Translators in the *TTP*', 39–62; Bove, Moreau and Ramond, 'Le *Traité politique*: une radicalisation conceptuelle?', 27–44; Moreau, 'La notion d'*imperium* dans le *Traité politique*', 355–66.

[228] *TP* II, 6; CWS II, 509.

[229] *TP* II, 8; CWS II, 511.

potestate), and is under his own right (*sui juris*) to the degree that he can resist violence, avenge the harm inflicted upon him and live fully in accordance with his own insight (*ingenium*).[230] There are four possibilities: A has power over B if (1) A has tied up B, (2) taken away his weapons of defence, (3) instilled fear in him, or (4) won B over to himself by a benefit so that B would rather obey A than himself and prefers to live according to A's wishes over his own. In the first two scenarios, A only has power over B's body, while in the final two scenarios both B's body and mind (*mens*) are in his power, albeit only as long as the hope or fear lasts. A person's faculty of judgement (*iudicandi facultas*) can likewise fall under the right and thus the power of another person, especially when the mind is deceived by another. It follows, then, that the mind is under its own right (*sui juris*) when the mind can use reason properly. But since human power is determined not so much by the strength of the body as the strength of the mind, the people who are most under their own right (and who are therefore most free) are those who have the strongest mind and are most guided by reason.

When people are tormented by envy, hatred or anger, so Spinoza argues, then they are enemies, and since these affections come over them so frequently, people are by nature enemies. But the more people unite and have common rights, the more right they have. At this point, Spinoza inserts a list of definitions:

> This right, which is defined by the power of a multitude [*potentia multitudinis*], is usually called Sovereignty [*imperium*]. Whoever, by common agreement [*communis consensus*], has responsibility for public Affairs [*respublica*] – that is, the right of making, interpreting, and repealing laws, fortifying cities, and making decisions about war and peace, etc. – has this right absolutely.[231]

If this responsibility is entrusted to a council consisting of the common multitude (*communis multitudo*), it is called a democracy; if entrusted to a certain number of elected people, an aristocracy; and if entrusted to one person, a monarchy. Spinoza uses the classic terminology and threefold division, and his definitions appear to duplicate those of Hobbes. And yet there are a number of remarkable differences: the neutral, mathematical vocabulary

---

[230] For the significance, meaning and translation of the concept of *ingenium*, see Moreau, 'Les passions du social: "personnalité de base" et *ingenium*', 303–26. See also Lantoine in his study of the related concept of *habitus*: *L'intelligence de la pratique*, e.g. 156–8.

[231] *TP* II, 17; *CWS* II, 514.

SPINOZA'S REVERSAL

(no images of sea-monsters); the (Italian) Aristotelian reflection on act and potency (which appears to be absent in Hobbes); and, finally, certain omissions, and in particular Hobbes's view that the multitude dissolves into one people/the sovereign when it transitions into a political state.[232] It is worth noting that Spinoza is *not* talking about a transition from the natural condition to the political state; there is actually no such transition, since in his view people have always lived in a civil community.

From there, Spinoza goes on to turn the meaning of sin and obedience on its head. As we recall, sin and merit are, according to Spinoza's own insistence, the theme of the *Ethica*, while the connection which the *TTP* had drawn between faith and obedience had aroused the particular ire of his critics. Here all of these things converge. In the natural state there is no sin (*peccatum*). Due to the natural right, no one is obligated to anyone else to live a specific life unless he wants to, nor does anyone judge what is good and bad except according to his own insight (*ex suo ingenio*). Nothing is forbidden by natural right, except what no one is able to do. As a result, one can only conceive of sin in a state; this is the only place where common right is used to determine what is good and evil. Normally people call 'sin' (*peccatum*) what is contrary to sound reason (*sana ratio*), and 'obedience' (*obsequium*) the constant will to moderate one's appetite (*appetitus*) according to the prescription of reason. Spinoza would agree, if only human freedom consisted in the licentiousness (*licentia*) of appetite and human bondage (*servitus*) in the dominion of reason. But that is not how things are. A 'but' announces another break, the reversal which Spinoza completes. *But* (*Sed*) since human freedom is greater the more a person is led by reason and controls his appetites, we can only call a rational life 'obedience' and a weakness of mind (*impotentia mentis*) 'sin' in a most improper sense.[233] Finally, justice (*Justitia*) and injustice (*injustitia*) only make sense in a sovereignty (*imperium*).[234] For there is nothing in all of nature that properly belongs to one person and not to another or that can be claimed by one or the other. This brings Spinoza's summary of the *Ethica* to a close.

Conversely, Spinoza in the *Ethica* – more specifically, in the 2nd scholium with proposition 37 in part IV – also offers a synopsis of his *Tractatus politicus*, the quintessence of his political theory. Every person exists by the supreme natural right and does those things that flow with that supreme natural right from the necessity of his own nature. On the basis of his own insight

---

[232] Hobbes, *De cive*, VI; *Leviathan*, XVI.
[233] *TP* II, 20; *CWS* II, 515.
[234] *TP* II, 23; *CWS* II, 515.

(*ex suo ingenio*), each person considers his own advantage and pursues the preservation of what he loves and the destruction of what he hates. If people live according to the guidance of reason, everyone could exercise their natural right without injuring anyone. But since they are subject to the affects 'which far surpass man's power [*potentia*], or virtue [*virtus*]', they are often drawn in different directions, and at the moment they require one another's aid, they are opponents. But in order that they might 'live harmoniously and be of assistance to one another, it is necessary for them to give up their natural right and to make one another confident that they will do nothing which could harm others'.[235] But how is this possible, Spinoza wonders. How can people, who are inconstant, liable to change and subject to the affects come to trust one another and earn their trust? To answer this question, Spinoza directs his readers to proposition 7, once again in part IV, which says that a passion can only be controlled by a more powerful and contrary passion, and to proposition 39 of part III, which establishes that everyone refrains from harming another out of fear for greater harm. A society (*societas*) can be established on this law (*lex*) if it appropriates the right of each individual to judge good and evil: it must therefore have the authority to prescribe a common way of life, to enact laws and to maintain these laws not by reason, which, we recall, cannot restrain the passions, but by threats.

> This Society [*societas*], maintained by laws and the power it has of preserving itself, is called a State [*civitas*], and those who are defended by its law, Citizens. From this we easily understand that there is nothing in the state of nature which, by the agreement of all, is good or evil; for everyone who is in the state of nature considers only his own advantage, and decides what is good and what is evil from his own insight [*ex suo ingenio*], and only in so far as he takes account of his own advantage. He is not bound by any law to submit to anyone except himself. So in the state of nature no sin [*peccatum*] can be conceived. But, in the Civil state, of course, it is decided by common agreement [*omnium consensu*] what is good or what is evil. And everyone is bound to submit to the State [*civitas*]. Sin, therefore, is nothing but disobedience, which for that reason can be punished only by the law of the State [*civitatis jure*]. On the other hand, obedience is considered a merit in a Citizen, because on that account he is judged worthy of enjoying the advantages of the State. Again, in the state of nature there is no one who by common consent is Master of anything,

---

[235] *Ethica* IV, 37, Schol. 2; CWS I, 567; see Balibar, 'L'*Éthique*: une anthropologie politique', *Spinoza politique*, 139–63.

nor is there anything in Nature which can be said to be this man's and not that man's. Instead, all things belong to all. So in the state of nature, there cannot be conceived any will to give to each his own, or to take away from someone what is his. I.e., in the state of nature nothing is done which can be called just or unjust. But in the civil state, of course, where it is decided by common consent what belongs to this man, and what to that [, things are done which can be called just or just]. From this it is clear that just and unjust, sin and merit, are extrinsic notions, not attributes that explain the nature of the Mind.[236]

*

3. At the beginning of Chapter 3, Spinoza once again defines the various concepts he has used, in a way that is illustrative of his language-critical method of exposition. Every time a shift takes place, he lists the definition, if necessary in a new translation. He searches, weighs and deliberates his terminological choices. In connection with a theme that is determined by the affects, such linguistic rigour is of supreme importance. The order of each sovereignty (*imperium*) he now calls 'civil state' (*status civilis*), the whole body of the state 'Commonwealth' (*civitas*) and the common business that depends on the policy of the sovereign 'Public Affairs' (*respublica*). The people are called 'citizens' (*civis*) insofar as they enjoy civil rights, and 'subjects' (*subditos*) insofar as they are bound to 'established practices' (*instituta*).[237] The right of a state is the right of nature, determined not by the power (*potentia*) of each person (*uniuscujusque*), but by the power of the multitude which is led as if by one mind (*multitudo, quae una veluti mente ducitur*).[238] What applies to anyone in the natural state applies also to the soul and body of the state which has right in proportion as it has power, and, what is more, every subject has less right in proportion as the Commonwealth (*civitas*) itself is more powerful. If the Commonwealth (*civitas*) grants someone a right (*ius*), and thus also the power (*potestas*) to live according to his own insight (*ingenium*), then it returns this power (*potestas*)

---

[236] *Ethica* IV, 37, Schol. 2; CWS I, 567–8. Translation modified. Insertion in square brackets from Curley. In relation to the thesis that possession cannot exist or be conceived in the natural state, see also Hobbes's 'Annotation' in *De cive*, VI, where he writes that a 'multitude' cannot 'possesse', which is one of the reasons why it must be transformed into 'one person/one people' (English version, 92). This view is likewise posited and approved in *Theophrastus redivivus*, II, 854–60 (see above, Chapter II.4, 56–8), and in Languet's *De la puissance*, 130–1 (see above, Chapter I.1, 8–10).

[237] *TP* III, 1; CWS II, 517.

[238] *TP* III, 2; CWS II, 517.

228 DEMOCRATIC THOUGHT FROM MACHIAVELLI TO SPINOZA

which was given to it. If it gives it to two or more people, then it divides the political authority and everything reverts to the natural state. Consequently, it is inconceivable for the established practice of the Commonwealth (*civitatis institutum*) to grant to each citizen that he should live according to his own insight (*ex suo ingenio*).[239] The natural right by which each person is his own judge therefore necessarily ceases in the civil order. Spinoza says exactly the same thing as Hobbes. But then follows this strange passage: 'I say explicitly "by the established practice of the Commonwealth" [*ex civitatis instituto*], for (if we consider the matter properly) each person's Right of nature does *not* cease in the civil order.'[240] For both in the natural state and in the civil state, each person looks to his own advantage and is led by the laws of nature. In both states, people are moved to do this or that guided by hope or fear. The difference between the two conditions is that in the civil order everyone fears or enjoys the same thing, although this does *not*, of course, eliminate each person's ability to judge. Here Spinoza can be found saying the opposite of Hobbes.

The dialectical process continues in what follows. Each citizen should not be permitted to interpret the laws. Citizens are not their own judge but are subject to the control of the commonwealth and must therefore carry out the civil commands. The will of the commonwealth must be considered the will of all. Even if a subject thinks a decree of the commonwealth to be unfair, he is nevertheless bound to carry it out. At the same time, one might object that to subject oneself completely to someone else's judgement – i.e. the civil order – is contrary to the dictate of reason. Spinoza counters that reason teaches nothing contrary to nature and that reason teaches us to seek peace, from which it follows that the more a man is led by reason, the more free he is and the more steadfastly he will observe the laws of the commonwealth. The harm of having to do something with which they do not agree is outweighed by the advantages and it testifies to reason when someone chooses the lesser of two evils. Spinoza then supplies three arguments which serve to overthrow the Hobbesian position and turn its meaning on its head. First, just as in the natural state the man who is guided by reason is his own master, so a Commonwealth will also be the most powerful and under its own right (*sui juris*), if it is founded on and directed by reason. For the right of the commonwealth is 'determined by the power of the multitude which is led as

[239] *TP* III, 3; *CWS* II, 518.
[240] *TP* III, 3; *CWS* II, 518 (italics mine). Here we see the same argumentative structure found in *TTP* XVI and especially XVII, where Spinoza observes that the argument first construed remains 'merely theoretical'; see above 2.3, 181.

SPINOZA'S REVERSAL

229

if by one mind [*Nam Civitatis Jus potentia multitudinis, quae una veluti mente ducitur, determinatur*]'[241]. Yet this union of minds is only conceivable if the commonwealth aims most at what sound reason teaches to be useful to *all* men (*omnibus hominibus*). Secondly, subjects are not under their own right (*sui juris*) but are under the right of the commonwealth, insofar as they fear or love the commonwealth. Therefore, the things no one can be induced to do by reward or threat do *not* belong to the right of the commonwealth. In particular, the *ability to judge* does not fall under the power of authority, since no one can surrender it.[242] And, thirdly, the more people resent a thing, the less it belongs within the right of the commonwealth. Since the right of the commonwealth is defined by the common power of the multitude (*Jus Civitatis communi multitudinis potentia definitur*), its power and thus its right *diminish* to the extent that *more* people *conspire* against it (*ut plures in unum conspirent*).[243] The greater reason the commonwealth has for fear, the less it is under its own right.

The reversal which Spinoza completes not only has a direct connection to the anthropology and ontology he had set out in his *Ethica*, but is also closely related to the work of Machiavelli. Spinoza adapts the essential components and argumentative structure from *Il Principe* and the *Discorsi* and integrates them into his theoretical repertoire, often using the same examples. In *Discorsi* III, 6, Machiavelli devotes a lengthy chapter to conspiracies, which he describes using his well-known method from two opposing perspectives (i.e. the perspective of the conspirator and the perspective of the sovereign attacked by the conspiracy), shifting between one and the multitude, and which prove successful or else are uncovered, neutralised and fail. The success or failure of conspiracies is largely similar to that of rebellions: there is the period preceding the plan, the moment of execution and the period that follows. Time plays an integral role in the preparation of the plan and its execution, as do secrecy, unawareness and concealment versus knowledge, exposure and detection. The virtue (*virtù*) of the actors (both conspirators and their target) is determinative for the execution of the plan and the period which follows, whether the scheme is of one or a multitude, whether it targets a monarch or a republic. The situation in the period which follows the execution is similar to that of a rebellion: those who attain power by way of a conspiracy must be able to preserve themselves, as the conspiracy is only the impulse. Machiavelli also makes clear – and this also brings us to the

---

[241] *TP* III, 7; CWS II, 520.
[242] *TP* III, 8; CWS II, 520.
[243] *TP* III, 9; CWS II, 521.

230 DEMOCRATIC THOUGHT FROM MACHIAVELLI TO SPINOZA

point Spinoza wants to make – that the more people conspire, the more the power of the states *diminishes*.

> Princes therefore have no greater enemy than conspiracy, for when a conspiracy is made against them, either it kills them or it brings them infamy. For if it succeeds, they are dead; if it is exposed, and they kill the conspirators, it is always believed that it was the invention of the prince to vent his avarice and cruelty at the expense of the blood and property of those whom he has killed.[244]

*

4–5. In the two chapters that follow, the notion of the state depending on the trust and approval of its subjects (love and trust, not fear) is fleshed out further. Fear exists on the side of the state, which after all depends on the power (*potentia*) of the multitude (*multitudo*). Spinoza shows what this view means concretely, examining the duties of the commonwealth in Chapter 4. People commonly wonder whether the state can sin and if it is consequently bound to laws. Of course this is so, Spinoza immediately responds, for if it were not bound by 'any laws, *or* rules, [. . .] then we'd have to think of [the Commonwealth], not as a natural thing, but as a fantasy', that is, it would not exist. 'The Commonwealth sins, then, when it does, or allows to happen, what can be a cause of its ruin', when it commits errors which prevent it from persevering. Spinoza reminds his readers of the different ways of speaking, and that he is speaking as a philosopher or physician when the latter treats nature as if it is able to sin. When he says that people are not under their own right but under the right of the commonwealth, he does *not* mean 'that they lose their human nature and take on a different nature'.[245] Nor does he mean that the state has the right to compel people to go against their nature and to relinquish their own capacity of judgement, as when they show respect (*reverentia*) for what actually moves them 'to laughter

[244] Machiavelli, *Discorsi* III, 6, 443: 'Non hanno pertanto i principi il maggiore nimico che la congiura: perché, fatta che è una congiura loro contro, o la gli ammazza, o la gli infama. Perché, se la riesce, e' muoiono; se la si scuopre, e loro ammazzino i congiurati, si crede sempre che la sia stata invenzione di que principe per isfogare l'avarizia e la crudeltà sua contro al sangue e la roba di quegli che egli ha morti.' Machiavelli likewise addresses conspiracies in *Il modo che tenne il duca Valentino* and in *Il Principe* XVIII (see above, Chapter I.3, 20–1; I.4, 29–30). For the direct relationship between this passage in the *TP* and Machiavelli's writings, see also Gebhardt's commentary at the relevant passage in G V, 91; 140.

[245] *TP* IV, 4; *CWS* II, 526–7.

SPINOZA'S REVERSAL   231

or disgust'. It is impossible for those in power 'to run, drunken or naked, through the streets with prostitutes, to play the actor, to openly violate or disdain the laws he himself has made', without as a consequence losing their claim to such respect.[246] The murder, robbery and violation of subjects and the abduction and rape of young girls 'turn fear into indignation, and hence turn the civil order into a state of hostility'.[247] Once again, Spinoza measures the views of Machiavelli by the touchstone of Hobbes's argument in *Leviathan*, which here yields a dialectical progression that takes him one step back in the opposite direction of what has just been described above. For, so he writes, if we understand sin as what is rightly prohibited by civil right, that is, if we use the term in its proper meaning (*genuino sensu*),

> we can't say in any way that the Commonwealth is bound by laws or can sin. For the rules and causes of fear [*metus*] and respect [*reverentia*] the Commonwealth [*civitas*] is bound, for its own sake, to observe don't concern the civil Law [*jura civilia*], but the Law of nature [*jus naturale*].[248]

In Chapter 5, Spinoza moves in a forward direction again, now turning to examine each form of state under the best circumstances. Up to this point, he has only looked at how right (or power) is established, but not everything that occurs with right occurs on that account in the best possible manner. There is a difference between cultivating a field by right and in the best way, and in the same way there is a difference between ruling and administering public affairs by right and ruling and administering public affairs in the best possible way. According to Spinoza, we can easily understand the best condition of each state from the goal of the civil condition, primarily peace and the security of life. The best state is therefore the one in which people live in harmony and where the laws are not violated. 'For certainly we should impute rebellions, wars, and contempt for, or violation of, the laws not so much to the wickedness of the subjects [*subditorum*] as to the corruption of the state [*pravo imperii statui*]. Men aren't born civil [*civilis*]; they become civil.'[249] The opposite it also true. Just like

> 'the subjects' vices [*vitia subditorum*], and their excessive license [*licentia*] and stubbornness [*contumacia*], are to be imputed to the Commonwealth

---

[246] Ibid; *CWS* II, 527.
[247] Ibid.
[248] *TP* IV, 5; *CWS* II, 527.
[249] *TP* IV, 2; *CWS* II, 529. Cf. Machiavelli, *Discorsi* III, 29.

[*civitas*], so, on the other hand, their virtue [*virtus*] and constant observance of the laws [*observantia legum*] are to be attributed most to the virtue of the Commonwealth [*civitas*] and its absolute right [*juri absoluto*].[250]

To illustrate the point, Spinoza recalls the exceptional power/virtue of Hannibal, whose army never experienced any rebellion. Here he is clearly inspired by Machiavelli, who in *Il Principe* 17 and *Discorsi* III, 21 extols Hannibal's *virtù* because 'although his army was composed of various kinds of men, no dissension ever arose in it, either among them or against him'.[251] In the context of both passages, Machiavelli seeks to understand how it is that radically opposing approaches can both be effective and precisely what it is in which the *virtù* consists, apparently neutral with respect to what is generally understood as good and evil. In *Discorsi* III, 21 he therefore adduces two contradictory examples: Scipio, who won over to himself the inhabitants of the Spanish territory he was invading by his mild humanity; and Hannibal, who entered Italy and left no form of cruelty, violence, plundering and deception untried, but still managed to get the people to join him. In his investigation of how it is possible that someone who perpetrates violence can win people over to himself, Machiavelli recognises several different causes, the most important one nevertheless being the fact that 'men are driven by two principal things, either by love or by fear; so whoever makes himself loved commands, as does he who makes himself feared'.[252] On the face of it, it even appears as if 'whoever makes himself feared is more followed and more obeyed than whoever makes himself loved'.[253] Yet the two cases also show that *both* approaches have positive as well as negative consequences. Those who seek to be loved excessively become a laughing stock, and those who seek to instil fear excessively are

---

[250] *TP* V, 3; *CWS* II, 529–30.

[251] Machiavelli, *Discorsi* III, 21, 475: 'che nel suo esercito ancoraché composto di varie generazioni di uomini, non nacque mai alcuna dissensione, né infra loro medesimi, né contro di lui'; *Il Principe* XVII, 164: 'avendo uno esercito grossissimo, misto di infinite generazioni di uomini, condotto a militare in terra aliena, non vi surgessi mai alcuna dissensione, né in fra loro, né contro al principe, così nella cattiva come nella sua buona fortuna'. Cf. Gebhardt who references – without further commentary – Titus Livius (Livy), these two passages from Machiavelli and De la Court's *Politike Discoursen*; see G V, 142.

[252] Machiavelli, *Discorsi* III, 21, 474: 'gli uomini sono spinti da due cose principali: o dallo amore o dal timore, talché cosí gli comanda chi si fa amare, come colui che si fa temere'.

[253] Ibid. 'anzi il più delle volte è più seguito e più ubbidito chi si fa temere che chi si fa amare'.

eventually hated. The moderate middle course likewise fails to represent a solution: it is impossible to steer a middle course, between being loved and feared. Both approaches easily degenerate into excess, and the only available option is compensation by an exceptional *virtù*. Machiavelli illustrates that too using the same examples. Scipio's soldiers in Spain rose up in revolt against him, but he was able to solve this problem by responding with a certain degree of violence (entirely against his nature and his will) and by neutralising his overly ambitious and restless captains. Hannibal's *virtù*, in contrast, consisted in his ability to lead an enormous and highly complex army without ever encountering an insurrection. Yet it is also true that the Roman people never hated anyone as much as Hannibal, and that 'they never forgave [him], though he was disarmed and exiled, until at last they caused his death'.[254] In short, *virtù* does not mean good and laudable, nor evil and despicable, nor even a middle course. Machiavelli describes Scipio's and Hannibal's example neutrally, without giving preference to the one or the other, and both involve success and failure. Yet the *virtù* with the most lasting effect remains that of Scipio, who only resorted to violence when pushed to the brink, but still did so when required to.

We recognise the spirit of these reflections in the two side notes Spinoza makes, which serve both to confirm and to nuance his position. The first side note is that a 'Commonwealth whose subjects, terrified by fear, don't take up arms', as in the case of the Italians who came to face Hannibal, 'should be said to be without war, but not at peace'. In other words, when 'the peace of a Commonwealth [*civitas*] depends on its subjects' lack of spirit [*inertia*] – so that they're led like sheep, and know only how to be slaves – it would be more properly called a wasteland [*solitudo*] than a Commonwealth [*civitas*]'.[255] This observation directly targets Hobbes, who defines peace simply and within a logic of measurability as the privation of war.[256] Such a view of politics leads to tyranny which, so Spinoza objects, treats people 'as no more than cattle'.[257] His overall argument is therefore similar to that of Hobbes, although it differs on this decisive and fundamental point for which he draws on Machiavelli, from whom he also borrows an example: the institutions of the commonwealth *cannot* depend on fear, since fear is just a highly temporary emergency measure for a crisis situation and must rapidly be transformed

---

[254] Machiavelli, *Discorsi* III, 21, 475: 'ad Annibale mai, ancora che disarmato e disperso, perdonarono, tanto che lo fecioro morire'.

[255] *TP* V, 4; CWS II, 530.

[256] Hobbes, *Leviathan*, XIII; *De cive*, I; see also Gebhardt's commentary in G V, 142.

[257] *TP* VII, 25; CWS II, 557.

234   DEMOCRATIC THOUGHT FROM MACHIAVELLI TO SPINOZA

into trust, love and goodwill. The second side note is Spinoza's observation that the best state (*imperium*) is the one in which people live harmoniously. What he means is 'a *human life*, one defined not merely by the circulation of the blood, and other things common to all animals, but mostly by reason, the true virtue and life of the Mind'.[258]

To close this general analysis in which fear and dread are contrasted with political order and reason, Spinoza uses a reference that will initially not surprise anyone: 'Machiavelli, ever shrewd, has shown in detail the means a Prince must use to stabilize and preserve his rule, if all he craves is to be master.'[259] Yet in that same sentence, after the comma, he immediately dismantles the certainty of that cliché: 'Why he did this may not be clear.'[260] The surprise comes in the second, highly complex sentence, in which Spinoza deploys a wide array of hypothetical constructions, litotes and barbs:

> If his purpose was good, as we must believe of a wise man, it seems to have been to show how imprudent many people are to try to remove a Tyrant from their midst, when they can't remove the causes of the prince's being a Tyrant. On the contrary, they give the prince more reason to fear, and so more reason to be a Tyrant.[261]

Ever careful and yet resolute, he in the third sentence summarises the goal envisioned with the *TP*, the reason for Machiavelli's example:

> Perhaps Machiavelli also wanted to show how much a free multitude [*multitudo*] should beware of entrusting its well-being absolutely to one person. Unless the prince is so vain that he thinks he can please everyone, he must fear treachery every day. So he's forced to look out for himself, and to set traps for the multitude, rather than look out for their interests.[262]

Spinoza then brings this theme to a close with a clause that, perhaps for reasons of caution, was left out in the Dutch *Nagelate Schriften*: 'I'm the more inclined to believe this about that very prudent man because it's clear he was on the side of freedom, and gave very good advice for protecting it.'[263]

---

[258] *TP* V, 5; CWS II, 530.
[259] *TP* V, 7; CWS II, 531.
[260] *TP* V, 7; CWS II, 531.
[261] Ibid.
[262] Ibid.
[263] Ibid.; *Nagelate Schriften*, 329.

4.2 Experience

6–7. From there, Spinoza discusses the different forms of state concretely, beginning in Chapters 6 and 7 with monarchy. He continues with the same motif and patterns himself after Machiavelli's *Principe*, a treatise on monarchy which systematically demonstrates that a monarchy can only exist if it is supported, willed and approved by the multitude, and if the sovereign has come from the multitude – in other words, if it has the marks of a free republic. Spinoza repeats a number of matters, for instance that people by nature pursue a civil order – on their own they do not have the necessary power to defend themselves and to see to their needs – but that they are by nature also such that they are not driven most to what is of the greatest use to them. This explains the need for the art of achieving harmony and loyalty (*opus arte ad concordiam, & fidem*), and the state must be set up so that 'everyone – both those who rule and those who are ruled, [. . .] whether they want to or not [*omnes, tam qui regunt, quam qui reguntur, velint nolint*]' – does what promotes the common well-being and life according to the dictates of reason.[264] For this reason, Spinoza argues that the common well-being may *not* be committed absolutely to any one person who, like everyone else, experiences negative emotions on a daily basis or else is subject to weakness, loss of focus, illness and despondency. But if one believes, like Spinoza, that a lasting state is the best guarantee for well-being and peace, then experience appears to teach that power (i.e. institutional or political power) *should* indeed be conferred on one person. For no state has stood so long as that of the Turks – an example Spinoza may well have taken from De la Court – while no state appears to have been less lasting than popular or democratic states.[265] Yet Spinoza immediately counters this anticipated objection with a variation on the first side note from the preceding chapter: 'if slavery, barbarism, and being without protection are to be called peace,

---

[264] *TP* VI, 3; *CWS* II, 532. The Renaissance notion of politics as art, conceived *ad arte* (invented or established with a purpose or goal, based on an ideal project which is brought to realisation) is clearly present in Spinoza as well as in the *Theophrastus redivivus*, both under the influence of Machiavelli who in turn was influenced by the Renaissance visual arts, vernacular (*in volgare*) literature and, philosophically, the Paduan Averroist school. A typical feature of this approach is its neutral, detached consideration of the whole (with a view to both rulers and subjects) and at the same time its respect for the concrete, diverging observational perspectives (of rulers and subjects); see also Chapter I above, and Lavaert, *Het perspectief van de multitude*.

[265] De la Court, *Consideratien van Staat*, 140–85.

236   DEMOCRATIC THOUGHT FROM MACHIAVELLI TO SPINOZA

nothing is more wretched for men than peace'.[266] Absolute monarchy promotes slavery and peace does not consist in the privation of war but in the
unity and harmony of minds. The point, according to Spinoza, is that the
idea of committing power to a single person is a mistake, since any one
person is not equal to such a task. Every absolute monarchy is really just a
covert aristocracy, which is the worst kind. Since a king fears the citizens
more than his enemies, he will look out for himself more than he will look
after the interests of his subjects. In short, the more civil right is entrusted
to a king, the less powerful he is and the more wretched the condition of
his subjects, while conversely a king is most under his own right and his
rule most stable when he is most attentive to the well-being of the multitude (*cum maxime multitudinis saluti consulit*). In §9 to §31, Spinoza then
sets out the foundations that best serve the well-being of the multitude in
a monarchy, offering a host of concrete examples drawn from De la Court's
Consideratien van Staat and *Politike Discoursen*; Machiavelli's *Discorsi*, *Il
Principe* and *L'arte della Guerra*; and other works on his bookshelf such
as those of Tacitus, Livy and Curtius. Spinoza also takes examples from
Hobbes's *Leviathan* and *De cive*, although he most often twists them to their
opposite intended political meaning or else uses them to form an anticipated objection which he then goes on to refute.

At this point, we may tentatively conclude that it is the same pattern we
found in *Il Principe*. In his treatment of monarchy, Spinoza exposes its disadvantages and shows that a monarchy can only persevere if it assumes the
form of sovereignty by the multitude, that is, as a democracy. He shifts the
goal to the freedom of the multitude, the perspective to that of the common
people as the subject or actor; he refutes the objections, as when people
claim that the plebeians show no restraint or fear, sow terror, witness excessive humility or thirst for power, for 'everyone shares a common nature', it
is common to all.[267] The multitude can preserve its freedom under a king,
so long as it sees to it that his power 'is determined only by the power of the
multitude, and is preserved by the multitude's support'.[268]

*

8–11. In Chapters 8, 9 and 10, Spinoza turns to aristocracy, investigating
the conditions under which this form of state can persevere. According
to the aforementioned letter, these chapters, along with the mere four

[266] *TP* VI, 4; CWS II, 533.
[267] *TP* VII, 27; CWS II, 559.
[268] *TP* VII, 31; CWS II, 563.

SPINOZA'S REVERSAL 237

paragraphs of Chapter 11, were the ones Spinoza was working on during the final months of his life.[269] In an aristocracy, the rule is not by one person, but by multiple persons selected from the people. Yet an aristocracy must not be mistaken for a democracy, in which every person has the right to vote and qualifies to hold power; for in an aristocracy, the power is only attributed by 'choice' to several people – literally an elite company – who form a council. Spinoza insists that such a council must be sufficiently large. In this somewhat strange claim that the elite must be large in number, we recognise the view of Machiavelli who did not even bother to investigate a 'rule of the best' (*ottimato*) because it degenerates so easily to a 'rule of the few' (*governo de' pochi*), which must be avoided at all costs.[270] When a rule is transferred to a sufficiently large council, it closely approaches absolute rule, by which Spinoza means a rule resting with the multitude (*multitudo*). Once again, he continues by going back and forth between anticipated objections and responses based on his own view, which method is familiar to us from his investigation of monarchy and in fact from the work of De la Court on which he once again draws heavily.[271] In an aristocracy, the power never returns to the multitude, the multitude is never consulted, and the foundations do not rest on the vigilance of the multitude since they are prevented from offering advice and from voting. In practice, aristocratic rule is *not* absolute, the only reason being 'that the multitude is terrifying to its rulers. So it maintains some freedom for itself. If it doesn't claim that freedom for itself by an explicit law, it still claims it tacitly and maintains it.'[272] From the perspective and objective of rule, the freedom of the multitude must therefore be suppressed as much as possible, and since the council – in Spinoza's view – consists of many members, the chances of it degenerating to a machine of violence are slim. The multitude of councillors ought to guarantee that the council follows reason.

---

[269] *Ep.* LXXXIV [to N.N.]; *CWS* II, 488; see above, 271.

[270] There is so little on aristocracy in Machiavelli's writings that the entries for *ottimato*, *governo d'ottimati* and *governo di pochi* – the term *aristocrazia* does not occur at all – in the 'Indice analitico' of the modern edition of his collected works do not even add up to a single line; see *Opere* III, 1051–273. Machiavelli writes about monarchy in *Il Principe* and about democracy in *Discorsi*, but of course the case studies transcend their thematic boundaries so that the theme of rule by an elite does appear in both, with Machiavelli rejecting it decidedly. See also Lavaert, *Het perspectief van de multitude*, 227–9.

[271] For De la Court, see Visentin, 'Between Machiavelli and Hobbes', 227–48.

[272] *TP* VIII, 4; *CWS* II, 567.

238 DEMOCRATIC THOUGHT FROM MACHIAVELLI TO SPINOZA

In spite of this, Spinoza, as we read in Chapter 9, actually prefers another model in which several cities with an aristocratic form of government unite and together form a larger whole. At first sight, their union is without effect on the internal relationship between the state and the multitude it governs. Spinoza follows Machiavelli's plea for the formation of a larger political entity from the separate city states (i.e. a united Italy), but the argumentation in regard to the aristocratic state as such (which, as we have already recalled, is not actually explicitly addressed in Machiavelli) is unclear. In this regard, the *TP* has the appearance of a compilation of sources, from Machiavelli and especially from De la Court. As Gebhardt remarks in his commentary, Spinoza also follows the latter's view as he explicitly formulated it in the next-to-last chapter of the *Consideratien van Staat*, in particular that 'an aristocracy, which closely approaches popular [rule], is clearly the best [form of] government'.[273] De la Court pursued the democratisation of Dutch aristocracy, and it is a theme perfectly suited to Spinoza's argument here. But in terms of argumentative style and structure, we find ourselves far removed from the first five chapters.

In Chapter 10, Spinoza considers whether an aristocratic state can be dissolved from some inherent defect, and once again he turns to Machiavelli for an answer. As 'that most acute Florentine' noted in the *Discorsi*, a state, like the human body, is in constant change, suffering decline and requiring treatment.[274] For that reason, it is necessary that a state return to the principle on which it was established. If this does not happen, 'the defects [*vitia*] increase to the point where they can't be removed unless the sovereignty itself is removed with them'.[275] The Roman solution to this problem was

---

[273] Gebhardt, 'Kommentar', G V, 168; De la Court, *Consideratien van Staat*, 563–7: '[. . .] een Aristokratie, die allernaast aan de Populaare komt, gewisselik de beste regeering is'; see also Chapter IV.3, 84–93.

[274] Machiavelli, *Discorsi* III, 1, 416–17. Tommasini suggests that Machiavelli bases himself on Galen in this passage. It is worth noting that the key term *virtù* means nothing other than what Galen and the physicians referred to as *virtus*, and Tommasini points out that Spinoza adopts precisely this definition in *Ethica* IV, Def. 8 ('By virtue [*virtus*] and power [*potentia*] I understand the same thing, i.e. [. . .] that virtue, insofar as it is related to man, is the very essence, *or* nature, of man, insofar as he has the power [*potestas*] of bringing about certain things, which can be understood through the laws of his nature alone.'): *La vita e gli scritti di Niccolò Machiavelli nella loro relazione col Machiavellismo*, II, I, 39; see also Vivanti's note in Machiavelli, *Opere* I, 1065.

[275] *TP* X, 1; CWS II, 596. For the notion of return to the principle/beginning, see Esposito who contrasts Machiavelli's idea with the Platonic *topos*: the beginning is the place of conflict where the passions exist and collide; see *L'ordine e il conflitto*, 200–1. Spinoza

SPINOZA'S REVERSAL   239

the brief appointment, every five years, of a dictator who had the right to investigate and judge the deeds of senators and public officials, deciding on any punishments, and restoring the sovereignty to its principle. But this solution was a failure. The main problem with Machiavelli's proposal for the institution of a dictator and for a state's return to its principle is that such a situation produces fear not only for bad men but also for the good. And when this happens, the sovereignty is in the greatest danger.

In Chapter 11, Spinoza finally turns to democracy, an absolute sovereignty in which every citizen (i.e. every person with citizen rights) can claim the right to vote and to stand for political office. We can only guess at how the text might have evolved. In the four existing paragraphs of this chapter, he rather surprisingly has very little to say about the multitude, although elsewhere throughout the *TP* he does mention it frequently in the context of democratic rule. But here he speaks of all people who have citizen rights because they have parents who are citizens, were born on the country's soil, served the republic or obtained citizen rights by law.[276] While Spinoza consistently ties citizenship to an undefined multitude throughout the work, here in the opening paragraphs of this chapter he introduces excluding conditions to the notion of citizenship.

In the second paragraph, Spinoza explicitly lists the possible conditions to which the right of citizenship may be subject: it can be restricted to adults who have reached a certain age, or only the first-born, or only those who contribute a certain sum of money to the commonwealth. One possible consequence is that the resulting council ends up being smaller than in an aristocracy, although Spinoza insists we can still call it a democracy because the councillors are not 'chosen' by the council but are destined to their status by 'law' (*cives, qui ad regendam Rempublicam destinantur, non a supremo Concilio, ut optimi, eliguntur, sed lege ad id destinantur*).[277] While throughout the *TP* the undefined number of the *multitudo* had functioned as the foundation for the establishment of the right (that is, power), he now appeals to the law (*lex*) as foundation. Are these themes that Spinoza intended to refute later on, components that he had not yet managed to incorporate and adapt to his own purposes? One might wonder whether an aristocracy is actually better, he even writes, because there in principle the best (*optimi*) are chosen, while in the democratic state which he has sketched out people are eligible for

follows in Machiavelli's footsteps for the constituent principle of power and conflict, but sees no benefits in the Italian political theorist's own example.

[276] *TP* XI, 1; *CWS* II, 601–2.
[277] *TP* XI, 2; *CWS* II, 602.

240 DEMOCRATIC THOUGHT FROM MACHIAVELLI TO SPINOZA

selection by virtue of their age or place of birth, or on account of the wealth they can contribute, etc. – all occasional factors. For it is the occasional and unfounded factors (i.e. the factors not borne or desired by a multitude) he wants to banish. At the same time, we do here recognise Spinoza's dialectical and contrapuntal style. As always, he counters this anticipated objection with a 'but': *but* (*sed*) experience teaches us that in an oligarchy the election of councillors depends completely on the will of a certain few. In such a state, things go most unfortunately.

In the third paragraph, Spinoza continues his argument: in a democratic state, absolutely everyone must receive the right to vote and to stand for political office, the only condition being that they subject themselves to the laws of their land, are under their own right and live honourably. With this one condition, Spinoza excludes from the quantitatively undefined concept of multitude precisely that category which gives it a potentially concrete content – in particular, the foreigners, women, hirelings (servants, maids, labourers), and anyone who was discredited by reason of crime or a scandalous life. How is this passage to be reconciled with the argument that Spinoza had been constructing throughout the *TP*?

In the fourth and final paragraph, Spinoza zooms in on the category of women, and offers a dialectical argument similar to what we saw in Chapter 6, where he discussed all the pros and cons of a monarchy with reference to the Turkish empire. Someone may ask whether women fall under the authority of men by nature or by custom. For if this is only by custom (which is an artefact, fiction, construction), then there is no reason compelling us to exclude women from politics.[278] But if we go by experience, then their situation may be comparable to that under Turkish rule, which proved so durable and stable that it itself amounted to an argument against every form of freedom, against every other form of rule and especially against democracy, so that we would have to conclude that women are too weak to rule. In his analysis of the rule of the Turks, Spinoza, as we saw, then went on to dismantle that misguided argument slowly and carefully. For his present analysis of women, the problem on the face of it appears to be the absence of an available counterexample, since there is no place where women rule over men. On top of this, wherever he looked he would have seen men who allow themselves to be guided by their lust, desire, jealousy, etc. It is quite

---

[278] *Theophrastus redivivus* likewise speaks about women, but the tenor of the text goes in a radically different direction: *TR*, VI. 4, 893; see also Chapter II.5, 63–5. As has been noted, this clandestine work also connects political institutions with fiction/art; see above, n. 264 and Chapter II.

clear that, both textually and in terms of the line of argument, Spinoza takes his point of departure here in De la Court, who in his *Consideratien van Staat* likewise begins his investigation of democracy by treating women and their subjection to men.[279] Yet it is hardly likely that the extant material in this chapter, along with Spinoza's additions (which, however sparse they may be, still do tend in another direction than De la Court), represented the final shape of the argument. But, as we know, the rest is missing.

4.3 [. . .]

The abrupt ending and the bewildering anomaly in Chapter 11 ultimately take little away from either the internal coherence of the *TP* or its cohesion with Spinoza's other works. In the first five chapters, he develops theoretical principles for a political theory that contain the quintessence of the *TTP* and *Ethica*, this time neither covert nor clandestine. The inner logic and structure of the theoretical construction are rigid and strong. The premises are accounted for, the propositions demonstrated, and what he subjects to renewed investigation are precisely those elements from the *TTP* which his opponents had attacked most fiercely. All antitexts responded to Spinoza's association of religion and obedience, his equation of God and nature, and his assimilation of right and power. As a result, appetite becomes the hinge on which the entire human condition turns, the freedom of the will is denied, and all people are considered equal (and of equal worth). There is no natural hierarchy, no reason why one person should have more than another – and this scandalises and even frightens his opponents. The link between faith and obedience turns religion into a political art, neutralises its religious-metaphysical import, and issues in a courageous nothing or in the multitude and/or diversity of religions. In other words, the *TP* comes as a logical response to the objections of Spinoza's opponents, and the same is true for the reference to Machiavelli and the positive role he plays here. If God or nature is the same thing, namely a word for the necessity of the universe, there is no good or evil in it, no sin or norm, and we human beings are the ones who devise such rules and laws. And although Spinoza himself

---

[279] De la Court, *Consideratien van Staat*, 434; see also Gebhardt, 'Kommentar', G V, 196. For these final paragraphs and the so-called 'black page' in Spinoza, see Gatens, 'The Condition of Human Nature', 47–60; Gullan-Wuhr, 'Spinoza and the Equality of Women', 91–111; James, 'Politically Mediated Affects', 61–77; Matheron, 'Femmes et serviteurs dans la démocratie spinoziste', *Études sur Spinoza*, 181–200; Sharp, 'Eve's Perfection. Spinoza on Sexual (In)Equality', 93–110.

242 DEMOCRATIC THOUGHT FROM MACHIAVELLI TO SPINOZA

claims not to be trying to invent a new form of state (where Pierre-François Moreau observes that *l'experience est close*, 'the experience is closed'), it is precisely this view of God/nature and the human condition, combined with the lessons drawn from Machiavelli, that lead him to a radically new political theory aimed at equal freedom and self-determination.[280]

In spite of this, there is a change that takes place between the *TTP* and the *TP*. On the one hand, the reactions of Spinoza's critics led him to search for the essence of his ideas and to formulate them more purely, resulting in what we already find in the *TTP* becoming more explicit, radicalised and systematised – this is something to which I will return shortly. On the other hand, his reflection on the principial level in the *Ethica* – a project initiated prior to the *TTP*, and resumed upon its publication – brought him to the field of politics, for it is there that the important questions present themselves. In the *TP*, in departure from the *TTP*, the theme is treated independently of the pressing questions that were being debated at the time and without relation to the concrete political events. In that context, Moreau emphasises the importance of the date: during the composition of the *TTP*, the free republic was under threat, while during the composition of the *TP* (after the French invasion), the freedom had already been lost.[281] This led Spinoza to ask the same question as Machiavelli had asked after 1513: why is it that a civil state – the free republic – cannot persevere, and how can it be brought to do so? In the *TP*, Spinoza is not looking for an answer to one concrete issue, such as the harm religion and state may suffer as a result of freedom, but his goal is to examine the complex political question as a whole.

The most remarkable difference between the two treatises, according to Moreau and Alexandre Matheron, is that Spinoza in the *TTP* discusses the origin of the state in terms of a contract (i.e. like Hobbes) but that he no longer does so in the *TP*.[282] Both Moreau and Matheron, however, hasten to nuance their observation. According to Moreau, this is a textual rather than a fundamental difference. And according to Matheron, Spinoza always thought that the existence and legitimacy of a political society demands

---

[280] Moreau, *Spinoza et le spinozisme*, 91.

[281] Moreau, 'Le *Traité politique*: une radicalisation conceptuelle?', 33–4.

[282] Ibid. 33–5; Matheron, 'Le problème de l'évolution de Spinoza du *TTP* au *TP*', *Études sur Spinoza*, 258–70. See also Matheron, *Individu et communauté*, 287–354 and Negri, *Spinoza sovversivo*, 296–312. In the reading of the *TTP* and *TP* we have proposed here, we rarely if ever explicitly referenced the pioneering studies on these themes, although they did play a highly inspirational role for me. They include the work of Balibar, Matheron, Moreau and Negri; see the bibliography for full publication details.

approval from the subjects, and if someone wants to refer to this phenomenon as a 'contract', it would indeed make Spinoza a contract thinker. But
at the same time, Spinoza always considered right the same thing as power,
and in that sense he never was a contract thinker.[283] Here Matheron's view
approaches that of Antonio Negri: If Spinoza speaks in terms of a contract
in the *TTP*, it is because he has not yet discovered how else one can escape
from the state of nature. This is something he only discovers through writing the *TTP*. The intolerance and productivity of the imagination in the
phenomenon of religion are matters he developed conceptually in book
III of the *Ethica*, 'which in turn facilitated the more global and radical
non-contractualism of the *TP*'.[284] Moreau, Matheron, and Negri, as well as
Étienne Balibar, all point to an aspect that finds confirmation in our own
reading: Spinoza's thought is a thought in motion. He was led to the radical
conceptualisation we encounter in the *TP* not only by the reactions to the
TTP, or the debates with correspondents and friends, and the changing
events, but also by the very composition of the *TTP* itself.

The reading we have proposed here reveals that the conceptual shift
which takes place between the *TTP* and the *TP* makes explicit, radicalises
and systematises three elements that were already present in the former. The
first is the idea that God and nature are the same thing, that there is in nature
no norm, sin or right, and that we human beings ourselves devise and make
the rules in a free and open spirit with respect to nature (and its laws), to
other natural things, and thus also to one another. The second is the view on
the status of language (an institution, artefact, fiction), which leads to that
view of philosophy as criticism or unmasking, in contrast to theology, where
precision of words, logical order, and trajectories are of essential importance.
As such, Spinoza effects a 'reversal' which is only possible on the basis of
the neutralising shift of meaning or translation of several concepts he effects
(and, as Hobbes says, what consequently changes is not the natural thing,
but our words, our fictions).[285] The third is the 'leftist' reading of Hobbes,
which comes to expression in the context of the question of the multitude,
the idea that natural right continues to apply also in the civil state, and the

---

[283] Matheron, 'Le problème de l'évolution', 258.

[284] Ibid. 269.

[285] For the theme of language and its connection to the imagination, see Moreau, *Spinoza.
L'expérience et l'éternité*, Chap. II, 307–78. Moreau likewise refers to the 'neutrality'
of the imagination. In Negri's *L'anomalia selvaggia*, imagination plays a fundamental role. See also Balibar, who argues that the most important aspect of Spinoza's
democracy consists in the freedom of communication: 'L'*Éthique*, une anthropologie
politique', *Spinoza politique*, 162–3.

244 DEMOCRATIC THOUGHT FROM MACHIAVELLI TO SPINOZA

necessity of freedom of thought and speech. We have already treated the first at length. In what follows, we will therefore offer a brief commentary on the second and the third.

While throughout the *TP* Machiavelli is named explicitly as an example and cited or paraphrased, concrete references to Hobbes are absent. At the same time, there is no doubt that Spinoza follows the argumentation of *De cive* (as well as *Leviathan*) step by step, at times even paraphrasing it. Moreover, he, like Koerbagh and Van den Enden, further develops Hobbes's view of the use and abuse of language, and also applies it, more so than Hobbes himself and even against Hobbes's own view. Language is an institution, like a fiction, and it can be used properly, to recall thoughts and to communicate them to others; it can also be used improperly, to seduce oneself and others to pleasure; and it can be abused improperly, to deceive, mislead, and suppress.[286] On the basis of this view, Spinoza develops in the *TP* a political theory based on the reasoning of Hobbes which is translated, whose significance is shifted so as to be reversed at decisive moments and applied for a radically different end. The distinctions Spinoza draws (between, for instance, natural power/*potentia* and political power/*potestas*), the concepts he deploys and connects them with (natural power with the multitude, and political power with the established government/state), the translations in neutral terms (citizenship, citizens), and finally what he omits (there is not just *one* people), are intricately connected and shape this movement of reversal. The right of citizenship is the right of nature which is determined by the power – not of each individual, but of the multitude which is led by a single mind, as it were. This harmony, however, is only conceivable if the civil state pursues what sound reason recognises as useful for *all* people. Here the faculty of judgement is *not* subject to the authority of the sovereign, since no one can surrender it. And since the right of citizenship is determined by the communal power of the multitude, the power and, consequently, the right of the citizens *decreases* proportional to the *increase* in the people who oppose it and rebel. As Spinoza wrote in his letter to Jelles, the difference between Hobbes and him is that he is of the view that the natural power of the multitude remains, regardless of the specific form of state, and moreover that this natural power is necessary for the sake of peace and freedom. If this is not so, that state completely misses its goal.

While Spinoza during the writing of the *TTP* was still sceptical of the faculty of judgement of the multitude (which is ignorant, tends to make the wrong choice, and represents a threat to the free republic), experience has

[286] Hobbes, *Leviathan*, IV, Of Speech.

now taught him that the judgement of theologians and even that of philosophers is less trustworthy. The condition of the multitude is the condition of everyone. There is, therefore, only one remedy for ignorance of politics and of all other matters of importance to us, which is that *as many as possible* assume the duty of knowledge, of fashioning and expressing their views, 'publicly running the risk of knowledge'.[287]

There is a logical coherence between the three motives that make up the goal of Spinoza's argument: Natural right (the power of the multitude) continues to apply in the civil state. Freedom of (thought and) speech is necessary for the sake of – and therefore flows from – the fact that every social institution is relative, contingent and susceptible to improvement. Multitude (and, consequently, diversity) is a real and natural phenomenon, while the fiction of one people involves compulsion and is problematic. This coherence constitutes the radicality of Spinoza.

[287] Balibar, 'L'*Éthique*, une anthropologie politique', 163: 'courir publiquement le risque de l'intelligence'; for Van den Enden, see the beginning of this chapter above, 166–7; 187–8.

VIII

Une mauvaise rhapsodie, un artifice

1. A revolutionary thesis

In 1683, six years after Spinoza's death and the posthumous publication of his *TP*, the Rotterdam autodidact Adriaen Verwer published a refutation of the *Ethica* that was to play a decisive role during the first several decades of the eighteenth century and beyond. The arguments he used to critique Spinoza's hypothetical thought in *'t Mom-Aensicht der Atheistery Afgerukt door een Verhandeling van den aengeboren stand der menschen* were taken over nearly verbatim by Bernard Nieuwentyt in his posthumously published *Gronden van zekerheid* (1720), and, as some have claimed, even laid the foundation for logical empiricism.[1] *'t Mom-Aensicht* played an important role in the dissemination of Locke's empiricism and contributed to the development of a scientific comparative linguistics. Contrary to what one might initially think, Verwer's epistemological and linguistic refutation actually touches on the essential aspects of Spinoza's political radicality, and it does so using a new motif, namely deceit. As such, Verwer takes us back to Spinoza's sources from the past, to his contemporary allies, to the heirs operating in his spirit, and also to his moderately enlightened critics who transported him into a future where his ideas concerning freedom and equality were transformed into something else.

Verwer distinguishes two radically opposing trajectories within the history of thought according to their respective views on the human 'innate state'

---

[1] Jongeneelen, 'Disguised Spinozism in Adriaen Verwer's Momaensicht', 15–21; Nieuwentyt, *Gronden van zekerheid, of de regte betoogwyse der wiskundigen*, 1720; Ducheyne, 'Curing Pansophia through Eruditum Nescire: Bernard Nieuwentijt's (1654–1718) Epistemology of Modesty'.

(*aengeboren stand*).[2] The one view understands people as dependent on a higher principle which is 'distinguished [from them] materially and has of old been called *God*', while the other conceives of them as independent of such a principle and as self-determining.[3] In the eyes of the proponents of the dependence-thesis, as Verwer calls them, the allies of independence are atheists or God-deniers. He situates himself within the former camp, that is, among the Jews, Christians, Muslims, most civilised pagans, and, in particular, the theologians, Erasmus, Calvin, Grotius, and the political treatises based on the Bible and the Code of Justinian.[4] They all consider the extraordinary things which occur or have been observed in this world as coming from God. Human beings stand in an 'innate relationship or respect towards God', and whatever preserves this relationship is good and anything that tears it apart is bad.[5] The proponents of the independence-thesis, on the other hand, claim that good and evil are not innate and do not exist in nature. This latter view, so Verwer charges, can be found in the political treatises of Machiavelli, Vanini, Hobbes and Spinoza.[6] Since Spinoza gave the most radical expression to the independence-thesis, Verwer proposes to attack it by refuting the *Ethica*. What bothers him most is the fact that Spinoza disguises his radical views using words and a language that have the appearance of moderation and seem to fit the orthodox tradition – a deceit. For that reason, Verwer deems it necessary first to offer a translation of the *Ethica*, before exposing its true meaning and significance.

To that end, Verwer returns first of all to the 'short argument' in which Spinoza sets forth his independence-thesis 'unfeigned', in particular the 2nd scholium to proposition 37 in part IV, which we have already cited in an earlier chapter.[7] Verwer reads and translates the text step by step, a process yielding him the following most important independence-theses: In the natural state, people pursue their own advantage; they judge something and deem it good or evil only on the basis of their own advantage. They only obey themselves and submit to their own feelings and ideas alone. For this reason, there is no sin in the natural state. People are independent of all powers that are distinct from or above them, or, in the words of Verwer, they are independent of God. This means that for Spinoza, dependence

---

[2] Verwer, '*t Mom-Aensicht der Atheistery Afgerukt*, 1683, 5.

[3] Ibid. n.p. [*2v].

[4] Ibid. 6; 15–16.

[5] Ibid. 15.

[6] Ibid. 6.

[7] See Chapter VII.4.1, 225–7.

248   DEMOCRATIC THOUGHT FROM MACHIAVELLI TO SPINOZA

obtains only in a political society. Verwer for his part claims that Spinoza does not demonstrate but simply presupposes the independence-thesis, especially in his concept of God as the 'universe' (*al*) in which 'universal thought' (*algemene denking*) and 'universal extended materiality' (*algemene uitgestrekte stoffelijkheid*) have been forged together and under which all individual 'thoughts' (*denkingen*) and 'corporeal things' (*lichamelijke stoffen*) can be subsumed.[8] In all his writings, Spinoza simply understands God as this 'universe'. The foundation underlying his subsequent argument is 'that all things exist properly as they exist according to the supreme and ultimate power – that is, as we have added in explanation, that nothing can be other than it is'.[9]

Even though this principle only speaks of what 'is' and excludes every norm or 'ought' from the argument, as Verwer aptly observes, the problem of this line of reasoning is its hypothetical character, such that it lacks reality and overthrows the foundation of politics and justice. The envisioned goal of his translation is to unmask, and consequently he looks for the core of the dispute in its purest form, the principle of the argument which he can then topple. There are two things happening here. First, Verwer translates the argument to its most radical form. Secondly, while translating he encounters a significant number of points on which he actually agrees, meaning that his philosophy does not in that sense differ all that drastically from Spinoza's; he too situates himself on the enlightened side of the spectrum. Furthermore, Verwer uses typically modern strategies, such as 'translation' to unmask the deceit and 'reversal' to change the meaning of linguistic concepts, although he does not apply them to the canon or to standard authors of reference but to Spinoza and his new philosophy. This at once clarifies and confuses the matter. Moreover, the dividing line separating the countermovement from moderate Enlightenment thought ends up becoming razor-thin.

Verwer categorically rejects the hypothetical basis for Spinoza's geometric thought, charging that mathematics must have an applied character and an empirical basis. Concretely, he rejects the hypothetical thought for its atheism, that is, its autonomous and self-determining character, as it comes to expression in the field of politics. Since Spinoza holds that right and power coincide in the 'innate state', there is 'nothing [. . .] that is good or evil by the agreement of all', and there can be no sin except in the civil state, 'where what is good or bad is determined by common consent'; people themselves determine what is good and bad, for there is 'nothing' outside of them by

[8] Verwer, '*t Mom-Aensicht*, 53.
[9] Ibid. 64.

which they could make such a determination.[10] This claim may be read as a direct critique of the theory of Grotius, which was generally accepted at the time.[11] Verwer, for his part, does base himself on Grotius's 'principle of freedom and equality', which can only be followed if you have knowledge not only of 'the right of a citizen' and 'the right of a nation', but also of God, 'the foundation of our very dependence'.[12] Taking his point of departure in the absolute equality in the innate nature of all people, Spinoza gives a new meaning to such concepts as 'sin', 'merit', 'justice', 'injustice' and 'human freedom'. Earlier we saw that the reversal he completed was a reversal of Hobbes, but Verwer shows that it is even more a reversal of Grotius. Spinoza understands the equality in human nature mathematically and neutrally: there is no hierarchy, such that every norm, every external transcendent criterion or external determination, must be removed from ethical, political and legal concepts. He does not deny God but his transcendence, and he reduces the criteria for action and determination to the terrain of immanence – that is, to people, to a *multitude*. As such, politics becomes a matter of conflict and struggle, as well as rational dialogue and agreements that are supremely sustainable in spite of their inherently temporal character. Spinoza is not predisposed to revolutionary activity, nor does he speak in terms of 'equal freedom' as *maître* Van den Enden does, and his suspicions towards the mobs which can be whipped up into a one-headed monster are at a fundamental level. Yet this takes nothing away from the fact that the ethical, political and legal implications of his independence-thesis, of the idea that all people are equal and free, or, as the *De jure ecclesiasticorum* formulates it, that there is no freedom without equality and no equality without freedom, are radically revolutionary and liberating. The moment a citizen refuses to obey, that refusal is just.

[10] Ibid. 52.

[11] On this point, Verwer's critique runs parallel to that of Van Blyenbergh, who in his *De waerheyt van de christelijcke godts-dienst* contrasts Grotius with Spinoza's rejection of Christian teaching; see above, Chapter VII.3.2, 200–4; see also Verbeek in 'Spinoza on Aristocratic and Democratic Government', 145–60. On the relationship between Spinoza and Grotius, see Secretan, 'Fonction du politique et *jus circa sacra* dans les controverses hollandaises du début du XVIIe siècle', 167–85, and Fukuoka, *The Sovereign and the Prophets*.

[12] Verwer, *'t Mom-Aensicht*, 78–88.

2. L'Esprit de Spinosa/Traité des trois imposteurs

While Nieuwentyt was trying to assuage the unrest provoked by these wild ideas with his rational and careful *Gronden van zekerheid*, in 1719 the city of Amsterdam saw the appearance of an anonymous work which sought on the contrary to bring that same independence-thesis to radical development. The work was printed under the title *La Vie et l'Esprit de Monsieur Benoit de Spinosa* and it combined two texts: a biography of Spinoza, and a treatise on the essence of his philosophy. We know that the biography (*La Vie*) was authored by Jean-Maximilien Lucas, a French journalist, Huguenot, and refugee living in Holland, and that it was published that same year in the July–December issue of the *Nouvelles littéraires*.[13] But we know very little about *L'Esprit*, and none of it with any certainty. We do not know when and where the text was composed, nor the identity of its author. It is an unconventional essay written in a lively pamphlet style, claiming to set forth the quintessence of Spinoza's ideas simply and straightforwardly. No work caused as much upheaval as this bellicose essay, not even Spinoza's own treatises. Paul Vernière has suggested that it too was probably authored by Lucas, a view that finds some support in its contents, in certain remarks in *La Vie* as well as the copyist's preface (*Préface du copiste*), and in the studies of Meinsma, Meyer, Dunin-Borkowski and, more recently, Benítez, Charles-Daubert and Schröder.[14] Miguel Benítez drew up a complete inventory of the extant manuscripts (as well as the many lost manuscripts), and for dating it he appealed to the testimony of Arpe, Tentzel and Struve.[15] Françoise Charles-Daubert based her study on a meticulous archaeology of the different manuscripts and editions, as well as the testimony of Marchand and others.[16] Winfried Schröder similarly used textual analyses together with the testimony of Tentzel, Struve, Budde and Reimmann.[17] It is clear

---

[13] The *Vie de Spinosa* was published by Henri Du Sauzet in the July–December 1719 issue of the *Nouvelles littéraires*; see *Dictionnaire des journaux* online, vol. X, 42–74.

[14] Vernière, *Spinoza et la pensée française avant la Révolution*, vol. II, 365: 'Quant au véritable auteur, apologiste maladroit mais informé de Spinoza, pourquoi ne pas y voir encore Jean-Maximilien Lucas, malgré l'érudit hollandais Meijer qui ne peut admettre l'athéisme d'un disciple?' In the footnote he draws a line to the hypothesis of Marchand, who had suggested that Vroese is the author: 'Il est possible que Vroese ait été le détenteur d'un manuscrit de Lucas, ce qui concilierait toutes les thèses.'

[15] Benítez, *La Face cachée des Lumières*, 303–4.

[16] Charles-Daubert, *Le 'Traité des trois imposteurs' et 'L'Esprit de Spinosa'*; Marchand, Art. 'Impostoribus', *Dictionaire historique*, vol. 1, 312–29.

[17] Schröder, 'Einleitung', in *Traktat über die drei Betrüger*, VII–XLIII; Budde, *Theses theologicae de atheismo et superstitione*, 111–13; Reimmann, *Versuch einer Einleitung*

that the essay was written much earlier than 1719, presumably not long after the publication of Spinoza's *Opera Posthuma*, somewhere in the 1680s, when Verwer's and Blyenbergh's refutations were coming into print. One complicating factor is the existence of different textual versions. The earliest printed edition is the *Esprit* of 1719; a Latin translation was published in 1721; then in 1768 another French edition appeared, most probably the work of Baron d'Holbach, under the title *Traité des trois imposteurs*; after which another six editions came on the market before the turn of the century, all bearing the latter title. These printed editions were accompanied by countless manuscripts that were already circulating before the first edition of 1719. One manuscript was found in the library which Baron Hohendorf left at his death in Vienna in 1719; another was discovered among a bundle of manuscripts owned by Boulainvilliers which appears to date from 1712, judging at least by the title page to the latter's *Essay de Métaphisique dans les Principes de B. de Spinosa* with which it was bound. Each of these editions and manuscripts presents a slightly different text. There is one treatise, but it exists in numerous variations. The *Esprit* is the prototype of a living and collective – and polemical – text appropriated by a *multitude* of anonymous authors, adapted by them to different degrees according to their respective insights or strategic goals, and disseminated in clandestine fashion to a formidable audience. The text is itself likewise the product of such a revolutionary act: a compilation of fragments appropriated, translated or paraphrased silently from existing libertarian writings, primarily from Spinoza (*TTP* and *Ethica*), but also from Hobbes (the Latin version of *Leviathan*), from Vanini, and through him, from Machiavelli. The *Esprit* positively incorporates the independence-thesis, whose genealogy Verwer had established, in its most radical expressions and then develops it. In the spirit of Spinoza, the *Esprit* goes a step beyond Spinoza.

The contents are explosive. Religion and traditional moral and metaphysical frameworks constructed on the dependence-thesis are unmasked as the servants of political constellations and governing powers. The idea of God is torn down and neutralised, revelation and miracles are undermined, the fear of punishment in the hereafter and that hereafter itself are both eliminated, and the legitimacy of the ecclesiastical authorities'

---

in die Historie der Theologie insgemein und der jüdischen Theologie ins besondere, 647; Struve, *Dissertatio historico-litteraria de Doctis Impostoribus*, 16–24; Tentzel, *Curieuse Bibliothec*, 493–5. In Tentzel's work we find a quotation from a letter of Johann Wilhelm Petersen, written in 1700, which includes a detailed and concrete description of the table of contents of the *Esprit/Traité*. On this basis, we can establish 1700 as the *terminus ad quem* for its composition.

252 DEMOCRATIC THOUGHT FROM MACHIAVELLI TO SPINOZA

political power is shattered. The main theme is the political origin of the religions, and on this point the *Esprit* follows the tradition of the 'Politiques' (Machiavelli, Charron, Naudé and Vanini) and applies the motif of deceit.[18] In the previous chapter, we saw how the countertexts compared the *TTP* with the work of the 'Machiavellians' or 'pseudo-politicians' who 'connect all religions with political art' in order to subdue the masses and scare off rebels.[19] Spinoza's scepticism regarding prophecy and his denial of miracles serve the truth and the unmasking of deceit, he completes a reversal. But once the motif of the unmasking of deceit is introduced, the concept of truth itself is unhinged, there are sides and perspectives to consider, reality is duplicated into a being that is hidden and a semblance (or feigned being) that must be preserved (for the one) or shattered (for the other), and people speak from two sides of their mouth – whether the deceiver and violator of the truth, or else the advocate of the truth, so as to evade the deceiver's violence. For the counter-reaction confirms the deceit with greater force and violence than ever before.

Deceptive processes of power and, in response, the unmasking critique are of all times and perhaps as human as religion and deceit themselves.[20] What, concretely, is the author talking about? There is an old legend which speaks of a book about the deceit of the three monotheistic religions, *De tribus impostoribus*, the book of the three imposters. This legend goes back to an elusive story for which the earliest evidence is found in the 1239 papal bull against Frederick II, king of Sicily, who was reported to have said that 'the whole world is misled by three deceivers: Moses, Jesus, and Mohammed'.[21]

---

[18] Charles-Daubert, Le "Traité des trois imposteurs" et "L'Esprit de Spinosa", 110. See also Cavaillé, 'Libertinage ou lumières radicales', 61–104.

[19] See Chapter VII.3.3, 215–6. See also Verbeek, who focuses on this Spinoza-libertines-Machiavelli genealogy but pairs it with an interpretation of Spinoza's political theory as a premodern, conservative and 'Machiavellian' *might is right*-defence from the perspective of the powerful elite, against the multitude. In his reading, Spinoza rejects the 'modern' tradition of Grotius, Locke and Pufendorf, who all attempt to establish a secular morality and legal sphere in which a central place is reserved for individual rights: 'Spinoza on Aristocratic and Democratic Government', 145–60; Verbeek, 'Spinoza on Natural Rights', 257–75.

[20] This is a recurring theme among thinkers who focus on the relationship between practices of language and practices of power; see, e.g., Foucault's programmatic *L'ordre du discours*, but also the Preface which Kant wrote for the first edition of his *Kritik der reinen Vernunft* (Critique of Pure Reason, 1781).

[21] 'a tribus barattatoribus [. . .] scilicet Christo Iesu, Moyse et Machometo, totum mundum fuisse deceptum'; see Schröder, 'Einleitung', XII–XIII; Niewöhner, *Veritas sive Varietas. Lessings Toleranzparabel und das Buch von den drei Betrügern*. The notion of

As such, Frederick II's method and ideas represented a threat to the politics and power of Pope Gregory IX. He saw government as an art (*ad arte*), considered the world changeable, and attached little value to faith but was highly interested in the science of the philosophers, most of them Arabic, who were assembled at his court.[22] He was reluctant to embark on a crusade until the pope excommunicated him, then continued to hesitate, and when he did finally head to Jerusalem, he went out in a spirit of dialogue, compromise and peace. He gained political success, bolstered his power and earned himself a following, but the situation also intensified his conflict with the pope. The latter responded in classical fashion by carefully constructing a blasphemous counterimage of him. As Charles-Daubert has observed, the blasphemy of the three deceivers at once thematises and illustrates the intrinsically political origin of religion.[23] The deceit unmasked by Frederick is turned against him, and he is represented as a deceiver and traitor of the faith. Piero della Vigna, his secretary, is said to have recorded his words in a blasphemous work called *De tribus impostoribus*. This fiction later became a legend and went on to live a life of its own; Boccaccio, Pomponazzi, Bruno, Rabelais, Machiavelli, Aretino, Campanella and Vanini are only the most prominent names among the many suspected of authoring this mythical work. It has also been linked to Averroes, the first to have uttered the blasphemous idea, although this only serves to emphasise the indebtedness of Italian Renaissance thinkers formed in the Paduan school to Islamic philosophy.

There is little doubt that the *Esprit de Spinosa*, which also circulated under the title *Traité des trois imposteurs*, was written after 1677. It is an artefact: someone once had the idea to write this book which was most unsettling to everyone, although no one had ever seen or read it. And, given its title, disruptive contents and composing parts, it must have been the lesson of Spinoza – i.e. both his work and its reception – that moved a 'disciple' to

---

religions owing their existence to the deceit of their founders was already widely spread in the Islamic world; see Bonnerot, 'L'"imposture" de l'Islam et l'esprit des Lumières', 101–14.

[22] Cf. Mack Smith, *Storia della Sicilia medievale e moderna*, 9–84; 749. In his groundbreaking *Die Kultur der Renaissance in Italien* (1860), Burckhardt likewise points to the importance of the Sicilian King Frederick II for the formation of the notion of a state 'as the outcome of reflection and calculation, the state as a work of art', and the influence of the Saracens for making him comfortable with a 'thoroughly objective treatment of affairs' such that the 'first ruler of the modern type' came to sit upon a throne; see *The Civilisation of the Renaissance in Italy*, 4–5.

[23] Charles-Daubert, *Le "Traité des trois imposteurs" et "L'Esprit de Spinosa"*, 13.

254 DEMOCRATIC THOUGHT FROM MACHIAVELLI TO SPINOZA

write it. This suggestion finds confirmation in the prefatory *Avertissement*, whose very first line immediately locates the publication of *La Vie et L'Esprit de Spinosa* in the tradition of the 'strong spirits' (*esprits forts*) and reads like an entry in Koerbagh.[24] The way religion's defenders treat their opponents (i.e. the philosophers), with contempt for and by suppression of the books in which the latter develop their counterarguments, does not speak to their advantage. If they really were convinced of their cause, would they fear its downfall if they only defended it with sound arguments? And if they were so full of the confidence which the truth offers to those who fight for it, would they take recourse in false prejudices and misguided means to secure its victory? Furthermore, there is the irony that the publication of this monstrous essay will give 'competent people' (*habiles Gens*) the ability to overturn Spinoza's corrupt system.[25]

In *De waerheyt van de christelijcke godts-dienst* (1674), Van Blyenbergh writes that atheism was known to have struck deep roots in the minds of the people, for instance in that 'accursed book *De Tribus impostoribus*'.[26] Like many authoritative sources, Van Blyenbergh situates the book of the three imposters, whose title continued to be cited only in Latin up to that time, somewhere in the sixteenth century. In his *Quaestiones celeberrimae* of 1623, Mersenne thus mentions a friend who had read it and recognised in it the style of Aretino, and Voetius was to repeat these words in his *De atheismo* of 1639.[27] In his *Appendix ad Commentationem de Antichristo* of 1641, however, Grotius argues that people were already talking about the book before

---

[24] 'Avvertissement', in Charles-Daubert, *Le "Traité des trois imposteurs" et "L'Esprit de Spinosa"*, 619: 'Il n'y a peut-être rien qui donne aux *Esprits forts* un prétexte plus plausible d'insulter à la Religion, que la manière dont en agissent avec eux ses Deffenseurs.'; 's'ils etoient assûrez de sa bonté, craindroient-ils qu'elle ne succombât en ne la soûtenant que par de bonnes raisons? Et s'ils étoient pleins de cette ferme confiance qu'inspire la *Vérité* à ceux qui croyent combattre pour elle, auroient-ils recours à de faux avantages, & à de mauvaises voyes pour la faire triompher?' The similarities with Koerbagh can be illustrated, for instance, with the entry 'Excommuniceerde' in *Een Bloemhof*, 285–9. See also above, Chapter VI.1, 138–9; Mignini, '*Een ligt schijnende in duystere plaatsen*: Adriaan Koerbagh tra averroismo e libertinismo', 167–200.

[25] Charles-Daubert, 'Avvertissement', 619.

[26] Blyenbergh, *De waerheyt van de christelijcke godts-dienst*, n.p. [a1].

[27] Mersenne, *Quaestiones celeberrimae in genesim*, as cited in Charles-Daubert, *Le "Traité des trois imposteurs" et "L'Esprit de Spinosa"*, 17–19; Voetius, *De atheismo*, in *Selectarum disputationum theologicarum*, 216–17: 'Illic vulgatus est horribilis liber de Tribus Impostoribus auctore Petro Aretino, ut vult Mersennus supra cit.'

Aretino's birth and alludes to the story of Frederick II.[28] No one appears to have read the book himself, but everyone knows someone who claims to have seen it or held the text in his hands. Like most contemporaries, Van Blyenbergh bases himself on these vague rumours, but for his refutation of atheism he focuses on two contemporary works of which he himself did indeed have first-hand knowledge: Koerbagh's *Een Bloemhof*, with its feigned title; and Spinoza's *TTP*, whose 'erudite abominations' and 'pile of concepts forged in hell' surpass even Machiavelli.[29]

Beginning in the 1680s, the notion of deceit plays a growing role in the countertexts attacking those who equate God and nature, but they still rarely mention the book of the three imposters. Van Blyenbergh does not mention it in his *Wederlegging van de Ethica of Zede-Kunst van Benedictus de Spinosa* of 1682, even though the major theme of his refutation is the radical naturalistic view of God and the human soul. It is likewise absent in Verwer's genealogy of the independence-thesis, though one might have expected it there. The existence of the work came to be increasingly questioned, such that intellectuals reached the consensus that it never actually existed. As such, a shift took place from the old myth to a new idea holding that *L'Esprit* was devised by contemporary deceivers who were also circulating it. For instance, in his article on 'Aretin' in his *Dictionaire historique et critique* Bayle adds a 'Remarque' in which he questions the well-known story of Mersenne, charging that 'it seems very unlikely the work ever existed'.[30] In support of this view, he appeals to Bernard de la Monnoye's dissertation, which was sent to him by mail in 1693 and was to be published in 1715 in part IV of the *Menagiana*.[31] In his 'Spinoza' article, Bayle, ever well-informed and himself a French refugee in Holland, says nothing at all about the motif of the deceit of the religions, nor does he mention the Spinoza texts of Lucas, a fellow French exile. For composing the Spinoza article of 1697, however, he bases himself partly on 'a manuscript sent to the bookseller', as

---

[28] Grotius, *Appendix ad interpretationem locorum N. Testamenti quae de Antichristo agunt*, 133. See also Bayle, Art. 'Aretin', *Dictionaire historique et critique*, vol. 1, Rem. G, 304; Guichard, *Histoire du socinianisme*, 32–4; Schröder, in his edition of Müller's *De imposturis religionum (De tribus impostoribus)*, 21; 240.

[29] Blyenbergh, *De waerheyt*, n.p. [a1–a2].

[30] Bayle, Art. 'Aretin', vol. 1, Remarque G, 304. We find a similar remark in *Naudeana et Patiniana ou singularitez remarquables, prises des conversations de Mess. Naudé & Patin*, 129: 'Je n'ai jamais vu le Livre de tribus impostoribus, & je crois qu'il n'a jamais été imprimé, & tiens pour mensonge tout ce qu'on en a dit.'

[31] Bayle, Art. 'Aretin', Remarque G, 304; De la Monnoye, 'Lettre à Monsieur Bouhier', *Menagiana* IV, 283–4; 298–9.

256 DEMOCRATIC THOUGHT FROM MACHIAVELLI TO SPINOZA

he remarks in the margin, most likely in reference to *La Vie*.[32] When, several months before his death, he reads Colerus/Köhler's Spinoza biography, he writes in a letter that on a number of points the German biographer is even better informed than he: 'Mr. Colerus had the time to investigate each and every detail over the course of many years.'[33] Bayle's letter situates the other biography much earlier, illustrates his incessantly critical stance towards his sources, his doubt and modesty, his constant pursuit of improvement. Yet it also raises questions about his place in the detours he makes, and we still do not find a single word about an *Esprit de Spinosa/Traité*. The motif of deceit only arises in the second edition of Bayle's dictionary (1702), and there he ascribes it to Spinoza. Anyone who wants to discover the tricks and ambiguities Spinoza used to disguise his atheism, he writes, 'only needs to consult Christian Kortholt's *De Tribus Impostoribus magnis*, printed in Kiel in 1680, in duodecimo. There the author has assembled various passages from Spinoza and exposed all their venom and artifice.'[34]

L'Esprit may well represent a response to the *De Tribus Impostoribus magnis*. As in *'t Mom-Aensicht* and the other countertexts from the 1670s and 1680s, Kortholt reverses the motif of the three imposters and – inspired by Mersenne and Voetius – locates it in a genealogy which extends back to antiquity (Lucian, Epicurus, Lucretius) and the Italians (Machiavelli, Aretino and Vanini), branches out into France, England, Holland and Germany, before reaching its apex in Cherbury, Hobbes and Spinoza. In a biographical entry on Lucas from 1918, Willem Meyer noted that *L'Esprit* appears to be a reaction to Kortholt's work.[35] He bases this suggestion on his study of the figure and writing of Lucas. In departure from today, in the late nineteenth and early twentieth centuries there was near unanimity concerning the authorship and date of *La Vie* and *L'Esprit*.[36]

---

[32] Bayle, Art. 'Spinoza', vol. 3, note c, 255.

[33] Bayle, 'Lettre à M. xxx à Rotterdam, le . . . d'avril 1706', in *Écrits sur Spinoza*, 165.

[34] Bayle, Art. 'Spinoza', Remarque M, 259; Kortholt, *De tribus impostoribus magnis liber*, n.p. [*6r–8v]. See also Lagrée, 'Christian Kortholt (1633–1694) et son *De tribus impostoribus magnis*', 169–83.

[35] Meyer, 'Lucas, Jean Maximilien', 935–6.

[36] Many questions surrounding textual history and authorship remain unanswered, as evident in the essays by and in Berti, Charles-Daubert and Popkin (eds), *Heterodoxy, Spinozism, and Free Thought in Early-Eighteenth-Century Europe* (1996). Furthermore, many of the hypotheses postulated in that collected volume have since been abandoned in more recent studies, sometimes even by the same author, as in the case of Charles-Daubert. Popkin situates an embryonic form of the *Esprit/Traité* around the middle of the seventeenth century, and Charles-Daubert, with her thesis of an urtext which she dated to c. 1672, initially followed suit. Berti follows Marchand and

Meinsma, Freudenthal, Meyer and Dunin-Borkowski all held the view that the adventurous pamphlet-writer Lucas, author of the *Quintessences*, a notorious opponent of Louis XIV, co-founder of *La gazette raisonné*, and a fellow refugee and acquaintance of Bayle, wrote both *La Vie*, immediately after 1677 and before 1680, and *L'Esprit*, after 1678 but before 1688. All of them also saw similarities between *La Vie* and *L'Esprit* in terms of the relationship between the published text of 1719, the earlier manuscripts, and a basic text whose existence they posited, which were reason enough for them to insist on a common author for both. Finally, there is the verifiable accuracy of the biography in *La Vie*, together with the quality of the manuscripts in which both works are included compared to the inadequacy of the manuscripts in convolute volumes only incorporating either *La Vie* or *L'Esprit*. At the same time, they did acknowledge the doubts evoked in contemporary testimonies. Meinsma, for instance, draws attention to the ambiguous formulation in the 'copyist's preface' to the 1719 edition: 'One could say, and perhaps with certainty, that the entire piece is the work of the late Mr. Lucas, of *Quintessens* fame.'[37] Meyer points to Bayle who, as always, only confuses the matter for us. He suggested that Bayle sought to clarify the matter for the circle of his friends, yet without revealing his true view to the uninitiated.[38] Stanislaus von Dunin-Borkowksi did not doubt that Lucas authored both *La Vie* and *L'Esprit*, although he did question whether this political adventurer had really grasped anything of Spinoza's work. There is only one reason to doubt his authorship, so Dunin-Borkowski writes, and that is the authority of Prosper Marchand who considered it impossible for the 'genius jester' (*génie bouffon*) to write such a treatise and therefore suggested other potential authors in

---

situates the composition of the work much later, with Jan Vroese. It is certain that Charles Levier, a member of the *Chevaliers de la Jubilation*, played an important role in the edition of 1719, and this leads Jacob to situate the origins of the treatise in those same years and to ascribe a role to Toland, the English commonwealth-men, and the Freemasons (see also Jacob, *The Radical Enlightenment*). Schwarzbach and Fairbairn suggest that the *Esprit/Traité* is dependent on Schramm's 1709 work, which served as an intermediary source for the Vanini quotations. Israel is inclined to follow Lucas in his *Radical Enlightenment*, 695–6, as is Schröder, who in his 'Einleitung', XII–XXVIII, as well as in his *Ursprünge des Atheismus*, 452–64, offers convincing arguments against the other attributions and any attempt to date the work outside the period 1678–1700. See also Raimondi, 'Vanini e il "De tribus impostoribus"', 265–90; Steenbakkers, *Spinoza's* Ethica *from Manuscript to Print*, 10–11.

[37] Meinsma, *Spinoza en zijn kring*, XVI–XVII.
[38] Meyer, 'Lucas, Jean Maximilien', 935–6; Meyer, 'Wer war Lucas', 270–8.

258   DEMOCRATIC THOUGHT FROM MACHIAVELLI TO SPINOZA

the 'Impostoribus' article of his *Dictionaire historique*.[39] Marchand for his part does confirm a dating that leaves Lucas an option, traces the story of the different attributions, editions and manuscripts, and concludes that the treatise *Des trois imposteurs* is of recent manufacture, the work of an 'accomplished Spinozist' (*Spinosiste achevé*), which was fabricated shortly before it began to circulate, that is, somewhere in the last 'forty or fifty years', around 1690.[40] The book of the three imposters is just 'a bad rhapsody [. . .] fabricated in secret by one of these wretched compilers [. . .] an artifice, which has been put to use'.[41]

3. Unmasking deceit

The *multitude* of traces, clues, manuscripts and variants form a labyrinth in which one can easily lose one's way, although they bring Marchand to a rather precise date, the notion of the artifice, the positing of a basic text, and rather apt comparisons. As noted, the *Esprit/Traité* consists almost entirely of a compilation of paraphrases and translated fragments from, once again, a *multitude* of seventeenth-century heterodox writings, the most recent being Spinoza's *Ethica* (1677) and the oldest Vanini's *De admirandis naturae* (1619). There is a strong affinity between Spinoza and Vanini, connected as they are by the *Politiques* and an ideology-critical perspective on religion in the spirit of Machiavelli. This connection was confirmed in the reading we have offered over the past several chapters. On the basis of an immanent ontology (i.e. there is nothing outside of nature, no interaction from the other side), religion is depicted as a political fiction and the deceit perpetrated by religions as an instrument of political oppression. Theoretical immanentism, the equation of God and nature, and the motif of deceit can all be found on the main genealogical stem of *L'Esprit/Traité*. The comparison Marchand drew to the manuscript *Theophrastus redivivus* is therefore an apt one. Both texts contain the same message, both are surrounded by various uncertainties appealing to the imagination, and copies of both were found in Baron de Hohendorf's library. The *Theophrastus redivivus* could easily pass

[39] Dunin-Borkowski, 'Nachlese zur ältesten Geschichte des Spinozismus', 61–2; *Der junge De Spinoza*, 46–51; Marchand, Art. 'Impostoribus', *Dictionaire historique, ou Mémoires critiques et littéraires*, 325.

[40] Marchand, ibid.

[41] Marchand, ibid, 321. This conclusion finds confirmation in Johann Wilhelm Petersen's 1700 letter, with its detailed and concrete description of the table of contents of the *Esprit/Traité*, which was cited by Wilhelm Ernst Tentzel in the *Curieuse Bibliothec* of 1704: see Schröder, 'Einleitung', XVII–XVIII.

for the treatise of the three imposters and has the marks of a purposefully (*ad arte*) fabricated text which offers a wide array of representative fragments from erudite heterodox works extending from antiquity to the early seventeenth century, assembled with a lively commonsense criticism of the religious and political authorities that has a very familiar ring to it even to us today. Dunin-Borkowski went a step further when he claimed to see more *Theophrastus* than Spinoza in the *Esprit*, together with yet more evidence for his view that the *Esprit* does not include anything that the author did not copy from somewhere else. Chapters 1 and 2 contain a watered-down version of the *TTP*, Chapters 2 and 3 fragments from amateur religio-philosophical writings circulating in manuscript form at the time, like the *Theophrastus redivivus*. Dunin-Borkowski even suggested that Lucas drew everything from the latter work, indirectly. So too Chapter 5, which treats of the human soul, is entirely indebted to another work, although it bears no signs of Spinoza's views on human psychology. Chapter 6 offers proofs against the existence of the devil which had acquired the status of commonplaces by that time through the circulation of freethinker manuscripts, though one searches in vain for the arguments Spinoza uses in his *Korte Verhandeling*.[42] The only remaining chapter is Chapter 4, entitled 'Perceptible and evident truths' (*Vérités sensibles et évidentes*), and it is the only one that is reminiscent of a Spinoza text, and even then only vaguely so.

Current scholarship has a somewhat different perspective. Schröder has demonstrated that there are clear substantive analogies between *Theophrastus redivivus* and *L'Esprit/Traité*, but cautions that there is nothing suggesting it is a paraphrase or translation, so that this thesis must be discarded.[43] But does the question of a direct relationship really matter in a case involving a revolutionary, collective and anonymous text like *L'Esprit/Traité*? Its theoretical immanentism, and in its wake the motif of deceit, confronts the pursuit of knowledge with the futility of life hereafter and the complex *multitude* of the actual, living reality. As a result of the immanentist perspective

---

[42] Dunin-Borkowski, 'Nachlese zur ältesten Geschichte des Spinozismus', 65–6. Vernière disagrees, arguing that while there may be no reference to Chapter 25 on the demons, the theory of the soul partly goes back to Chapter 23 of the *Korte Verhandeling* and Chapter 6 of *L'Esprit* appropriates the demonology developed by Spinoza in that same treatise. Moreover, some of the common views on God which we read in the first two chapters can be traced back directly to Chapter 24. All of this is reason enough for Vernière to identify the *Esprit*, like *La Vie*, as being of Dutch origins, and in fact to locate both texts in Rieuwertsz's Spinoza-archive: Vernière, *Spinoza et la pensée française avant la Révolution*, vol. II, 364.

[43] Schröder, 'Einleitung', XXXVI–XXXVII.

260 DEMOCRATIC THOUGHT FROM MACHIAVELLI TO SPINOZA

and the rejection of the dependence-thesis, the traditional concept of truth is cut loose from its moorings, the questions change and so do the methods and criteria. This is physics: when the transcendent ordering principle is removed, the focus of knowledge shifts to the *multitude* of perspectives and views, the envisioned goals, the advantages and disadvantages for the one individual/collective or the other, the discontinuities and common denominators, briefly, the ethical and political questions. The majority of early modern ideas assembled in the *Traité* – from Hobbes, Lamy, La Mothe Le Vayer – could perfectly co-exist with a Christian worldview, but this does not hold for Vanini's unmasking of the religions of revelation (even though it does not exclude a natural religion) and even less so for Spinoza's philosophy (which abandons the notion of a personal God).[44]

According to Charles-Daubert, the author of *L'Esprit* follows the classic structure of antireligious discourse also encountered in *Theophrastus redivivus* and his explicit goal is to get his readers to cast off the yoke of religions because they foster ignorance and fear. He attempts to achieve this by demonstrating that God is not an avenger, that the eternity of the soul is an invention of poets and theologians, and that demons do not exist. His readers will liberate themselves from their fear of punishment in the hereafter once they recognise that this is an invention of political lawgivers whose purpose is to suppress them. The anonymous writer uses Spinoza more than he actually follows him, and at any rate radicalises the message of the *TTP* by applying the arguments of Machiavelli and Vanini to it. He follows the notion which Naudé had set out in his *Considérations politiques sur les coups d'Estat*, arguing that Christ, Mohammed and Moses are all deceivers, which is an idea foreign to Spinoza although ultimately that hardly matters.[45] For a libertine reader/author like the anonymous Lucas, Spinoza's interpretation of the Mosaic law as a civil law cannot be read as anything but an attempt to turn Moses into a deceiver. The same is true for *Ethica* I: the passages added in the *Esprit* to its translation of the Appendix do not come from the *Ethica* but from Vanini's *De admirandis naturae*. With his critical analysis of Scripture, Spinoza offered a scientific foundation for what the *libertins érudit* had already achieved via another road and method.[46]

According to Paganini, the convergence of the French *libertins érudits* (like *Theophrastus*) and a philosophy that is incompatible with the

---

[44] Ibid.

[45] Charles-Daubert, 'L'image de Spinoza dans la littérature clandestine et l'*Esprit de Spinoza*', 59–67; Naudé, *Considérations politiques sur les coups d'Estat*, 1639/1667.

[46] Charles-Daubert, 'L'image de Spinoza', 64.

Christian view (like that of Hobbes and Spinoza) gave the libertine views a new systematic shape.[47] Our own reading suggests that this convergence furthermore allowed the libertine views to transform into a politically revolutionary mission. Hobbes and Spinoza have two different theories on religion, both of them leaving their traces in the *Esprit/Traité*: the former locates fear at the centre of the origin of religion, while the latter sees the alternation of hope and fear as the cause of superstition. Paganini stresses the materialism of the *Esprit*, which he describes as a rereading of Spinoza through the lens of Hobbes, the first to recognise the equivalence of 'substance' and 'body'.[48] With respect to Spinoza, he highlights the systematic and consistently developed character of his atheism. But how does Hobbes's materialism relate to Spinoza's atheism? And, more importantly, what does that relationship mean for the notion of political and social liberation? Spinoza connects a Hobbesian naturalism to a democratic republican vision based on freedom and equality; that perspective differs from the perspective of Hobbes and issues in an alternative view on fear, deceit and oppression. The opposite appears to be true in *Esprit*, which is like a rereading of Hobbes in the 'leftist' spirit of Spinoza and Vanini.

Dunin-Borkowski found the vulgarising superficiality of *L'Esprit* rather irksome. Yet the latter actually goes a step beyond Spinoza precisely because its unmasking message is expressed in a language accessible to all. Not only are Latin passages from the aforementioned philosophers silently collected, translated and paraphrased, but the *Esprit/Traité* also transforms itself into a consistent and new text with its own style. It does not mention its sources by name (with the exception of Charron and Naudé in the chapters added by Levier for the printed *Esprit*, which are nevertheless absent from the Hohendorf and Boulainvilliers manuscripts, nor can they be found in the printed *Traité*, such that they do not belong to what one might call the 'basic text'), and all layers of authorship have been anonymised.[49] In the absence of notes and references to the underlying sources or authors, the text does not present itself as a theoretical treatise but adopts the physiognomy of a battle manifest whose aim is to clarify the import and essence of the new ideas for a *multitude* of people. The *Esprit* goes a step beyond Spinoza, but

---

[47] Paganini, *Introduzione alle filosofie clandestine*, 70–1. Malcolm too writes that Hobbes has a much greater presence in the *Esprit/Traité* than commentators have commonly assumed; see 'Hobbes and the European Republic of Letters', in *Aspects of Hobbes*, 488–92. See also n. 56 below.

[48] Paganini, *Introduzione*, 81; Hobbes, *Leviathan*, Chap. 34.

[49] Charles-Daubert, *Le "Traité des trois imposteurs" et "L'Esprit de Spinosa"*, 100–5.

262 DEMOCRATIC THOUGHT FROM MACHIAVELLI TO SPINOZA

still continues 'in his spirit', as it were. After all, once Spinoza had passed away, his *Ethica* had been published and the countermovement was set in motion, what better way to spread these revolutionary ideas than by acting like him and by adopting that of which he was accused as a positive motif? And what better way to achieve this than to assume the motif of deceit and to follow in the footsteps of those scorned *Politiques*, themselves the target of that countermovement?[50]

Spinoza was not the only one to pave the way for the *Esprit/Traité*, for the writers from his circle did the same. The motif of deceit as a cornerstone of the 'reason of state' is criticised by Van den Enden and Koerbagh and then reversed. De la Court's position is in that regard somewhat ambiguous and fluctuates. On the one hand, there is the plagiarism of Wassenaar's *Bedekte konsten* in the *Naeuwkeurige consideratie*, the pessimism regarding the *multitude*. Starting with the second edition of the *Consideratien van Staat*, the initial enthusiasm for a democracy drops and gradually transforms into a defence of aristocracy – an aristocracy of the multitude, indeed, but still one at odds with the spirit of Machiavelli. On the other hand, there is the rich anthology of material drawn from Machiavelli, so that the *Consideratien* and *Politike Discoursen* might even be said to breathe Machiavelli's spirit. There is the naturalistic intellectual framework, the view on religion and language, the unmasking and the strategy of reversal, the erudite compilation style, the collection, appropriation and application of a multitude of sources for his own specific goals, the translation for a wide audience. De la Court's political reflections served as an example to the Dutch radical scene of Koerbagh, Van den Enden and Spinoza. The massive critique and condemnation which met the *TTP* moved Spinoza to compose the *TP* and to apply that process of reversal one more time. As we have shown in the preceding chapters, this procedure governs his entire corpus, and he applies it both to the tradition and to his immediate interlocutors, such as Descartes, Hobbes and Grotius. He rejects the prejudice of the free will, and posits and demonstrates the interchangeability of God and nature, from the *Korte verhandeling*, through the *TTP*, and down into the *Ethica* and *TP*. The naturalist foundation, religion as a political art, and his view on the use and abuse of language are ideas that Spinoza – along with De la Court, Van den Enden, the author of *De jure ecclesiasticorum* and Koerbagh – takes over from Hobbes. In the consequences he draws from there he not only goes beyond Hobbes, but also against the latter's political views. Earlier on we drew attention to Spinoza's letter to Jelles from 2 June 1674, in which he wrote that he differed from

---

[50] Ibid. 110. See also Lagrée, 'Spinoza l'imposteur libertin?'.

Hobbes in that he 'always [left] natural Right unimpaired'. This means that the *multitude* with its natural *potentia*/power on which an institutionalised governmental power is based and therefore depends does not completely transform and dissolve into one nation (which is a fiction) and its sovereign. As a result, the success of a sovereign depends on the extent to which that sovereign is open to improvement and accedes to the interests of the *multitude* of common people, who support and approve him for that very reason. The greatest threat in that context is the deceit manifesting itself when falsities and prejudices are spread about by so-called religions, self-styled scholars and mystifying language. This theme, which occupies a central place in Spinoza, Koerbagh and Van den Enden, is taken over quite literally in *L'Esprit*. Deceit means that common people are not treated equally, it means inequality and thus oppression and coercion and the absence of freedom. The victims of that deceit may indeed be able to break through by showing the courage to think for themselves, to fashion knowledge themselves, and to seize upon the freedom to philosophise as their duty. They have the ability to do all these things. This notion was expressed most clearly by Van den Enden, who published his political works anonymously in Dutch and in a style that did not address the elite alone but each and every person.[51] He likewise participated in plans for an actual revolt against Louis XIV, who was also the political enemy of Jean-Maximilien Lucas, the quasi-anonymous professional writer, amateur philosopher, obscure anti-hero, illegal exile, author of the *Quintessens*, *La Vie de Spinosa* and, most probably, also *L'Esprit*.

4. The effectual truth for everyone

We know next to nothing about the fortunes of *L'Esprit*/*Traité* in the period intervening between its redaction in 1678–88 and the moment it began to circulate in 1712. In the absence of factual documentation and with very few witnesses, we can only take recourse to textual-substantive and logical

---

[51] The plea for vernacular writing has nothing to do with nationalism. Van den Enden pleads for the use of *a* vernacular language (e.g. French) in education in the Delaware colony; see above, Chapter V.4, 130–1. This view, which was shared by Koerbagh, Van den Enden and Lodewijk Meyer, is often described as a matter of language purism, but that is beside the point. It is clear that their concern is for a translation strategy which both facilitates dissemination to a wide audience (and which, in a Kantian sense, subjects the theory to a public, critical investigation) and can be applied to the strategy of unmasking and reversal. Cf. Lavaert, "Entre clandestinité et sphère publique. Le cas Koerbagh', 33–48; Lavaert, 'La traduction comme intrigue philosophique et stratégie des Lumières', 109–26.

264   DEMOCRATIC THOUGHT FROM MACHIAVELLI TO SPINOZA

arguments to say anything that surpasses pure speculation. Starting in 1712, the problem is actually reversed, as the *multitude* of tangible traces and clues now impede the quest for the true course of events. The work represents a revolutionary mission text which spreads its message to a wide audience, does not fret about philosophical subtleties, originality or scientific rigour, and is future-oriented. It is, moreover, a living text which was appropriated, adapted and disseminated by a *multitude* of readers, copyists and authors, ultimately circulating in numerous manuscripts and editions, in different variants.[52] There is, first of all, the printed edition of 1719 with the title *La Vie et L'Esprit de Mr. Benoit de Spinosa*, where *L'Esprit de monsieur Benoit de Spinosa* – i.e. the second composing part of the work – consists of twenty-one chapters. There is also a printed edition from 1768, most probably the work of d'Holbach, which only includes the latter treatise, albeit under the title *Traité des trois imposteurs* and with six chapters. Hohendorf's manuscript, which dates from before 1719, likewise consists of six chapters, is bound together with *La Vie de feu Monsieur de Spinosa* and bears the title *L'Esprit de Monsieur de Spinosa*.[53] The Boulainvilliers manuscript, which possibly dates from 1712, consists of *La Vie de feu Mr. de Spinosa*, Boulainvilliers's own *Essay de metaphisique dans les Principes de B. de Spinosa* and *L'Esprit de Mr. Spinosa*. The manuscript bundle as a whole bears the title *La métaphisique et l'Ethique de Spinosa, son Esprit, et sa Vie*.[54] The table of contents in this manuscript of the *Esprit* lists nine titles, although they run parallel to the subsection headings in the six chapters of the Hohendorf manuscript and the later d'Holbach edition. After comparing these two printed editions with the above two manuscripts (and several others), Charles-Daubert concluded that Chapters 1, 2, 4, 5 and 6 are stable, but that the text of Chapter 3 is unstable, contains the most variants, and has the appearance of the *Traité des trois imposteurs* being inserted into the *Esprit/Traité*.[55] The textual variants led Charles-Daubert to posit the existence of an 'original' treatise consisting exclusively of Chapters 1, 2 and 4 (which treat the same theme, primarily God and the false ideas concerning God constructed by the religions). The majority of material in these three chapters goes back

---

[52] See Benítez, 'La diffusion du Traité des trois imposteurs au XVIIIe siècle', 137; Benítez, 'Une Histoire interminable: origine et développement du *Traité des Trois imposteurs*', 53–74.

[53] For the text of *L'Esprit de Spinosa*, *Traité des trois imposteurs* and the Hohendorf manuscript, we refer to Charles-Daubert's edition, 643–713; 715–52; 459–542.

[54] Anonymous [Ms Boulainvilliers], *L'esprit de Mr. de Spinosa*, in *La Métaphysique et l'Ethique de Spinosa. Son Esprit et sa Vie*, Paris-Arsenal, sign. Ms. 2236, 333–402.

[55] Charles-Daubert, *Le "Traité des trois imposteurs" et "L'Esprit de Spinosa"*, 110–12.

UNE MAUVAISE RHAPSODIE, UN ARTIFICE 265

to Spinoza, some to Vanini and through him to Machiavelli. Chapter 3 can be traced back to the Latin edition of Hobbes's *Leviathan*, as well as Vanini and La Mothe Le Vayer. Chapter 5 derives from Lamy, and Chapter 6 once again the Latin *Leviathan*.[56] In the following, we will focus on Chapters 1, 2 and 4 – placed side by side, they can be read as the contrapuntal components of a fugal ricercar.

*

Counterpoint 1

In the first section of Chapter 1, which treats of God, the author writes that it is important for all people to know the truth; this is almost exactly the same formulation we find in the opening of Koerbagh's *Een Ligt*.[57] And yet, so the author continues, there are few who use this advantage, whether from laxity, lack of courage or a perceived inability. They prefer to be satisfied with the prejudices which they have learned in their youth and which have shaped them; this is the source of all the prevalent but misguided ideas about God, the soul and the mind, the traditional themes of religion. After constructing these erroneous ideas about God, they mobilised every available means to convince the people of them, to strip them of the possibility to investigate them for themselves, or to turn them against the philosophers who could expose these errors for them. The champions of these absurdities have been so successful in their endeavour that resistance is not without danger. There is too much at stake for them, and so they will do everything in their power

---

[56] Cf. Schröder, 'Einleitung', XXVIII–XXXVII; 'Kommentierende Anmerkungen', 143–61; Charles-Daubert, 'L'image de Spinoza dans la littérature clandestine et l'*Esprit de Spinoza*', 51–74. Malcolm too stresses that large parts of Chapter 3 are a translation of cap. 12 of the Latin *Leviathan*, where Hobbes ascribes the origin of religion to fear and discusses how the epistemological confusion led to the invention of the concept of a 'spirit' and to the manipulation of the people's psychology by the priests. Chapter 6 is in its entirety drawn from cap. 45, where Hobbes treats the pagan ideas regarding spirits and demons which were transmitted to Christendom. As for the thesis of God's corporality, it was copied by the anonymous pamphleteer from cap. 3 of the Appendix to the Latin *Leviathan*, where the authority of Tertullian is invoked. And in Chapter 1 he copied a passage from cap. 32, where Hobbes presents one of his most destructive arguments, namely that when someone claims to have received a direct revelation from God, no one has a divine obligation to accept what that person says since the only reason for accepting it would be human. Through the great popularity of the *Esprit/Traité*, the most radical element of Hobbes's intellectual legacy was spread throughout Europe. See Malcolm, 'Hobbes and the European Republic of Letters', 491–3.

[57] Koerbagh, *Een Ligt*, 56; see also Chapter VI.5, 153–4.

266 DEMOCRATIC THOUGHT FROM MACHIAVELLI TO SPINOZA

to keep the people in their ignorance, such that they remain passive and do not revolt against the oppression and abuse they are enduring. If only the people understood the abyss into which their ignorance was bringing them, they would not hesitate to cast off the yoke of these ignoble leaders. Reason is the only light a person must follow, and if the people were not as incapable of reasoning as they are often said to be, those who teach reason must break down the prejudices. This is an idea we encounter quite literally in d'Holbach's *Essai sur les préjugés* – and we have in fact paraphrased that sentence from his 1768 printed edition of the *Esprit/Traité*, which only preceded the publication of his *Essai* by two years.[58]

The *Esprit/Traité* proceeds from the notion of equality, and that basis serves its most important motif, which is the deconstruction of prejudices. This is the same motif we find in Spinoza, based on the same foundation. Spinoza develops the arguments for this motif slowly, beginning in the *TTP* with a certain scepticism regarding the *multitude*, and down into the *Ethica* and the *TP* where he recognised that *multitude* is the universal condition. No such gradual development takes place in the *Esprit/Traité*, for it rather completes the entire move in the first three sections, immediately transporting Spinoza to the Enlightenment and the future. In sections 4, 5 and 6, the *Esprit/Traité* largely paraphrases parts of Chapter 2 from Spinoza's *TTP*. We only need a little bit of sound reason to recognise that God is not subject to jealousy or wrath, justice or compassion. These are not attributes of God, and the teaching of the prophets is wrong. In fact, prophets are just regular people: they have been born as women or men, embrace life like we do, and have no special endowment of mind or intellect different from the *multitude* of people. The prophets say that God is speaking to them, but they acknowledge that this happens in their dreams. And is anything more natural or human than to dream? Everyone dreams. But even if we assume for the sake of argument that God speaks to people in dreams or through their imagination, what remains suspicious is that those who tell such stories are the victim of deceit, convince themselves of something, or are out to deceive others. In the midst of these paraphrases from *TTP* 2, the author of the *Esprit/Traité* slips in an idea from Vanini, who is in turn paraphrasing Machiavelli,

---

[58] *Traité des trois imposteurs* I, §3, 716; d'Holbach, *Essai sur les préjugés*, 10–11; 44–6. The people are capable of knowledge and truth because there is no difference between human beings. The erudite elite are just as subject to fear and imagination as the common people are. This notion of equality can be traced back to Machiavelli, *Istorie Fiorentine* III, 13; *Discorsi* I, 11; see above, Chapter I.2, 4–12.

UNE MAUVAISE RHAPSODIE, UN ARTIFICE 267

about unarmed and armed prophets (Jesus and Moses).[59] Furthermore, he sees signs of deceit or illusion in the many contradictions that fill the prophets: at one time they understand God as a corporeal and material being who is subject to human passions, but at another time they describe him as a being that is totally distinct from matter and altogether incomprehensible. Here we still hear echoes of *TTP* 2, but the text also anticipates the next chapter which for its part goes back largely to the Appendix to *Ethica* I. As for the textual variants and instability, we can note that it is only in the text of section 6 that the *Esprit* diverges to some extent from the *Traité* and the two manuscripts, albeit without altering the meaning in any way.

*

Counterpoint 2

Sections 1 through 9 of Chapter 2 consist of a summary, paraphrases and literal translations from the Appendix of *Ethica* I. In the beginning, the author also introduces Hobbes's notion regarding the origin of religion: ignorance of physical causes elicits fear in people who resist that fear by imagining a being for themselves that has the power to protect them. They are then swept along by this phantasy, and they give it an independent existence as well as attributes that turn back on them, so as to threaten them and inspire them with fear. This view on the significance of religion is an old one and could already be found in antiquity, in Cicero, Tacitus or Lucretius, for instance, and it would in fact have been puzzling had the *Esprit* omitted it, considering how well adapted it is to Spinoza's message. But we find no positive perspective on fear here, nor does fear constitute a means for coercing people to acquiescence. On the contrary, the central idea of these nine sections is the quintessence of Spinoza's *Ethica*: Once people have fashioned this idea about God, they begin to imagine that God looks like human beings and that he does everything with a certain goal. They are born in ignorance and the only natural knowledge they have at birth is their pursuit of self-preservation. Combined, their ignorance and their pursuit of self-preservation turn childish prejudice into the superstition by which they imagine God and nature to function like people do. But nature has no end; ends are a purely human fiction.

---

[59] Machiavelli, *Il Principe* VI, 7. The notion of Moses as an armed prophet and the unarmed Jesus returns in *Theophrastus redivivus*; see above, Chapter II.3, 54–5. See on this also Strauss, *Thoughts on Machiavelli*.

268   DEMOCRATIC THOUGHT FROM MACHIAVELLI TO SPINOZA

In section 10, which represents section 1 of the next chapter (Chapter 3) in the *Esprit*, the initial question as to what God is, is posed again, and the author responds that this term stands for 'universal being'. Or, to use the words of Paul, everything is God and everything follows from his essence. The text in the Hohendorf and Boulainvilliers manuscripts is substantively and verbally close to the *Esprit*, although structurally it must be situated closer to d'Holbach's *Traité*. The reference to Paul occurs only in the *Traité*, while the earlier *Esprit* and the manuscripts offer a philosophical, materialist exposition in line with Spinoza's concept of God in *Ethica* I. More specifically, we recognise here proposition 3 (if things have nothing in common with one another, one of them cannot be the cause of the other) and a truncated version of the scholium to proposition 15 (there is only one substance, namely God, or nature). The materialist view concerning 'substance' as well as 'God, or nature' is entirely in line with the account Koerbagh gives in *Een Bloemhof* and *Een Ligt*.[60] We moreover recognise in abbreviated form a notion Spinoza had first formulated geometrically in the Appendix to his *Korte Verhandeling*: 'Nature is known through itself, and not through any other thing', and its existence belongs to its essence, so that outside it there is no essence or being.[61] This concept of God is seized upon in *Ethica* II and in the next part of the Appendix to the *Korte Verhandeling*, where Spinoza treats the relationship between the infinite 'nature, or God' and the finite human soul. In his letter to Oldenburg from 1 December 1675, which was cited earlier, Spinoza likewise appealed to the words of Paul, doing so, in fact, in the context of his definition of God as 'immanent cause'.[62] Obviously, d'Holbach deemed it worthy of inclusion.

---

[60] We recognise the phrase from Vanini in what Koerbagh writes in *A Light*, 58; 474: 'Being (which is called God)', 'the whole of nature is God, nature is not above God'. In *Een Bloemhof* the term *substantie* is translated as 'onderstandigheyd' (lit. 'sub-sistence') and *essentie* is defined as 'wesen / wesenheyd [. . .] dat is God / waar van alle onderstandige of afhangige wesens afhangig zijn' (lit. 'being / beingness [. . .] that is God / on which all subsistent or dependent beings depend'): 609; 275. See above, Chapter VI.4&5, 152–7. The phrase from Vanini is likewise quoted in *De jure ecclesiasticorum*, specifically in its defence of 'the natural state in which nature, that is God, has placed us all': 20.

[61] *KV*, App., 4 Cor.; *CWS* I, 152.

[62] *Ep*. LXXIII [to Henry Oldenburg]; *CWS* II, 467. Many pantheists can be found appealing to the words of Paul in Acts 17: 38: 'In him we live and move and have our being.' See, e.g., Toland, *Pantheisticon*, 55. There is much that suggests the author of the *Esprit/Traité* only used a small selection of Spinoza texts from the *Opera posthuma* (which must therefore have been available to him), including this letter. This is one argument for dating the work after 1677; see Schröder, 'Kommentierende Anmerkungen', 146.

'These ideas are clear, simple, and the only ones that a sound mind can fashion about God. And yet few are satisfied with such simplicity.'[63] They prefer a God who is just and avenges himself, who rewards and punishes like kings. They give him hands and feet, eyes and ears, and yet they insist that this being is not material. In section 11 of the *Traité* and *Esprit* manuscripts, or section 2 of Chapter 3 in the published *Esprit*, certain phrases and clauses from various passages of the *TTP* and *Ethica* are assembled – they appear to be partly a translation of a section from Dialogue 50 in Vanini's *De admirandis naturae*.[64] We will examine this fragment in the different textual

[63] *L'Esprit de Spinosa* III, §2, 653: 'Ces sentiments sont simples, & même les seuls qu'un bon & sain Entendement puisse se former de Dieu. Cependant il y en a peu qui se contentent d'une telle simplicité.'; *Traité des trois imposteurs* II, §11, 723: 'Ces idées sont claires, simples & les seules mêmes qu'un bon esprit puisse se former de Dieu. Cependant il y a peu de gens qui se contentent d'une telle simplicité.'

[64] In the three printed texts, the full text of the relevant passage reads as follows: Vanini, *De admirandis naturae*, IV, 50, 1362: 'In unica Naturae lege, quam ipsa Natura, quae Deus est (est enim principium motus) in omnium Gentium animis inscripsit. Caeteras vero leges non nisi figmenta et illusiones esse asserebant, non a Cacodaemone aliquo inductas (fabulosum namque illorum genus dicitur a Philosophis), sed a Principibus ad subditorum paedagogiam excogitatas et a sacrificulis, ob honoris et auri aucupium, confirmatas, non miraculis, sed Scriptura, cuius nec originale ullibi adinvenitur, quae miracula facta recitet et bonarum ac malarum actionum repromissiones polliceatur, in futura vita, ne fraus detegi possit.'; *L'Esprit de Spinosa* III, §2, 655: 'Oui, telle est la Folie & la stupidité des Chrétiens, qu'ils aiment mieux passer leur Vie à idolatrer un Livre, qu'ils tiennent d'un Peuple ignorant, un Livre, où il n'y a ni ordre, ni méthodologie, que personne n'entend, tant il est confus & mal conceu, & qui ne sert qu'à fomenter les Divisions entre eux, telle est, dis-je, leur Folie, qu'ils aiment mieux adorer ce Phantôme, que d'écouter la Loy naturelle, que Dieu, c'est à dire la nature, entant qu'elle est le principe du Mouvement, a écritte dans le Cœur des Hommes. Toutes les autres Loyx ne sont que des fictions humaines, & de pures illusions forgées, non par les Démons, ou par les mauvais Esprits, qui ne furent jamais qu'en idée, mais par l'adresse des Princes & des Ecclésiastiques, ceux là, pour donner plus de poids à leur Authorité, ceux cy, pour s'enrichir par le débit d'une infinite de Chiméres, qu'ils vendent cher aux Ignorans. [. . .] Ainsi le Peuple, toujours flottant entre l'Espérance & la crainte, est retenu dans son Devoir par l'Opinion qu'il a, que Dieu n'a fait les Hommes, que pour les rendre éternellement heureux ou malheureux.'; *Traité des trois imposteurs* II, §11, 724: 'Les Juifs & les Chrétiens, aiment mieux consulter ce grimoire que d'écouter la loi naturelle que Dieu, c'est-à-dire la Nature, en tant qu'elle est le principe de toutes choses, a écrit dans le cœur des hommes. Toutes les autres loix ne sont que des fictions humaines, & de pures illusions mises au jour, non par les Démons ou mauvais Esprits, qui n'existerent jamais qu'en idée, mais par la politique des Princes & des Prêtres. Les premiers ont voulu par-là donner plus de poids à leur autorité, & ceux-ci ont voulu s'enrichir par le débit d'une infinité de chimeres qu'ils vendent cher aux ignorans.' The two manuscripts do not show any textual variants of note vis-à-vis the printed *Esprit*,

270 DEMOCRATIC THOUGHT FROM MACHIAVELLI TO SPINOZA

versions. The central claim in Vanini, namely that 'the law of nature which nature itself, which is God, since it is the principle of motion, has inscribed in the soul of men', is rendered as follows in *L'Esprit*: 'the law of nature which God, that is, nature, since it is principle of motion, has written in the heart of men'. It is clear that this is a translation, quite a literal one, although one can also detect a shift that is not without consequences. The clause we find in Vanini's text, 'nature itself, which is God', can also be given a non-naturalist reading, but such a reading is impossible for the latter, inverted form: 'God, that is, nature'. In both texts, nature (or God) is the principle of motion and the law of nature is innate to all: in Vanini it is 'inscribed in the soul', but in *L'Esprit* it is 'written in the heart'. All other laws and religions, in both Vanini and *L'Esprit*, are nothing but 'fictions and illusions', with the latter specifying that they are 'human'. In both fragments, we read that the laws/religions, with the exception of natural law/religion, have not been introduced by 'evil spirits', since Vanini and the philosophers consider them just a 'fable' while *L'Esprit* says they 'have never existed except as an idea'. In both, religions have been devised by 'princes and priests' to expand their political power and riches at the cost of the ignorant *multitude*.

If we compare the text of the *Esprit* with the *Traité*, we only see a small shift, primarily in the clause according to which nature is 'the principle of all things': philosophically, the formulation is less precise, nor does it approach the academic vocabulary d'Holbach himself mobilises in his *Système de la nature* (1770). The differences are even more apparent in regard to the Bible. In a lengthy sentence *L'Esprit* posits that Christians 'prefer to pass their lives idolizing a book which they have taken over from an ignorant people, a book without order, without methodology, which no one understands, is highly confused and poorly organized, and only feeds the conflicts, such [. . .] is their insanity'. The *Traité* immediately equates 'Jews and Christians' and merely says that they 'prefer to consult this magical book', where the omission of the extraneous material actually serves to bolster the message. A remarkable feature is that the term 'deceit', for which Vanini opts, has been replaced in the two variants by 'illusions' sold at a high cost to the 'ignorant' by the 'princes and priests'. In spite of this, the motif of deceit does occur several lines down in both the *Esprit* and the *Traité*. The Bible holds forth rewards and punishments for good and evil deeds in the hereafter out of fear that the

so that it suffices to note the relevant chapter and page numbers: Boulainvilliers, II, §11, n.p. [350v]; Hohendorf, II, §11, ed. Charles-Daubert, 495. For a comparative study of the two published texts, see also Lavaert, 'La traduction comme intrigue philosophique', 109–26.

UNE MAUVAISE RHAPSODIE, UN ARTIFICE   271

deceit will be uncovered; this is a faithful translation of Vanini. And thus the 'people who constantly sway between hope and fear' are bound to keep their duties by the opinion that God only created human beings so that they might be eternally happy or unhappy. This clause alludes to Spinoza's view concerning the origin of religion, which is different from the explanation we find in Hobbes and also Vanini.[65] In a single movement, it recapitulates the essence of the spirit that breathes throughout the entire *Ethica* and has been formulated in the Appendix to *Ethica* I – Spinoza's most important critique, which holds that the view according to which God (or nature) rewards or punishes like a human sovereign is an illusion or deceit.

*

Counterpoint 3

The anonymous author also uses Chapter 4 in the *Traité* and the Hohendorf and Boulainvilliers manuscripts of the *Esprit*, or Chapter 8 in the printed *L'Esprit* edition, to translate Spinoza's argument to its essence. Since Moses, Jesus and Mohammed are as they have been described in the preceding chapters (which are longer in the printed *Esprit*, refer extensively and by name to Naudé and Charron, devote more attention to Mohammed, and also treat Numa-Pompilius as a fourth, added member), it is not in their laws and texts that one must look for the true idea of God. In section 2, the author once again combines this with a translation of a part from Dialogue 50 in Vanini's *De admirandis* – this fragment too we will examine in its three variants.[66] In

---

[65] Vanini speaks only of 'the fear which introduced the Gods in the world', and then cites the phrase 'Primos in orbe Deos fecit timor' from Statius, *Thebaïs*, III, 661, which he nevertheless erroneously attributes to Lucretius. We do, however, find similar views expressed in Lucretius; see Vanini, *De admirandis* IV, 50, 1362; 1770. The saying from Vanini/Statius is analogous to Hobbes's account of the origin of religion (*Leviathan*, XII), but differs from Spinoza's view. According to Spinoza, it was not just fear but the fluctuation between hope and fear that brought religion to the world. Statius was widely read in Renaissance Italy and cited by Dante, Boccaccio, etc. It is furthermore remarkable that *L'Esprit*/*Traité* presents Spinoza's view and does not translate Vanini, thereby deviating from Hobbes just before embarking on Chapter 3 (or Chapter 4 in the printed *L'Esprit*) which draws heavily on the Latin version of *Leviathan*.

[66] Vanini, *De admirandis naturae*, IV, 50, 1344: 'Deus simplex est, nulla igitur in eo distinctio; qua de re nulla erit in eo causarum comparatio. Neque homo est – inquiunt – propter Deum. Nullius indigus Deus est.'; *Esprit*, XVIII, §2, 184–5: 'Dieu est un Etre simple, ou une Extension infinie, qui ressemble à ce qu'il contient, c'est-à-dire qui est matériel, sans être néanmoins ni juste, ni miséricordieux, ni jaloux ni rien de ce qu'on s'imagine, & qui par conséquent n'est ni Punisseur, ni Rémunérateur.'; *Traité* IV, §2,

272   DEMOCRATIC THOUGHT FROM MACHIAVELLI TO SPINOZA

the d'Holbach edition/translation, the sentence that breathes the spirit of Spinoza, 'God is a simple being, or an infinite extension, a being which looks like what it contains, that is, which is material', is translated with a clear and simple sentence that repeats the main message: 'God who [. . .] is nothing but nature' – where the part 'a being which is material' of the *Esprit* has been replaced by an account of how this material being can be understood, namely as 'the assembly of all beings, all properties, and all energies' and which 'is necessarily the immanent cause, not distinguished from its effects'. In Vanini we find a phrase which, if we may permit ourselves this anachronism, situates itself halfway between Spinoza and d'Holbach: 'God is simple, there is therefore no distinction in him and thus no causal relationship of any kind.' A shift takes place from Vanini to the *Esprit/Traité*, from something that can first still be given a pantheistic reading to an explicitly immanent and earthly view of reality. From the *Esprit* to the *Traité*, the contents remain the same, but the latter takes some distance from the analytical style and transposes – that is, translates – philosophical concepts to a non-theoretical and non-academic register. The distinctions drawn by Spinoza, for instance in the scholium to proposition 29 of *Ethica* I between *natura naturans*, substance and *natura naturata*, the concrete individual things in reality, are lost in both translations; the anonymous author/translator as well as the translator/publisher appear to consider them irrelevant here. Or perhaps they thought that Spinoza was in this one instance confused: the distinction appears on the face of it to be more or less irreconcilable with d'Holbach's interpretation, according to which there is only an assembly of concrete things, properties and energies, but no *natura naturans*. Alternatively, one could translate the concept of 'nature', as the sentence continues in d'Holbach and as Spinoza himself does in proposition 18 of *Ethica* I, as immanent cause (that is, not distinguished from its effects). Or else one could understand nature as in the *Esprit*, as matter (that is, once again, as a cause not distinguished from its effects). In either case, the notion of a first metaphysical cause or origin in time has no place, and in that sense the translations by d'Holbach and in the *Esprit* are both right.[67] The authors of the *Esprit/Traité* are writing for

743: 'Dieu n'étant, comme on a vu, que la nature, ou, si l'on veut, l'assemblage de tous les êtres, de toutes les propriétés & de toutes les énergies, est nécessairement la cause immanente & non distincte de ses effets; il ne peut être appelé ni bon, ni méchant, ni juste, ni miséricordieux, ni jaloux; ce sont des qualités qui ne conviennent qu'à l'homme; par conséquent il ne sauroit ni punir ni récompenser.'

[67] Schröder's interpretation diverges slightly from the view expressed here in the sense that he sees a greater distance between Spinoza's metaphysical premises in the *Ethica* and the *Esprit*, and between the *Esprit* and d'Holbach's *Traité*. Aside from his

a common audience that needs to know these things, without requiring all the argumentative details leading to such knowledge. Nonetheless, each of them, like Spinoza, wrestles to understand the difficult relationship between concrete beings, ideas and energies, and that which is common to all beings, ideas and energies, and how that commonality can be expressed using intelligible language. In other words, each of them wrestles with the relationship between that which is *common* to the multitude of people (some such thing must exist if you deny a natural hierarchy and thus proceed from the natural *equality* of all human beings), and the concrete *multitude* of separate, individual people (that is, their *freedom*). Concepts such as 'nature' or 'matter' are ultimately no less mysterious than 'God'. The term 'immanent cause', on the contrary and notwithstanding the theoretical ring to it, expresses the core of the matter quite accurately: a cause which is not distinguished from its effects, or, to put it in scholastic terms once again, a *natura naturans* which cannot be distinguished from *natura naturata*.

As we have already observed on several occasions, the theme of the interchangeability of God and nature governs Spinoza's entire corpus. He does not understand this interchangeability as unity or identity in the form of a corporeal mass, as he writes in that oft-cited letter to Oldenburg, but rather, in his own words, in the sense that 'God is the immanent cause of all things.'[68] Christians, and modern Christians in particular, see nature or God as a corporeal mass which assumes the form of a human being with an end, and they base themselves for this idea on miracles, that is, on 'ignorance', which is the root of all evil. In his work, Spinoza *opposes* this ignorance. After all, none of the kings will oppose it.

Spinoza translates and integrates Vanini's insight into a coherent and consistent whole, in the process eliminating all assumptions of a natural hierarchy. It is clear that he has read Hobbes, and he proceeds from the same naturalist perspective. Throughout the *Ethica* we find expressions of a neutral, scientific and highly consistent naturalism. These remind us – as they undoubtedly did Spinoza as a reader of Hobbes – of Vanini, who had cult status among progressive seventeenth-century intellectuals. In academic manuals and anti-atheistic writings, he was consistently cited as an example. He had a reputation as a naturalist, atheist and freethinker who was executed for his heretical ideas and, in the face of death, delivered

---

'Einleitung' (as cited above), see also Schröder, *Ursprünge des Atheismus*, 321–42; 'Panthéisme – spinozisme – matérialisme athée', 133–40.

[68] *Ep.* LXXIII [to Henry Oldenburg]; CWS II, 467. See also above, Chapter VII.3.3, 214–5.

274 DEMOCRATIC THOUGHT FROM MACHIAVELLI TO SPINOZA

a revolutionary speech in which he stood up for the oppressed and con-demned the wicked collaboration between priests and princes. The exe-cution of Vanini was reported in periodicals like the *Mercure François*, and the accounts of his unfortunate end also served to spread his ideas more widely.[69] The press he received, together with the many references to him, turned his ideas into commonplaces or a paradigm, and no one at that time needed to have read his works to be able to cite him. In the Praefatio to *Ethica* IV we read a passage that can partly pass as a translation of the frag-ment in question from *De admirandis*. Spinoza summarises the current state of his investigation and points the reader to the Appendix to part I, where he has shown 'that Nature does nothing on account of an end. That eternal and infinite being we call God, *or* Nature, acts from the same necessity from which he exists.'[70] The reason or cause why 'God, *or* Nature, acts and exists' is one and the same. God or nature does not exist for the sake of an end, he does not act purposively, his existence has no beginning or goal, and con-sequently his acts have no beginning or goal. God or nature is the infinite essence or substance, that whose concept does not require the concept of another thing, from which it must be formed.[71] Between parts I and II he meticulously set forth the relationship between the idea of infinite sub-stance and the concrete individual things, including finite human beings and their spirit or soul, so as to understand the nature of that spirit/soul on that basis. From the very outset, he is very clear about not intending to write a metaphysics or a proof for the existence of God, and instead he wants to delineate the topics and prepare the ground for an account of human freedom, determination (self-determination), capacity and power. This is the purpose the conceptual distinctions serve. Accordingly, he posits that God, the substance, does not pertain to the essence of man.[72] Substance (which is one/unique) literally means that without which the (multitude of) finite people cannot exist, but whose concept itself does not require another thing to exist – and since human beings (and their souls) are finite, substance does not pertain to their essence or nature. As such, Spinoza has expressed – and he also formulates it explicitly in the second scholium to proposition 10 in part II – that substance, which is that without which individual things cannot exist or be conceived, does *not* pertain to the essence of those individual things. In other words, if individual things,

---

[69] See Chapter I.1, 5–7.
[70] *Ethica* IV, Praef.; CWS I, 544.
[71] *Ethica* I, Def. 3 and 6.
[72] *Ethica* II, 10; CWS I, 454.

people and thoughts exist, then the concept of substance follows from it, but not vice versa. This excludes the view which sees substance as a creator or as a being which acts with a goal (*ad arte*) and praises or punishes as human beings do. When he looks back in the Praefatio, he goes on to speak of the *perfectum* and *imperfectum*, which are concepts or modes of thinking, and then of good and evil. These too are concepts, not positive attributes in things. They are concepts which people fashion by comparing things with one another and through which one thing can seem good to us, or bad, or indifferent.[73] These characteristics therefore cannot be spoken of substance (nature, or God). Returning to the *Traité*, we can note that the phrase that God 'cannot be called good or bad' is given further explanation with the phrase 'these are qualities that are only applicable to man'. The theoretical-philosophical issue is therefore anthropological, ethical and inherently political in character.

The nature of this character is posited using ever clearer terms in the following sections, and the question as to what God is, is instantly related to such issues as advantage and power, in ever more unmistakable terms. One ought not to think that the universal (or, according to the *Esprit*, the simple and extended) Being 'which people commonly call God is more concerned about a human being than about an ant, a lion, or a stone'.[74] For this Being, there is no beautiful or ugly, good or bad, perfect or imperfect. These distinctions come from the imagination, due to ignorance, and they are fed and preserved by those who stand to gain from them. This is why a wise person 'cannot believe in God, hell, spirits or devils as people generally speak of them. All these great words have been forged to blind and intimidate the common people.' All that is being related about these things has its origins in 'the imagination of poets and the deception of priests'.[75] And after such

---

[73] In *Een Ligt* Koerbagh follows the same line of argument, according to which religious indifference and moral neutrality coincide: 206. See also Chapter VI.5, 160.

[74] *Esprit de Spinosa* XVIII, §3, 703: 'il ne faut pas croire, que cet *Etre simple & étendu*, qui est ce qu'on nomme communément DIEU, fasse plus de cas d'un *Homme* que d'une *Fourmi*, d'un *Lion* que d'une *Pierre*"; *Traité des trois imposteurs* IV, §3, 743–4: 'Il ne faut donc pas croire que l'Etre universel qu'on nomme communément Dieu fasse plus de cas d'un homme que d'une fourmi, d'un lion plus que d'une pierre.'

[75] *Esprit de Spinosa* XVIII, §4, 703–4: 'Ainsi tout Homme qui fera un bon usage de sa Raison, ne croira ni *Ciel* ni *Enfer*, ni *Ame*, ni DIEU ni *Diables*, de la manière dont on en parle communément. Tous ces grands mots n'ont été forgez que pour aveugler, ou pour intimider le Peuple.'; §6, 704: 'que les *Poëtes* ont inventé'; *Traité des trois imposteurs* IV, §4, 744: 'Ainsi tout homme sensé ne peut croire ni Dieux, ni Enfer, ni Esprits, ni Diables, de la maniere qu'on en parle communément. Tous ces grands mots n'ont été forgéz que pour éblouir ou intimider le vulgaire.'; §6, 744: 'Tout ce qu'on en dit

276 DEMOCRATIC THOUGHT FROM MACHIAVELLI TO SPINOZA

discourses were devised to impress those who are ignorant or mentally weak, they were transformed into articles of faith by those who stood to gain most from the preservation of this opinion.

It is no coincidence that the fragments that represent a direct translation or paraphrase of a Spinoza text can all be traced back to *TTP* 2, the Appendix to *Ethica* I, the Praefatio of *Ethica* IV and the letter to Oldenburg. The *TTP* is a case apart, but in the other texts Spinoza abandons his analytical style and uses common language to explain what his work really is about, its aim, its target and what is at stake.[76] As we have seen, they are also all fragments in which Spinoza adopts Vanini's critique of political theology and its sociopolitical vision, both rendered famous by the academic countertexts and the journalistic biographies. Spinoza himself therefore makes an appearance as the "anonymous" of the *Esprit*, he translates, paraphrases and appropriates Vanini's text and integrates it into his own work. This makes Vanini the author of choice for translation or paraphrase, appropriation, and integration into the *Esprit*, in the spirit of Spinoza, without any references. This happens *ad arte*, it is a strategy, a translation-strategy. Spinoza is repeated, the effect of his operation is doubled. Furthermore, the translation-strategy systematises the message so as to become more explicit and to be reduced to its essence. The same operation is then repeated in the *Traité*, where it is moreover directed to an audience composed of common people, the *multitude*.

n'est que l'effet de l'imagination des Poëtes & de la fourberie des Prêtres.' These passages look like a condensed synthesis / paraphrase of the politically motivated critique which Machiavelli levels against the church and priests throughout the *Discorsi*; see above, Chapter I.5, 32–41.

[76] On the two styles of writing Spinoza uses in the *Ethica*, see Deleuze, *Pourparlers 1972–1990*, 223–5: 'Lettre à Réda Bensmaïa, sur Spinoza'.

IX

Quodlibet
In the Spirit of Machiavelli

Remarkably, the *Traité/Esprit* does not refer to the *TP* even though it is precisely in the latter work that Spinoza draws an explicit connection to the *Politiques* and to Machiavelli and expands the immanent worldview to a complete moral neutrality and religious indifference. In the *TP* Spinoza arrives at the 'geometric' essence, as it were. He is no longer addressing a concrete problem, such as the threat to the freedom to philosophise, or, conversely, the necessity of such freedom for the commonwealth, but he addresses the complex matter of politics as such. He does not present any new findings that were absent from the *TTP*, nor does he invent any new political forms, and the structure of his argument is the same. He reads Hobbes, offers a similar account of religion and the formation of political communities, develops the argument to its most extreme consequence and finally adds a simple 'but' which has the effect of shifting the entire structure. Hobbes's account is purely theoretical and ultimately takes little to no account of experience or reality, no 'effectual truth'. In the *TP* Spinoza initially follows Hobbes even more closely than he had in the *TTP*, as the latter's sense for Euclidean aesthetics must have exercised an irresistible draw on him. The insight that political knowledge must be shaped by constant reference to experience establishes the necessity of the neutral boldness, to which we are accustomed in mathematics, for the human passions. Yet that same insight and neutral boldness ultimately leads Spinoza to a reversal of Hobbes. And this brings him to Machiavelli, as he himself explicitly observes. The shift of focus to the field of immanence means that the multitude with its natural power, the struggle and conflict (which can issue in violence), the knowledge, imagination and language (which enable deception) all become decisive factors that the theory must address (which very thing Hobbes, for his part, had sought to avoid and exclude).

278   DEMOCRATIC THOUGHT FROM MACHIAVELLI TO SPINOZA

Anachronistically speaking, we might say that in the *TP* Spinoza goes beyond even the *Esprit*/*Traité*.

The *Esprit* remains partly in the clutches of a particularistic approach to the religion-deceit-monarchy triad and of a pessimism towards the multitude. This can be attributed to the elitist arrogance of learned erudition and a life of contemplative reflection. But it can also be attributed to a political bias. In Chapter 7 we saw that the experience of the *TTP* caused Spinoza to change his mind. While he during writing, between 1665 and 1670, had still been sceptical of the multitude's capacity to judge, after the publication of the treatise he came to experience that the judgement of the erudite elite, both theologians and philosophers, was even less worthy of trust. The human condition is one and universal, and the condition of the multitude is the condition of all. And this is why the antidote to lies, falsities and political ignorance is to assume the duty of gaining knowledge, and forming and expressing thoughts, with *as many as possible*. As a result, the *TP* studies the inherent structure of every form of state (monarchy, aristocracy, democracy) and investigates the best way for it to function for all parties (i.e. both rulers and subjects). In this work, Spinoza draws the logical consequences of the insights he had presented in the *TTP* and *Ethica*, strips the arguments of all that is irrelevant (i.e. whatever has reference to the person), and searches for common denominators in the complex game of perspectives and interests. This process brings him to the essence, to Machiavelli and to a radical reversal. At the same time, the neutrality can yield doubts about the politically revolutionary content of his theoretical reversal. After all, Spinoza's work lends itself very well to eclectic use, especially when there are common enemies. In an article on the relationship between Spinoza and the French libertines, Paul-Laurent Assoun wondered aloud 'how such flirtation between a "republican" thought and a thought that is by nature oligarchic and championed by the French aristocracy could ever be possible'.[1] The answer is obvious: because the republicans and the old aristocracy were political allies in their resistance to the absolutist ambitions of the king. This finds confirmation in the conspiracy involving Franciscus van den Enden and the Chevalier de Rohan: while the latter sought to unleash a revolt of the Norman nobility, the former wanted 'to establish a certain state in Holland'.[2]

There was much in Spinoza's teaching with which the aristocratic libertines could identify, so Assoun writes. If we consider the four great themes of

---

[1] Assoun, 'Spinoza, les libertins français et la politique', 198.
[2] See Chapter V.1&4 above, 107–14; 134–6.

the *TTP* – i.e. the war on superstition, the critique of religion as a political deceit, the relativisation of the Christian religion from a global perspective, and the insight that people can be dehumanised by this deceit (self-deceit) in that they are not free to use their own capacity of judgement – then the outcome is clear: the libertines could do no other than to recognise Spinoza as one of their own.[3] Beginning in 1670, Spinoza became something of an institution in libertine circles – and his status only grew when, in 1678, Saint-Glain's French translation appeared and the *Ethica* started to be disseminated.[4] Yet we could just as well turn the story around. It may have been that Spinoza was himself inspired to what the libertines recognised (and in which they later also saw themselves confirmed) by the reading of libertine ideas, whether directly or in the countertexts. What pleads for the latter alternative is that the similarities become increasingly concrete in the movement from the *TTP* to the *Ethica* to the *TP*, in which the same Vanini fragments are assembled, the categorical (ontological and anthropological) reversal is radically effected, and the connection to Machiavelli becomes increasingly close and explicit. As Spinoza's ideas were being sharpened, he returned to the principle (with Vanini and Machiavelli's naturalism as his source), but he also gradually appropriated the radical ideas and gave them his own specific formulation. It is especially where we hear his own voice that we recognise the similarities with *De jure ecclesiasticorum*, along with the work of Koerbagh and Van den Enden. Everything suggests that we are dealing with a knowledge that found its nourishment in the living reality, the context, the pushback from the countertexts, and the examples, adherents and teachers, and that this multitude of perspectives did not shape

---

[3] Assoun points to the ten libertine maxims as they were set out by the Jesuit François Garasse in *Doctrine curieuse des beaux esprits de ce temps* (1623): 'Spinoza, les libertins français et la politique', 175–8. In this work, Garasse offers a lengthy and detailed refutation of Vanini as one of the most evil and thus exemplaric atheist libertines after Machiavelli: 986. See also Carparelli, 'Vanini e la "Prudenza" di Cristo', 210–20; Cavaillé, *Postures libertines*; Foucault, 'Sources italiennes du libertinisme français dénoncées par les religieux Garasse et Mersenne autour de 1620', 1–14; Schmeisser, 'Garasse contre Vanini', 231–47. See also Chapter I.1, 5–8.

[4] Cf. Vernière who juxtaposes the stories of the way Bayle and Boulainvilliers became acquainted with Spinoza in a single chapter. Until Bayle managed to obtain a copy of Saint-Glain's translation in the French principality of Sedan, he only had access to indirect voices and refutations: see *Spinoza et la pensée française avant la Révolution*, vol. I, 287–306. See also Lagrée, 'Spinoza l'imposteur libertin?', 193–209. The date of publication for Saint-Glain's translation (1678) coincides with and thus confirms the date we are following here, that is, between 1678 and 1688: see above, Chapter VIII.2, 250–8.

280   DEMOCRATIC THOUGHT FROM MACHIAVELLI TO SPINOZA

this knowledge in a single direction, but multilaterally and in a dialectic process. The vibrancy, contrapuntal confluence and mutual tension also facilitate the bias: Spinoza's *TTP* is put to use politically by the aristocratic libertines, not for the sake of and even against his specific political theory (as we see it reach its essence in the *TP*), but as a weapon in the ideolog-ical critique (on the church and priests) and the political critique (on the absolutism of the king). In an article on Spinoza in the French press from 1678 to 1705, Pierre Clair calls for attention to the absence of the political theme in the seventy-three Spinoza-hits he unearthed. In the debates sur-rounding Spinoza, the main issue is religion; in matters of political theory, the primary reference is Hobbes.[5]

All of this appears to slot into place like a perfectly cut puzzle – i.e. it suits the aristocratic elite very well – even though the puzzle pieces appear to change and to lead to new positions as they are being laid. This emerges, for instance, when we consider the aristocrat Boulainvilliers who played an important role in the introduction of Spinoza's work to France and is intimately connected to the *Esprit*.[6] He became acquainted with the Dutch philosopher through Saint-Glain's French translation of the *TTP* and initially, before 1696, he only wanted to refute it. But family problems forced him to abandon the project for some time, at a point when he had only reached the first six chapters and been restricted to the theological question. Around 1700 he started writing an *Abrégé d'histoire universelle* in which his Christian position remains intact, although it also shows clear traces of his reading of the *TTP*. Like other readers (in France and elsewhere), Boulainvilliers was initially not struck by the novelty of Spinoza's theoretical work, but rather showed a preoccupation with his text-critical hermeneutic, biblical exposition, and connection to the tradition of religious deceit.[7] But as Vernière has shown, while Boulainvilliers started as an opponent of Spinoza and sought to refute him, he gradually applied himself to the study of radical thought and ultimately became convinced of it. When he in 1704 was searching for a Hebrew grammar, he chanced upon the *Opera posthuma* and thus the

---

[5] Clair, 'Spinoza à travers les journaux en langue française à la fin du XVIIe siècle', 205; see also Assoun, 'Spinoza, les libertins français et la politique', 172–3.

[6] Assoun, 'Spinoza, les libertins français et la politique', 175. See Chapter VIII.4, 263–4.

[7] In that sense, Boulainvilliers's response is comparable to that of the libertines: his inter-est in Spinoza's work was uniquely motivated by its close connection to the tradition of religious deceit found in Vanini, Machiavelli or Hobbes. Cf. Cavaillé, 'Libertinage ou Lumières radicales', 61–74. For the story of Boulainvilliers, see Vernière, *Spinoza et la pensée française*, 311–16.

Ethica. But to refute the *Ethica* it is first necessary to create clarity, and this is why Boulainvilliers found it necessary to translate this unreadable 'mathematical dryness' into normal language.[8] His intention was merely to create a paraphrase for personal use, but, once again out of his conviction regarding the language-critical and hermeneutical reading method of the *TTP*, he could only effect such a paraphrase once he had actually translated the text. It was this growing familiarity with this difficult text, garnered through the work of translation in an intellectual effort stretching out over multiple years, that led to a result familiar to translators, who inescapably develop a sympathy for the thought they are discovering and dissecting to its bare essence.[9] Boulainvilliers was the first to adopt a full Spinozism, a complete and coherent system rather than a partial religious and political critique – a world of difference compared to the first French readers/commentators, in particular Bayle.[10] Assoun too speaks of a turn he finds illustrated in the 'overtranslation' (*surtraduction*) which Boulainvilliers effected in his translation of the Appendix to *Ethica* I, a passage that had the function of an introduction to the *TTP* among libertines, as it indeed does in the *Esprit*. By adding the brief qualifying phrase 'with respect to final causes' (*au sujet des causes finales*) to the word 'prejudice', he bolstered Spinoza's critique on a view of God or nature

[8] In his *Réfutation de Spinoza* (in fact *Essai de Métaphysique dans les principes de B. . . de Sp . . .*), Boulainvilliers writes that he wants to rid the *Ethica* of 'cette sécheresse mathématique qui en rend la lecture impraticable, même à la moitié des savants, afin que le système rendu dans une langue commune et réduit à des expressions ordinaires pût être en état d'exciter une indignation pareille à la sienne et procurer par ce moyen de véritables ennemis à de si pernicieux principes', 155; see also Vernière, *Spinoza et la pensée française*, 315–17.

[9] Vernière, *Spinoza et la pensée française*, 316. The manuscript of Boulainvilliers's *Ethica* translation was discovered by Colonna d'Istria in the Bibliothèque municipale of Lyon (fonds généraux, n° 5.165). In the text accompanying his edition of the translation (*Éthique*, 1907), Colonna d'Istria writes that Boulainvilliers first produced a French translation on the basis of a manuscript he obtained in 1704: 'Introduction', V–XLIII and 'Appendice II', 367–71. Like Vernière, Assoun bases himself on Colonna d'Istria's commentary. Mori, however, has questioned whether this translation is the work of Boulainvilliers, noting the latter was sufficiently versed in Latin to work directly with the original text and that he was too careful to try to disseminate the *Ethica* among a wide audience. Mori draws his most important objection from Simon, *Henri de Boulainvilliers: historien, politique, philosophe, astrologue*, who pointed out that the Lyon manuscript is not an autograph and that Boulainvilliers's name could have been written on the cover as a sales trick: see 'Boulainvilliers a-t-il traduit l'*Éthique*?', 37–9. While Mori's argument is reason for caution, Vernière's account remains plausible.

[10] See Assoun, 'Spinoza, les libertins français et la politique', 196–7.

282 DEMOCRATIC THOUGHT FROM MACHIAVELLI TO SPINOZA

who has goals or acts as a judge, and drew all the attention to the essence of the matter.[11]

The movement of reversal effected by Boulainvilliers after Spinoza's own example is something we likewise encounter, albeit less clearly so and with some differences, in the *Esprit/Traité*. His manuscript copy from 1712 shows many similarities with the d'Holbach edition of 1768, and in terms of structure it even resembles it more than the Lucas edition from 1719. In that movement of reversal, the focus shifts from questions of origin and the past to goals and the future, from knowledge among a few to the free capacity of judgement of the multitude, from an emphasis on metaphysics to the common political-historical domain. Spinoza does what Machiavelli had already done before him, his critique of politics and religion does not remain isolated in the form of purely speculative questions (which can only be answered speculatively) but is integrated into a fundamental and systematic code switch to the field of immanence. It is the *questions* that change for a thought that pursues effectual truth, aims at the future and proceeds from the axiom that political power depends on the power of the multitude. In his 'Boulainvilliers lecteur de Spinoza', Laurent Bove has shown how this shift emerges clearly from this French thinker's historical works. In them we find 'a Machiavellian Boulainvilliers, reader of the *Tractatus politicus*', who does for history what Spinoza had done for political philosophy.[12]

In this genealogy, the insights and writings of Machiavelli function as a revolutionary intermediary. The shift to the immanent is paired with a religious indifference and moral neutrality which can be detected in the duality – both good and evil, neither good nor evil – and fluctuation – between effective power and chance/God/nature, between hope and fear – structuring historical and political human existence. This fluctuation between fear and hope is what causes religion, and it dominates political life. Yet the similarity is not complete, the relationship is complex and in constant motion, the result temporal, provisional, never definitive and always open to improvement. Furthermore, what takes precedence is the

[11] Ibid. 197.

[12] Bove, 'Boulainvilliers lecteur de Spinoza', 373–88. Commentaries on the relationship between Boulainvilliers and Spinoza (e.g. Vernière) are completely silent about the historical texts, while Michel Foucault, who treats these historical texts extensively in his lecture series *Il faut défendre la société* (1976), conversely does not say anything about Spinoza. See his 'Cours du 25 février 1976', 149–67. On Boulainvilliers and Spinoza, see also Mori, *L'ateismo dei moderni*, 121–33; Benítez, 'Un spinozisme suspect: à propos du Dieu de Boulainvilliers', 17–28.

perspective of the free multitude, that is, the multitude which is guided more by hope than by fear.

Machiavelli's *Principe* does for morality what Spinoza's work does for faith, so the Prussian King Frederick II wrote in the preface to his *Antimachiavel* from 1741.[13] Just like Spinoza tore down the edifice of religion, so Machiavelli corrupted politics and attempted to destroy the precepts of good morality. Spinoza's mistakes were merely speculative errors, so Frederick adds, but Machiavelli's mistakes were worse because they had practical consequences for life. With these words, this absolutist monarch testified to his penetrating insight into the import of political theories and confirms the genealogy we have sketched out in this monograph. He understood what kind of thinking really threatens tyranny and the champions of government by a few. A speculative critique on religion and metaphysics remains trapped in speculation and is therefore relatively innocuous. He also understood perfectly well what the best counter-strategy was, in particular a reconfirmation of the deceptive fiction. As a consequence, Frederick aimed the arrows of his refutation at the principle which he finds in Machiavelli and which occupies a central place in Spinoza's *TP*. In this way, the king contributed to the construction of the counterimage of a speculative, apolitical Spinoza who is stripped of his critical and revolutionary significance. He likewise repeated the construction of the counterimage of a monstrous Machiavelli, in which oppressive violence and deceit are once again developed into a system, in which struggle and conflict are once more traced back to war, politics is yet again reduced to the dynamics of orders and obedience, and inequality – and, therefore, unfreedom – is restored as principle. This is a lie *ad arte* indeed.

---

[13] Frédéric II, *Anti-Machiavel, ou Essai de critique sur le Prince de Machiavel, publié par Mr. de Voltaire*, IV: 'Le Prince de Machiavel est en fait de Morale ce qu'est l'Ouvrage de Spinosa en matière de Foi. Spinosa sapoit les fondements de la Foi, & ne tendoit pas moins qu'à renverser l'édifice de la Religion; Machiavel corrompit la Politique, & entreprit de détruire les préceptes de la saine Morale. Les erreurs de l'un n'étoient que des erreurs de spéculation, celles de l'autre regardoient la pratique. Cependant il s'est trouvé que les Théologiens ont sonné le tocsin & crié aux armes contre Spinosa, qu'on a réfuté son Ouvrage en forme, & qu'on a constaté la Divinité contre ses attaques, tandis que Machiavel n'a été que barcelé par quelques Moralistes, & qu'il s'est soutenu malgré eux & malgré sa pernicieuse Morale, sur la chaire de la Politique, jusqu'à nos jours.'

Appendix
The Manuscript *Finis est in Holandia*

Editorial note

The original manuscript which we first transcribe and then translate into English is found in the court file for the *Procès Rohan* and held at the Archives Nationales (Paris), V/4/1474, 342r–344v. The court file includes a total of three appended manuscripts: one two-page manuscript pertaining to administrative matters (69r–69v); one manuscript with six pages entitled *La noblesse et le peuple de Normandie* (71r–72v); and, finally, the manuscript *Finis est in Holandia* which likewise numbers six pages. Since the first two manuscripts are not relevant to the discussion in this monograph, we have opted to edit and translate only the third manuscript.

Each of the six pages of the manuscript *Finis est in Holandia* has been initialled by Franciscus van den Enden; on the first five, he wrote 'F. A. D. Enden', and on the sixth and final page 'François Affinius vanden Enden'. It is not known who authored the manuscript. It is, however, clear that this is an autograph and not a copy; copies of this court file are held by the department of manuscripts of the Bibliothèque nationale de France (Fr. 7576, Fr. 7629, Fr. 16556). According to statements given by Van den Enden during his interrogation on 26–7 September and 2 October 1674 (*Procès Rohan*, 77r–99v), the text reflects what he dictated or explained to Latréaumont – that is, it represents a translation of the essence of his *Vrye Politijke Stellingen* (see above, Chapter V, 110–3; 134–6). Van den Enden therefore does not deny that the content derives from him, but he is adamant that he did not himself write the manuscript. The orthographic and grammatical errors in the manuscript (cf. the footnotes with the transcription below) indeed indicate that Van den Enden, a professional teacher of Latin, could not have written it. Instead, it was quite likely written by Latréaumont, who had conspired against Louis XIV together with the Chevalier de Rohan, the

APPENDIX

Marquise de Villars, the Chevalier de Préau and Van den Enden, and who also had the manuscript in his possession at the time of his arrest.

In the transcription, we follow the orthography of the manuscript; where we do correct grammatical or orthographical errors, we have added a footnote. Capital letters at the beginning of sentences have been inserted silently. Abbreviations have been resolved, marked by square brackets ([. . .]).

Transcription

[342r] Finis est in Holandia[1] erigere Statum quemdam populi armis insupera-
bilem, semper florentem, semper crescentem per unionem et conspirationem
in unum commune bonum et aequalem communemque omnium libertatem.

Primo die conuocentur cives inermes in parochias[2] et ibi proponatur
libertas et subsignatio eius. Scilicet quod non alium noscant superiorem
nisi nobilitatem et populum liberum non suspendantur omnia officia juris-
dictiones judicia etc. donec populus cum nob[ilitate] ipse[3] sibi rectores
elegerit qui secundum leges a se constituendas et quando lubuerit innouan-
das eos regat. Quam ad rem cum opus sit sanctorum armorum praesidio
in singulis parochiis[4] compareant [342v] duodecim nobiles qui praesint
singulis cohortibus prouisionaliter. Ut illos disponant ad comparendum
post meridiem in armis ut jam sibi serio eligant ducem legatum et vexilli-
ferum occultis suffragiis, et qui plurima habebit cohortis suae suffragia erit
dux, qui plura post illum legatus et tertius vexillifer. Et hi duces et legati
numero sexcentorum[5] constituunt consilium militare. Qui die praefixo
congregati eligent ex singulis parochiis[6] duodecim ex ditioribus et pruden-
tioribus qui trecenti electi constituent consilium ciuile, quod consilium
aget secundum instructionem [343r] a communitate dandam de opibus,
censu annuo ciuitatis, de prouisione, de ornamentis, de fortificationibus
urbis et conseruatione eorum,

de viduis orphanis pauperibus (sine contemptu) prospiciendis

de familiis declinantibus ad paupertatem

de conseruatione sanitatis peste et morbis contagiosis praeueniendis

de officinis, artibus mechanicis,[7] mercatura

de officiis seruilibus et utilibus in commodum reipublicae

de litibus et jure ciuium inter se

de criminalibus et furto homicidio et super omnia de peccantibus[8] contra
libertatem [343v] communem

---

[1] Ms: holandia
[2] Ms: parrochias
[3] Ms: ibse
[4] Ms: parrochiis
[5] Ms: sexencentorum
[6] Ms: parrochiis
[7] Ms: mecanicis
[8] Ms: depecantibus

APPENDIX   287

Translation

[342r] The goal is to establish in Holland a certain state which cannot be conquered by weapons, is always flourishing and growing, through the union and concord into a single commonwealth and the equal and common freedom of all.

On the first day, the citizens are to be convoked in the districts, and freedom and the guarantee of that freedom will be proposed to them. And so, since they recognise no other government except the nobility and free people, no office, jurisdiction, sentence, etc., will be suspended until the people themselves, together with the nobility, have chosen for themselves leaders who have decided to renew them according to the laws instituted by them and at a time of their pleasing. To that end, when necessary there will appear, with the aid of invincible weapons [342v], twelve noblemen in the individual districts who will provisionally command the individual regiments.[1] So that they might be led to present themselves in the afternoon, in their armour, for the real election by secret ballot of their deputy leader and standard-bearer, the one who receives the most votes of his regiment will become the leader, the one with the next most votes the deputy leader, and the third the standard-bearer. And these leaders and deputy leaders, six hundred in total, form the military council. They will assemble on a previously established day and choose from the individual districts twelve of the wealthier and wiser men who, three hundred in total, form the civil council. This council is to act according to the community's instructions [343r] in regard to the resources, annual state taxes, care, ornamentation, and fortification of the city and their conservation,

the provision for widows, orphans, and poor (without contempt)
the families falling into poverty
healthcare by the prevention of plague and contagious diseases
the workshops, mechanical arts, merchantry
the duties serviceable and useful to the well-being of the republic/politics
conflicts and justice among the citizens
crimes, theft, murder, and above all those who offend the common freedom [343v]

---

[1] Van den Enden's vocabulary here shows clear influences from the Roman military tradition. He uses the term *cohors*, and even though the term 'cohort' does exist in English, we have opted to render it as 'regiment' (since a *cohors* is, literally, a tenth part of a Roman legion). So too we have decided to translate *legatus* – 'legate' in English – as 'deputy leader'.

288 APPENDIX

de matrimonio et multiplicatione prolis

contra lenones, adulteros et laedentes castimoniam ciuium

de instructione puerorum in artibus liberalibus et maxime in cognitione libertatis communis

de foederibus et contractibus cum aliis ciuitatibus populis et nationibus

et de omnibus quae spectant regimen ciuitatis

imo de ipso tempore quando arma sint exercenda sed exercitium armorum totum spectat ad consilium militare.

Consilium hoc militare debet magnam habere communicationem cum ciuile, et contra [344r] ita ut semper sint quatuor ad minimum commissarii ex altero in altero et nihil proponatur populo nisi ex consensu utriusque consilii.

Hi consiliarii singulis annis renouabuntur non elegendi iterum nisi post vacationem biennii in numerum ciuium nemo admittitur nisi sit viginti[9] unius anni natus et qui non seruiuerit in militia tribus annis, quod si quis aetatem viginti[10] et unius anni attigerit et non seruiuerit cogetur annos seruitii implere antequam admittatur. Omnes nobiles ecclesiastici[11] et incolae pagorum erunt ciues istius ciuitatis cui pagi annexi sunt nota nos nullam facere distinctionem inter catholicos[12] et reformatos modo se praestent bonos ciues et libertatis communis propugnatores et non [344v] miscant[13] rem religionis cum republica.

---

[9] Ms: vinginti
[10] Ms: vinginti
[11] Ms: eclesiastici
[12] Ms: catolicos
[13] Ms: misciant

marriage and the multiplication of offspring

fornicators, adulterers, and those who offend the chastity of the citizens

the education of children in the free arts and in particular in the knowledge of common freedom

the alliances and agreements with other states, peoples and nations

and all other things pertaining to the rule of the state

and indeed the time for weapons exercises which are to be carried out, although the whole exercise of weapons [as such] is the concern of the military council.

This military council is to communicate very closely with the civil council, and conversely [344r] there must always be at least four commissioners from the one council in the other and nothing may be proposed to the people except with the agreement of both councils.

These councillors will be renewed every year; they may not be elected again except after a two-year leave. Only those are admitted to the number of the citizens who are twenty-one years old and have served in the army for three years. But if someone has turned twenty-one and has not served in the army, that person is to be forced to complete the years of service prior to admission. All nobles, ecclesiastics and residents of the districts will be citizens of the civil state to which those districts belong. It should be noted that we make no distinction between Catholics and Reformed, if only they prove themselves good citizens and defenders of the common freedom, and do not [344v] mix matters of religion with matters of state.

Bibliography

Manuscripts

Anonymous [Boulainvilliers, Henri de], *L'esprit de Mr. de Spinosa*, in *La Métaphisique et l'Ethique de Spinosa. Son Esprit et sa Vie*, 1712, Paris-Arsenal, Sign. Ms. 2236, 195–331.

Monnikhoff, Johannes, 'Voor-reeden', Ms B 75G16, Koninklijke Bibliotheek The Hague.

Procès Rohan, Archives Nationales, V/4/1474.

[Enden, Franciscus van den], *Finis est in Holandia*, in *Procès Rohan*, ibid. [342r–344v].

Spinoza, Benedictus de, *Godgeleerde Staatkundige Verhandelinge*, Ms. A 75G15, Koninklijke Bibliotheek The Hague, [100–422].

Primary sources

Alberti, Leon Battista, *De pictura*, ed. Lucia Bertolini, Florence, Edizioni Polistampa, 2011.

Alighieri, Dante, *Tutte le opere*, ed. Luigi Blasucci, Florence, Sansoni, 1965.

Amelot de la Houssaye, Abraham Nicolas, 'Préface', in *Le Prince de Machiavel traduit et commenté de A. N. Amelot*, Amsterdam, Wetstein, 1683, n.p. [*3r–*6r].

Anonymous [Nicolas Barnaud], *Le Réveille-Matin des François et de leurs voisins, composé par Eusebe Philadelphe Cosmopolite, en forme de Dialogues*, Edinburgh [Lausanne?], Jacques James, 1574.

Anonymous [Nicolas Barnaud], *Der Francoysen ende haerder nagebueren Morghenwecker door Eusebium Philadelphum*, Overgheset door Jan Fruytiers, Dordrecht, s.n., 1574.

BIBLIOGRAPHY 291

Anonymous [Hubert Languet], *Vindiciae contra tyrannos: sive, de Principis in Populum, Populique in Principem legitima potestate. Stephano Junio Bruto Celta Auctore*, Edinburgh [Basel], s.n., 1579, in *Nicolai Machiauelli Florentini Princeps*, Frankfurt, Lazarus Zetzner, 1608.

Anonymous [Hubert Languet], *De la puissance legitime du prince sur le peuple, et du peuple sur le prince. Traité tres utile & digne de lecture en ce temps, escrit en Latin par Estienne Iunius Brutus, & nouvellement traduit en François*, s.l., s.n., 1581 [facsimile, Geneva, Droz, 1979].

Anonymous, *Theophrastus redivivus* [1659], ed. Guido Canziani and Gianni Paganini, Florence, La Nuova Italia, 1981.

Anonymous, *Theophrastus redivivus*, VIe Traité: De la vie selon la nature, in Jacques Prévot, Laure Jestaz and Hélène Ostrowiecki-Bah (eds), *Libertins du XVIIe siècle*, Paris, Gallimard, 2004, 217–404.

Anonymous [Adriaan Koerbagh?], *'t Samen-spraeck tusschen een Gereformeerden Hollander en Zeeuw*, see Koerbagh.

Anonymous [pseud.: Lucius Antistius Constans], *Lucii Antistii Constantis De Jure Ecclesiasticorum, Liber Singularis. Quo docetur: quodcunque Divini Humanique Iuris Ecclesiasticis tribuitur, vel ipsi sibi Tribuunt, hoc, aut falso impieque illis Tribui, aut non aliunde, quam a suis, hoc est, ejus Reipublicae sive Civitatis Prodiis, in qua sunt constituti, accepisse*, Alethopoli [Amsterdam], apud Cajum Valerium Pennatum, 1665.

—, *Du Droit des Ecclésiastiques*, ed. Hans Blom, Véronique Butori, Jacqueline Lagrée, Pierre-François Moreau and Christian Lazzeri, Caen, Université de Caen, 1991.

Anonymous, *Homo politicus, consiliarius novus, officiarius et aulicus, secundum hodiernam praxin, Auctore pacifico a Lapide*, Cosmopoli, s.n., 1668.

Anonymous, *De Koeckoecx-zangh Van de Nachtuylen Van het Collegie Nil Volentibus Arduum &c.*, Zwolle, s.n., 1677/8.

Anonymous [Johann Joachim Müller], *De imposturis religionum (De tribus impostoribus) Von den Betrügereyen der Religionen*, ed. Winfried Schröder, Stuttgart-Bad Cannstatt, Frommann-Holzboog, 1999.

Anonymous, *Rencontre de Bayle, et de Spinoza dans l'autre monde*, Cologne, 'P. Marteau', [1711] 1713.

Anonymous, *Unschuldige Nachrichten von alten und neuen theologischen Sachen &c.*, Leipzig, Johann Friedrich Braun, 1714.

Anonymous, *L'esprit de Monsieur de Spinosa* (Ms. Hohendorf), in Françoise Charles-Daubert, *Le "Traité des trois imposteurs" et "L'Esprit de Spinosa". Philosophie clandestine entre 1678 et 1768*, Oxford, Voltaire Foundation, 1999, 483–542.

292 BIBLIOGRAPHY

Anonymous, *La vie et l'esprit de Mr. Benoit de Spinosa*, s.l., s.n., 1719, in Charles-Daubert, *Le "Traité des trois imposteurs" et "L'Esprit de Spinosa"*, 1999, 617–713.

Anonymous, *Traité des trois imposteurs*, s.l., s.n., 1768, in Charles-Daubert, *Le "Traité des trois imposteurs" et "L'Esprit de Spinosa"*, 1999, 715–52.

Anonymous, *Traktat über die drei Betrüger. Traité des trois imposteurs (L'esprit de Mr. Benoit de Spinosa)*, ed. Winfried Schröder, Hamburg, Felix Meiner Verlag, 1992.

Anonymous, *Trattato sui tre impostori. La vita e lo spirito del signor Benedetto de Spinoza*, ed. Silvia Berti, Turin, Einaudi, 1994.

Anonymous, *Réponse à la Dissertation de M. de la Monnoye sur le* Traité des trois imposteurs, The Hague, Henri Scheurleer, 1716.

Anonymous, *Il celebre e raro trattato de' tre impostori* 1798, ed. Luciano Guerci, Turin, Edizioni dell'Orso, 1996.

Asher, Georges Michael, *A Bibliographical and Historical Essay on the Dutch Books and Pamphlets Relating to New Netherland and to the Dutch West-India Company and to Its Possessions in Brazil, Angola, etc.*, Amsterdam, Frederik Muller, 1854–67.

Assonville de Bouchault, Guillaume d', *Atheomastix, sive adversus religionis hostes universos (politicos maxime) dissertatio*, Antwerp, Joannes Moretus, 1598.

Bacon, Francis, *The Advancement of Learning* 1605, ed. G. W. Kitchin, London, J. M. Dent & Sons Ltd [1915] 1973.

—, *The New Organon* 1620, ed. Fulton H. Anderson, Indianapolis, The Bobbs-Merrill Company, 1960.

—, *The Essays or Counsels, civill and morall* 1625 (*Sermones Fideles* 1641) in Francis Bacon, *Essays*, Oxford, Oxford University Press, 1930.

—, *Sermones Fideles Ethici, Politici, Œconomici: Sive Interiora Rerum. Accedit Faber Fortunæ &c.*, Leiden, Hackius, 1641.

Batelier, Johannes, *Vindiciae miraculorum, per quae divinae Religionis et fidei Christianae veritas olim confirmata fuit adversus profanum auctorem. Tractatus theologico politici*, Amsterdam, Johan Jansz Waesberge, 1674.

Baumgarten, Siegmund Jakob, *Nachrichten von einer Hallischen Bibliothek*, Bd. 3, Halle, s.n., 1749.

Bayle, Pierre, 'Lettre 69: Pierre Bayle à Vincent Minutoli, 15 décembre 1674', in *Œuvres diverses*, t.4, The Hague, Husson et al., 1727, 550–1.

—, *Nouvelles de la République des Lettres*, Janvier 1686, in *Œuvres diverses*, t.1, The Hague, Husson et al., 1727, 740–1.

BIBLIOGRAPHY 293

—, *Het leven van B. De Spinoza, met eenige Aanteekeningen over zyn Bedryf, Schriften, en Gevoelens: door den Heer Bayle, &c.* [. . .] *Vertaalt door F. Halma*, Utrecht, Willem vande Water, 1698.

—, *Dictionaire historique et critique*, Amsterdam & al., Pierre Brunel et al., 5me éd., 1740.

—, *Écrits sur Spinoza*, ed. Françoise Charles-Daubert and Pierre-François Moreau, Paris, Berg International Éditeurs, 1983.

Berkel, Abraham van, 'Voor-reden', in Hobbes, *Leviathan of van de stoffe*, 1667, n.p. [*3r–*6v].

Beverland, Adriaan, *De peccato originali* [. . .] *Dissertatio*, s.l., s.n., 1679.

Blyenbergh, Willem van, *De waerheyt van de christelijcke gods-dienst en de authoriteit der H. Schriften, beweert tegen de argumenten der ongodtsdienstige, of een wederlegginge van dat godt-lasterlijcke boeck, genoemt Tractatus theologico-politicus*, Leiden, Daniel van Gaesbeeck, 1674.

—, *Wederlegging van de Ethica of Zede-Kunst van Benedictus de Spinosa. Voornamentlijk omtrent het Wesen ende de Natuur van God en van onse Ziel. &c*, Dordrecht, By de Weduwe van Jasper, en by Dirck Goris, 1682.

Boecler, Johann Heinrich, *Bibliographia historico-politico-philologica curiosa, quid in quovis scriptore laudem censuramve mereatur exhibens cui praefixa celeberrimi cuiusdam viri de studio politico bene instituendo dissertatio epistolica postuma*, Germanopoli, s.n., 1677.

Botero, Giovanni, *Della Ragione di Stato 1589*, ed. Chiara Continisio, Rome, Donzelli, 2009.

Boulainvilliers, Henri de, Refutation de Spinoza (in fact *Essai de Métaphysique dans les Principes de B . . . de Sp . . .*), in Boulainvilliers et al., *Réfutation des erreurs de Benoît de Spinosa. Par M. de Fenelon &c.*, Brussels, Foppens, 1731, 1–320.

Bozio, Tommaso, *De antiquo et novo statu Italiae. Libri IV adversus Machiavellum*, Rome, Guglielmo Facciotto, 1554.

Bredenburg, Johannes, *Enervatio Tractatus theologico-politici; una cum demonstratione geometrico ordine disposita, naturam esse Deum &c.*, Rotterdam, Isaac Naeranus, 1675.

Brucioli, Antonio, *Dialogo di Antonio Brucioli della morale philosophia*, Venice, Bartolomeo Zanetti, 1st ed., 1526; 2nd ed., 1537.

Brucker, Johann Jakob, *Historia critica philosophiae*, IV/2, Leipzig, Breitkopf, 1744.

Brun, Jean [Braun, Johann], *La veritable religion des Hollandois. Avec une apologie pour la religion des Estats Généraux des Provinces Unies. Contre le libelle diffamatoire de Stoupe qui a pour titre La religion des Hollandois*, Amsterdam, Abraham Wolfgang, 1675.

294 BIBLIOGRAPHY

Budde, Johann Franz, *Theses theologicae de atheismo et superstitione*, Jena, Bielcke, 1717.

—, *Traité de l'athéisme et de la superstition*, Amsterdam, J. Schrueder & P. Mortier, 1756.

Campanella, Tommaso, *L'ateismo trionfato overo riconoscimento filosofico della religione universale contra l'antichristianesimo macchiavellesco*, 1607–8, 2 vols, ed. Germana Ernst, Pisa, Edizioni della Normale, 2004.

—, *Ad divum Petrum Apostolorum principem triumphantem. Atheismus triumphatus seu reductio ad religionem per Scientiarum veritates* [. . .] *contra Antichristanismum Achiteophellisticum*, Rome, Bartolomeo Zanetti, 1631.

Catalogus van de tractaten, pamfletten, enz. over de geschiedenis van Nederland, aanwezig in de bibliotheek van Isaac Meulman. Bewerkt door J.K. van der Wulp &. Tweede deel 1649–1688, Amsterdam, Van Munster & zoon, 1867.

Catarino, Ambrogio [Lancelotto Politi], *Enarrationes*, Rome, Blado, 1552.

Cauze de Nazelle, Jean Charles du, *Mémoires du temps de Louis XIV*, see Daudet.

Clapmar, Arnold, *De Arcanis Rerumpublicarum Libri sex*, Amsterdam, Elzevir, 1605/41.

Clément, Pierre, *La conspiration du chevalier de Rohan*, Paris, Didier, 1856.

—, *Trois drames historiques*, Paris, Didier, 1857.

Colerus, Johannes, *Korte, dog waarachtige Levens-Beschryving van Benedictus de Spinoza*, Amsterdam, Jacob Lindenberg, 1705.

—, *Korte, dog waaragtige Levens-Beschryving, van Benedictus de Spinosa*, in Freudenthal, *Die Lebensgeschichte Spinoza's*, 1899, 35–104.

Conring, Hermann, *Animadversiones politicae in Nicolai Machiavelli librum de Principe*, Helmstedt, Müller, 1661.

Court, Johan/Pieter de la, *Consideratien en exempelen van staat, Omtrent De Fundamenten van allerley regeringe. Beschreven door V. H.*, Amsterdam, Ian Iacobsz Dommekracht, 1660.

—, *Consideratien van Staat, Ofte Politike Weeg-Schaal beschreven door VH.*, Amsterdam, Iacob Volckerts, 1661.

—, *Consideratien van Staat, Ofte Politike Weeg-Schaal, Waar in met veele Reedenen, Omstandigheden, Exempelen en Fabulen werd ooverwoogen; Welke forme der Regeeringe, in speculatie gehoud op de practijk, onder de menschen de beste zy. Beschreven door V. H. In deese derde editie naawkeurig ooversien, merkelik vermeerdert, en in veelen klaarder gestelt*, Amsterdam, Dirk Dirksz, 1662.

—, *Politike Discoursen, handelende in ses onderscheide boeken van Steeden, Landen, Oorlogen, Kerken, Regeeringen en Zeeden. Beschreven door D.C.*, Leiden, Pieter Hakius, 1662.

[Court, Johan/Pieter de la], *Naeuwkeurige consideratie van staet, Wegens de Heerschappye van een vrye en geheymen staets-regering. Over de gantsche Aertbodem. Aengewezen door V.D.H.*, Amsterdam, Ioan Cyprianus vander Graft, 1662.

Daudet, Ernest (ed.), *Mémoires du temps de Louis XIV par Du Cause de Nazelle*, Paris, Plon, 1899.

Descartes, René, *Brieven*, vertaling J. H. Glazemaker, Amsterdam, Tymon Houthaak, 1661.

Desmarets, Samuel: see Maresius.

Donck, Adriaen van der, *Beschryvinge Van Nieuw-Nederlant, (Gelijck het tegenwoordigh in Staet is) Begrijpende de Nature, Aert, gelegentheyt en vruchtbaerheyt van het selve Landt &.*, Amsterdam, Evert Nieuwenhof, 1656.

Duijkerius, Johannes, *Het leven van Philopater & Vervolg van 't leven van Philopater*, ed. Gerardine Maréchal, Amsterdam, Rodopi, 1991.

Durand, David, *The Life of Lucilio (alias Julius Cæsar) Vanini. Burnt for Atheism at Thoulouse. With an Abstract of his Writings. [. . .] Translated from the French into English*, London, W. Meadows, 1730.

Dürr, Johannes Konrad, *Oratio De praeposterâ et impiâ libertate Philosophandi* (30/6/1671), in *Actus Panegyricus impositae merentibus*, Jena, Christoph Enoch Buchta, 1672, n.p. [A4r–D1r].

Du Sauzet, Henri (ed.), *Nouvelles littéraires* 1, 1715–20, *Dictionnaire des journaux 1600–1789* online, Voltaire Foundation, n° 1039, http://diction naire-journaux.gazettes18e.fr/journal/1039-nouvelles-litteraires-1.

Edelmann, Johann Christian, *Abgenöthigtes Jedoch Andern nicht wieder aufgenöthigtes Glaubens-Bekentniß* 1746, in *Sämtliche Werke*, ed. Walter Grossmann, Stuttgart-Bad Cannstatt, Frommann-Holzboog, 1969ff.

[Enden, Franciscus van den], *Kort verhael van Nieuw-Nederlants Gelegentheit, Deughden, Natuerlijke Voorrechten, en byzondere bequaemheidt ter Bevolkingh: Mitsgaders eenige requesten, Vertoogen, Deductien, enz. ten dien einden door eenige Liefhebbers ten verscheide tijden omtrent 't laatst van 't Jaer 1661. gepresenteert aen A.A. heeren Burgemeesteren dezer Stede, of der zelver E.E. Heeren Gecommitteerde, enz.*, s.l., s.n., 1662.

—, *Vrye Politijke Stellingen, en Consideratien van Staat, Gedaen na der ware Christenens Even gelijke vryheits gronden, strekkende tot een rechtschape, en ware verbeeteringh van Staat, en Kerk. Alles kort / en beknopt / onder verbeeteringh / voorgestelt / door Een Liefhebber van alle der welbevoeghde Borgeren Even gelyke vryheit, en die, ten gemeenebeste, Meest Van Zaken Houdt. 't Volks welvaert is de hooghstc Wet, En des zelfs stem, is Gods stem. Het eerste deel*, Amsterdam, Pieter Arentsz. Raep, 1665.

BIBLIOGRAPHY

—, *Vrije Politijke Stellingen*, ed. Wim Klever, Amsterdam, Wereldbibliotheek, 1992.

—, *Philedonius*, ed. Marc Bedjaï, Paris, Éditions Kimé, 1994.

—, *Philedonius*, in Omero Proietti, *Philedonius, 1657*, 2010, 182–289.

Feuerbach, Ludwig, *Pierre Bayle. Ein Beitrag zur Geschichte der Philosophie und Menschheit*, Berlin, Akademie-Verlag, 1967.

Francesca, Piero della, *De prospectiva pingendi*, ed. G. Nicco-Fasola, Florence, Le Lettere, 1984.

Frederik II, *Anti-Machiavel ou essai de critique sur le Prince de Machiavel, publié par Mr. de Voltaire*, The Hague, s.n., 1740.

Freytag, Friedrich Gotthilf, *Analecta litteraria de libris rarioribus*, Leipzig, Weidemann, 1750.

Galilei, Galileo, *Capitolo Contro il portar la toga. Against the Donning of the Gown*, ed. Lucia Tongiorgi Tomasi, Pisa, Edizioni ETS, 2009.

Garasse, François, *La doctrine curieuse des beaux esprits de ce temps. Contenant plusieurs maximes pernicieuses à la religion, à l'État, et aux bonnes mœurs*, Paris, Sebastien Chappelet, 1623.

Gentili, Alberigo, *De Legationibus libri tres*, London, Thomas Vautrollerius, 1585.

Gentillet, Innocent, *Discours sur les moyens de bien gouverner & maintenir en bonne paix un Royaume ou autre Principauté, divisez en trois Livres [. . .]. Contre Nicolas Machiavel Florentin*, Geneva, Jacob Stoer, 1576.

Goeree, Willem, *De kerklyke en weereldlyke Historien; Uyt d'Aal-Ouwde Aardbeschryving &.*, Leiden, Johannes van Abkoude, [1705] 1730.

Graevius, Johann Georg, *Oratio funebris in obitu V.C. et doctissimi Regneri Mansveldii [. . .] Jun. 1671*, Utrecht, Van Dreunen, 1671.

Grotius, Hugo, *Appendix ad interpretationem locorum N. Testamenti quae de Antichristo agunt*, in *De imperio Summarum Potestatum Circa Sacra*, Amsterdam, Cornelius Blaeu, 1641.

Guichard, Anastase, *Histoire du socinianisme, divisee en deux parties*, Paris, François Barois, 1723.

Hobbes, Thomas, *De cive. The English Version*, entitled in the first edition *Philosophical Rudiments Concerning Government and Society* (London, 1651), ed. Howard Warrender, Oxford, Clarendon Press, 1983.

—, *Leviathan, or The Matter, Forme, & Power of a Common-wealth Ecclesiasticall and Civill*, London, Andrew Crooke, 1651 (ed. Crawford Brough Macpherson, Penguin Books, 1968; ed. Edwin Curley, Hackett Publishing Company, 1994).

—, *Leviathan of van de stoffe, gedaente, ende magt vande kerckelycke ende wereltlycke regeeringe*, Amsterdam, Jacobus Wagenaar, 1667.

Holbach, Paul-Henri Thiry d', *Système de la nature*, I, II (1781), Paris, Fayard, 1990.

[Holbach, Paul-Henri Thiry d'], *Essai sur les préjugés, ou, De l'influence des opinions sur les mœurs & sur le bonheur des hommes*, London [Amsterdam, Rey?], 1770.

Index librorum prohibitorum, Sacred Congregation of the Roman Inquisition, Rome, 1559.

Jahn, Johann Christian Gottfried, *Verzeichnis der Bücher so gesamlet Johann Christian Gottfried Jahn*, Frankfurt/Leipzig, Johann Samuel Heinsius Erben, 1757.

Knorr, Christian Friedrich (Resp. et auct.) / Musaeus, Johannes (praes.), *Tractatus Theologico-Politicus, Quo Auctor Quidam Anonymus, conatu improbo, demonstratum ivit, Libertatem Philosophandi [. . .] tolli non posse. Ad veritatis lancem examinatus*, Jena, Bauhofer, 1st ed., 1674; *Spinosismus, Hoc est, Tractatus theologico-politicus, quo Benedictus Spinoza &c.*, Wittenberg, Meisel, 2nd ed., 1708.

Knutzen, Matthias. *Schriften und Materialien*, ed. Winfried Schröder, Stuttgart-Bad Cannstatt, Frommann-Holzboog, 2010.

[Koerbagh, Adriaan?], *'t Samen-spraeck tusschen een Gereformeerden Hollander en Zeeuw. Waer in de Souverainiteyt van Holland ende West-Vriesland Klaer ende Naecktelijck werd vertoont. Tot Refutatie van den verresen Barnevelt; bedunckelijcken Brief; 't Samen-spraeck tusschen een Rotterdammer en Gelderman, Kaats-Bal en andere onlangs uytgegevene Laster-schriften, belangende een Formulier van 't Bidden, &c. Eerste Deel. Door Vrederyck Waermont*, Middelburg, Antoni de Vrede, 1664.

Koerbagh, Adriaan, *'t Nieuw Woorden-Boek der Regten: ten dele uyt de Schriften van H. en W. de Groot versamelt ende ten dele nu eerst uyt het Latyn in Nederduyts overgeset*, Amsterdam, By de Weduwe van Jan Hendriksz Boom, 1664.

—, *Een Bloemhof van allerley lieflijkheyd sonder verdriet, geplant door Vreederyk Waarmond / ondersoeker der waarheyd / Tot nut en dienst van al die geen die der nut en dienst uyt trekken wil. Of Een vertaaling en uytlegging van al de Hebreusche / Griecksche / Latijnse / Franse / en andere vreemde bastaart-woorden en wijsen van spreeken, die ('t welk te beklaagen is) soo inde Godsgeleertheyd / regtsgeleertheyd / geneeskonst / als in andere konsten en wee-tenschappen / en ook in het dagelijks gebruyk van spreeke / inde Nederduytse taal gebruykt worden / gedaen*, Amsterdam, s.n., 1668.

—, *Een Ligt schynende in Duystere Plaatsen: Om te verligten de voornaam-ste saaken der Gods geleertheyd en Gods dienst / ontsteeken door Vreederijk Waarmond / ondersoeker der Waarheyd*, Amsterdam, s.n., 1668.

298   BIBLIOGRAPHY

—, *Een ligt schijnende in duystere plaatsen*, ed. Hubert Vandenbossche, Brussel, Centrum voor de studie van de Verlichting VUB, 1974.

—, *A Light Shining in Dark Places, to Illuminate the Main Questions of Theology and Religion*, ed. Michiel Wielema, Leiden/Boston, Brill, 2011.

—, *Een licht dat schijnt in duistere plaatsen*, modern Dutch translation by Michiel Wielema, Nijmegen, Vantilt, 2014.

Kortholt, Christian, *De tribus impostoribus magnis liber*, Kiel, Richelius, 1680.

Kuyper, Frans, *Arcana atheismi revelata, philosophice et paradoxe refutata, examine Tractatus theologico-politici*, Rotterdam, Isaac Naeranus, 1676.

La Boétie, Etienne de, *Discours de la servitude volontaire*, Paris, Flammarion, 1983.

La Croze, Mathurin Veyssière de, *Entretiens sur divers sujets d'histoire, de littérature, de religion et de critique*, Cologne [Amsterdam], 1711.

La Monnoye, Bernard de, *Lettre à Monsieur Bouhier, Président au Parlement de Dijon, sur le prétendu livre des trois imposteurs*, in *Menagiana* (16/5/1712), 3e éd., vol. IV, Paris, F. Delaulne, 1715.

Lange, Joachim, *Causa Dei et religionis naturalis adversus atheismum*, Halle, Orphanotropheum, 2nd ed., 1727.

La Place, M. (Pierre Antoine) de (ed.), *Nouveau choix de pièces tirées des anciens Mercures, et des autres journaux*, t. 90, Paris, Pissot, Duchesne, Lambert & Cellot, 1760–4.

Leibniz, Gottfried Wilhelm, *Essais de Théodicée*, ed. Jacques Brunschwig, Paris, Garnier-Flammarion, 1969.

—, *Nouveaux essais sur l'entendement humain*, ed. Jacques Brunschwig, Paris, Garnier-Flammarion, 1966.

—, *Allgemeiner politischer und historischer Briefwechsel. Erster Band 1668–1676*, Darmstadt, Otto Reichl Verlag, 1923.

—, *Sämtliche Schriften und Briefe* I, Berlin, De Gruyter, 2006.

Lilienthal, Michael, *Theologische Bibliothec*, Königsberg, Hartung, 1741.

Machiavelli, Niccolò, *L'arte della Guerra*, Florence, Bernardo di Giunta, 1521.

—, *I Discorsi*, Florence, Bernardo di Giunta, 1531.

—, *I Discorsi*, Rome, Antonio Blado, 1531.

—, *Il Principe, La vita di Castruccio Castracani da Lucca, Il modo che tenne il duca Valentino per ammazar Vitellozo, Oliverotto da Fermo, il signor Pagolo et il duca di Gravina Orsini in Senigaglia*, Rome, Antonio Blado, 1532.

—, *Istorie Fiorentine*, Rome, Antonio Blado, 1532.

—, *Il Principe, La vita di Castruccio Castracani da Lucca, Il modo che tenne il duca Valentino per ammazar Vitellozo, Oliverotto da Fermo, il signor Pagolo et il duca di Gravina Orsini in Senigaglia*, Florence, Bernardo di Giunta, 1532.

BIBLIOGRAPHY 299

—, *Nicolai Machiavelli Princeps*, Basel, Petrus Perna, 1560.

—, *Le Prince de Nicolas Machiavel secretaire et citoyen florentin* [. . .] *traduit de l'Italien en François avec la vie de l'auteur mesme par Jaq. Gohory* [. . .] *suivi de Discours &c.*, Paris, Robert le Mangnier, 1571.

—, *Nicolai Machiauelli Florentini Princeps ex Sylvestri Telii Fulginatis traductione diligenter emendates. Adiecta sunt eiusdem argumenti aliorum quorundam contra Machiavellum scripta, de potestate & officio Principum contra Tyrannos. Quibus denua accessit Antonii Possevini iudicium de Nicolai Machiauelli & Ioannis Bodini scriptis*, Frankfurt, Lazarus Zetzner, 1608.

—, *Tutte le opere di Nicolo Machiavelli cittadino e secretario fiorentino divise in V parti et di nuovo con somma accuratezza ristampate*, s.l., s.n., 1550 [1610–29].

—, *Nicolai Machiavelli Princeps aliaque nunnulla ex italico latine nunc demum partim versa, partim infinitis locis sensus melioris ergo castigata curante Hermanno Conringio*, Helmstedt, Müller, 1660.

—, *Le Prince de Machiavel traduit et commenté de A. N. Amelot*, Amsterdam, Weststijn, 1683.

—, *The Chief Works and Others*, trans. Allan Gilbert, 3 vols, Durham, NC, Duke University Press, 1965.

—, *Florentine Histories*, trans. Laura F. Banfield and Harvey C. Mansfield Jr, Princeton, Princeton University Press, 1988.

—, *Discourses on Livy*, trans. Harvey C. Mansfield and Nathan Tarcov, Chicago, University of Chicago Press, 1996.

—, *Opere I* (*I primi scritti politici; Decennali; Il Principe; Discorsi sopra la prima deca di Tito Livio; Dell'arte della guerra; Scritti politici "post res perditas"*), ed. Corrado Vivanti, Turin, Einaudi-Gallimard, 1997.

—, *The Prince*, trans. Harvey C. Mansfield, Chicago, University of Chicago Press, 2nd ed., 1998.

—, *Opere II* (*Lettere; Legazioni e commissarie*), ed. Corrado Vivanti, Turin, Einaudi, 1999.

—, *De principatibus. Le Prince*, ed. Jean-Louis Fournel and Jean-Claude Zancarini, Paris, PUF, 2000.

—, *Opere III* (*Rime varie; Canti carnascialeschi; Capitoli; L'asino; Favola; Teatro; Scritti letterari in prosa; Dialogo sulla nostra lingua; La vita di Castruccio Castracani; Istorie Fiorentine*), ed. Corrado Vivanti, Turin, Einaudi, 2005.

Mansvelt, Regnerus van, *Adversus anonymum Theologo-politicum liber singularis, in quo omnes et singulae Tractatus theologico-politici dissertationes examinantur et refelluntur*, Amsterdam, Abraham Wolfgang, 1674.

Marchand, Prosper, *Dictionaire historique, ou Mémoires critiques et littéraires, concernant la vie et les ouvrages de divers personnages distingués, particulièrement dans la république des lettres*, The Hague, Pierre de Hondt, 1758.

300   BIBLIOGRAPHY

—, Art. 'Impostoribus', *Dictionaire historique*, in Berti, Charles-Daubert and Popkin (eds), *Heterodoxy, Spinozism, and Free Thought*, 1999, 476–524.

Maresius, Samuel, *Vindiciae dissertationis suae nuperae de abusu philosophiae Cartesianae*, Groningen, T. Everts, 1670.

Marx, Karl, 'Brief 87 Marx an Engels 25/9/1857', in MEW 29, 192–3 (cf. *Ex libris Karl Marx und Friedrich Engels. Schicksal und Verzeichnis einer Bibliothek*, Berlin, Dietz Verlag, 1967, 134; ill. 286).

Masch, Andreas Gottlieb, *Verzeichnis der erheblichsten freidenkerischen Schriften*, in Masch, *Abhandlung von der Religion der Heiden und der Christen*, Halle, Bauer, 1753.

Mehlig, Johann Michael, *Das erste schlimmste Buch, oder historisch-Critische Abhandlung von der religionslästerlichen Schrift De Tribus Impostoribus*, Chemnitz, Johann Christoph Strössel, 1764.

Melchior, Johann, *Epistola Ad Amicum, Continens Censuram. Libri, cui titulus: Tractatus Theologico-Politicus*, Utrecht, Cornelius Noenaert, 1671.

Mémoires historiques et authentiques sur La Bastille, Dans une Suite de près de trois cens Emprisonnements, détaillés & constatés par des Pieces, Notes, Lettres, Rapports, Procès-verbaux, trouvés dans cette Forteresse, & rangés par époques depuis 1475 jusqu'à nos jours, &c., t. I, London/Paris, Buisson, 1789, 74–112.

Mercure François, 5, 1619, http://mercurefrancois.ehess.fr/index.php?/categ ory/61.

Mersenne, Marin, *Quaestiones celeberrimae in genesim, cum accurata textus explicatione &c.*, Paris, Sébastien Cramoisy, 1623.

—, *L'impiete des deistes, athees, et libertins de ce temps, combatuë & renuersee*, Paris, Pierre Bilaine, 1624.

Meyer, Lodewijk, *Philosophia S. Scripturae Interpres, Exercitatio paradoxa*, Eleutheropoli [Amsterdam], s.n., 1666.

—, *De Philosophie d'Uytleghster der H. Schrifture. Een wonderspreuckigh Tractaet*, Vrystadt [Amsterdam], s.n., 1667.

Moreri, Louis, *Le Grand Dictionaire historique*, Lyon and Paris, Jean Girin et al., 1687ff.

Müller, Johann, *Atheismus devictus Das ist Ausführlicher Bericht Von Atheisten / Gottesverächtern / Schrifftschändern / Religionsspöttern / Epicureern / Ecebolisten / Kirchen- und Prediger-Feinden / Gewissenlosen Eydbrüchigen Leuten / und Verfolgern der Recht-Gläubigen Christen*, Hamburg, Nauman & Wolffen, 1672.

Musaeus, Johannes, *Spinozismus, hoc est Tractatus theologico politicus*, Jena, Literis Bauhoferianis, 1674, see Knorr.

BIBLIOGRAPHY   301

—, *Ableinung Der ausgesprengten abscheulichen Verleumbdung* [. . .]: *Welcher beygefüget ist Eine notwendige Vertheidigung der H. Schrifft Wider in besagten Chartequen / die zu Ende beygedruckt sind / enthaltene Lästerungen derselben*, Jena, Johann Bielcke, 2nd ed., 1675, in Matthias Knutzen, *Schriften und Dokumente*, ed. Winfried Schröder, Stuttgart-Bad Cannstatt, 2010, 91–284.

Naudé, Gabriel, *Bibliographia politica*, Venice, Franciscus Baba, 1633.

—, *Considérations politiques sur les coups d'Etat*, Rome, s.n., 1639.

—, *Bibliographia politica et Casparis Scioppii Paedia Politices ut & ejusdem argumenti alia. Nova editio reliquis omnibus emendatior cura Hermanni Conringii*, Frankfurt, Müller, 1673.

—, *Naudeana et Patiniana, ou singularitez remarquables prises des conversations de Mess. Naudé et Patin*, Paris, Fl. & P. Delaulne, 1701; Amsterdam, F. Van der Plaats, 1703.

Nieuwentyt, Bernard, *Gronden van zekerheid, of de regte betoogwyse der wiskundigen. So in het Denkbeeldige, als in het Zakelyke: Ter Wederlegging van Spinosaas denkbeeldig Samenstel &c.*, Amsterdam, Joannes Pauli, 1720.

Nifo, Agostino, *De regnandi peritia*, Napoli, In aedibus Dominae Catherinae de Siluestro, 1523.

—, *Libellus de rege et tyranno*, Naples, s.n., 1526.

Osorio, Jeronimo, *De nobilitate civili libri duo; Ejusdem de nobilitate Christiana libri tres*, Olyssipone [Lisboa], Apud Ludovicum Rodericum, *De nobilitate christiana* [1542] 1552, in *Nicolai Machiauelli Florentini Princeps*, 1608, 164–78.

Panzer, Georg Wolfgang, *Bibliotheca Thomasiana* . . ., vol. 1, Nuremberg, Wolfgang Schwarzkopf, 1765, 309–10 (no. 2724)

Plokhoy, Pieter Cornelisz., *Kort en klaer ontwerp, dienende tot Een onderling Accoort, om Den arbeyd, onrust en moeyelijckheyt, van Alderley-handwerckluyden te verlichten &c.*, Amsterdam, Otto Barentsz. Smient, 1662.

Pole, Reginald, *Apologia ad Carolum Quintum*, 1539, in *Epistolarum Reginaldi Poli S.R.E. Cardinalis et aliorum ad ipsum collectio*, I, ed. Angelo Maria Querini, Brescia, Italia, Rizzardi, 1744, 66–171.

Possevino, Antonio, *Iudicium de Nicolai Machiauelli & Ioannis Bodini scriptis*, 1592, in *Nicolai Machiauelli Florentini Princeps*, 1608, 195–205.

Post, S. D., 'De aantekeningen van Pieter de la Ruë. Een 18e-eeuwse bron voor receptieonderzoek op letterkundig gebied', *De Nieuwe Taalgids* 86, 1993, 405–20.

Rappolt, Friedrich, *Programma ad audiendam orationem inauguralem* (29/5/1670), in *Opera Theologica, Exegetica, Didactica, Polemica*, Leipzig, s.n., 1693, 2160–8.

302 BIBLIOGRAPHY

—, *Oratio contra Naturalistas &c. Junii a. 1670*, in *Opera Theologica, Exegetica, Didactica, Polemica*, Leipzig, s.n., 1693, 1383–1407.

Raynaud, Theophil, *Erotemata de malis ac bonis libris, deque iusta aut iniusta, eorundem confixione*, Lyon, Jean-Antoine Huguetan & Marc Antoine Ravaud, 1653.

Reimarus, Hermann Samuel, *Dissertatio schediasmati de machiavellismo ante Machiavellum*, Wittenberg, Gerdes, 1719.

Reimmann, Jakob Friedrich, *Versuch einer Einleitung in die Historie der Theologie insgemein und der jüdischen Theologie ins besondere*, Magdeburg, Christoph Seidel, 1717.

—, *Historia universalis atheismi et atheorum falso et merito suspectorum* (1725), ed. Winfried Schröder, Stuttgart-Bad Cannstatt, Frommann-Holzboog, 1992.

Reiser, Anton, *De origine, progressu et incremento antitheismi, seu atheismi, epistolaris dissertatio, ad clariss. virum Theophilum Spizelium*, Augsburg, Gottlieb Goebel, 1669.

Ribadeneyra, Pietro, *Della religione del Prencipe Christiano contra li machiavellisti*, Bologna, Pierre Tozzi, 1622.

Riedel, Carl, *Renati des Cartes et Benedicti de Spinoza praecipua opera philosophica*, Leipzig, Hermann Hartung, 1843.

Rou, Jean, *Mémoires inédits*, see Waddington.

Saintes, Amand, *Histoire de la vie et des ouvrages de B. de Spinosa, fondateur de l'exégèse et de la philosophie modernes*, Paris, Jules Renouard et Cie, 1842.

Schwindel, Georg, *Theophili Sinceri Nachrichten Von lauter alten und raren Büchern*, Nürnberg, s.n., 1731.

Spinoza, Benedictus de, *Tractatus theologico-politicus continens dissertationes aliquot, quibus ostenditur libertatem philosophandi non tantum salva pietate, & reipublicae pace posse concedi: sed eandem nisi cum pace reipublicae, ipsaque pietate tolli non posse*, Hamburg [Amsterdam], Henricus Künrath [Jan Rieuwertsz], 1670.

—, *Opera posthuma*, Amsterdam, s.n., 1677 [facsimile ed. Pina Totaro, Macerata, Quodlibet, 2008].

—, *De Nagelate Schriften*, Amsterdam, s.n., 1677.

—, *De rechtzinnige theologant of godgeleerde staatkundige verhandelinge*, Hamburg [Amsterdam], Henricus Koenraad [Jan Rieuwertsz], 1693.

—, *Een rechtsinnige theologant of godgeleerde staatkunde*, Bremen, Jurgen van der Weyl, 1694.

—, *Éthique*. Traduction inédite du Comte Henri de Boulainvilliers (1658–1722), ed. François-Marie Colonna d'Istria, Paris, Librairie Armand Colin, 1907.

BIBLIOGRAPHY 303

—, *Opera* I–V, ed. Carl Gebhardt, Heidelberg, Carl Winter Universitätsverlag, 1972–87.

—, *The Collected Works of Spinoza* I, ed. Edwin Curley, Princeton/Oxford, Princeton University Press, 1985.

—, *The Vatican Manuscript of Spinoza's Ethica*, ed. Leen Spruit and Pina Totaro, Leiden/Boston, Brill, 2011.

—, *The Collected Works of Spinoza* II, ed. Edwin Curley, Princeton/Oxford, Princeton University Press, 2016.

Spitzel, Gottlieb, *Felix literatus ex infelicium periculis et casibus &c.*, Augsburg, Koppmayer, 1676.

Stensen, Niels, 'Denunciation of Spinoza's Philosophy to the Holy Office (Rome, 4 September 1677) ACDE, SO, Censurae librorum, 1680–1682, Folia extravangantia n. 2, n.n. (autograph)', in *The Vatican Manuscript of Spinoza's Ethica*, ed. Spruit and Totaro, 2011, 68 and 72.

Stolle, Gottlieb, *Anleitung zur Historie der Gelahrtheit*, Jena, Meyer, 1727.

—, *[Reisetagebuch 1703], Beyträge zur Kenntniss des 17. und 18. Jahrhunderts aus den handschriftlichen Aufzeichnungen Gottlieb Stolle's. Mitgeteilt von G. E. Guhrauer*, in *Allgemeine Zeitschrift für Geschichte* 7, 1847, 385–436; 481–531.

—, *Der Bericht der Stolle-Hallmannschen Reisebeschreibung 1704*, in Gebhardt, *Spinoza – Lebensbeschreibungen und Dokumente*, 1998, 125–48.

Stouppe, Jean-Baptiste, *La religion des Hollandois, Représentée en plusieurs Lettres écrites par un Officier de l'Armée du Roy, à un Pasteur & Professeur en Theologie de Berne*, Paris, François Clousier & Pierre Auboüin, 1673.

—, *De gods-dienst der Hollanders, Vertoont in verscheide Brieven, geschreven door een Amptenaar in 's Konings Leger, Aen een Leeraar ende Professor in de God-geleertheid der Stad Berne*, Amsterdam, Cyprianus vander Gracht, 1673.

Struve, Burchard Gotthelff, *Dissertatio historico-litteraria de Doctis Impostoribus*, Jena, Müller, 1710.

Sue, Eugène, *Latréaumont* [1837], Paris, Garnier, 1979.

Tarabaud, Mathieu Mathurin, *Histoire critique du philosophisme anglois* II, Paris, Duprat-Duverger, 1806.

Tentzel, Wilhelm Ernst, *Curieuse Bibliothec. De ersten Repositorii fünfftes Fach*, Frankfurt/Leipzig, Philipp Wilhelm Stock, 1st ed., 1704.

Thomasius, Christian, *Historia contentionis inter imperium et sacerdotium breviter delineata &c. in usum auditorii Thomasiani*, Halle, Renger, 1722.

Thomasius, Jacob, *Programma adversus anonymum, de libertate philosophandi* [1670], in Jacob Thomasius, *Dissertationes LXIII varii argumenti*, ed. Christian Thomasius, Halle, Zeitler, 1693, 571–81.

304 BIBLIOGRAPHY

Toland, John, *Pantheisticon. Sive formula Celebrandae Sodalitatis Socraticae*, Cosmopoli, s.n., 1720.

Trinius, Johann Anton, *Freydenker-Lexicon*, Leipzig/Bernburg, C.G. Cörner, 1759–65 [reprint, ed. Franco Venturi, Turin, Bottega d'Erasmo, 1966].

Uffenbach, Zacharias Konrad von, *Bibliothecae Uffenbachianae tomus I* [II, III], Frankfurt/Main, Andreae, 1729–30.

—, 'Brief aan Valentin Löscher, 14/7/1714', in *Commercii epistolaris Uffenbachiani selecta*, ed. J. G. Schelhorn, Ulm/Memmingen, Gaum, 1753, 152f.

—, *Merkwürdige Reisen durch Niedersachsen Holland und Engeland*, II, Frankfurt and Leipzig, s.n., 1753.

Vanini, Lucilio [Giulio Cesare], *Amphitheatrum aeternae providentiae* (*Anfiteatro dell'eterna provvidenza*), 1615, in Vanini, *Tutte le opere*, ed. Francesco Paolo Raimondi and Mario Carparelli, Milano, Bompiani, 2010, 320–771; 1557–1634.

—, *De admirandis naturae reginae Deaeque Mortalium Arcanis* (*I meravigliosi segreti della natura, regina e dea dei mortali*), 1616, in Vanini, *Tutte le opere*, ed. Raimondi and Carparelli, 2010, 772–1553; 1634–1818.

Velthuysen, Lambertus van, 'Lambertus van Velthuysen med.dr. aan de zeer geleerde en aanzienlijke heer Jacob Ostens', in Curley (ed.), *The Collected Works of Spinoza*, II, 2016, 374–85.

Verwer, Adriaen, *'t Mom-Aensicht der Atheistery Afgerukt door een Verhandeling van den aengeboren stand der menschen, Vervattende niet alleen een Betoogh van de Rechtsinnige Stellinge; maer ook voornamentlijk een Grondige Wederlegging van de tegenstrijdige Waen-gevoelens en in 't bysonder van de gehele Sede-konst, van Benedictus de Spinoza*, Amsterdam, Wilhelmus Goeree, 1683.

Voetius, Gijsbert, *De atheismo* [1639], in *Selectarum disputationum theologicarum pars prima*, Utrecht, Waesberge, 1648.

Vogt, Johann, *Catalogus historico-criticus librorum rariorum*, Hamburg, Herold, 1753.

Voltaire, François Marie Arouet, *Épitre à l'auteur du livre des trois imposteurs* [1769], in *Œuvres complètes*, vol. 10, Paris, Garnier, 1877, 402–5.

—, *Dictionnaire philosophique*, Art. 'Athéisme', in *Œuvres complètes*, vol. 17, Paris, 1878, 461–76.

Waddington, Francis (ed.), *Mémoires inédits et Opuscules de Jean Rou* (*1638–1711*), Paris/The Hague, Agence centrale de la société/Nijhoff, 1857.

Wagner, Tobias, *Examen elencticum atheismi speculativi*, Tübingen, Johann Henrick Reis, 1677.

Wassenaer, Geraard van, *Bedekte Konsten in regeringen en heerschappien. Die bykans gebruyckt worden, en waer door Koningen en Princen, Edelen en Steden, die het hooghste gebiedt hebben, haer Staedt en Heerschappie vast stellen,* Utrecht, Gysbert van Zyll & Dirck van Ackersdyck, 1657.

Zedler, Johann Heinrich, *Grosses vollständiges Universal-Lexikon Aller Wissenschaften und Künste,* Halle and Leipzig, Johann Heinrich Zedler, 1732ff.

Secondary sources

Abensour, Miguel, *La Démocratie contre l'État. Marx et le moment machia-vélien,* Paris, Félin, 2004.

Adam, Antoine, *Le mouvement philosophique dans la première moitié du XVIIIe siècle,* Paris, SEDES, 1967.

Addante, Luca, 'Radicalismes politiques et religieux', in Berns, Staquet and Weis (eds), *Libertin!,* 2013, 29–50.

Agamben, Giorgio, *Stasis. La guerra civile come paradigma politico. Homo sacer, II, 2,* Turin, Bollati Boringhieri, 2015.

Akkerman, Fokke, *Spinoza's tekort aan woorden. Humanistische aspecten van zijn schrijverschap.* Mededelingen vanwege Het Spinozahuis 36, Leiden, Brill, 1977.

—, *Studies in the Posthumous Works of Spinoza on Style, Earliest Translation and Reception. Earliest and Modern Edition of Some Texts.* PhD dissertation, University of Groningen, 1980.

Albertini, Rudolf von, *Das florentinische Staatsbewusstsein im Übergang von der Republik zum Prinzipat,* Bern, Francke Verlag, 1955.

Althusser, Louis, *Machiavel et nous,* in *Écrits philosophiques et politiques tome II,* Paris, Stock/Imec, 1995, 39–168.

—, *Solitude de Machiavel,* Paris, PUF, 1998.

Altwicker, Norbert, 'Spinoza. Tendenzen der Spinoza-Rezeption und -Kritik', in Altwicker (ed.), *Texte zur Geschichte des Spinozismus,* Darmstadt, Wissenschaftliche Buchgesellschaft, 1971, 1–58.

—, 'Spinozas Theologisch-politischer Traktat und Politischer Traktat in der philosophischen Forschung der letzten fünfzig Jahre', in Spinoza, *Opera* V, 1987, 265–446.

Ansaldi, Saverio, 'Conflit, démocratie et multitudes: l'enjeu Spinoza-Machiavel', *Multitudes* 27, 2007, 217–25.

Aron, Raymond, *Machiavel et les tyrannies modernes,* Paris, Gallimard [1946] 1993.

BIBLIOGRAPHY

Assmann, Jan, *Herrschaft und Heil. Politische Theologie in Altägypten, Israel und Europa*, Munich/Vienna, Carl Hanser Verlag, 2000.

Assoun, Paul-Laurent, 'Spinoza, les libertins français et la politique (1665–1725)', *Cahiers Spinoza* 3, 1980, 171–208.

Audier, Serge, *Machiavel, conflit et liberté*, Paris, Vrin, 2005.

Baeck, Leo, *Spinozas erste Einwirkungen auf Deutschland*, Berlin, Mayer & Müller, 1895.

Bal, Mieke, *Narratology: Introduction to the Theory of Narrative*, Toronto, University of Toronto Press, 2009.

Balibar, Etienne, 'Jus, Pactum, Lex: Sur la constitution du sujet dans le *Traité Théologico-Politique*', *Studia Spinozana* 1, 1985, 105–42.

—, *Spinoza et la politique*, Paris, PUF, 1985.

—, *La crainte des masses. Politique et philosophie avant et après Marx*, Paris, Galilée, 1997.

—, *Spinoza politique. Le transindividuel*, Paris, PUF, 2018.

Balsamo, Jean, 'Le plus meschant d'entre eux ne voudroit pas estre Roy. La Boétie et Machiavel', *Montaigne Studies* 11, 1999, 5–27.

Barker, Ernest, 'The Authorship of the Vindiciae contra tyrannos', *Cambridge Historical Journal* 3/2, 1930, 164–81.

Barot, Emmanuel, '1378 ou l'émergence de la question moderne du sujet révolutionnaire', in Weil, *La révolte des Ciompi*, 2013, 61–80.

Bedjaï, Marc, 'F. Van den Enden, maitre spirituel de Spinoza', *Revue de l'histoire des religions* 3, 1990, 289–31.

—, *Métaphysique, éthique et politique dans l'œuvre du docteur Franciscus van den Enden (1602–1674)*. Thèse de doctorat (sous la direction de A. Matheron), Paris 1 BU Pierre Mendès-France, 1990.

—, 'Métaphysique, éthique et politique dans l'œuvre du docteur Franciscus van den Enden (1602–1674). Contribution à l'étude des sources des écrits de B. de Spinoza', *Studia Spinozana* 6, 1990, 291–313.

—, 'Le docteur Franciscus van den Enden, son cercle et l'alchimie dans les Provinces-Unies du XVIIème siècle', *Nouvelles de la République des Lettres*, 1991, 19–50.

—, 'Pour un État populaire ou une utopie subversive', in Méchoulan (ed.), *Amsterdam XVIIe siècle*, 1993, 194–213.

—, 'Les circonstances de la publication du Philedonius (1657)', in Van den Enden, *Philedonius*, 1994, 9–55.

Benítez, Miguel, 'Un spinozisme suspect: à propos du Dieu de Boulainvilliers', *Dix-huitième siècle* 24, 1992, 17–28.

—, 'La diffusion du Traité des trois imposteurs au XVIIIe siècle', *Revue d'histoire moderne et contemporaine* XL, 1993, 137–51.

—, *La Face cachée des Lumières. Recherches sur les manuscrits philosophiques clandestins de l'âge classique*, Paris/Oxford, Universitas/Voltaire Foundation, 1996.

—, 'Une histoire interminable: origine et développement du *Traité des trois imposteurs*', in Berti, Charles-Daubert and Popkin (eds), *Heterodoxy, Spinozism and Free Thought*, 1996, 53–74.

—, 'Le corpus des traités manuscripts philosophiques clandestins: un regard critique', in McKenna and Mothu (eds), *La Philosophie clandestine à l'Age classique*, 1997, 17–38.

Berns, Thomas, *Violence de la loi à la Renaissance. L'originaire du politique chez Machiavel et Montaigne*, Paris, Kimé, 2000.

—, 'Conflit, guerre, violence et corruption', *Multitudes* 13, 2003, 135–9.

—, 'L'averroïste et le Machiavélien', in Berns, Staquet and Weis (eds), *Libertin!*, 2013, 265–74.

Berns, Thomas, Anne Staquet and Monique Weis (eds), *Libertin! Usage d'une invective aux XVIe et XVIIe siècles*, Paris, Garnier, 2013.

Bertelli, Sergio Piero Innocenti, *Bibliografia Machiavelliana*, Verona, Valdonega, 1979.

Berti, Silvia, '"La Vie et l'Esprit de Spinosa" (1719) e la prima traduzione francese dell' "Ethica"', *Rivista storica italiana* 93, 1986, 6–46.

—, 'L'Esprit de Spinoza: ses origines et sa première édition dans leur contexte spinozien', in Berti, Charles-Daubert and Popkin (eds), *Heterodoxy, Spinozism, and Free Thought*, 1996, 3–51.

—, *Anticristianesimo e libertà. Studi sull'illuminismo radicale europeo*, Bologna, Il Mulino, 2012.

Berti, Silvia, Françoise Charles-Daubert and Richard H. Popkin (eds), *Heterodoxy, Spinozism, and Free Thought in Early-Eighteenth-Century Europe. Studies on the* Traité des trois imposteurs, Dordrecht/Boston/London, Kluwer Academic Publishers, 1996.

Bianchi, Lorenzo, 'Fascino del potere e servitù volontaria', *Studi storici* 21, 1980, 819–33.

—, 'Sapiente e popolo nel "Theophrastus redivivus"', *Studi storici* 24, 1983, 137–64.

—, '"Nullo modo autem mors timendus est": paura e ragione secondo il Theophrastus redivivus', in Lucia Valenzi (ed.), *Storia e paura. Immaginario collettivo, riti e rappresentazione della paura in età moderna*, Milan, Franco Angeli, 1992, 43–54.

Bianchi, Lorenzo and Alberto Postigliola (eds), *Dopo Machiavelli/Après Machiavel*, Naples, Liguori, 2008.

308   BIBLIOGRAPHY

Bloch, Olivier, 'Theophrastus Redivivus', in Jean-Pierre Schobinger (ed.), *Grundriss der Geschichte der Philosophie. Die Philosophie des 17. Jahrhunderts. Bd 2: Frankreich und Niederlande*, Basel, Schwabe, 1993, 258–70.

—(ed.), *Le matérialisme du XVIIIe siècle et la littérature clandestine*, Paris, Vrin, 1982.

Blom, Hans Willem, *Spinoza en de la Court*. Mededelingen XLII vanwege het Spinozahuis, Leiden, Brill, 1981.

—, 'Le contexte historique du *De jure ecclesiasticorum*', in *Du droit des Ecclésiastiques*, ed. Blom, Butori, Lagrée, Moreau and Lazzeri, 1991, IX–XXI.

—, *Causality and Morality in Politics; the Rise of Naturalism in Dutch Seventeenth-Century Political Thought*, PhD dissertation, University of Utrecht, 1995.

Blom, Hans Willem and Ivo W. Wildenberg, *Pieter de la Court in zijn tijd. Aspecten van een veelzijdig publicist (1618–1685)*, Amsterdam/Maarssen, APA-Holland Univerisity Press, 1986.

Blom, Frans and Henk Looiesteijn, 'Ordinary People in the New World: The City of Amsterdam, Colonial Policy, and Initiatives from Below', in Jacob and Secretan (eds), *In Praise of Ordinary People*, 2013, 203–35.

Bock, Gisela, Quentin Skinner and Maurizio Viroli (eds), *Machiavelli and Republicanism*, Cambridge, Cambridge University Press, 1990.

Boehm, Rudolf, '"Dieses war die Ethic und zwar Niederländisch, wie sie Spinoza anfangs verferttiget". Spinozas "Korte Verhandeling" – eine Übersetzung aus einem lateinischen Urtext?', *Studia Philosophica Gandensia* 5, 1967, 175–206.

Boer, Pim den, 'Adriaan Koerbagh and the Comparative History of Concepts – The Past and the Future', *History of Concepts Newsletter* 6, 2003, 20–3.

—, 'Le dictionnaire libertin d'Adriaen Koerbagh', in Secretan, Dagron and Bove (eds), *Qu'est-ce que les Lumières "radicales"?*, 2007, 105–29.

Bonnerot, Olivier H., 'L'imposture de l'Islam et l'esprit des Lumières', in J. P. Schneider et al. (eds), *Études sur le XVIIIe siècle*, Strasbourg, publications de la faculté des lettres de Strasbourg, 1980, 101–14.

Bordoli, Roberto, 'Account of a Curious Traveller on the Libertijnen Milieu of Amsterdam', *Studia Spinozana* 10, 1994, 175–82.

—, *Ragione e scrittura tra Descartes e Spinoza. Saggio sulla "Philosophia S. Scripturae Interpres" di Lodewijk Meyer e sulla sua recezione*, Milan, FrancoAngeli, 1997.

—, 'Tra democrazia apparente e tirannia. Spinoza e la letteratura repubblicana', *Intersezioni. Rivista di storia delle idee* XXXII/3, 2012, 331–54.

BIBLIOGRAPHY 309

—, 'The Monopoly of Social Affluence. The Jus circa sacra around Spinoza', in Lavaert and Schröder (eds), *The Dutch Legacy*, 2017, 121–49.

Borghero, Carlo, '"Ragione classica" e libertinismo', *Giornale critico della filosofia italiana* 81, 2002, 367–88.

Bossers, Anton, 'Nil Volentibus Arduum, Lodewijk Meyer en Adriaan Koerbagh', *Opstellen over de Koninklijke Bibliotheek en andere Studies*, Hilversum, Verloren, 1986, 374–83.

Bostrenghi, Daniela (ed.), *Hobbes e Spinoza. Scienza e politica*, Naples, Bibliopolis, 1992.

Bostrenghi, Daniela, Venanzio Raspa, Cristina Santinelli and Stefano Visentin (eds), *Spinoza. La potenza del comune*, Hildesheim/Zurich/New York, Olms, 2012.

Boucheron, Patrick, *Léonard et Machiavel*, Paris, Verdier, 2008.

Bove, Laurent, *La stratégie du conatus. Affirmation et résistance chez Spinoza*, Paris, Vrin, 1996.

—, 'Le réalisme ontologique de la durée chez Spinoza lecteur de Machiavel', in Bove (ed.), *La recto ratio. Criticiste et spinoziste?*, Paris, PUF, 1999, 47–64.

—, 'Boulainvilliers lecteur de Spinoza. Analyse politique et forme paradoxale de la radicalité dans la première moitié du XVIIIe siècle', in Secretan, Dagron and Bove (eds), *Qu'est-ce que les Lumières "radicales"?*, 2007, 373–88.

—, 'Politique: "j'entends par là une vie humaine". Démocratie & orthodoxie chez Spinoza', in Yann Moulier Boutang (ed.), *Politiques des multitudes. Démocratie, intelligence collective & puissance de la vie à l'heure du capitalisme cognitif*, Paris, Éditions Amsterdam, 2007, 517–24.

Bove, Laurent, Pierre-François Moreau and Charles Ramon, 'Le *Traité politique*: une radicalisation conceptuelle?', in Jaquet, Sévérac and Suhamy (eds), *La multitude libre*, Paris, Éditions Amsterdam, 2008, 27–44.

Bredekamp, Horst, *Thomas Hobbes: Der Leviathan. Das Urbild des modernen Staates und seine Gegenbilder. 1651–2001*, Berlin, De Gruyter, 2012.

Brummer, Rudolf, *Studien zur französischen Aufklärungsliteratur im Anschluss an J. A. Naigeon*, Breslau, Priebatsch, 1932.

Bunge, Wiep van, 'On the Early Dutch Receptions of the *Tractatus Theologico-Politicus*', *Studia Spinozana* 5, 1989, 225–52.

—, 'Van Velthuysen, Batelier and Bredenburg on Spinoza's Interpretation of the Scriptures', in Cristofolini (ed.), *L'hérésie spinoziste*, 1991, 49–65.

—, 'The Absurdity of Spinozism: Spinoza and his First Dutch Critics', *Intellectual News* 2, 1997, 18–26.

BIBLIOGRAPHY

—, *From Stevin to Spinoza. An Essay on Philosophy in the Seventeenth-Century Dutch Republic*, Leiden, Brill, 2001.

—(ed.), *The Early Enlightenment in the Dutch Republic, 1650–1750*, Leiden/Boston, Brill, 2003.

—, 'Introduction', in Koerbagh, *A Light Shining in Dark Places*, 2011, 1–38.

—, *Spinoza. Past and Present. Essays on Spinoza, Spinozism, and Spinoza Scholarship*, Leiden/Boston, Brill, 2012.

Bunge, Wiep van and Wim Klever (eds), *Disguised and Overt Spinozism Around 1700*, Leiden/New York/Cologne, Brill, 1996.

Bunge, Wiep van et al. (eds), *The Dictionary of Seventeenth and Eighteenth-Century Dutch Philosophers*, Bristol, Thoemmes, 2003.

Bunge, Wiep van et al. (eds), *The Continuum Companion to Spinoza*, London/New York, Continuum, 2011.

Burckhardt, Jacob, *The Civilisation of the Renaissance in Italy* (1860), trans. S. G. C. Middlemore, London, Swan Sonnenschein & Co., 1892.

Burke, Peter, *The Italian Renaissance*, Cambridge, Polity Press, 1986.

Busson, Henri, *La religion des classiques (1660–1685)*, Paris, PUF, 1948.

Cambi, Franco, 'Gli Orti Oricellari: un cenacolo formativo del Rinascimento', *Educazione. Giornale di pedagogia critica* 4/1, 2015, 7–28.

Cantimori, Delio, 'Rhetoric and Politics in Italian Humanism', *Journal of the Warburg Institute*, 1937–8, 83–102.

Canziani, Guido, 'La critica della 'civiltà' nel *Theophrastus redivivus* (II): ordine naturale e legalità civile', in Gregory et al. (eds), *Ricerche su letteratura libertina*, 1981, 297–303.

Canziani, Guido and Gianni Paganini, 'Introduzione', in *Theophrastus redivivus*, 1981, XV–CXXIII.

Caporali, Riccardo, Vittorio Morfino and Stefano Visentin (eds), *Spinoza: individuo e moltitudine*, Cesena, Il Ponte Vecchio, 2007.

Carparelli, Mario, 'Dalla definizione alla demolizione del concetto di Dio tra teologia e filosofia', in Vanini, *Tutte le opere*, 2010, 1821–47.

—, 'Vanini e la "Prudenza" di Cristo: da Cardano a d'Holbach', *Problemata* 4/3, 2013, 210–20.

Catalogus van de bibliotheek der Vereniging Het Spinozahuis te Rijnsburg, Leiden, Brill, 1965.

Cavaillé, Jean-Pierre, 'Le prince des athées. Vanini et Machiavel', in Sfez and Senellart (eds), *L'enjeu Machiavel*, 2001, 59–72.

—, 'Libertinage ou lumières radicales', in Secretan, Dagron and Bove (eds), *Qu'est-ce que les Lumières "radicales"?*, 2007, 61–104

—, *Postures libertines. La culture des esprits forts*, Toulouse, Anacharsis, 2011.

BIBLIOGRAPHY 311

—, 'Combat antireligieux et athéisme dans le Theophrastus Redivivus (1659)', *Les Dossiers du Grihl. Les dossiers de Jean-Pierre Cavaillé, Libertinage, athéisme, irréligion. Essais et bibliographie*, Online 1/9/2015, https://journals.openedition.org/dossiersgrihl/261.

Chabod, Federico, *Scritti su Machiavelli*, Turin, Einaudi, 1964.

Charbonnel, Jean-Roger, *La pensée italienne au XVIe siècle. Le courant libertin*, Paris, Champion, 1919.

Charles-Daubert, Françoise, 'Les principales sources de L'Esprit de Spinosa', in Groupe de recherches spinozistes 1, *Lire et traduire Spinoza*, Paris, Presses de l'Université de Paris Sorbonne, 1989, 61–108.

—, 'L'image de Spinoza dans la littérature clandestine et l'*Esprit de Spinoza*', in Bloch (ed.), *Spinoza au XVIIIe siècle*, 1990, 51–74.

—, 'Les Traités des trois imposteurs aux XVIIe et XVIIIe siècles', in Guido Canziani (ed), *Filosofia e religione nella letteratura clandestina. Secoli XVII e XVIII*, Milan, FrancoAngeli, 1994, 291–336.

—, 'Les libertins érudits dans 'L'esprit de Spinosa', in McKenna and Mothu (eds), *La philosophie clandestine*, 1997, 415–24.

—, *Le "Traité des trois imposteurs" et "L'Esprit de Spinosa". Philosophie clandestine entre 1678 et 1768*, Oxford, Voltaire Foundation, 1999.

Clair, Pierre, 'Spinoza à travers les journaux en langue française à la fin du XVIIe siècle', *Cahiers Spinoza* 2, 1978, 207–39.

Colonna d'Istria, François-Marie, 'Introduction'; 'Appendice II & III', in Spinoza, *Éthique*, 1907, VII–XLIII; 367–74.

Cristofolini, Paolo (ed.), *L'hérésie spinoziste. La discussion sur le* Tractatus theologico-politicus, *1670–1677, et la réception immédiate du Spinozisme*, Amsterdam/Maarssen, APA-Holland University Press, 1991.

—, 'Le parole-chiave del *Trattato politico* e le traduzioni moderne', in Totaro (ed.), *Spinoziana*, 1997, 23–38.

—, 'Spinoza et le "très pénétrant florentin"', in Cristofolini, *Spinoza edonista*, Pisa, ETS, 2002, 25–40.

Curley, Edwin, 'A Good Man is Hard to Find', *Proceedings and Addresses of the American Philosophical Association* 65, 1991, 29–45.

—, '*I Durst Not Write So Boldly*', in Bostrenghi (ed.), *Hobbes e Spinoza*, 1992, 497–594.

—, 'Troublesome Terms for Translators in the Tractatus theologico-politicus', in Totaro (ed.), *Spinoziana*, 1997, 39–62.

—, 'Editorial Prefaces', in Spinoza, *The Collected Works of Spinoza*, II, ed. Curley, 2016.

Curley, Edwin and Pierre-François Moreau (eds), *Spinoza: Issues and Directions*, Leiden/New York/København/Köln, Brill, 1990.

312   BIBLIOGRAPHY

Damisch, Hubert, *L'origine de la perspective*, Paris, Flammarion, 1987.

Daussy, Hugues, *Les huguenots et le roi: le combat politique de Philippe Duplessis-Mornay (1572–1600)*, Geneva, Droz, 2002.

Deborin, Abram, 'Die Weltanschauung Spinozas', in August Thalheimer and Abram Deborin, *Spinozas Stellung in der Vorgeschichte des dialektischen Materialismus*, Vienna/Berlin, Verlag für Literatur und Politik, 1928, 40–74.

Deleuze, Gilles, *Spinoza et le problème de l'expression*, Paris, Minuit, 1968.

—, *Spinoza. Philosophie pratique*, Paris, Minuit, 1981.

—, *Pourparlers 1972–1990*, Paris, Minuit, 1990/2003.

Del Lucchese, Filippo, 'S'accoutumer à la diversité. Figures de la multitude chez Machiavel et Spinoza', *Multitudes* 13, 2003, 141–9.

—, *Tumulti e indignatio. Conflitto, diritto e moltitudine in Machiavelli e Spinoza*, Milan, Ghibli, 2004.

—(ed.), *Storia politica della moltitudine. Spinoza e la modernità*, Roma, Derive Approdi, 2009.

—, 'The Revolutionary Foundation of Political Modernity: Machiavelli, Spinoza, and Constituent Power', in Melamed and Sharp (eds), *Spinoza's Political Treatise*, 2018, 190–203.

Del Lucchese, Filippo, Fabio Frosini and Vittorio Morfino (eds), *The Radical Machiavelli: Politics, Philosophy, and Language*, Leiden/Boston, Brill, 2015.

Den Uyl, Douglas J., *Power, State and Freedom. An Interpretation of Spinoza's Political Philosophy*, Assen, Van Gorcum, 1983.

Dethier, Hubert, 'De kritiek van de godsdienst als maatschappijkritiek. Vanini's utopistische toekomstvisie', *Tijdschrift voor de studie van de Verlichting* 2, 1974, 170–93.

—, 'Introduction à l'étude de l'oeuvre de Pietro Pomponazzi (1462–1525) et de Giulio Cesare Vanini (1585–1619)', *Tijdschrift voor de studie van de Verlichting en van het vrije denken* 14/15, 1986/7, 102–40.

Dethier, Hubert and Hubert Vandenbossche (eds), *Woordenboek van Belgische en Nederlandse Vrijdenkers* I & II, Brussels, VUB, 1979/82.

Dierse, Ulrich, 'Die Machiavelli-Rezeption und -Interpretation im 19. Jahrhundert, besonders in Deutschland', in *Ethica & Politica / Ethics and Politics* XVII 3, 2015, 116–48.

Dijn, Herman De, 'Was Van den Enden het meesterbrein achter Spinoza?', *Algemeen Nederlands Tijdschrift voor Wijsbegeerte* 1, 1994, 71–4.

Dionisotti, Carlo, *Machiavellerie. Storia e fortuna di Machiavelli*, Turin, Einaudi, 1980.

Donné, Boris, *Vanini, portrait au noir*, Paris, Éditions Allia, 2019.

Dotti, Ugo, *Niccolò Machiavelli. La fenomenologia del potere*, Milan, Feltrinelli, 1979.

Ducheyne, Steffen, 'Curing Pansophia through Eruditum Nescire: Bernard Nieuwentijt's (1654–1718) Epistemology of Modesty', *HOPOS: The Journal of the International Society for the History of Philosophy of Science* 7/2, 2017, 272–301.

Dunin-Borkowski, Stanislaus von, *Der junge De Spinoza. Leben und Werdegang im Lichte der Weltphilosophie*, Münster, Aschendorffsche Buchhandlung, 1910.

—, 'Nachlese zur ältesten Geschichte des Spinozismus', *Archiv für Geschichte der Philosophie* 24, 1911, 61–98.

—, *Spinoza nach dreihundert Jahren*, Berlin/Bonn, Dümmlers Verlag, 1932.

—, *Aus den Tagen Spinozas. Geschehnisse, Gestalten, Gedankenwelt*, Münster, Aschendorffsche Verlagsbuchhandlung, 1933.

—, *Spinoza. Band III. Aus den Tagen Spinozas. II. Teil. Das neue Leben*, Münster, Aschendorffsche Verlagsbuchhandlung, 1935.

Esposito, Roberto, *Ordine e conflitto. Machiavelli e la letteratura politica del Rinascimento italiano*, Naples, Liguori, 1984.

—, *Living Thought: The Origins and Actuality of Italian Philosophy*, trans. Zakiya Hanafi, Stanford, CA, Stanford University Press, 2012.

Flam, Leopold, 'De Toland à d'Holbach', *Tijdschrift voor de studie van de Verlichting* 1, 1973, 33–50.

—, *Filosofie van de eros*, Antwerpen, Ontwikkeling, 1973.

Fontana, Alessandro, *L'exercice de la pensée. Machiavel, Leopardi, Foucault*, Paris, Publications de la Sorbonne, 2015.

Foucault, Didier, *Un philosophe libertin dans l'Europe baroque. Giulio Cesare Vanini*, Paris, Champion, 2003.

—, 'Sources italiennes du libertinisme français dénoncées par les religieux Garasse et Mersenne autour de 1620', Journées d'étude FRAMESPA-Il Laboratorio 14/12/2012, *Autour du libertinisme – circulations transalpine de la littérature philosophique (XVIIe–XVIIIe siècles)*, https://halshs.archives-ouvertes.fr/halshs-01717252/document, 1–14.

Foucault, Michel, *L'ordre du discours*, Paris, Gallimard, 1971.

—, *"Il faut défendre la société"*. Cours au Collège de France (1975–6), Paris, Gallimard, 1997.

Fournel, Jean-Louis and Jean-Claude Zancarini, 'Commentaires et notes', in Machiavel, *De principatibus. Le Prince*, 2000, 213–509.

Francès, Madeleine, *Spinoza dans les pays néerlandais de la seconde moitié du XVIIe siècle*, Paris, Librairie Félix Alcan, 1937.

Freudenthal, Jakob, *Die Lebensgeschichte Spinoza's in Quellenschriften, Urkunden und nichtamtlichen Nachrichten*, Leipzig, Veit, 1899.

314 BIBLIOGRAPHY

—, *Die Lebensgeschichte Spinoza's*, ed. Manfred Walther, Stuttgart-Bad Cannstatt, Frommann-Holzboog, 2006.

Fukuoka, Atsuko, *The Sovereign and the Prophets. Spinoza on Grotian and Hobbesian Biblical Argumentation*, Leiden/Boston, Brill, 2018.

Galli, Carlo, *Contingenza e necessità nella ragione politica moderna*, Rome-Bari, Laterza, 2009.

Gallicet Calvetti, Carla, *Spinoza lettore del Machiavelli*, Milan, Vita e pensiero, 1972.

Garin, Eugenio, *Dal Rinascimento all'Illuminismo. Studi e ricerche*, Pisa, Nistri-Lischi, 1970.

Gatens, Moira, 'The Condition of Human Nature', in Melamed and Sharp (eds), *Spinoza's Political Treatise*, 2018, 47–60.

Gatti, Hilary, *Ideas of Liberty in Early Modern Europe. From Machiavelli to Milton*, Princeton, Princeton University Press, 2015.

Gatto, Alfredo, 'La fictio del sacro. Il Theophrastus Redivivus e il fondamento della sovranità politica', *Giornale Critico di Storia delle Idee* 5, 2011, 67–83.

Gebhardt, Carl, 'Einleitung zu den beiden Traktaten', in Spinoza, *Opera* V, 1987, 238–41.

—, 'Kommentare *TTP*; *TP*', in Spinoza, *Opera* V, 1987, 1–132; 133–96.

—, *Spinoza – Lebensbeschreibungen und Dokumente*, ed. Manfred Walther, Hamburg, Felix Meiner Verlag, 1998.

Genette, Gérard, 'Discours du récit', in Genette, *Figures III*, Paris, Seuil, 1972, 67–282.

Gengoux, Nicole, 'L'athéisme du "Theophrastus", une éthique naturelle au fondement de la morale évangélique', *Libertinage et philosophie* 11, 2009, 229–54.

—, 'Fortune et infortune du "Theophrastus redivivus"', *La lettre clandestine* 18, 2010, 293–315.

—, *Un athéisme philosophique à l'Âge classique: le* Theophrastus redivivus, *1659*, 2 vols, Paris, Champion, 2014.

Gengoux, Nicole and Pierre-François Moreau (eds), *Entre la Renaissance et les Lumières, le* Theophrastus redivivus (*1659*), Paris, Champion, 2014.

Gensini, Stefano, 'The Linguistic Naturalism of Theophrastus redivivus (1659?)', *Historiographia Linguistica. International Journal for the History of the Language Sciences* XXIII, 1996, 301–20.

Gerber, Adolph, *Niccolò Machiavelli: Die Handschriften, Ausgaben und Übersetzungen seiner Werke im 16. und 17. Jahrhundert*, Gotha, Gotha-Perthes, 1912–13.

Giancotti Boscherini, Emilia, *Lexicon Spinozanum*, 2 vols, The Hague, Martinus Nijhoff, 1970.

Gilbert, Felix, *Machiavelli e il suo tempo*, Bologna, Il Mulino, 1964.

Ginzburg, Carlo, *Miti emblemi spie. Morfologia e storia*, Turin, Einaudi, 1986.

—, *Wooden Eyes: Nine Reflections on Distance*, trans. Martin Ryle and Kate Soper, London, Verso, 2005.

—, *Paura, reverenza, terrore. Cinque saggi di iconografia politica*, Milan, Adelphi, 2015.

—, *Nondimanco. Machiavelli, Pascal*, Milan, Adelphi, 2018.

Gobert, Catherine, 'La généalogie de l'histoire des Ajaoïens', *La Lettre clandestine* 16, 2008, 225–59.

Goldenbaum, Ursula, 'Die *Commentatiuncula de judice* als Leibnizens erste philosophische Auseinandersetzung mit Spinoza nebst der Mitteilung über ein neuaufgefundenes Leibnizstück', *Labora diligenter, Studia Leibnitiana* Sonderheft 29, Wiesbaden, Steiner, 1999, 61–127.

Gootjes, Albert, 'The First Orchestrated Attack on Spinoza: Johannes Melchioris and the Cartesian Network in Utrecht', *Journal of the History of Ideas*, 79, 1, 2018, 23–43.

Gramsci, Antonio, *Note sul Machiavelli sulla politica e sullo stato moderno*, Rome, Riuniti, 1977.

Gregory, Tullio, *Theophrastus Redivivus. Erudizione e ateismo nel seicento*, Naples, Morano, 1979.

—, '"Omnis philosophia mortalitatis adstipulatur opinioni": quelques considérations sur le *Theophrastus redivivus*', in Bloch (ed.), *Le matérialisme du XVIIIe siècle*, 1982, 213–18.

—, *Etica e religione nella critica libertina*, Naples, Guida, 1986.

Gregory, Tullio et al. (eds), *Ricerche su letteratura libertina e letteratura clandestina nel Seicento*, Florence, La Nuova Italia, 1981.

Grunert, Frank (ed.). *Concepts of (Radical) Enlightenment. Jonathan Israel in Discussion.* Kleine Schriften des IZEA 5/2014, Halle, Mitteldeutscher Verlag, 2014.

Grunwald, Max, *Spinoza in Deutschland*, Berlin, Calvary & Co, 1897.

Gullan-Wuhr, Margaret, 'Spinoza and the Equality of Women', *Theoria* 68, 2008, 91–111.

Haitsma Mulier, Eco O.G., *The Myth of Venice and Dutch Republican Thought in the Seventeenth Century*, Assen, Van Gorcum, 1980.

—, 'De naeuwkeurige consideratie van de gebroeders De la Court. Een nadere beschouwing', *BMGN Low Countries Historical Review* 99/3, 1984, 396–407.

BIBLIOGRAPHY

—, 'A Controversial Republican: Dutch Views of Machiavelli in the Seventeenth and Eighteenth Centuries' in Bock, Skinner and Viroli (eds), *Machiavelli and Republicanism*, 1993, 247–64.

Hale, John Rigby, *Machiavelli and Renaissance Italy*, London, The English University Press, 1961.

Han-Ding, Hong, *Spinoza und die deutsche Philosophie. Untersuchung zur metaphysischen Wirkungsgeschichte des Spinozismus in Deutschland*, Aalen, Scientia Verlag, 1989.

Hardt, Michael and Antonio Negri, *Assembly*, Oxford, Oxford University Press, 2017.

Heck, Paul van, 'In het spoor van Machiavelli: De Politike Discoursen (1662) van Johan en Pieter De la Court', *Lias* 27, 2000, 277–318.

Heertum, Cis van, 'Reading the Career of Johannes Koerbagh: The Auction Catalogue of His Library as a Reflection of his Life', *Lias* 38, 2011, 1–57.

Horkheimer, Max, *Anfänge der bürgerlichen Geschichtsphilosophie* (1930), in Horkheimer, *Gesammelte Schriften 2: Philosophische Frühschriften 1922–1932*, Frankfurt, Fischer [1987] 2012, 177–268.

Israel, Jonathan, *Radical Enlightenment. Philosophy and the Making of Modernity 1650–1750*, Oxford, Oxford University Press, 2001.

—, 'The Early Dutch Enlightenment as a Factor in the Wider European Enlightenment', in Van Bunge (ed.), *The Early Enlightenment in the Dutch Republic*, 2003, 215–30.

—, *Enlightenment Contested. Philosophy, Modernity, and the Emancipation of Man 1670–1752*. Oxford, Oxford University Press, 2006.

—, 'The Early Dutch and German Reaction to the *Tractatus Theologico-Politicus*: Foreshadowing the Enlightenment's More General Spinoza Reception?', in Melamed and Rosenthal (eds), *Spinoza's Theological-Political Treatise*, 2010, 72–100.

—, 'Spinoza and the Religious Radical Enlightenment', in Sarah Mortimer and John Robertson (eds), *The Intellectual Consequences of Religious Heterodoxy, 1600–1750*, Leiden/Boston/Cologne, Brill, 2012, 184–204.

Israel, Jonathan and Martin Mulsow (eds), *Radikalaufklärung*, Berlin, Suhrkamp, 2014.

Jacob, Margaret C., *The Radical Enlightenment. Pantheists, Freemasons and Republicans*, London/Boston/Sidney, Allen & Unwin, 1981.

Jacob, Margaret C. and Catherine Secretan (eds), *In Praise of Ordinary People. Early Modern Britain and the Dutch Republic*, New York, Palgrave Macmillan, 2013.

Jacobs, Jaap, *The Colony of New Netherland. A Dutch Settlement in Seventeenth-Century America*, Leiden/Boston, Brill, 2004.

BIBLIOGRAPHY   317

James, Susan, *Spinoza on Philosophy, Religion, and Politics. The Theologico-Political Treatise*, Oxford, Oxford University Press, 2012.

—, 'Politically Mediated Affects: Envy in Spinoza's Tracatus Politicus', in Melamed and Sharp (eds), *Spinoza's Political Treatise*, 2018, 61–77.

Jaquet, Chantal, Pascal Sévérac and Ariel Suhamy (eds), *La multitude libre. Nouvelles lectures du* Traité politique, Paris, Éditions Amsterdam, 2008.

Jongeneelen, Gerrit H., 'An Unknown Pamphlet of Adriaan Koerbagh', *Studia Spinozana* 3, 1987, 405–15.

—, 'La philosophie politique d'Adrien Koerbagh', *Cahiers Spinoza* 6, 1991, 247–67.

—, 'Adriaan Koerbagh, een voorloper van de Verlichting?', *Geschiedenis van de wijsbegeerte in Nederland* 5, 1994, 27–34.

—, 'Disguised Spinozism in Adriaen Verwer's *Momaensicht*', in Van Bunge and Klever (eds), *Disguised and Overt Spinozism*, 1996, 15–21.

Kahn, Victoria, 'Machiavelli's Afterlife and Reputation to the Eighteenth Century', in John M. Najemy (ed.), *The Cambridge Companian to Machiavelli*, Cambridge, Cambridge University Press, 244–5.

Kessler, Eckhardt, 'Humanistische Denkelemente in der Politik der italienischen Renaissance', *Wolfenbütteler Renaissance Mitteilungen* 7, 1983, 34–44; 85–92; 89.

Klever, Wim, 'Spinoza and Van den Enden in Borch's Diary in 1661 and 1662', *Studia Spinozana* 5, 1989, 311–25.

—, 'Proto-Spinoza Franciscus van den Enden', *Studia Spinozana* 6, 1990, 281–8.

—, 'A New Source of Spinozism: Franciscus Van den Enden', *Journal of the History of Philosophy* 29/4, 1991, 613–31.

—, 'Inleiding', in Van den Enden, *Vrije Politijke Stellingen*, 1992, 11–119.

—, *Mannen rond Spinoza 1650–1700. Presentatie van een emanciperende generatie*, Hilversum, Verloren, 1997.

Kordela, Kiarina A. and Dimitris Vardoulakis, Dimitris (eds), *Spinoza's Authority Volume I: Resistance and Power in* Ethics, London/New York, Bloomsbury, 2018.

Kors, Alan Charles, *Atheism in France, 1650–1729. Volume I: The Orthodox Sources of Disbelief*, Princeton, Princeton University Press, 1990.

Kossman, Ernst Heinrich, *Politieke Theorie in het zeventiende-eeuwse Nederland*, Amsterdam, Noord-Hollandse Uitgevers Maatschappij, 1960.

—, *Political Thought in the Dutch Republic. Three Studies*, Amsterdam, Koninklijke Nederlandse Akademie van Wetenschappen, 2000.

Kozul, Mladen, *Les Lumières imaginaires. Holbach et la traduction*, Oxford, Voltaire Foundation, 2016.

Krop, Henri, 'The *Philosophia S. Scripturae Interpres* between Humanist Scholarship and Cartesian Science: Lodewijk Meyer and the Emancipatory Power of Philology', in Lavaert and Schröder (eds), *The Dutch Legacy*, 2017, 90–120.

Lagrée, Jacqueline: 'Louis Meyer et la *Philosophia S. Scripturae Interpres*': projet cartésien, horizon spinoziste', *Revue des Sciences philosophiques et théologiques* 71/1, 1987, 31–43.

—, 'Christian Kortholt (1633–1694) et son *De tribus impostoribus magnis*', in Cristofolini (ed.), *L'hérésie spinoziste*, 1991, 169–83.

—, 'Du magistre spirituel a la "Medicina Mentis": ou du rapport entre le "jus circa sacra", le magistère spirituel et la liberté de penser chez Grotius, Hobbes, Constans, Spinoza', in Bostrenghi (ed.), *Hobbes e Spinoza*, 1992, 595–621.

—, *Spinoza et le débat religieux*, Rennes, Presses universitaires de Rennes, 2004.

—, 'Spinoza l'imposteur libertin?', in Berns, Staquet and Weis (eds), *Libertin!*, 2013, 193–209.

Lagrée, Jacqueline and Pierre-François Moreau, 'Spinoza ou la puissance de la traduction', in Jacques Moutaux and Olivier Bloch (eds), *Traduire les philosophes*, Paris, Sorbonne, 2000, 377–91.

Lanson, Gustave, 'Questions diverses sur l'histoire de l'esprit philosophique en France avant 1750', *Revue d'histoire littéraire de la France* 19, 1912, 1–12; 293–317.

Lantoine, Jacques-Louis, *L'intelligence de la pratique. Le concept de disposition chez Spinoza*, Lyon, ENS Éditions, 2019.

Laudani, Raffaele, *Disobbedienza*, Bologna, Il Mulino, 2010.

Laursen, John Chris, 'Review of Marcellino Rodriguez Donis, *Materialismo y ateismo. La filosofia de un libertino del siglo XVII*', *Fragmentos de filosofia* 6, 2008, 171–4.

—, 'Cynicism in the *Theophrastus redivivus*', in Gengoux and Moreau (eds), *Entre la Renaissance et les Lumières*, 2014, 47–64.

—, 'Spinoza et les "mensonges officieux" dans les manuscrits clandestins', *La Lettre clandestine* 26, 2018, 81–98.

Lavaert, Sonja, *Het perspectief van de multitude. Agamben, Machiavelli, Negri, Spinoza, Virno*, Brussels, VUBPress, 2011.

—, 'Radical Enlightenment, Enlightened Subversion, and Spinoza', *Philosophica* 89, 2014, 49–102.

—, '"Lieutenants" of the Commonwealth: A Political Reading of *De jure ecclesiasticorum*', in Lavaert and Schröder (eds), *The Dutch Legacy*, 2017, 150–64.

—, 'The Logic of Conflict, against the Logic of War', in Danny Praet (ed.), *Philosophy of War and Peace*, Brussels, VUBPress, 2017, 105–19.

—, 'Entre clandestinité et sphère publique. Le cas Koerbagh', *La Lettre clandestine* 26, 2018, 33–48.

—, 'Koerbagh, Adriaan', in Secretan and Frijhoff (eds), *Dictionnaire des Pays-Bas au siècle d'or*, 2018, 409–11.

—, 'Metafysica van het subject, een misleidende spraakverwarring', in Paul Willemarck (ed.), *Wat moet? En wat is nodig? Over de filosofie van Rudolf Boehm*, Antwerp/Apeldoorn, Garant, 2018, 141–72.

—, 'La traduction comme intrigue philosophique et stratégie des Lumières. De Vanini au *Traité des trois imposteurs*, en passant par Spinoza et son *Esprit*', *La Lettre clandestine* 27, 2019, 109–26.

—, 'Multitude. De omkering van Spinoza, in de geest van Machiavelli', in Yoni Van den Eede and Karl Verstrynge (eds), *De maakbare moraal. Visies op ethiek en humanisme*, Brussels, VUBPress, 2019, 71–108.

—, 'Prelude voor een democratische revolutie. Het politiek-filosofische project van Frans van den Enden', in Henri Krop (ed.), *De kring van Spinoza, een balans van veertig jaar onderzoek*, Rijnsburg, Uitgeverij Spinozahuis, 2019, 63–74.

Lavaert, Sonja and Winfried Schröder (eds), *The Dutch Legacy. Radical Thinkers of the 17th Century and the Enlightenment*, Boston/Leiden, Brill, 2017.

Lazzeri, Christian, 'L. A. Constans entre Hobbes et Spinoza', in *Du droit des Ecclésiastiques*, ed. Blom, Butori, Lagrée, Moreau and Lazzeri, 1991, XXIIV–XLI.

Leeuwenburgh, Bart, *Het noodlot van een ketter. Adriaan Koerbagh (1633–1669)*, Nijmegen, Vantilt, 2013.

Lefort, Claude, *Le travail de l'œuvre Machiavel*, Paris, Gallimard, 1972.

Lenger, Marie-Thérèse, *Contribution à la bibliographie des éditions anciennes (XVIe et XVIIe siècles) des œuvres de Machiavel: catalogue critique conservés dans les bibliothèques belges*, Brussels, 1973.

Licata, Giovanni (ed.), *L'averroismo in età moderna (1400–1700)*, Macerata, Quodlibet, 2013.

Linde, Antonius van der, *Benedictus Spinoza. Bibliografie*, The Hague, Martinus Nijhoff, 1871.

Lupoli, Agostino, 'La nozione di "popolo corrotto" ("corrupted people") in Machiavelli e Hobbes', in Bianchi and Postigliola (eds), *Dopo Machiavelli*, 2008, 153–85.

McCormick, John P., *Machiavellian Democracy*, Cambridge, Cambridge University Press, 2011.

320   BIBLIOGRAPHY

Macek, Josef, *Machiavelli e il machiavellismo*, Florence, La Nuova Italia, 1980.
Macherey, Pierre, *Avec Spinoza. Études sur la doctrine et l'histoire du Spinozisme*, Paris, PUF, 1992.
McKenna, Antony, 'Spinoza in Clandestine Manuscripts: a Bibliographical Survey of Recent Research', in Van Bunge and Klever (eds), *Disguised and Overt Spinozism*, 1996, 305–20.
McKenna, Antony and Alain Mothu (eds), *La Philosophie clandestine à l'Age classique*, Oxford, Voltaire Foundation, 1997.
Mack Smith, Denis, *Storia della Sicilia medievale e moderna*, Rome/Bari, Laterza, 2000.
Malcolm, Noel, *Aspects of Hobbes*, Oxford, Oxford University Press, 2002.
Malettke, Klaus, *Opposition und Konspiration unter Ludwig XIV. Studien zu Kritik und Widerstand gegen System und Politik des französischen Königs während der ersten Hälfte seiner persönlichen Regierung*, Göttingen, Vandenhoeck & Ruprecht, 1976.
Matheron, Alexandre, *Anthropologie et politique au XIIe siècle. Études sur Spinoza*, Paris, Vrin, 1985.
—, *Individu et communauté chez Spinoza*, Paris, Minuit, 1988.
—, 'Le problème de l'évolution de Spinoza du *Traité théologico-politique* au *Traité politique*', in Curley and Moreau (eds), *Spinoza: Issues and Directions*, 1990, 258–70.
—, 'À propos de Spinoza. Entretien avec Laurent Bove & Pierre-François Moreau', in Yann Moulier Boutang (ed.), *Politiques des multitudes*, 2007, 499–516.
—, *Études sur Spinoza et les philosophies de l'âge classique*, Lyon, ENS éditions, 2011.
Maury, Alfred, 'Une conspiration républicaine sous Louis XIV – Le Complot du Chevalier de Rohan et de Latréamont', *Revue des deux mondes* 76, 1886, 376–406.
Mauthner, Fritz, *Der Atheismus und seine Geschichte im Abendlande*, I–IV, Stuttgart/Berlin, Deutsche Verlagsanstalt, 1920–3.
Méchoulan, Henry (ed.), *Amsterdam XVIIe siècle. Marchands et philosophes: les bénéfices de la tolérance*, Paris, Éditions Autrement, 1993.
Meinecke, Friedrich, *Die Idee der Staatsräson in der neueren Geschichte*, Munich, Oldenbourg Verlag, 1957.
Meininger, Jan V. and Guido Van Suchtelen, *Liever met wercken, als met woorden. De levensreis van doctor Franciscus van den Enden*, Weesp, Heureka, 1980.
Meinsma, Koenraad Oege, *Spinoza en zijn kring. Historisch-kritische studiën over Hollandse vrijgeesten*. Utrecht, Hes Publishers [1896] 1980.

Melamed, Yitzhak and Michael Rosenthal (eds), *Spinoza's Theological-Political Treatise. A Critical Guide*, Cambridge, Cambridge University Press, 2010.

Melamed, Yitzhak and Hasana Sharp (eds), *Spinoza's Political Treatise. A Critical Guide*, Cambridge, Cambridge University Press, 2018.

Menzel, Adolph, 'Machiavelli und Spinoza', *Zeitschrift für das Privat- und öffentliche Recht der Gegenwart* 29, 1902, 566–77.

—, *Beiträge zur Geschichte der Staatslehre*, Vienna/Leipzig, Hölder-Pichler-Tempsky, 1929.

Merleau-Ponty, Maurice, 'Note sur Machiavel', in Merleau-Ponty, *Signes*, Paris, Gallimard, 1960, 267–83.

Mertens, Frank, 'Franciscus van den Enden: tijd voor een herziening van diens rol in het ontstaan van het Spinozisme?', *Tijdschrift voor Filosofie* 56, 1994, 718–38.

—, *Franciscus van den Enden's Brief Account*. 2 vols, PhD Universiteit Gent, 2006.

—, 'Franciscus van den Enden' in Van Bunge et al. (eds), *The Continuum Companion to Spinoza*, 2011, 68–71.

—, *Van den Enden en Spinoza*, Voorschoten, Uitgeverij Spinozahuis, 2012.

—, 'Van den Enden and Religion', in Lavaert and Schröder (eds), *The Dutch Legacy*, 2017, 62–89.

Meyer, Willem, 'Wer war Lucas?', *Archiv für Geschichte der Philosophie* 11/4, 1898, 870–8.

—, 'Lucas, Jean Maximilien', *Nieuw Nederlandsch biografisch woordenboek*, Deel 4, 1918, 934–6.

Mignini, Filippo, 'Een ligt schijnende in duystere plaatsen: Adriaan Koerbagh tra averroismo e libertinismo', in Licata (ed.), *L'averroismo in età moderna*, 2013, 167–200.

Moreau, Pierre-François, 'La notion d'*imperium* dans le *Traité politique*', in Emilia Giancotti (ed.), *Spinoza nel 350° anniversario della nascita*, Naples, Bibliopolis, 1985, 355–66.

—, *Spinoza. L'expérience et l'éternité*, Paris, PUF, 1994.

—, 'Machiavel ou la philosophie', *Revue philosophique de la France et de l'Étranger* 189, 1999, 3–6.

—, 'Althusser et Machiavel: la consistance de l'État', in Sfez and Senellart (eds), *L'enjeu Machiavel*, 2001, 141–8.

—, *Spinoza et le spinozisme*, Paris, PUF, 2003.

—, *Spinoza. État et religion*, Lyon, ENS Éditions, 2005.

—, 'È legittima la resistenza allo Stato?', *Quaderni materialisti* 5, 2006, 49–61.

320

BIBLIOGRAPHY

—, 'Spinoza est-il spinoziste', in Secretan, Dagron and Bove (eds), *Qu'est-ce que les Lumières "radicales"?*, 2007, 289–97.

—, 'Les passions du social: "personnalité de base" et *ingenium*', in Eva Debray, Frédéric Lordon and Kim Sang-Ong-Van-Cung (eds), *Spinoza et les passions du social*, Paris, Éditions Amsterdam, 2019, 303–26.

Morfino, Vittorio, *Il tempo e l'occasione. L'incontro Spinoza Machiavelli*, Milan, LED Edizioni, 2002.

—, *Il tempo della moltitudine. Materialismo e politica prima e dopo Spinoza*, Rome, Manifestolibri, 2005.

—, 'La question du conflit chez Machiavel: de Gramsci et Althusser à Negri', in Zarka and Ion (eds), *Machiavel: le pouvoir et le peuple*, 2015, 175–92.

Mori, Gianluca, 'Boulainvilliers a-t-il traduit l'Éthique ?', *La Lettre clandestine* 3, 1994, 37–9.

—, *L'ateismo dei moderni. Filosofia e negazione di Dio da Spinoza a D'Holbach*, Rome, Carocci, 2016.

Nadler, Steven, *Spinoza. A Life*, Cambridge, Cambridge University Press, 1999.

—, 'Benedictus Pantheissimus' in G. A. J. Rogers, Tom Sorell and Jill Kraye (eds), *Insiders and Outsiders in Seventeenth-Century Philosophy*, New York, Routledge, 2010, 238–56.

—, *A Book Forged in Hell. Spinoza's Scandalous Treatise and the Birth of the Secular Age*, Princeton/Oxford, Princeton University Press, 2011.

Namer, Émile, *Machiavel*, Paris, PUF, 1961.

—, *La Vie et l'œuvre de J. C. Vanini, prince des libertins*, Paris, Vrin, 1980.

Negri, Antonio, *Descartes politico o della ragionevole ideologia*, Milan, Feltrinelli, 1970.

—, *L'anomalia selvaggia. Saggio su potere e potenza*, Milan, Feltrinelli, 1981.

—, *Il potere costituente. Saggio sulle alternative del moderno*, Rome, Manifestolibri [1992] 2002.

—, *Spinoza sovversivo* (1992), in Negri, *Spinoza*, Rome, DerriveApprodi, 1998, 286–378.

—, 'Nécessité & liberté chez Spinoza: quelques alternatives', in Moulier Boutang (ed.), *Politiques des multitudes*, 2007, 525–34.

—, *Spinoza: une hérésie de l'immanence et de la démocratie*. Mededelingen vanwege het Spinozahuis 97, Uitgeverij Spinozahuis, 2009.

—, 'A Different Power to Act', in Kordela and Vardoulakis (eds), *Spinoza's Authority*, 2018, 135–46.

Niewöhner, Friedrich, *Veritas sive Varietas. Lessings Toleranzparabel und das Buch von den drei Betrügern*, Heidelberg, Lambert Schneider Verlag, 1988.

BIBLIOGRAPHY

Nobbs, Douglas, *Theocracy and Toleration: A Study of the Disputes in Dutch Calvinism from 1600 to 1650*, Cambridge, Cambridge University Press, 1938, 245–50.

Nowicki, Andrzej, 'Studia nad Vaninim', *Euhemer* 50, 1966, 23–32.

—, 'Vanini in de zeventiende eeuw en het begrippeninstrumentarium om zijn aanwezigheid in de cultuur te bestuderen', *Tijdschrift voor de studie van de Verlichting* 2, 1974, 132–46.

O'Callaghan, Edmund Bailey, *History of New Netherland; or, New York under the Dutch*, 2 vols, New York, Appleton, 1855.

Olesti, Joseph, 'Presencia de la Boétie en el spinozismo ?', *Astrolabio* 16, 2015, 89–105.

Ostrowiecki-Bah, Hélène, 'Le paratexte du *Theophrastus redivivus*', in McKenna and Mothu (eds), *La Philosophie clandestine*, 1997, 267–78.

—, 'Theophrastus Redivivus. VIe traité: De la vie selon la nature. Notice', in Prévot, Jestaz and Ostrowiecki-Bah (eds), *Libertins du XVIIe siècle*, 2004, 1490–1516.

—, *Le Theophrastus redivivus, érudition et combat antireligieux au XVIIe siècle.* Paris, Champion, 2012.

Otto, Rüdiger, *Studien zur Spinozarezeption in Deutschland im 18. Jahrhundert*, Frankfurt/Main, Peter Lang, 1994.

Paganini, Gianni, 'La critica della civiltà', in Gregory et al. (eds), *Ricerche su letteratura libertina*, 1981, 83–118.

—, 'L'anthropologie naturaliste d'un esprit fort. Thèmes et problèmes pomponaciens dans le Theophrastus redivivus', *XVIIe siècle* 149, 1985, 349–78.

—, '"Legislatores et impostores". Le *Theophrastus redivivus* et la thèse de l'imposture des religions au milieu du XVIIe siècle', in Didier Foucault and Jean-Pierre Cavaillé (eds), *Sources antiques de l'irreligion moderne: le relais italien, XVe-XVIIe siècles*, Toulouse, Collection de l'E.C.R.I.T. 6, 2001, 181–218.

—, 'Il Theophrastus redivivus e Vanini: una lettura selettiva', in Giuseppe Bentivegna et al. (eds), *Filosofia scienza cultura*, Soveria Mannelli, Rubbettino, 2002, 685–98.

—, 'Un athéisme d'ancien régime? Pour une histoire de l'athéisme à part entière: l'héritage de la pensée de la renaissance et l'incrédulité moderne', in Pierre Lurbe and Sylvie Taussig (eds), *La question de l'athéisme au dix-septième siècle*, Turnhout, Brepols, 2004, 105–30.

—, 'Tirannia, sovranità e "disobbedienza" nel pensiero di Hobbes', *Collegium Philosophicum* VIII–IX, 2005, 77–89.

—, *Introduzione alle filosofie clandestine*, Rome/Bari, Laterza, 2008.

324 BIBLIOGRAPHY

—, 'Clandestine Philosophy Before and After the Beginning of the Enlightenment', in Hubertus Busche (ed.), *Departure for Modern Europe. A Handbook of Early Modern Philosophy (1400–1700)*, Hamburg, Felix Meiner Verlag, 2011, 976–85.

—, 'Qu'est-ce qu'un libertin radical? Le *Theophrastus redivivus*', in Berns, Staquet and Weis (eds), *Libertin!*, 2013, 213–30.

Panofsky, Erwin, *Die Perspektive als symbolische Form*, Leipzig, Teubner, 1927.

Pedullà, Gabriele, 'Il divieto di Platone. Niccolò Machiavelli e il discorso dell'anonimo plebeo (*Ist. Fior.* III, 13)', in Jean-Jacques Marchand and Jean-Claude Zancarini (eds), *Storiografia repubblicana fiorentina (1494–1570)*, Genova, Franco Cesati editore, 2003, 209–66.

Petry, Michael John, 'Hobbes and the Early Dutch Spinozists', in Cornelis De Deugd (ed.), *Spinoza's Political and Theological Thought*, Amsterdam/Oxford/New York, North-Holland Publishing Company, 1984, 150–70.

Pincin, Carlo, *Sul testo del Machiavelli. I "Discorsi sopra la prima Deca di Tito Livio"*, in *Atti dell'Accademia delle scienze di Torino. II. Classe di scienze morali, storiche e filologiche*, vol. 96, 1961–2, dispensa I, 71–178; 163–4.

Pintard, René, *Le libertinage érudit dans la première moitié du XVII siècle*, Paris, Boivin, 1943.

Pocock, John Greville Agard, *The Machiavellian Moment. Florentine Political Thought and the Atlantic Republican Tradition*, Princeton, Princeton University Press, 1975.

Pollock, Frederick, 'Spinoza et le machiavélisme', *La revue politique internationale* 11, 1919, 3–11.

Popkin, Richard H., 'Spinoza and the Three Imposters', in Curley and Moreau (eds), *Spinoza: Issues and Directions*, 1990, 347–58.

Préposiet, Jean, *Spinoza et la liberté des hommes*, Paris, Gallimard, 1967.

Procacci, Giuliano, *Studi sulla fortuna del Machiavelli*, Rome, Istituto Storico Italiano per l'Età Moderna e Contemporanea, 1965.

—, *Machiavelli nella cultura europea dell'età moderna*, Rome/Bari, Laterza, 1995.

Proietti, Omero, 'Le 'Philedonius' de Franciscus van den Enden et la formation rhétorico-littéraire de Spinoza (1656–1658)', *Cahiers Spinoza* 6, 1991, 9–82.

—, *Osservazioni, note e congetture sul testo latino e nederlandese del Tractatus politicus*, Dipartimento di filosofia e scienze umane. *Quaderni di ricerca e di didattica* XIII, Macerata, Università di Macerata, 1995.

—, 'La tradizione testuale del *Tractatus politicus*. 'Examinatio' per un'edizione critica', in Totaro (ed.), *Spinoziana*, 1997, 125–53.

BIBLIOGRAPHY 325

—, 'Gerarchia mariana. Nuovi documenti su Franciscus van den Enden', *La Cultura*, 2010, 423–58.

—, *Philedonius, 1657: Spinoza, Van den Enden e i classici latini*, Macerata, Eum, 2010.

Proietti, Omero and Giovanni Licata, *Il carteggio Van Gent-Tschirnhaus (1679–1690). Storia, cronistoria, contesto dell'*editio posthuma *spinoziana*, Macerata, EUM, 2013.

Rahe, Paul A., *Against Throne and Altar: Machiavelli and Political Theory under the English*, Cambridge, Cambridge University Press, 2008.

Raimondi, Fabio, 'Les "tumultes" dans *Le Prince* et dans les *Discours*. Notes pour un lexique machiavélien des luttes', in Zarka and Ion (eds), *Machiavel: le pouvoir et le peuple*, 2015, 157–74.

Raimondi, Francesco Paolo, 'Vanini e il "De tribus impostoribus"', in Raimondi, *Ethos e cultura. Studi in onore di Ezio Riondato* I, Padua, Antenore, 1991, 265–90.

—, 'Bibliografia vaniniana (XX sec.)', in Raimondi (ed.), *Giulio Cesare Vanini*, 2000, 203–36.

—, '*Simulatio* e *dissimulatio* nella tecnica vaniniana della composizione del testo', in Raimondi (ed.), *Giulio Cesare Vanini e il libertinismo*, Lecce, Congedo, 2000, 77–126.

—, 'Monografia introduttiva', in Vanini, *Tutte le opere*, 2010, 320–771.

Ravà, Adolfo, 'Spinoza e Machiavelli', in Ravà, *Studi su Fichte e Spinoza*, Milan, 1958, 91–113.

Rehmann, Jan, 'Power ≠ Power: Against the Mix-Up of Nietzsche and Spinoza', *Critical Sociology* 45/2, 2017, 1–14.

Reitz, Tilman, 'Der politische Traktat in der Diskussion der Gegenwart', in Wolfgang Bartuschat, Stephan Kirste and Manfred Walther (eds), *Naturalismus und Demokratie*, Tübingen, Mohr Siebeck, 2014, 171–202.

Richardson, Brian, 'The Prince and its Italian Readers', in Martin Coyle (ed.), *Niccolò Machiavelli's The Prince. New Interdisciplinary Essays*, Manchester/New York, Manchester University Press, 1995, 18–39.

Röd, Wolfgang, 'Van den Hoves "Politische Waage" und die Modifikation der Hobbesschen Staatsphilosophie bei Spinoza', *History of Philosophy* VIII, 1970, 29–48.

Rodríguez Donis, Marcelino, 'Nature, plaisir et mort dans le Theophrastus redivivus', in Jean Salem (ed.), *L'atomisme au XVIIe et XVIIIe siècles*, Paris, 1999, 73–97.

—, 'Deux épicuriens face à face: l'anonyme du "Theophrastus redivivus" et Gassendi', in *La lettre clandestine* 13, 2004, 193–231.

—, *Materialismo y ateísmo. La filosofía de un libertino del siglo XVII*, Sevilla, Universidad de Sevilla, 2008.

Ruffo-Fiore, Silvia, *Niccolò Machiavelli. An Annotated Bibliography of Modern Criticism and Scholarship*, New York, Greenwood Press, 1990.

Russo, Luigi, *Machiavelli*, Rome/Bari, Laterza [1945] 1988.

Saada, Julie (ed.), *Hobbes, Spinoza, ou, les politiques de la parole*, Lyon, ENS Éditions, 2009.

Saar, Martin, *Die Immanenz der Macht. Politische Theorie nach Spinoza*, Frankfurt/Main, Suhrkamp, 2013.

Sacerdoti, Gilberto, *Sacrificio e sovranità. Teologia e politica nell'Europa di Shakespeare e Bruno*, Turin, Einaudi, 2002.

Salatowsky, Sascha, 'Socinian Headaches: Adriaan Koerbagh and the Antitrinitarians', in Lavaert and Schröder (eds), *The Dutch Legacy*, 2017, 165–203.

Sasso, Gennaro, *Niccolò Machiavelli*, Bologna, Il Mulino, 1980.

Schmeisser, Martin, 'Garasse contre Vanini. Biologie, transformisme et anthropocentrisme dans le *De admirandis*', in Berns, Staquet and Weis (eds), *Libertin!*, 231–47.

Schnepf, Robert, 'Enlightened Radicals: A Possible Difference between Spinoza and Van den Enden' in Grunert (ed.), *Concepts of (Radical) Enlightenment*, 2014, 95–111.

Schröder, Winfried, *Spinoza in der deutschen Frühaufklärung*, Würzburg, Königshausen & Neumann, 1987.

—, 'Einleitung', in *Traktat über die drei Betrüger. Traité des trois imposteurs*, 1992, VII–XLIII.

—, 'Sur quelques traductions anciennes et parfois inconnues du 'Traité des trois imposteurs', *La Lettre clandestine* 2, 1993, 63–4.

—, 'Spinoza im Untergrund. Zur Rezeption seines Werks in der "littérature clandestine"', in Hanna Delf, Julius Schoeps and Manfred Walther (eds), *Spinoza in der europäischen Geistesgeschichte*, Berlin, Hentrich, 1994, 142–61.

—, 'Einleitung', in *De imposturis religionum*, 1999, 7–77.

—, 'Einleitung'; 'Kommentar', in Knutzen, *Schriften & Dokumente*, 2010, 7–32; 60–74.

—, *Ursprünge des Atheismus. Untersuchungen zur Metaphysik- und Religionskritik des 17. und 18. Jahrhunderts*, Stuttgart-Bad Cannstatt, Frommann-Holzboog, 2012.

—, 'Der Insipiens im 18. Jahrhundert: Aufklärung und Atheismus', in Ulrich Kronauer and Andreas Deutsch (eds), *Der "Ungläubige" in der Rechts- und Kulturgeschichte des 18. Jahrhunderts*, Heidelberg, Universitätsverlag Winter, 2015, 249–64.

—, 'Panthéisme – spinozisme – matérialisme athée. La métaphysique du *Traité des trois imposteurs*', *La Lettre clandestine* 24, 2016, 133–40.

Schwarzbach, Bertram Eugene and Andrew W. Fairbairn, 'Sur les rapports entre les éditions du Traité des trois imposteurs et la tradition manuscrite de cet ouvrage', *Nouvelles de la République des Lettres* II, 1987, 111–36.

—, 'History and Structure of Our Traité des trois imposteurs', in Richard H. Popkin (ed.), *Travaux du séminaire de Leide*, Leiden, 1–31/7/1990, 75–129.

—, 'Notes sur deux manuscrits clandestins', *Dix-huitième siècle* 22, 1990, 433–40.

Secretan, Catherine, 'Partisans et détracteurs de Hobbes dans les Provinces Unies au temps de Spinoza', *Bulletin de l'Association des Amis de Spinoza* 2, 1979, 2–13.

—, 'Premières réactions néerlandaises à Hobbes au XVIIe siècle', *Annales d'histoire des Facultés de Droit* III, 1986, 137–65.

—, 'La réception de Hobbes aux Pays-Bas au XVIIe siècle', *Studia Spinozana* 3, 1987, 27–46.

—, 'La démocratie absolue, ou le défi politique des Lumières radicales', in Secretan, Dagron and Bove (eds), *Qu'est-ce que les Lumières "radicales"?*, 2007, 343–53.

—, 'Fonction du politique et *jus circa sacra* dans les controverses hollandaises du début du XVIIe siècle. Johannes Uytenbogaert et Hugo Grotius', *Revue d'histoire du Protestantisme* I, 2016, 167–85.

Secretan, Catherine, Tristan Dagron and Laurent Bove (eds), *Qu'est-ce que les Lumières "radicales"? Libertinage, athéisme et spinozisme dans le tournant philosophique de l'âge classique*, Paris, Éditions Amsterdam, 2007.

Secretan, Catherine and Willem Frijhoff (eds), *Dictionnaire des Pays-Bas au Siècle d'or. De l'Union d'Utrecht à la Paix d'Utrecht (1579–1713)*, Paris, CNRS éditions, 2018.

Senellart, Michel, *Machiavélisme et raison d'État*, Paris, PUF, 1989.

Sfez, Gérald, *Machiavel, le prince sans qualités*, Paris, PUF, 1998.

—, *Machiavel, la politique du moindre mal*, Paris, PUF, 1999.

Sfez, Gérald and Michel Senellart (eds), *L'enjeu Machiavel*, Paris, PUF, 2001.

Sgard, Jean, 'Jean Lucas 1646–1697', in *Dictionnaire des journalistes (1600–1789)*, Voltaire Foundation, http://dictionnaire-journalistes.gazettes18e.fr/journaliste/531-jean-lucas.

Sharp, Hasana, 'Eve's Perfection. Spinoza on Sexual (In)Equality', in Melamed and Sharp (eds), *Spinoza's Political Treatise*, 2018, 93–110.

Simon, Renée, *Henri de Boulainvilliers: historien, politique, philosophe, astrologue 1658–1722*, Paris, Boivin, 1942.

328   BIBLIOGRAPHY

Simonutti, Luisa, 'Bibliographie primaire, 1670–1677', in Cristofolini (ed.), *L'hérésie spinoziste*, 1991, 253–4.

Skinner, Quentin, *Machiavelli*, Oxford, Oxford University Press, 1981.

Solmi, Edmondo, 'Leonardo e Machiavelli', in Solmi, *Scritti vinciani*, Florence, La Voce, 1924, 201–39; Florence, La Nuova Italia, 2nd ed., 1976, 535–71.

Spini, Giorgio, *Tra Rinascimento e Riforma: Antonio Brucioli*, Florence, La Nuova Italia, 1940.

Spink, John Stephenson, 'La diffusion des idées matérialistes et anti-religieuses au début du XVIIIe siècle: le "Theophrastus redivivus"', *Revue d'histoire littéraire de la France* I, 1937, 248–55.

—, *French Free-Thought from Gassendi to Voltaire*, London, University of London Athlone Press, 1960.

Spruit, Leen and Pina Totaro, 'Introduction', in Spruit, Leen and Totaro (eds), *The Vatican Manuscript of Spinoza's* Ethica, 2011, 6–26.

Steenbakkers, Piet, *Spinoza's* Ethica *from Manuscript to Print*, Utrecht, Department of Philosophy, Utrecht University, 1994.

—, 'Spinoza leest Machiavelli', in Alex C. Klugkist and Jacob van Sluis (eds), *Spinoza: zijn boeken en zijn denken*, Voorschoten, Uitgeverij Het Spinozahuis, 2010, 35–54.

Stein, Ludwig, 'Neue Aufschlüsse über den literarischen Nachlass und die Herausgabe der Opera Posthuma Spinozas', *Archiv für Geschichte der Philosophie* 1, 1888, 554–65.

—, *Leibniz und Spinoza. Ein Beitrag zur Entwicklungsgeschichte der Leibnizischen Philosophie*, Berlin, Georg Reimer, 1890.

Strauss, Leo, *Thoughts on Machiavelli*, Glencoe, The Free Press, 1958.

Stuparich, Giani, *Machiavelli in Germania* (1915), Rome, Riuniti, 1985.

Suchtelen, Guido van, 'François van den Enden, précepteur de Spinoza', *Bulletin de l'Association des Amis de Spinoza* 1, 1979, 3–14.

—, 'Nil Volentibus Arduum. Les amis de Spinoza au travail', *Studia Spinozana* 3, 1987, 391–404.

Sutcliffe, Adam, *Judaism and Enlightenment*, Cambridge, Cambridge University Press, 2003.

Terpstra, Marin, *De wending naar de politiek. Een studie over de begrippen 'potentia' en 'potestas' bij Spinoza*, Nijmegen, s.n., 1990.

—, 'An Analysis of Power Relations and Class Relations in Spinoza's *Tractatus politicus*', *Studia Spinozana* 9, 1993, 79–106.

Thijssen-Schoute, Louise Caroline, *Lodewijk Meyer en diens verhouding tot Descartes en Spinoza*, Leiden, Brill, 1954.

—, *Nederlands Cartesianisme*, Amsterdam, Noord-Hollandsche Uitgevers Maatschappij, 1954.

Toffanin, Giuseppe, *Machiavelli e il "Tacitismo"*, Naples, Guida editori [1921] 1972.

Tommasini, Oreste, *La vita e gli scritti di Niccolò Machiavelli nelle loro relazioni col Machiavellismo*, Turin-Rome, Ermanno Loescher & C., 1883–1911.

Tosel, André, 'Pour une étude systématique du rapport de Marx à Spinoza', in Tosel, Pierre-François Moreau and Jean Salem (eds), *Spinoza au XIXe siècle*, Paris, Publications de la Sorbonne, 2004, 127–47.

Totaro, Pina (ed.), 'Niels Stensen (1638–1686) e la prima diffusione della filosofia di Spinoza nella Firenze di Cosimo III', in Cristofolini (ed.), *L'hérésie spinoziste*, 1991, 147–68.

—, *Spinoziana. Ricerche di terminologia filosofica e critica testuale*, Florence, Leo S. Olschki, 1997.

Tréhet, Olivier, 'Une république normande? La dernière conspiration politique importante du règne de Louis XIV', in Catherine Bougy and Sophie Poirey (eds), *Images de la contestation du pouvoir dans le monde normand (Xe–XVIIIe siècle)*, Caen, Presses Universitaires de Caen, 2007, 283–94.

Trucchio, Aldo, 'Il problema del ritorno alla democrazia: Spinoza lettore di Machiavelli', in Bianchi and Postigliola (eds), *Dopo Machiavelli*, 2008, 187–200.

Van Dalen, Jan Leendert, 'Willem Laurensz. van Blyenbergh', *De Tijdspiegel* 2, 1908, 307–29.

Vandenbossche, Hubert, *Spinozisme en kritiek bij Koerbagh*, Brussel, Centrum voor de Studie van de Verlichting VUB, 1974.

—, *Adriaan Koerbagh en Spinoza*. Mededelingen vanwege het Spinozahuis 39, Leiden, Brill, 1978.

—, 'Quelques idées politiques de Koerbagh', *Tijdschrift voor de studie van de Verlichting* 6, 1978, 223–40.

Van de Ven, Jeroen M. M., '"Van bittere galle by een gebonden": over de laat zeventiende-eeuwse Nederlandse vertalingen van Spinoza's *Tractatus Theologico-politicus*', in Henri Krop (ed.), *De kring van Spinoza, een balans van veertig jaar onderzoek*, Rijnsburg, Uitgeverij Spinozahuis, 2019, 107–18.

Verbeek, Theo, 'La demonizzazione di Vanini: Voetius, Schoock e Descartes', in Raimondi (ed.), *Giulio Cesare Vanini e il libertinismo*, 2000, 183–201.

—, *Spinoza's Theologico-Political Treatise. Exploring 'The Will of God'*, London/New York, Routledge, 2003.

—, 'Spinoza on Natural Rights', *Intellectual History Review* 17/3, 2007, 257–75.

BIBLIOGRAPHY

—, 'Hobbes, Spinoza, et la souveraineté de la Hollande', in Saada (ed.), *Hobbes, Spinoza, ou, les politiques de la parole*, 2009, 165–82.

—, 'Spinoza on Aristocratic and Democratic Government', in Melamed and Sharp (eds), *Spinoza's Political Treatise*, 2018, 145–60.

Vercruysse, Jeroom, 'Bibliographie descriptive des éditions du *Traité des trois imposteurs*', *Tijdschrift van de Vrije Universiteit Brussel* 17, 1974/5, 65–70.

—, 'Le Theophrastus redivivus au XIIIe siècle: mythe et réalité', in Gregory (ed.), *Ricerche su letteratura libertina*, 1981, 297–303.

Vernière, Paul, *Spinoza et la pensée française avant la Révolution*, I & II, Paris, PUF, 1954.

Versiero, Marco, 'Dall'eternità del mondo al governo delle città: Leonardo da Vinci, dopo Machiavelli', in Bianchi and Postigliola (eds), *Dopo Machiavelli*, 2008, 33–52.

Villari, Pasquale, *Niccolò Machiavelli e i suoi tempi*, Milan, Hoepli, 1895.

Virno, Paolo, *Parole con parole. Poteri e limiti del linguaggio*, Rome, Donzelli, 1995.

—, *Quando il verbo si fa carne. Linguaggio e natura umana*, Turin, Bollati Boringhieri, 2003.

Viroli, Maurizio, *From Politics to Reason of Sate. The Acquisition and Transformation of the Language of Politics*, Cambridge, Cambridge University Press, 1992.

—, *Il Dio di Machiavelli e il problema morale dell'Italia*, Rome/Bari, Laterza, 2005

Visentin, Stefano, *La libertà necessaria. Teoria e pratica della democrazia in Spinoza*, Pisa, Edizioni ETS, 2001.

—, 'Potere del nome e potenza del linguaggio nel Discorso sulla servitù volontaria di Etienne de La Boétie', *Isonomia*, 2007, 1–26.

—, 'Tra Machiavelli e Hobbes. A proposito di alcune interpretazioni dello Spinoza politico', in Daniela Bostrenghi and Cristina Santinelli (eds), *Spinoza. Ricerche e prospettive*, Naples, Bibliopolis, 2007, 535–62.

—, 'The Different Faces of the People: On Machiavelli's Political Topography', in Del Lucchese, Frosini and Morfino (eds), *The Radical Machiavelli*, 2015, 368–90.

—, 'Between Machiavelli and Hobbes. The Republican Ideology of Johan and Pieter De la Court', in Lavaert and Schröder (eds), *The Dutch Legacy*, 2017, 227–48.

Wade, Ira Owen, *The Clandestine Organization and Diffusion of Philosophic Ideas in France from 1700 to 1750*, New York, Octagon Books, 1967 [Princeton, 1st ed., 1938].

Walther, Manfred, 'From *potestas multitudinis* in Suárez to *potentia multitudinis*' in Spinoza, *Studia Spinozana* 16, 2008, 129–52.

Weil, Simone, 'Un soulèvement prolétarien à Florence au XVIe siècle', in Weil (ed.), *La révolte des Ciompi*, Toulouse, Les réveilleurs de la nuit, 2013.

Weststeijn, Arthur, *Commercial Republicanism in the Dutch Golden Age. The Political Thought of Johan & Pieter de la Court*, Leiden/Boston, Brill, 2012.

—, *De radicale Republiek. Johan en Pieter de la Court. Dwarse denkers uit de Gouden Eeuw*, Amsterdam, Bert Bakker, 2013.

Wielema, Michiel, 'The Two Faces of Adriaan Koerbagh', *Geschiedenis van de wijsbegeerte in Nederland* 12, 2001, 57–75.

—, 'Adriaan Koerbagh: Biblical Criticism and Enlightenment', in Van Bunge, (ed.), *The Early Enlightenment in the Dutch* Republic, 2003, 61–80.

—, *The March of the Libertines. Spinozists and the Dutch Reformed Church (1660–1750)*, Hilversum, Verloren, 2004.

—, 'Abraham van Berkel's Translations as Contributions to the Dutch Radical Enlightenment', in Lavaert and Schröder (eds), *The Dutch Legacy*, 2017, 204–26.

Wyzewa, Théodore de, 'Revues étrangères – Une biographie hollandaise de Spinoza', *Revue des deux mondes* 136, 1896, 696–707.

Zanini, Adelino, 'Machiavelli, l'etico contro il politico', *Belfagor* 39, 1984, 31–40.

Zarka, Yves Charles and Cristina Ion (eds), *Machiavel: le pouvoir et le peuple*, Paris, Mimesis, 2015.

Zenker, Kay, *Denkfreiheit. Libertas philosophandi in der deutschen Aufklärung*, Hamburg, Felix Meiner, 2012.

*

Index of names

Abensour, Miguel, 18n
Agamben, Giorgio, 51n, 58n, 143n
Akkerman, Fokke, 165n, 196n
Alberti, Leon Battista (1404–1472), 23n, 24
Alexander VI, pope [Rodrigo de Borja/Rodrigo Borgia] (1431–1503), 22
Alighieri, Dante (1265–1321), 24–5, 41, 61, 271n
Althusser, Louis, 18n
Amelot de la Houssaye, Abraham-Nicolas (1634–1706), 12n
Aretino, Pietro (1492–1556), 253–6
Ariosto, Ludovico (1474–1533), 61
Aristotle (384 BCE–324 BCE), 3, 10–11, 45, 51n, 153, 155
Arnauld, Antoine (1612–1694), 108n
Arpe, Peter Friedrich (1682–1740), 250
Asher, Georges Michael (1827–1905), 119n
Assmann, Jan, 51n
Assonville de Bouchault, Guillaume d' (†1598), 5n
Assoun, Paul-Laurent, 278–281
Audier, Serge, 27n
Averroes [Abû'l-Walîd Muhammad Ibn Ahmad Ibn Rushd] (1126–1198), 253

Bacon, Francis (1561–1626), 11–12, 165–6
Baeck, Leo (1873–1956), 212n
Bal, Mieke, 20n
Balibar, Etienne, 222n, 226n, 242n, 243, 245n
Balsamo, Jean, 11n
Barker, Ernest (1874–1960), 5n
Barot, Emmanuel, 15n, 18n
Batelier, Johannes (1593–1672), 184n, 188n, 194–5, 216

Baumgarten, Siegmund Jakob (1706–1757), 67n, 68n
Bayle, Pierre (1647–1706), 4n, 5n, 12n, 37n, 68, 107n–108n, 111n, 255–7, 279n, 281
Becchi, Ricciardo (1445), 35
Bedjaï, Marc, 108n, 111
Benítez, Miguel, 44n, 250, 264n, 282n
Berkel, Abraham van (1630–1688), 72n, 140–1, 143–8, 162
Berti, Silvia, 256n
Beverland, Adriaan (1650–1716), 108n
Bianchi, Lorenzo, 11n, 44n, 49n
Blado, Antonio (1490–1567), 2–3, 25n
Bloch, Olivier, 43, 44n, 46n
Blom, Frans, 111n, 123n
Blom, Hans Willem, 68n, 80n
Blyenbergh, Willem van (1632–1696), 168–9, 195n, 200–5, 249n, 251, 254–5
Boccaccio, Giovanni (1313–1375), 253, 271n
Bodin, Jean (ca.1520/1530–1596), 45
Boehm, Rudolf, 196
Boer, Pim den, 147n
Bonnerot, Olivier-Henri, 253n
Bordoli, Roberto, 68n, 70n, 72n, 139n, 141, 171n
Borgia, Cesare (ca.1475/1476–1507), 20–4, 35
Bostrenghi, Daniela, 182n
Botero, Giovanni (1544–1617), 5
Boucheron, Patrick, 24n
Boulainvilliers, Henri de (1658–1722), 251, 261, 264, 268, 270n, 271, 279n, 280–2
Bouwmeester, Johannes (1630–1680), 140
Bove, Laurent, 223n, 282
Boyle, Robert (ca.1626/1627–ca.1691/1692), 207

INDEX OF NAMES

333

Bredekamp, Horst, 58n
Bredenburg, Johannes (1643–1691), 188n, 194n, 209
Brucioli, Antonio (1498–1566), 3, 4n
Brun, Jean/Braun, Johannes (ca.1628–1708), 209–11
Bruno, Giordano (1548–1600), 253
Budde, Johann Franz (1667–1729), 250
Bunge, Wiep van, 111n, 139n, 141, 142n, 188n, 194n, 209n, 215
Burckhardt, Jacob (1818–1897), 253
Burgh, Albert Coenraadzoon (ca.1648/1650–1708), 208, 214
Butori, Véronique, 66n

Calvin, John (1509–1564), 247
Cambi, Franco, 4n
Campanella, Tommaso (1568–1639), 5, 45, 253
Cantimori, Delio, 3n
Canziani, Guido, 42n, 43, 44n–46n, 50n–52n, 56n, 58n–59n, 62
Carparelli, Mario, 279n
Cardano, Girolamo (1501–1576), 10, 45
Catarino, Ambrogio [Lancelotto Politi] (1484–1553), 4
Cauze de Nazelle, Jean Charles du (1649–1674), 109n, 110, 111n
Cavaillé, Jean-Pierre, 6n, 44n, 252n, 279n, 280n
Chabod, Federico, 20n, 21
Charles-Daubert, Françoise, 250, 252n, 253, 254n, 256, 260, 261n, 264, 265n, 270n
Charles I, Louis [Elector Palatine] (1617–1680), 194
Charron, Pierre (1541–1603), 10, 45, 252, 261, 271
Cicero, Marcus Tullius (106 BCE–43 BCE), 45n, 201, 267
Clair, Pierre, 280
Clapmar, Arnold (1574–1604), 81
Clement VII, pope [Giulio de' Medici] (1478–1534), 2n
Clément, Pierre (1809–1870), 109n, 110n
Colerus, Johannes (1647–1707), 67n, 68, 107n–108n, 198, 204n, 256
Colonna d'Istria, François-Marie (1864–1925), 281n
Conring, Hermann (1606–1681), 12n
Court, Johan de la (1622–1660), 34n, 47–8, 59n, 67–8, 75, 78–106, 115–16, 120n,

142–3, 150, 153n, 154, 162, 180–1, 232n, 235–8, 241, 262
Court, Pieter de la (1618–1685), 34n, 47–8, 59n, 67–8, 75, 78–106, 115–16, 120n, 142–3, 150, 153n, 154, 162, 180–1, 232n, 235–8, 241, 262
Cristofolini, Paolo, 223n
Curley, Edwin, 156n, 171n, 190n, 205n, 208n, 217n, 219n, 223n, 227n
Curtius, Quintus Rufus (1st century), 236

Damisch, Hubert, 24n
Datisius, Franciscus (17th century), 190, 192
Daussy, Hugues, 5n, 10n
Deborin, Abram (1881–1963), 43n
Deleuze, Gilles, 168n, 276n
Del Lucchese, Filippo, 18n, 222n
Descartes, René (1596–1650), 8, 11n, 61, 66n, 68n, 83, 104, 166, 168, 171, 181n, 188, 195, 201, 203–6, 262
Des Marets, Samuel see Maresius
Dionisotti, Carlo, 3, 4n, 13n
Donck, Adriaen van der (ca.1618–1655), 116–17
Donné, Boris, 6n
Ducheyne, Steffen, 246n
Duijkerius, Johannes (1661–1702), 171n
Dunin-Borkowski, Stanislaus von (1864–1934), 43n, 110, 250, 257, 258n, 259, 261
Durand, David (1680–1763), 8n
Dürr, Johannes Konrad (1625–1677), 184, 192, 195, 199
Du Sauzet, Henri (ca.1687–1754), 250n

Edelmann, Johann Christian (1698–1767), 150n
Enden, Franciscus van den (1602–1674), 1–2, 8, 28n, 34n, 43n, 47, 59n–60n, 78, 87, 99, 107–140, 142–3, 150–1, 153n, 154, 162, 166–7, 169, 181, 187–8, 208, 244–5, 249, 262–3, 278–9, 284–7
Ernst, Germana, 5n
Erasmus, Desiderius [of Rotterdam] (ca.1467/1469–1536), 247
Esposito, Roberto, 25, 27n, 238n
Eugen, Franz Prinz von Savoyen-Carignan (1663–1763), 43
Ezra/Esdras [the priest/scribe] (ca.480 BCE– ca.440 BCE), 148, 193

INDEX OF NAMES

Fairbairn, A.W., 257n
Fabritius, Johann Ludwig (1632–1696), 194
Ferrand, Louis (1645–1706), 43n
Feuerbach, Ludwig (1804–1872), 37n
Foucault, Didier, 279n
Foucault, Michel, 131n, 252n, 282n
Fournel, Jean-Louis, 24n
Francesca, Piero della (ca.1410/1420–1492), 23n
Frederick II, von Hohenstaufen (1194–1250), 252–5
Frederick II, of Prussia/the Great (1712–1786), 283
Freudenthal, Jakob (1839–1907), 67n, 187n, 194n, 196n, 200n, 257
Freytag, Friedrich Gotthilf (1687–1761), 68n
Fukuoka, Atsuko, 249n

Galen, Claudius [of Pergamon] (129–199), 45n, 238n
Galilei, Galileo (1564–1642), 61–3
Galli, Carlo, 27n, 31n, 32n
Garasse, François (1585–1631), 7, 45n, 279n
Garin, Eugenio, 11n, 44n
Gatens, Moira, 241n
Gatto, Alfredo, 45n
Gebhardt, Carl (1881–1934), 68n, 131n, 165n, 171n, 194n, 196n, 219n, 230n, 232n–233n, 238, 241n
Gengoux, Nicole, 43n–44n
Genette, Gérard, 20n
Gensini, Stefano, 50n
Gent, Pieter van (1640–1694), 196n, 204
Gentillet, Innocent (1535–1588), 4–5, 9
Gerber, Adolph (1856–1934), 3n–4n, 9
Gilbert, Felix, 13n
Ginzburg, Carlo, 24–5, 35n, 51n, 58n
Giunta, Bernardo (1487–1551), 2, 13n
Goeree, Willem (1635–1711), 107n–108n
Gohory, Jacques (1520–1576), 10, 12n
Goldenbaum, Ursula, 184n
Gootjes, Albert, 193n
Graevius, Johann Georg (1632–1703), 184n, 192
Gramsci, Antonio (1891–1937), 18n, 26n
Gregorius IX, pope [Ugolino dei Conti di Segni] (ca.1167–1241), 253
Gregory, Tullio, 43n, 58n–59n
Grotius, Hugo (1583–1645), 140, 203, 247, 249, 252n, 254, 255n, 262
Grunwald, Max, 198n

Guichard, Louis Anastase (†1737), 255n
Gullan-Wuhr, Margaret, 241n

Haitsma Mulier, Eco O.G., 80–2, 84
Han-Ding, Hong, 198n
Hannibal Barca (ca.247 BCE–183 BCE), 232–3
Herbert of Cherbury, Edward [baron] (1583–1648), 256
Heertum, Cis van, 139n
Heidegger, Johann Heinrich (1633–1698), 194n
Hobbes, Thomas (1588–1679), 35n, 57n, 58–60, 68n, 71–2, 76, 79, 80n, 83, 85n, 92n, 104, 128, 143–50, 153–4, 161–3, 171, 174, 180, 182n, 187–8, 191–2, 195, 203, 214n, 224–5, 227n, 228, 231, 233, 236, 242–4, 247, 249, 251, 256, 260–3, 265, 267, 271, 273, 277, 280
Hohendorf, Georg Wilhelm von (ca.1670–1719), 251, 258, 261, 264, 268, 270n, 271
Holbach, Paul-Henri Thiry [Baron] d' (1723–1789), 251, 264, 266, 268, 270–2, 282
Huygens, Christiaen (1629–1695), 208

Israel, Jonathan, 68n, 111n, 139n, 171n, 183n–184n, 187n, 193n–195n, 198n, 215n–216n, 257n

Jacob, Margaret C., 257n
James, Susan, 241n
Jelles, Jarig (1620–1683), 190–1, 195–7, 217n, 244, 262
Jesus of Nazareth [Christ] (ca. 5 BCE–ca.30 CE), 149, 159, 192, 252, 267, 271
Jongeneelen, Gerrit H., 139n, 141, 246n

Kahn, Victoria, 3n
Kant, Immanuel (1724–1804), 252n, 263n
Klever, Wim, 108n, 111, 115n, 119n, 139n, 171n
Knol, Jan Corneliszoon (†1672), 140
Knorr, Christian Friedrich (1646–1704), 198–9, 216
Knutzen, Matthias (1646–1674), 152n, 212–13
Koerbagh, Adriaan (1633–1669), 46–8, 59n, 98, 118, 131, 138–64, 167n, 170–1, 177, 181, 200, 203, 212–13, 244, 254–5, 262–3, 265, 268, 275, 279
Koerbagh, Johannes (1634–1672), 139–40
Kortholt, Christian (1633–1694), 256

INDEX OF NAMES

Kossman, Ernst Heinrich, 80, 100, 104
Krop, Henri, 107n, 171n
Kuyper, Frans (1629–1691), 215

Lagrée, Jacqueline, 66n, 68n, 72n, 165n, 171n, 256n, 262n, 279n
Lamy, Guillaume (1644–1683), 260, 265
La Boétie, Etienne de (1530–1563), 11
La Monnoye, Bernard de (1641–1728), 255
La Mothe le Vayer, François de (1588–1672), 260, 265
Languet, Hubert (1518–1581), 3, 5n, 9–10, 57n, 227n
Lantoine, Jacques-Louis, 224n
La Place, Pierre Antoine [M.] de (1707–1793), 110n
Latréaumont, Gilles Du Hamel de (1627–1674), 109–10, 112–13, 134, 135n, 139, 284
Laudani, Raffaele, 11n
Laursen, John Chris, 44n, 179n
Lavaert, Sonja, 27n, 107n, 122n, 126n, 131n, 140n, 196n, 235n, 237n, 263n, 270n
Lazzeri, Christian, 68n
Leeuwenburgh, Bart, 139n
Lefort, Claude, 18n, 27n
Leibniz, Gottfried Wilhelm (1646–1716), 67n, 68, 107n, 108n, 150n, 184, 190, 192–3, 204, 208, 215–16
Levier, Charles (†1734), 257n, 261
Licata, Giovanni, 196n, 204n
Lilienthal, Michael (1686–1750), 141n
Linde, Antonius van der (1833–1897), 198n
Livius, Titus [Livy] (ca.59 BCE–ca.17 CE), 21–2, 34, 39, 81, 95–6, 128n, 232n, 236
Locke, John (1632–1704), 246, 252n
Louis XIV (1638–1715), 108–9, 111n, 257, 263, 284
Looiesteijn, Henk, 111n
Lucas, Jean-Maximilien (1646–1697), 67n, 250, 255–60, 263, 282
Lucretius, Titus Carus (ca.99 BCE–ca.55 BCE), 45, 256, 267, 271n
Luther, Martin (1483–1546), 4, 186, 195, 198–9, 211, 215

Macek, Josef, 3n, 4n, 12n
Machiavelli, Niccolò (1469–1527), 1–41, 44–8, 52, 54–5, 57n–58n, 59, 61, 65n, 68, 79–80, 83, 85–6, 89–92, 94–6, 99, 106, 115–16, 119–20, 122n, 126, 128n, 131–2,

134, 154, 162, 187, 192, 200, 216, 218–19, 229–39, 241–4, 247, 251–3, 255–6, 258, 260, 262, 266–7, 276–83
Mack Smith, Denis, 253n
Maistre, Joseph de (1753–1821), 51n
Malcolm, Noel, 58n, 59n, 143n, 148, 261n, 265n
Malettke, Klaus, 111–12, 113n
Mansvelt, Regnerus van (1639–1671), 195–7, 205, 211, 215
Marchand, Prosper (1678–1756), 5n, 250, 256n, 257–8
Maresius, Samuel (1599–1673), 187, 193, 195n
Marx, Karl (1818–1883), 18n
Masch, Andreas Gottlieb (1724–1807), 68n
Matheron, Alexandre, 223n, 241n, 242–3
Maury, Alfred (1817–1892), 108, 110n, 112
Mauthner, Fritz (1849–1923), 139n
Meininger, Jan V., 108n
Meinsma, Koenraad Oege (1865–1925), 110, 111n, 116n, 139n, 171n, 190–1, 193n, 250, 257
Melchior, Johannes (1646–1689), 193, 195
Menzel, Adolph (1857–1938), 181n
Mersenne, Marin (1588–1648), 254–6, 279
Mertens, Frank, 107n–108n, 111n
Meyer, Lodewijk (1629–1681), 67–9, 75, 140, 163, 168–71, 176–7, 187, 196, 201, 204, 212, 263n
Meyer, Willem (1842–1926), 250, 256–7
Mignini, Filippo, 139n, 141, 163n, 254
Mohammed (ca.570–632), 89, 215, 252, 260, 271
Montaigne, Michel de (1533–1592), 10, 35n, 45
Moreau, Pierre-François, 44n, 66n, 68n, 70n, 165n, 171n, 223n–224n, 242–3
Morfino, Vittorio, 12n, 18n, 79n, 126n, 222n
Mori, Gianluca, 281n–282n
Moses [?], 36n, 53–4, 55n, 148–9, 213, 252, 260, 267, 271
Müller, Johann (1598–1672), 148n
Müller, Johann Joachim (1661–1733), 255n
Musaeus, Johannes (1613–1681), 198, 199n, 212–13, 216

Namer, Émile, 4n, 36n
Naudé, Gabriel (1600–1653), 10, 45, 252, 255n, 260–1, 271
Negri, Antonio, 11n, 18n–19n, 20, 61n, 222n–223n, 242n, 243

336 INDEX OF NAMES

Nieuwentyt, Bernard (1654–1718), 246, 250
Niewöhner, Friedrich, 252n
Nifo, Agostino (1473–1545), 3
Nobbs, Douglas, 68n
Numa-Pompilius (ca.750 BCE–ca.672 BCE), 271

Oldenburg, Henry (ca.1618–1676), 165–6, 169–70, 173, 176, 179, 207, 209, 214, 268, 273, 276
Olesti, Joseph, 11n
Osorio, Jeronimo (1506–1580), 4
Ostens, Jacob (1625–1678), 188, 189n, 190n
Ostrowiecki-Bah, Hélène, 44n, 46n, 49n
Otto, Rüdiger, 184n, 193n, 213n

Paganini, Gianni, 42n, 43, 44n–46n, 50n–52n, 56n, 58n–59n, 62, 260–1
Panofsky, Erwin, 24
Paul [apostle] (fl. ca.3–60), 196, 268
Pedullà, Gabriele, 15n, 18n
Perna, Pietro (1522–1582), 9
Petersen, Johann Wilhelm (1649–1727), 251n, 258n
Petrarca, Francesco (1304–1374), 61
Petry, Michael John, 85n
Pintard, René, 44n
Plato (427 BCE–347 BCE), 3, 15n, 18n, 45n, 201, 238n
Plekhanov, Georgi (1856–1918), 43n
Plokhoy, Pieter Corneliszoon (ca.1625–ca.1664/1670), 114, 122–5
Pole, Reginald (1500–1558), 4
Pomponazzi, Pietro (1462–1525), 3, 10, 45, 253
Popkin, Richard, 256n
Possevino, Antonio (1534–1611), 5, 9
Post, S.D., 141n
Procacci, Giuliano, 3n–4n, 11n–12n
Proietti, Omero, 108n, 111n, 196n, 204n, 217n
Pufendorf, Samuel von (1632–1694), 252n

Rabelais, François (ca.1483/1494–1553), 253
Raimondi, Fabio, 18n
Raimondi, Francesco Paolo, 6n, 257n
Ramond, Charles, 223n
Rappolt, Friedrich (1615–1676), 185–7, 192, 195, 216
Raynaud, Theophil (1583–1663), 4n
Rehmann, Jan, 222n
Reimmann, Jakob Friedrich (1668–1743), 67n–68n, 250

Reitz, Tilman, 222n
Ribadeneyra, Pietro (1526–1611), 5n
Richardson, Brian, 3n
Riedel, Carl (19th century), 66n, 68n
Rieuwertsz, Jan (ca.1616–1687), 204, 259n
Röd, Wolfgang, 85n
Rodriguez Donis, Marcellino, 44n
Rohan, Louis de [Chevalier de Rohan] (1635–1674), 108–12, 135n, 139, 278, 284
Rou, Jean (1638–1711), 109n
Rousseau, Jean-Jacques (1712–1778), 57n
Ruë, Pieter de la (1695–1770), 141n
Russo, Luigi, 35n, 36n
Ruzante, Angelo Beolco (1496–1541), 61

Saint-Glain, Gabriel de (1620–1684), 279–80
Saintes, Amand (1801–1878), 111n
Salatowsky, Sascha, 161n
Savonarola, Girolamo (1452–1498), 12, 35–6, 54
Scaliger, Joseph Justus (1540–1609), 42n
Schröder, Winfried, 44n, 48n, 152n, 212n, 250, 252n, 255n, 257n–258n, 259, 265n, 268n, 272n–273n
Schmeisser, Martin, 279n
Schmitt, Carl, 51n
Schramm, Johann Moritz (18th century), 257n
Schuller, Georg Hermann (ca.1650/1651–1679), 190–1, 204–8
Schwarzbach, Bertram Eugene, 257n
Scipio, Publius Cornelius [Scipio Africanus] (236 BCE–183 BCE), 232–3
Secretan, Catherine, 70n, 85n, 249n
Sextus Empiricus (ca.160–ca.210), 45
Sharp, Hasana, 241n
Simon, Renée, 281n
Simonutti, Luisa, 183n
Socrates (469 BCE–399 BCE), 201
Spinoza, Benedictus de/Baruch (1632–1677), 1–2, 8–12, 31n, 34n, 43n, 44–9, 59n, 66n, 67–9, 72–5, 79, 81, 97–8, 105–11, 116, 120, 126n, 128n, 131n, 139n, 140, 142, 143n, 162, 163n, 165–245, 246–83
Soderini, Piero di Tommaso (1450–1522), 12, 19, 24
Solmi, Edmondo (1874–1912), 24n
Spini, Giorgio, 3n
Spink, John Stephenson, 43n, 44
Spitzel, Gottlieb (1639–1691), 215–17
Spruit, Leen, 108n
Statius, Publius Papinius (ca.40–ca.96), 271

INDEX OF NAMES

Steenbakkers, Piet, 165n, 191n, 257n
Stein, Ludwig (1859–1930), 190, 191n, 204n
Stensen, Niels (1638–1686), 108n, 208–9
Stouppe, Jean-Baptiste (1623–1692), 210–11
Strauss, Leo, 36n, 267n
Struve, Burchard Gotthelff (1671–1738), 250, 251n
Suchtelen, Guido van, 108n
Sue, Eugène (1804–1857), 109–10, 112

Tacitus, Publius Cornelius (ca.56–ca.120), 10–11, 34–5, 79–81, 93n, 236, 267
Tarabaud, Mathieu Mathurin (1744–1832), 69, 74
Tegli, Silvestro (†1573), 9
Tentzel, Wilhelm Ernst (1659–1705), 250, 251n, 258n
Terpstra, Marin, 222n
Thales of Miletus (ca.624 BCE–545 BCE), 191
Theophrastus of Eresos (ca.371–ca.287), 44–5
Thijssen-Schoute, Louise Caroline, 67n, 139n, 171n
Thomasius, Christian (1655–1728), 69, 184–7
Thomasius, Jacob (1622–1684), 183–7, 192, 195, 216
Thucydides (ca.460 BCE–400 BCE), 35n
Toffanin, Giuseppe, 5n, 34n
Toland, John (1670–1722), 257n, 268n
Tommasini, Oreste (1844–1919), 15n, 238n
Totaro, Pina, 108n, 208n
Tschirnhaus, Ehrenfried Walther von (1651–1708), 196n, 204–9, 215
Tréhet, Olivier, 109n
Trinius, Johann Anton (1722–1784), 68n

Uffenbach, Zacharias Konrad von (1683–1734), 141n, 159
Uytenbogaert, Johannes (1557–1644), 70n

Van Dalen, Jan Leendert, 168n
Vandenbossche, Hubert, 139n, 141n
Van de Ven, Jeroen M.M., 171n

Vanini, Lucilio [Giulio Cesare] (1585–1619), 5–8, 11, 30n–31n, 45, 58, 181, 203, 247, 251–3, 257n, 258, 260–1, 265–6, 268–76, 279–80
Velthuysen, Lambertus van (1622–1685), 188–90, 194n, 205
Verbeek, Theo, 143, 181n, 249n, 252n
Vercruysse, Jeroom, 42n
Vernière, Paul, 111n, 250, 259n, 279n, 280, 281n–282n
Verwer, Adriaen (1655–1717), 246–9, 251, 255
Vigna, Piero della (ca.1190–1249), 253
Villari, Pasquale (1827–1917), 15n
Villars, Louise de [Marquise] (1647–1679), 109, 285
Vinci, Leonardo da (1452–1519), 23n, 24
Virno, Paolo, 50n–51n
Visentin, Stefano, 11n, 79n–80n, 85n, 120n, 206n, 222n, 237n
Vivanti, Corrado, 3n, 13n, 20n, 238n
Voet[ius], Gijsbert (1589–1676), 8, 181, 195n, 254, 256
Vogt, Johann (1695–1764), 68n, 141n
Voltaire, François-Marie Arouet (1694–1778), 283n
Vries, David Pieterszoon de (ca.1593–1655), 116
Vroese, Jan/Johan (†1725), 250n, 257n

Waddington, Francis (1828–1864), 109n
Wade, Ira Owen, 44n
Walther, Manfred, 222n
Wassenaer, Geraard van (ca.1589–1664), 81n
Weil, Simone, 15n, 18n
Weststeijn, Arthur, 68n, 72n, 79n–80n, 98, 106
Wielema, Michiel, 139n, 141, 143n, 157n, 158
Wolfe, John (ca.1548–1601), 9n
Wyzewa, Théodore de (1862–1917), 109n

Zancarini, Jean-Claude, 24n
Zenker, Kay, 183n, 192n, 198n

Anonymous texts

Arcana ecclesiasticorum, 69, 84

De imposturis religionum (De tribus impostoribus), 255n

De jure ecclesiasticorum, 10, 59n, 66–78, 83–4, 94, 106, 132, 154, 170, 174, 180–2, 184, 249, 262, 268n, 279

De la puissance legitime du prince sur le peuple, et du peuple sur le prince [Languet], 5n, 10n, 57n, 227n

Der Francoysen ende haerder nagebueren Morghenwecker door Eusebium Philadelphum, 11n

De tribus impostoribus, 8, 200, 252–7

Dialogues françois, 11

Esprit de Monsieur Benoit de Spinosa, 43n, 50n, 246–83

Essai sur les préjugés [d'Holbach], 266

Finis est in Holandia [Franciscus van den Enden], 109–14, 126–36, 284–9

Homo politicus, 116, 190–2

La noblesse et le peuple de Normandie, 110n, 112n, 284

La vie et l'esprit de Mr. Benoit de Spinosa, 67n, 250, 254, 256–9, 263–4

Le Réveille-Matin des François et de leurs voisins, composé par Eusebe Philadelphe Cosmopolite, en forme de Dialogues, 11

Naeuwkeurige consideratie van staet [De la Court], 79–84, 106n, 262

Rencontre de Bayle, et de Spinoza dans l'autre monde, 111n

Theophrastus redivivus, 7–8, 10, 42–65, 116n, 128n, 130n–131n, 154, 227n, 235n, 240n, 258–60, 267n

Traité des trois imposteurs, 47, 50n, 246–83

't Samen-spraeck tusschen een Gereformeerden Hollander en Zeeuw [Koerbagh], 140–3

Unschuldige Nachrichten von alten und neuen theologischen Sachen, 150–1

Vindiciae contra tyrannos [Languet], 5, 9–11, 57n